ORGANIC VEGETABLE GARDENING

No. 1660
$25.95

ORGANIC VEGETABLE GARDENING

BY BOB PERCIVAL

TAB BOOKS Inc.
BLUE RIDGE SUMMIT, PA. 17214

Also by the Author from TAB Books Inc.

No. 1460   *The How-To-Do-It Encyclopedia of Painting and Wallcovering*

FIRST EDITION

FIRST PRINTING

Copyright © 1984 by TAB BOOKS Inc.
Printed in the United States of America

Library of Congress Cataloging in Publication Data

Percival, Bob.
Organic vegetable gardening.
Includes index.
1. Vegetable gardening.   2. Organic gardening.
I. Title.
SB324.3.P43   1984   635'.0484   83-24224
ISBN 0-8306-0660-2
ISBN 0-8306-1660-8 (pbk.)

Contents

Acknowledgments

Thanks to Nada Jandrich, Linda Raymond, Michael Cain, Dee and Dave Blair, and Dorothy Thompson.

Introduction

Who loves a garden still his Eden keeps,
perennial pleasures, plants and whole-
some harvest reaps.

—Amos Bronson Alcott

The number of gardens in the United States increases each year. Vegetable gardening is the fifth most popular recreational activity in the country. Only watching television, listening to music, sewing, and going to movies top gardening as a recreational activity; all others take a back seat. In 1981 some 38 million American households had food gardens (according to Gardens for All, the national association for gardening based in Burlington, Vermont). Although this was 47 percent of all U.S. households, it does not equal the percentage of Americans who grew Victory Gardens during World War II. Still, the produce from these 1981 gardens had an estimated value of $15.5 billion dollars. The average gardener invests $20.00 in his garden. The average return is over $400.00 worth of vegetables. In fact, saving money, better-tasting

food, and pure enjoyment are the principal reasons most gardeners garden.

More importantly, the number of gardeners practicing organic or natural gardening techniques is increasing faster than the overall growth rate for gardening in general. What is going on? Nothing out of the ordinary—simply a desire by gardeners to make gardening as simple and safe as possible.

Every gardener, organic or otherwise, has his or her own definition of organic gardening. In general, organic gardeners will agree that their method of gardening is done without manufactured chemicals and is designed to work with nature instead of beating nature into submission. Organic gardening shies away from the use of chemical pesticides, fertilizers, and herbicides.

Natural gardening is a gentler way of gardening than chemical gardening. The emphasis is on building a naturally fertile soil so that plants can grow healthy without extra expense and work on the gardener's part. A healthy soil results in reduced insect damage and increased vegetable production. Many gardeners claim that vegetables grown organically taste better than their chemical counterparts.

Organic gardening fits right in with what gardeners consider important. By using the techniques in this book, you will be able to save a considerable amount of money. For instance, Chapter 15 will show you how to make many bug-chasing concoctions from materials already in your kitchen or from plants growing in your yard and garden. These are cheap pesticides. Why pay for expensive (and dangerous) chemical pesticides when you can make them for pennies?

Fertilizers are another good example of how organic gardening can save you money. Chapter 5 tells you how to turn the vegetative refuse found around your yard or community into a high-grade soil conditioner—free. Say goodbye to high-priced petroleum-based fertilizers forever.

Most gardening books tell you how the author gardens or how to garden a specific way. That gardener's method is thoroughly explained, and by the time you finish the book you are all set to practice that method. A single method of gardening, though, will not work for all gardeners in all parts of the United States. This book is different.

I share some of the tricks I have learned in my garden and answer many of the questions I frequently hear from students in the gardening class I teach each spring. This book is not limited to any single method. I explain several ways to do the various jobs and solve the problems you will be confronted with in your garden. Pick and choose the ones you think will work best for you. If the one you pick does not work out, alternatives are offered so you can dig right in with another technique.

Gardeners grow all kinds of vegetables. The tomato is by far the most popular, followed closely by onions, beans, cucumbers, peppers, lettuce, radishes, carrots, peas, and corn. Growing tips for all of these vegetables and many more—54 in all—are covered in Chapter 11. You'll also find techniques for irrigation, cultivation, tool selection and maintenance, soil types, nutrient cycles, and other important gardening topics.

I mentioned that gardeners like to grow their own food because of the better quality and taste of garden vegetables. This is true of chemical gardeners, but it is even more true of organic gardeners. Virtually all produce sold in supermarkets has been treated with chemicals. The pesticide industry is a $3.7 billion a year industry in the United States and it grows every year. Each of us receives more than our fair share of poison on the food we buy and eat, whether we want it or not. This is what this book is about—growing your own food without pesticides, herbicides or chemical fertilizers in order to cut down the number and volume of dangerous chemicals you are exposed to.

Imagine how much better your food will taste when you grow it without those chemicals! It makes me hungry enough to step out to my garden and pick a tomato right now. I can eat it without washing it first because there are no chemicals on it. What a treat! I hope this book will encourage you to grow vegetables the same way.

Chapter 1

Soil: Bedrock of the Garden

The farther we get away from the land, the greater is our insecurity.

—Henry Ford

When you ask a nongardener what soil is, he is likely to tell you it is dirt. Since dirt is matter in the wrong place, no word could be less applicable to soil which, as every gardener knows, is matter in the right place. Without soil the plant and animal life we take for granted would be impossible.

Good soil is the most precious commodity a gardener can have. Without it, the best tools, the most conscientious weeding and cultivation, and the best of seeds will not produce high-quality vegetables. Only good soil can do that.

Soil is more than the collection of minerals. It is a highly complex interrelationship of minerals, air, water, and vegetable and animal materials. Each of these soil components is constantly undergoing physical and chemical change. In fact, the soil is alive. The roots of the plants in your garden manage to become a part of this life for a short time and the end result is food for your table.

Although scientists have not figured out the soil's life entirely, they have labeled that mysterious process by which minerals in the soil find their way into plants "biochemical." The quality and quantity of your harvest is related directly to the health of your garden's soil.

Unfortunately, modern agriculture and chemical gardeners treat the living soil like dirt. They think of it as no more than a medium through which fertilizers can be force-fed to plants. These gardeners give little thought to how soil is formed or to how they can keep it full of life and vitality. They saturate the soil with harmful fertilizers, pesticides and herbicides (all of which have a skull and crossbones on the package) and then wonder why their soil becomes too lifeless, too worn out, to grow decent crops.

Organic gardeners have learned the secret of keeping their soil healthy. They work with nature instead of against it to build a sound soil in which lush, healthy plants grow as nature intended. Organic gardeners know that there are very few secrets to keeping soil in peak condition as long as their gardening practices harmonize with nature instead of trying to beat nature into submission with chemicals. Organic gardeners know that when the soil is healthy their garden will be also, since the soil is the foundation on which the rest of the garden is built.

Additionally, organic gardeners know that it takes time to build a healthy soil, and that it is especially hard to build a healthy soil from ground that has been abused by man. This chapter will acquaint you with soil so that, through diligent work, you too can speed up the centuries-long process nature uses to build soil. Later chapters will provide some specific ideas about how to improve your soil.

HOW SOIL IS FORMED

The earth has not always had the thin layer of material we call soil. Originally the earth's land masses were bare rock. The action of heat, cold, wind, rain, and glacial movement began the slow process of breaking the rock into finer particles. Water entered cracks in the rock. Through freezing and thawing, these cracks were expanded and loose rock broke off. Running water and wind worked the rock into finer and finer particles. Water dissolved some of the minerals present in the rock particles. These provided the basic nutrients for the microorganisms which contributed to the next round of soil formation.

Microorganisms—usually bacteria and fungi—lived in the water and air between the rock particles. These primitive life forms liberated carbon dioxide and organic and inorganic acids which also altered the original rock. Dead and decaying bodies of these organisms were the beginning of the organic material component of soil. As the organic material and fine rock particles mixed, primitive soil grew more fertile.

Primitive soils supported plant life that was increasingly more complex. Lichens and mosses covered the soil and exposed rock. Their root-like tentacles penetrated the cracks of the rock and the loose soil, aiding in the decomposition process. Slowly, the decomposing mosses enriched the soil and built it to a depth that allowed complex plants

like ferns to live.

In the next phase of soil evolution, ferns collected their energy from the sun through photosynthesis. When they died, the nutrient content of the soil was enriched. It became thicker and more able to support a wider variety of life. Microorganisms living in the soil continued breaking down both rock and decaying organic matter into nutrients useful by more complex plants such as shrubs and trees. Eventually, animals were incorporated into the system, eating the plants and returning their wastes to the soil.

This last stage is the place where we find the soil formation process today. The combination of chemical, physical and biological activity that formed the first soils millions of years ago continues today. Bedrock is still gradually turning into subsoil and then topsoil. The process is a slow one, and scientists estimate it takes up to 500 years to make an inch of soil.

Evolutionists hold this view of soil formation. Creationists believe that God created soil and we have been the benefactors ever since. Regardless of which school of thought you follow, soil is a living thing and should be treated as such. There are right ways and there are wrong ways to treat the soil. I'll cover the right way to treat soil in later chapters.

Soil Horizons

Soil, then, is a mixture of minerals, organic matter, water, air and living plants and animals. But soil is not uniform. It consists of a series of layers, one on top of another, from the surface to the bedrock. Soil scientists call these different layers "horizons." Each horizon has a distinct structure (Fig. 1-1).

The top layer, or A horizon, is what we commonly call topsoil. This layer has more organic material than lower layers of soil. Most of the decomposition of organic material into humus takes place in this layer of soil. To be considered fertile, topsoil should contain an abundance of nutrients in a form that plants can utilize for growth.

The next layer down, the B horizon, is commonly called subsoil, although most soil scientists consider it part of the topsoil. This layer contains

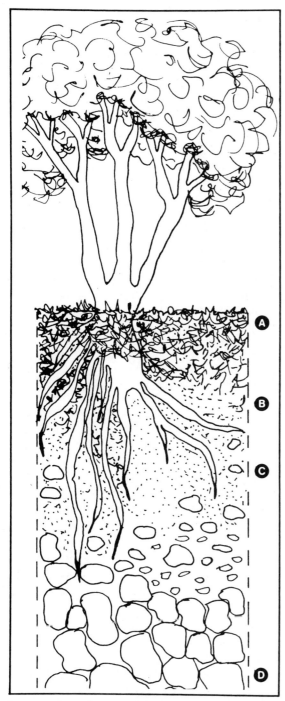

the same basic minerals as topsoil, but it lacks the organic material found in topsoil. Subsoil is often lighter in color than topsoil and it is often heavier in texture. This region is a storehouse of minerals such as iron, aluminum oxides and silicate clays. Many plants send roots down into the subsoil in search of these minerals.

Below the B horizon lies the C horizon, the true subsoil. This zone is not a zone of major biological activity. This soil layer may become topsoil as the layers above it are removed by erosion and weathering.

Finally, the D horizon, commonly called bedrock, lies at the bottom of the soil profile. The bedrock can be granite, limestone, sandstone, or some other parent material from which the upper levels of soil have formed. It is important to remember that the upper layers of soil, especially the A and B horizons, may not be made from the same material as the bedrock. Water, wind and glaciation may have deposited the upper soils over the bedrock. The C horizon usually contains some resemblance to the bedrock although it too may have been deposited and not formed directly from the D horizon.

The important thing to remember about soil horizons is that the deeper the first two layers of soil are, the more conducive to growth the soil will be. This is true because the biochemical activities which make nutrients available to plants occur in these two layers. The C and D horizons are usually so compacted that none but the strongest plants can send roots into them.

Average topsoil consists of 49 percent minerals, 25 percent air, 25 percent water and 1 percent organic matter. See Fig. 1-2. Of course, these guidelines are not absolute, since the parent material of the soil, the plants growing in it, its location and myriad other factors determine the actual makeup of topsoil.

Before discussing the three major types of soil (sand, silt and clay), there are a few terms you should become familiar with. Understanding these terms will make the discussions of different soil types and of many gardening practices more meaningful.

Fig. 1-1. Soil scientists classify the soil's layers into four basic horizons. They are: (A) topsoil, (B) lower topsoil, (C)subsoil, and (D) bedrock or parent material.

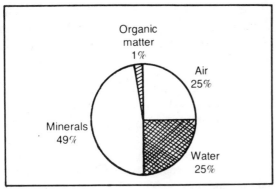

Fig. 1-2. A pie chart showing the average makeup of soil in percentages of organic matter, air, water, and minerals.

Texture

Soil texture is related to the size of the mineral particles making up the soil. Particle sizes in soil range from stones and gravel through sand and silt to clay. The three most important particle sizes in a soil are sand, silt, and clay (Fig. 1-3). Sand particles range in size from 1/50 to 1/500 of an inch in diameter. Silt particles range in size from 1/500 to 1/12,500 of an inch in diameter. Any particle less than 1/12,500 of an inch in diameter is considered a clay particle. Clay particles are so small that you cannot see them with an ordinary microscope, but the importance of clay is much greater than its size. These miniscule particles are highly reactive and are constantly taking on and giving off ions of other elements in the soil. This ionization process is how plants gather nutrients. Clay and humus are the two storehouses of soil nutrients. Sand, silt, clay, and to some extent humus, determine the texture of the soil.

You can get a good idea of your soil's texture by rubbing a pinch of the soil between your fingers or between the palms of your hands. Sand particles are gritty and easily felt. Silt has a flour or talcum-powder feel when dry. When wet, silt has a slightly plastic feel. Clay forms into hard pottery-like clods when dry, and is very plastic and sticky when wet. These three particle sizes—sand, silt and clay—occur in varying proportions in a soil, determining its texture. Many soil scientists use the texture triangle in Fig. 1-4 to determine a soils texture classification.

Structure

Structure refers to the groupings of the small sand, silt and clay particles (as well as the humus of a soil into larger composite pieces. These larger pieces are called granules or crumbs. Good granulation or crumb structure is important to soil structure. The ideal soil is made up of rounded soil crumbs that lie loosely together forming a porous soil through which water and air may enter and leave easily.

Porosity

Porosity is a combination of the structure and the texture of soil. Large particles of sand do not fit together as tightly as clay particles; therefore, there is space between the particles. These spaces fill with water or air or a combination of both. Clay particles pack so tightly together that they prevent air and water from moving between them. Air and water are important to the growth of plants as well as to the microorganisms living in the soil. Good soils have 40 to 60 percent of their bulk occupied by pore space.

Friability

Friability is a term used to describe the ability of a soil to be worked with a hoe or another cultivation tool. Another word for friability is "tilth." Because the friability of soil changes from day to day according to the moisture, air and humus content of the soil, you want to work the soil when it is at optimum friability to prevent damaging the soil. Clay soils, for instance, form clods that are nearly impossible to break up when worked while too wet.

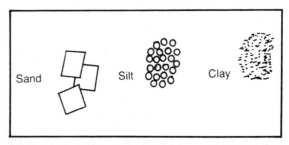

Fig. 1-3. The relative size of the three most common soil mineral particles (sand, silt, and clay) determine the texture of a soil.

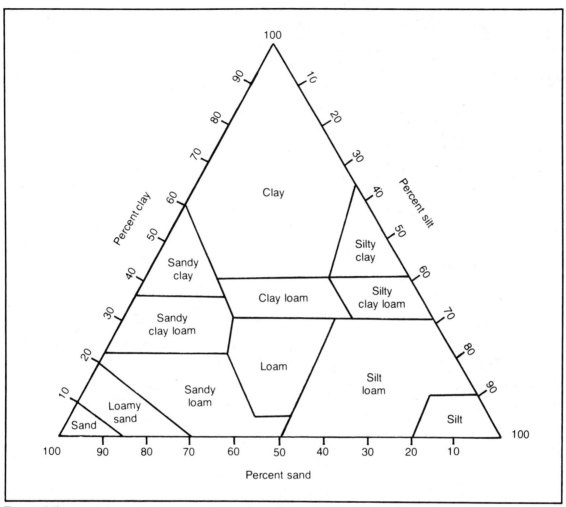

Fig. 1-4. Different soils have specific textures that are determined by the size of the mineral particles making up the soil. Clay loam, for example, has about 60 percent clay, 20 percent silt, and 20 percent sand.

These clods reduce the air-and water-holding capability of the soil and make root growth difficult. The trick to easy cultivation of a soil is catching it when the friability is at its peak.

Here is a simple test you can perform to give you an indication of soil friability. Grab a handful of moist soil and squeeze it tightly for 10 seconds. Drop the ball of soil from a height of 3 feet onto a hard surface. If the soil breaks into several pieces, it is workable. If the soil forms a ball that does not break into pieces, it will be too wet to work (Fig. 1-5). If you cannot pack a ball of soil, you have a sand soil that will be easy to work. Soils that are too dry to work cannot be packed into a ball either. Large quantities of organic matter added to clay or sandy soils will improve tilth.

Color

Although many believe that the darker a soil is the more fertile it is, this is not always the case. One cannot tell the fertility of a soil by its color alone.

Some soils, for example, may be dark because they contain high concentrations of manganese.

5

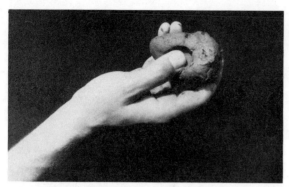

Fig. 1-5. Soil that forms a sticky ball is too wet to work. Wait until such soil dries to work it.

Others may be dark simply because they have been formed from black bedrock. Soil formed from rock produced in lava flows is black because the mineral component of the soil is black, not because of any abundance of nutrients.

A dark soil may also be the result of a soil containing a lot of humus in an advanced state of decay. The humus has lost most of its nutrients and will not be as productive as a soil supplied with fresh organic matter. Dark peat and muck soils, formed in a swamp, are examples of such soils. These soils are usually deficient in many important nutrients because of their extremely acid pH.

On the other hand, yellow and gray topsoils contain little organic material. Red soils are more productive than the yellow or gray soils because they contain iron oxide, an important source of iron, that is necessary for plant growth.

Regardless of a soil's color, it is its organic matter content that largely determines that soil's fertility.

What Weeds Tell About Soil

The native weeds growing near your garden, or where you want to place a garden, will tell you quite a few things about the nature of your soil. Table 1-1 will give you a few clues about your soil by the weeds growing on it.

SOIL TYPES

Although there are hundreds of scientific classifications for soil, all you really need to know to be a good gardener are three general types: sand, silt (or loam), and clay (Fig. 1-6). Each has certain characteristics that you should be aware of so you can practice the cultivation techniques that will make your soil perform its best for what you want to do—grow vegetables (Table 1-2).

Sand

Sandy soils are those that contain at least 50 percent of their weight in the form of sand particles. The mineral particles of this soil are visible to the naked eye and are irregular in shape. Because of this large particle size, sandy soils are very porous and their water-holding capacity is low. Sandy soils have good aeration and drainage, however, and they tend to be in a loose friable condition. Sandy soils can be worked early in the season since they dry quickly. On the other hand, this quick drying may cause problems during the summer when plants will have a difficult time finding water in the soil. Ample

Table 1-1. The Native Plants Growing in a Soil Can Give You a Hint about the Soil's Fertility, pH, and Drainage.

Plant	Soil
Cattails	Wet marshy soil—little chance of a productive garden.
Burdock, pigweed, lamb's quarters, purslane	Indicate soils with good organic matter content, fairly well drained and fertile.
Fennel, sorrel, mayweed, chamomile	Usually grow in soils lacking humus and fertility
Moss	Soils with a greenish tinge well into summer indicate land too wet for a good garden.
Broomsedge	Indicates a generally poor soil.
Bluegrass, alfalfa	Indicate a soil which is not overly acidic.
Clover	Good soil under this plant.
Walnut trees	These trees grow in good soil—usually in well drained river or creek bottoms.
Scrub oak, white cedar, huckleberry, hemlock, fir, blueberry, camellia, rhododendron, white birch, red cedar	These shrubs and bushes indicate acid soils.

Fig. 1-6. From the left, sand, clay, and silt are the three most common types of soil. Most soils are a combination of these three.

organic matter added to sandy soils will help hold water and produce crops of high quality. In most instances, sandy soils are not as fertile as silt or clay soils.

Clay

Soil takes on clay-like properties when the mineral content of the soil contains 40 percent or more clay. Because clay is a highly active material, these soils generally have adequate amounts of nutrients available for good plant growth. Unfortunately, the small size (less than 0.002 millimeters) of the clay particles causes poor porosity in the soil. Since clay particles tend to stick together, clay soils take on plastic characteristics when wet, only to dry to a cement-like hardness. These conditions produce a soil with poor drainage and aeration. A soil like this is hard to work. Clay soils tend to become tillable later in the year than sand or silt soils, but with ample organic material added on a regular basis these soils become easier to work. Clay is much more resistant to drought than sandy or silt soils.

Silt

Silts are made up of mineral particles ranging in size from sand to clay. Loam is the name given to a mixture of sand, clay and ample organic matter.

The loose, unconsolidated particles in silt soils form a medium that is generally considered the best for growing vegetables. This mix of small and large mineral particles with humus produces good texture, porosity and friability. Silt soils exhibit the best qualities of both sand and clay without the undesirable properties also associated with those soils. For instance, silt does not show the undesirable property of extreme looseness and low water-holding capacity of sand, nor does silt have the stickiness and compactness of clay soils. Silt loam soils are easy to work and resist drought better than most sand or clay soils. You are very fortunate if your soil falls into the silt classification.

Organic Matter

The term organic gardening can, in large part, trace its name to the fact that organic matter in a soil is a major determinant of that soil's fertility. Technically, anything with carbon in it is organic, but you would not want to pour motor oil on your garden even though oil is almost totally carbon. Organic gardeners define organic matter as any once-living plant or animal material (all of which contain carbon) that will decompose into humus. Keeping this decomposition process (which is carried out by the soil's microorganisms) active in the soil is the key to producing a healthy soil in which plants thrive (Fig. 1-7).

Although a distinct line between organic matter and humus cannot be drawn, the two materials are slightly different. Organic matter is a coarsely-textured, rough-looking material with its parent material in evidence. Straw, for example, is identifiable for a short time during the decomposi-

**Table 1-2. Common Soil Types Have
Varying Ratios of Clay, Sand and Silt.**

Soil	Percent Minerals
Clay	60% clay, 20% sand, 20% silt
Clayloam	40% clay, 30% sand, 35% silt
Loam	20% clay, 40% sand, 40% silt
Sandyloam	10% clay, 70% sand, 20% silt
Loam-sandy	5% clay, 85% sand, 10% silt
Siltloam	15% clay, 25% sand, 60% silt

Fig. 1-7. The return of organic matter to the soil and its decomposition into humus is the foundation on which organic gardening is based.

tion process, but before long it loses its identity and becomes humus. Humus is the fine, uniform in texture, not fiberous, amorphous material that remains at the end of the decomposition process (Fig. 1-8). Humus, whether made from straw or leaves, looks the same, unlike its parent material. The process of changing organic matter into humus is called humification. For our purposes, organic material and humus will be treated as much the same thing, since it is the actual humification process that does your soil the most good.

Feeding the soil with organic matter produces humic acids that change soil minerals to usable forms. These acids also produce humus which slowly releases nutrients as plant roots need them. Humic acids are natural chelating compounds—substances that hold ions of trace elements like iron, zinc, copper and magnesium for later utilization by plants. Without humic acids, the trace elements in the soil are fixed in forms unavailable to plants. With humic acids, the soil releases these plant nutrients as the soil warms up and as a plant's growth finally hits its stride. Bacteria and fungi break down the chelates and release the nutrients from organic matter in a form available to plants

On cultivated land organic matter is constantly breaking down and being used by soil organisms. When the edible portions of the crop plants are removed from the garden, there is less organic matter to fall back into the soil. Worn-out soils are those that have lost their organic matter. The soil is still rich in minerals, but these minerals are not available to plants because the bridge between mineral and plant—humus and organic matter—is missing. Few crops will grow in tired soils. The key to keeping your soil productive is returning ample organic material to the soil. This way, the biochemical exchange between minerals in the soil and plants will keep functioning.

There are many ways of getting organic matter into your soil. Some of the better known are: composting, mulching, green manuring, spreading animal manures, and by tilling organic matter directly into your garden. Each of these activities, as well as others, will be treated more thoroughly in later chapters. For now, suffice it to say that when you follow organic methods of composting and mulching, you provide your soil with enough organic material to keep the decomposition cycle active. In most cases, making it a habit to add organic material to the soil will allow your garden to correct most of its other problems by itself.

As organic matter decomposes in the soil it produces many marvelous benefits. Here are some of the more well-known benefits.

Organic Matter Feeds the Microorganisms in the Soil. When organic matter is added to the soil, microorganisms immediately set to work breaking down plant and animal tissues into a number of substances of use to other microorganisms as well as to plants. As the easily-decomposed material is used up, the more resistant compounds remain. These materials are slowly synthesized by microorganisms and held as part of their cell walls. Eventually, humus is formed.

Although the general requirements of soil organisms are the same as those of plants—energy, nutrients, water, suitable temperatures and an absence of harmful conditions—they do not need sunlight for energy. Instead, energy is drawn from the carbon in the organic material these organisms decompose. While the microbes are occupied breaking down the organic matter, several things happen that are beneficial to plants. Microorganisms protect plant life from harmful organisms; they adjust soil temperature and pH (the acid or alkaline level of the soil); they break down complex organic wastes into mineral nutrients which can be taken up by the plant roots; they liberate carbon dioxide which is taken up by plant leaves; and some of the microbes fix atmospheric nitrogen into a form usable by plants. Despite the wide range of knowledge about soil microorganisms, many benefits of microbal decomposition of organic matter are still a mystery.

It is known that any spoonful of soil rich in organic matter will have a population of microor-ganisms that is greater than the number of people on earth. There are thousands of different species of these microbes in that same spoonful of earth. Each has a specific function and each keeps the others in check. Scientists have found that when they inject a harmful organism into a microbe-rich soil, the intruder's effects are largely nullified by the organisms already living in the soil. Inject the same organisms into soil with few other forms of microbes and, lacking competition, the harmful organisms quickly run rampant. The addition of a wide variety of organic materials to soil encourages a diverse biological community. The greater the complexity of the community, the greater the stability of the community and the less chance harmful organisms have of attacking your plants. Of course, some organisms living in the soil are harmful, but these are of minor importance when compared to

Fig. 1-8. Humus has been called black gold because of its soil enriching properties. In true humus, the parent material is no longer identifiable.

the multitude of good things living there.

The top few inches of soil hold a countless variety of microbes. These microorganisms can be classified in two broad groups—aerobic and anaerobic. The former need air to survive; the latter thrive without it.

The top 5 inches of most soils contain 95 percent of the aerobic microbes found in soil. These microbes are the ones responsible for breaking down plant residues and other organic matter into humans. The anaerobic microbes live beneath this aerated zone and are usually associated with the subsoil. Both types of organisms are essential to good soil health.

Organic Matter Helps Make Nutrients in the Soil Available to Plant Roots by Breaking Them Down into a Form Plants Can Use. Organic matter has been called "the storehouse of the soil's nutrients" because as organic matter decomposes the microbes responsible for that decomposition produce wastes that are in reality the available form of nutrients so necessary for active plant growth. Additionally, the end result of decomposition—humus—is colloidal.

The minute particles of humus have a negative electrical charge that makes them very reactive. Cations (positively charged particles, many of them plant nutrients) are attracted to the humus particles and held in place instead of leaching from the soil as water passes through it. When plant roots contact the humus particles holding a nutrient, the root trades one of its own cations for the nutrient cation. This process, called cation exchange, is responsible for the transfer of mineral nutrients in the soil to plants. Recent research has proved that the exchange of cations is directly related to a soil's fertility. The rate of this exchange is also directly related to the organic matter content of a soil. The more organic material there is in a soil, the higher the cation exchange rate—which means a more fertile soil.

Although clay particles in a soil also exhibit colloidal properties, on a basis of weight the holding capacity of organic matter is greater than that of clay. In clay soils and soils that are especially sandy, the incorporation of organic matter is very important to the exchange of nutrients from the soil to the plant.

Organic Material Is an Important Source of the Three Macronutrients: Nitrogen, Phosphorus and Potassium. Organic materials, when green, contain from 5 to 6 percent nitrogen. This nitrogen is not available to plants until soil organisms digest the organic matter. One product of this digestion is the nitrates that plants absorb as food. An advantage of this slow release of nitrogen is that this precious nutrient is not leached from the soil as quickly as many chemical fertilizers are.

Although organic material contains less phosphorus than nitrogen the addition of organic matter influences the availability of this important mineral. Organic acids and humus tie up a lot of the iron and aluminum in a soil that would otherwise form an insoluble compound with phosphorus. While the iron and aluminum are tied up with the humus, the phosphorus is released and available for plants.

Like phosphorus and nitrogen, most of the potassium in a soil is unavailable to plants. It is normally bound up with the soil minerals. What little bit of potassium does become available to plants is quickly dissolved by water and carried out of the soil in the water. Fortunately, the humus particles that result from the incorporation of organic matter into the soil are negatively charged and are able to hold potassium particles in the soil until plant roots can absorb it.

The availability of many important micronutrients is also affected by the organic material in a soil. In fact, humus is well-endowed with almost all of the trace elements that are known to be needed by plants. Sulfur, for instance, is present in all plant and animal residues, but in a state unusable by plants. When microbes break down these organic materials, the sulfur is changed to a compound of sulfate which is readily absorbed by plants. Iron, normally a highly insolvent inorganic compound in most soils, forms a plant-usable iron-organic compound in the presence of humus. Boron, which leaches quickly from soil, is held through colloidal action by humus. Calcium magnesium and other metals, are likewise held by organic matter until called on by plants.

Organic Matter Improves the Physical Aspects of a Soil, Including Tilth, Aeration and Crumb Structure. Although organic matter is very active in the transfer of nutrients from soil to plant, its effects are most noticeable in terms of what it does to the friability of soil. In fact, humus has a chameleon-like ability to perform the seemingly impossible task of binding together the particles of loose sandy soils, while loosening the tightly bound particles present in clay soils.

Sandy, light soils will not hold much water because of the excess pore space between the large particles in this soil that allows the quick flow through of water. When organic matter is added the humus acts like a sponge, soaking up water and keeping it close to the plant roots where it is needed. This characteristic of humus can make sandy soils more drought resistant (Fig. 1-9).

In heavy clay soils humus acts as a buffer preventing the fine clay particles from binding together so tightly that air and water cannot penetrate to plant roots. Most clay soils are so tight that rain tends to form puddles and run off without entering the soil. Humus creates a porosity that allows the water to be held in the soil. This more porous structure also permits roots more room to grow, while making the cultivation of the soil much easier.

Perfect Soil

A perfect soil for your garden would be a deep silt loam with a good tilth and at least 5 percent humus. Water should percolate readily through the soil. This soil should contain 45 percent minerals, 25 percent water, and 25 percent air, see Fig. 1-10.

If the soil had a pH of 6.5 to 7.0 and had been fertilized with about 15 tons of rotted manure per acre (one-third ton per 1,000 square feet), and had been dressed with 2 tons per acre (100 pounds per 1,000 square feet) of rock phosphate two years ago, you would have soil that—as a gardener I know puts it—"You could stick a broken shovel handle in and it would take root."

Unfortunately, very few gardeners have soils like the one described above. Don't get discouraged if your soil does not measure up. With a little work and time, you can have a soil that produces well

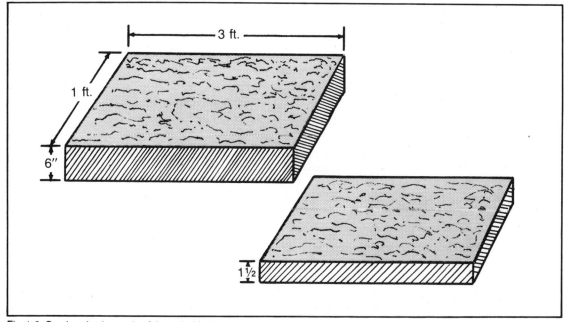

Fig. 1-9. One hundred pounds of dry soil with 4 to 5 percent organic matter can hold 165-195 pounds of water (left). This equals 4 to 6 inches of rain. The same amount of soil with only 1½ to 2 percent organic matter will hold only 35-45 pounds of water (right). This is only ½ inch of rain.

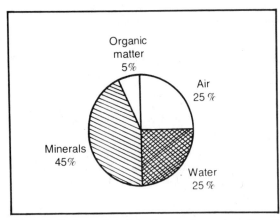

Fig. 1-10. Perfect soil contains 5 percent organic matter, 45 percent minerals, 25 percent water, and 25 percent air.

year after year. First, you need to know where your present soil stands in comparison to perfect soil. To find out, you will need to have your soil tested.

SOIL-TESTING METHODS

The steps that must be taken to produce a fertile soil depend entirely on the present condition of your soil. Some old-time farmers can gather a handful of soil, roll it between their fingers, and tell whether it is sand, silt, loam, or clay. A few can put a pinch on their tongues and tell whether it is acidic or alkaline. Still others can read the plants—both cultivated and weeds—growing in a field and determine which nutrients need to be added for optimum growth. Although many of these farmers' soil assessments are fairly accurate, they come nowhere near the accuracy of scientific soil tests.

A laboratory test of the soil is the first step any serious gardener should make when starting a new garden or embarking on a soil-improvement program. Soil tests are available through county extension agents in cooperation with nearby USDA state experimental stations, through state land-grant agricultural schools from a number of reliable privately owned testing laboratories (see the back of this book for addresses), and through the use of at-home soil testing kits and pH gauges.

The agricultural colleges in almost every state have soil testing services at very low cost to residents of that state. The service is usually conducted in cooperation with your county's extension service. You can contact your local agent to find out how, when and where to send your soil samples in for testing.

The tests offered by many land-grant universities, fertilizer companies and jack-of-all-trades laboratories are little more than a quick look at the three macronutrients and the pH level of your soil. The recommendations from these labs are couched in agribusiness jargon, and soil is considered little more than a support through which chemical fertilizers can be spoon-fed to plants.

Many reputable private companies and laboratories test soil. They charge more than the state-supported test services, but in most cases they will also tell you more about your soil. These labs are willing to make any test you are willing to pay for including analysis for organic matter, pesticides, and trace-element content of your soil.

Although far from perfect because of varying test procedures and equipment, the natural or organic soil-auditing labs go beyond the once-over-lightly of most agribusiness-influenced test labs. These natural labs delve into the humus content of the soil, macronutrients, pH, micronutrients, cation exchange rates, and the heavy metal content of the soil. They give their results in terms of natural fertilizers, which makes the job of correcting soil much easier. These labs also provide accurate readings of your soil's cation exchange rate for various micronutrients. For most home gardeners this more-technical information is of little use. If you depend heavily on your garden for food, however, or if you sell some of your produce and want maximum production, the more in-depth tests may be in order.

By using a do-it-yourself soil test kit you can learn a lot about your soil if you are up on your chemistry. A better method is sending your soil to a laboratory. Most labs have reviewed hundreds of tests for your area (this is especially true of land-grant schools) and can use this frame of reference to interpret their analysis when making recommendations for your soil. You cannot do that with a test kit.

It might be worthwhile, if you send your soil to one of these schools, to indicate on the information sheet you send with the sample that you would like an organic test. It is unlikely, but they may respond accordingly.

Regardless of who does the test on your soil, the "emperical" figures given you by the analysis represent no more than an attempt by the chemist to give you an approximation of the available nutrients in the top 6 inches of your soil at the time the sample was taken. At different times of the year the available nutrients in a soil vary greatly. Nitrogen, for example, is most active during the heat of summer when microbes are busily at work. During the winter little nitrogen is available.

Use soil test results only as a guideline. What is right in the laboratory may not be right in your garden. In general, the test results—even when couched in very general terms—will give you a direction for your soil building efforts. Look for gross abnormalities and work to correct them. Minerals that appear to be in balance on a soil test probably are, and you can assume that the soil is taking care of itself.

Collecting Soil

To get a soil sample that will provide you with an accurate test of your soil, you will have to do a little thinking and poking around in your garden. First, determine how many different soils you have. Variations in color, slope, soil texture and the native plants growing in the soil are good indicators of differing soils.

Plot the different soils in your yard on a map so that you will know which soil each test is associated with. If you have a small garden with only one type of soil, you will need only one sample. In this case, take about six samples evenly spaced around the garden, mix the soil and send it in as one test. If you have several small plots spread around your property and the soils look different, or they have been in production for different lengths of time, gather soil for a separate test from each plot.

The best time of year to take a soil sample is in the fall on a fairly dry day. Spring is just as good as far as the soil is concerned, but the lab may be busy in the spring, and you may get your results back too late for you to act on them. Also, if you take the

sample in the fall you will have time to add rock fertilizers should your soil need them. Adding rock fertilizers in the fall gives them time to break down a little and begin releasing nutrients by spring when the plants need the nourishment.

Taking a Soil Sample

Obtaining accurate results from the soil you have tested depends on how the sample is taken and handled before it reaches the lab. Sloppy sample taking will result in less-than-optimum results. A conscientious effort on your part to take the sample properly will enhance the accuracy of the test results.

The tools for taking a soil sample are few and simple. You will need a trowel, a shovel or sampling probe (Fig. 1-11), a bucket, a kitchen knife or clean

Fig. 1-11. A soil test probe will make taking soil samples easy. Do not touch the soil with your hands.

stick, and sample bags. Use only clean, rust-free tools and a plastic bucket when taking samples. Rust or metal from a metal bucket will influence your sample. At no time should you touch the sample with your hands, since this will also affect the sample.

After you have decided where you are going to gather samples, take a soil-sampling probe and twist it into the ground 6 to 8 inches. Pull up the probe and you will see a core of dirt (Fig. 1-11). Knock this dirt into a bucket. Gather several more samples from different locations in the same soil type and empty each sample into the bucket. Mix all the dirt together. Save enough dirt (about one cup) to fill the sample bag. Mark the sample with a number or letter and make a corresponding note on the soil map of your garden.

If you do not have a sampling probe, dig a hole 6 to 8 inches deep at each location where a sample is to be taken. Take your shovel and slice off a slab of dirt 1 to 2 inches thick from the side of the hole. Scrape away all but an inch-wide sliver of the dirt in the center of the shovel. Put this narrow strip of dirt in the bucket. Repeat this procedure at four or five locations around your garden, where the soil is similar, and then mix all the samples well with a stick or kitchen knife. Save about a cupful of the dirt and mark it on your map.

Prior to mailing, dirt samples should be placed in a shady location to dry. Do not use artificial heat, such as an oven, and do not allow dirt to dry in the sun or the sample will not accurately reflect the soil in your garden.

When the sample is reasonably dry, place it in a shipping bag (Fig. 1-12). You can get these from wherever you plan to have your soil tested by writing and asking for as many bags as you will need. If you are going to have the soil tested at your state's agricultural school, your county extension agent should have bags.

Mark each bag with your name and with a different number for each sample. Use a felt tip pen to mark the bag. (Pencil may rub off and a ball point pen will not write on a bag of dirt.) Fill out the file cards which accompany the bags so that the lab can make accurate recommendations. These informa-

tion sheets usually ask for your name and address, the type of test you want done, the type of plants you want recommendations for (garden, lawn, flowers, etc.), the sample numbers on each bag, and comments on past fertilization. Some labs will also ask for a sketch of your garden indicating where the samples were taken.

Fig. 1-12. Soil samples are shipped in sample bags. These bags are available from test labs and county extension agents.

Pack the bag or bags in a mailing carton and mail by parcel post, U.P.S. or return them to your dealer for mailing. Be sure to include a check or money order to cover the cost of the tests you want done.

Evaluating the Results

A few weeks after you send in your samples, you should receive recommendations for treating any soil deficiencies found by the lab. Tests done by state agricultural schools will probably return recommendations stating fertilizer requirements in chemical fertilizer terms. Private labs geared toward organic tests will be more specific in their organic fertilizer recommendations.

The state agricultural lab will send you something like this: "Use 200 pounds of limestone per 1,000 square feet. Fertilize with 10 pounds of 10-10-10 per 1,000 square feet at planting. Sidedress with three pounds of ammonia per 1,000 square feet during the growing season." Now, what does this mean in organic terms?

Suppose the size of your garden is 20 by 50 feet: 1,000 square feet. Follow the limestone recommendations: 200 pounds for 1,000 square feet. Use dolomite limestone, since it delivers extra magnesium. Next, forget about trying to find a 10-10-10 organic fertilizer—no such thing exists! Instead, nitrogen (the first number in the 10-10-10 equation) from manure. The optimum rate of manure application is about 15 tons per acre. Since 1,000 square feet is roughly one forty-third acre, 15 tons of manure divided by 43 is about one-third ton.

You'll need about 700 pounds of manure for 1,000 square feet of garden. The phosphorus and potassium (the second and third numbers in the 10-10-10 recommendation) and trace minerals will be provided by the manure. If you need more phosphorus and potassium—if, say, the lab recommendation is 10-20-25—then you can add 50 pounds each of rock phosphate and greensand or granite dust annually for three years. This addition of rock fertilizers will give you seven to eight years of fertilizer action.

Organic test labs will often return results in terms of natural fertilizers. Their recommendations will resemble those explained above.

Although many people recommend testing your soil every year, it is not necessary, especially when you add organic fertilizers. For instance, rock phosphate releases its nutrients over a period of several years so you will not have to add phosphorus each year. Chemical fertilizers, on the other hand, are good for less than a year. While you are working to improve your soil, have your soil tested every two years. When the tests keep coming back the same, the soil has been stabilized, and you can reduce the frequency of soil tests.

Soil is complex. The balance of minerals, organic matter, air and water that make your soil easy to work and loaded with plant nutrients may take years to achieve, but once you have coaxed your soil into shape, keeping it that way is relatively easy. The secret is working with nature instead of against it. Your soil is the foundation on which the pleasure of hundreds of delicious meals from your garden is grown.

Chapter 2

Cultivation Keeps Your Garden in Shape

Let us never forget that the cultivation of the earth is the most important labor of man.

—Daniel Webster

Thousands of years ago, when man first began domesticating food plants, he discovered that the good-tasting plants were not as strong as many other plants. He noticed that the food plants that were protected against the harsh realities of life in the wild produced more food, and decided to give them a home close to his own so that he could keep a watchful eye on them. More and more time was devoted to caring for the favored plants. In time, the plants came to depend on man's help as much as man depended on the plants. Cultivation came to be an important part of early man's life. To this day, cultivation remains an important part of human food production, even in the domestic wilds of a surburban backyard.

In its broadest sense, cultivation covers the entire process of preparing and using soil for growing crops. In its narrowest sense, cultivation means the care of the garden's surface—the breaking of soil and the control of weeds.

Cultivation has two primary purposes. The first is to prepare a firm, fine seedbed which will result in the best seed germination possible. Weed control is the second important purpose. Additionally, cultivation helps aerate the soil and improve drainage. Turning under green manures, cover crops, animal manure, and compost are also functions of cultivation.

Although mankind has been tilling the earth for thousands of years, no "best" way to cultivate has been developed. Many different types of cultivation exist because each gardener has his or her own way of doing things. Each gardener must also take into account the type of tools and amount of time available for cultivation, as well as the location, soil type, climate and size of the garden when deciding on a method of cultivation.

Organic gardeners know that the best way to ensure good production in the garden is by working with nature instead of against it. As unnatural as it may seem, cultivation in one form or another is necessary for a good garden. The domesticated vegetables we grow are just not as strong as native plants. Cultivation is required to give domesticated vegetables an edge.

There are as many opinions about the proper way to work soil as there are gardeners. At one extreme are those who advocate never turning the soil. At the other extreme are those who turn the soil as often as three times a year. The vast majority of gardeners find that a position somewhere in between is best for them.

Wherever you fall on this no-till/till spectrum, a new garden needs to be cultivated to get itself established. In most parts of the United States uncultivated soil is too tightly packed and lacking in nutrients for optimum plant growth. A gardener who wants the best production from the soil in the shortest possible time must resort to some sort of initial cultivation in order to prepare the soil for its first crops. It is mighty discouraging to wait for the soil to fix itself, since this process takes years under the best of conditions. Later, as organic material and added nutrients make the soil more fertile you will be able to reduce the amount of cultivation without harming production. But during the first few years of a new garden, cultivation will be an important part of your garden program.

This chapter covers some of the more popular methods of cultivation. Each has been proven as an effective gardening system, under certain circumstances and conditions. Many gardeners adhere strictly to one cultivation method. You may want to try different methods, even combining two or more, until you discover the practice which makes the most sense for you.

WHEN TO CULTIVATE

Regardless of the cultivation method you choose, the soil in your garden will respond more favorably at certain times than at others. Working a soil when it is not ready for cultivation will probably do more harm than good and chances are you will spend the remainder of the growing season trying to correct your mistakes. On the other hand, cultivating when the soil is ready will result in a soil that can be easily managed through the season.

Deciding when to cultivate is one of the more difficult problems facing a new gardener. If you have gardened in the same place for a few years, you have probably developed a feel for your soil. However, you might be puzzled by where all those clods come from or why the soil seems to turn to powder and blow away half way through the season. Both of these problems indicate that early cultivation was done at the wrong time.

Soil must have the correct temperature and moisure content for it to work up properly. Moisture is the most important determinant of when a soil can be worked. Although most soils are hard to work when wet, clay soils are by far the most difficult and suffer the greatest damage when worked wet. Working a clay soil when wet will produce clods which will become rock-hard when baked dry by the sun. Many a hoe has been dulled trying to break down these clods. On the other hand, after a clay soil has baked dry it is as easy to work as asphalt. The key to producing the best result through cultivation is working the soil when it tells you it is ready.

Perform this simple test to find out when your soil is ready to work. Grab a handful of soil and squeeze it into a ball in your hand. If you can crumble the ball into small pieces with gentle finger pressure, it is ready to work. If the ball is wet and sticky and you cannot break it apart, the soil is too moist to work. If you cannot press the dirt into a ball, it is probably too dry to work (Fig. 2-1).

Despite the warning against working a soil when wet, waiting until a clay or loam soil is extremely dry is just as big a mistake. Working a dry soil will break it into a powdery consistency. When rain wets this powder, a clay surface will turn into a concrete-hard crust. The only way to prevent this hardening of clay soils is by working them when they have the proper moisture content. Additionally, bringing the soil's organic matter content up to 5 percent will help its tilth. In any event, overworking a clay soil will result in crusting, which slows down seedling emergence and prevents rain from soaking into the lower soil levels.

In clay soils you can get a jump on spring cultivation by turning over the soil in the fall. Soil

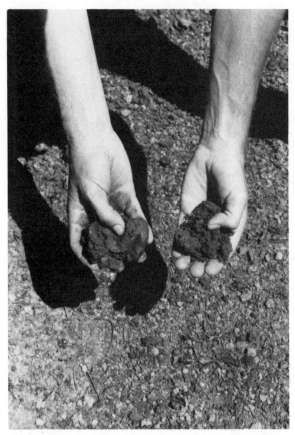

Fig. 2-1. The soil on the left is too wet to work. The soil on the right is just about perfect.

left exposed to freezing and thawing during the winter generally works easier the next spring. Winter freezes and thaws mellow the soil. Exposed soil also dries quicker in the spring. Be aware, however, that soil left exposed during the winter is subject to erosion. You can reduce erosion slightly by leaving the ground rough.

Sand and loam soils usually dry quickly in the spring; you will not need to turn them in the fall, unless you plan to plant a cover crop. As a general rule the less you work the soil the better, especially if your soil is low in organic matter. You can raise the organic content by turning organic materials into the soil every time you cultivate.

Many organic gardeners achieve the same effect as leaving their soil exposed all winter by planting a cover crop. The cover crop will protect the soil against erosion and, when turned under in the spring, does more to help the tilth and fertility of a soil than leaving it exposed to winter freezing and thawing.

A winter mulch that's at least 12 inches deep acts much like a cover crop. The mulch usually prevents the ground from freezing, keeps soil organisms like earthworms fairly active and adds to the organic content of the soil when the soil is turned in the spring. The way you leave your garden during the winter depends on how much time you have to work it in the fall, the severity of your winters, and how early you plan to get started the following spring.

Spring! It is time to get out there and cultivate your garden for the coming season. No doubt while driving around town you have noticed many different types, sizes and styles of gardens. Each gardener has adopted a method that works best with what they have. You too should choose the cultivation method that is best for you. Below are descriptions of several of the more popular methods of cultivation. When deciding on a cultivation method for your garden, take into account the type of tools you own, the amount of time you have and the location, soil type, climate and size of your garden. You may want to try only one method of cultivation or a combination of two or three, until you discover what works best for you.

PLOWING

If your garden is big, say half an acre or more, you may want to consider plowing as a cultivation method. Although plowing has been the accepted method of cultivation for hundreds of years it has come under fire recently because it is energy intensive, it encourages erosion, and it compacts the soil. While energy consumption and erosion are obvious problems, compaction may not show up in the top few inches of soil. Rather, a hardpan 8 to 10 inches below the surface—in the prime root growing zone—may develop. (See the hardpan section on the next page). Still, plowing remains a viable alternative for the gardener with a large garden.

This is the sequence for preparing soil by plowing. First, a tractor pulls a moldboard plow through the soil. The moldboard plow turns up a slice of soil as deep as the plow is set, moving the dirt eight to 12 inches to the left or right of the plow. Next, a disk is pulled over the turned soil breaking it into smaller pieces. Finally, the soil is smoothed with a harrow which breaks the soil into even finer pieces suitable for a seedbed.

Recently, a new method of plowing which does not disturb the soil as much as moldboard plowing has been developed, using a tool called a chisel plow. This plow has relatively narrow blades which are drug through the soil, loosening it without actually turning it over. Erosion is reduced and the danger of developing a hardpan through the extensive use of a moldboard plow is reduced. This method also leaves a residue of plant material on the soil's surface, slowing erosion.

On very rich soils loaded with organic material, a simple disk-and-harrow job may be all that is needed to produce a suitable seedbed. Remember, the fewer passes a tractor makes over the garden, the less compaction will result, and the less work will be required to prepare your garden for planting.

HARDPAN

Hardpan is a term used to describe soil that is too dense for roots to penetrate—indeed, it may even be so hard that water cannot percolate through it. If water cannot find its way through this layer chances are roots will not be able to either. Plant growth will suffer as a result (Fig. 2-2).

Hardpan can be a natural part of your soil or, as is often the case, it can be a result of repeated plowing at the same depth. An easy way to avoid plow-caused hardpan is to alter the plowing depth each season. Plow at 6 or 7 inches one season, 3 or 4 the next. Also, adding organic matter in the form of a ground cover will help reduce hardpan. Many ground covers have deep root systems which may be able to penetrate hardpan and make it a less serious problem. Organic gardeners seldom have problems with hardpan because the organic matter they add to the soil encourages earthworms. These natural rototillers are capable of burrowing through and loosening all but the severest hardpans.

If hardpan is currently a problem in your soil you can break it up mechanically by dragging what is known as a subsoiler through your garden. This plow-type device looks like an inverted T. The horizontal blades are set so that they are in the top level of the hardpan. As the blade moves through the soil it breaks up the hardpan, allowing deeper root penetration. Unfortunately, a subsoiler requires a very strong tractor. If hardpan is a real problem you may want to consider hiring a local farmer to do this work for you. You can then finish the cultivation job by yourself.

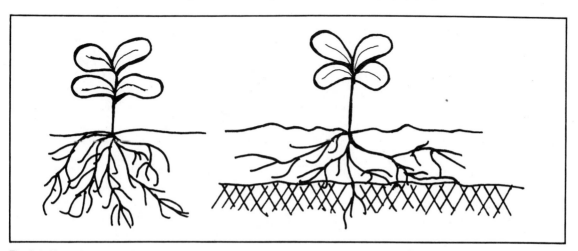

Fig. 2-2. Normal root growth pattern, left, and root growth cramped by a hardpan, right. Organic matter and earthworms will reduce this problem.

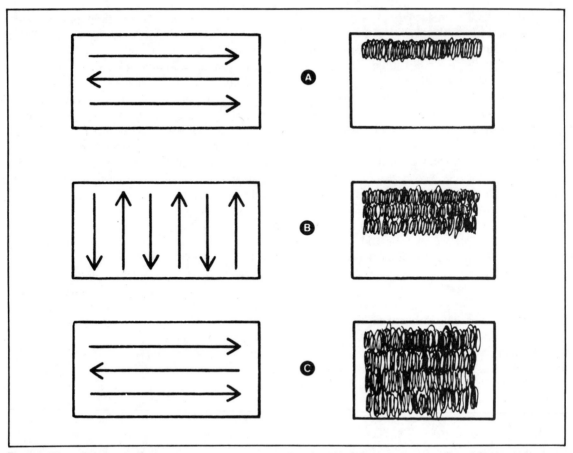

Fig. 2-3. When tilling, make the first pass shallow and in one direction (A). Subsequent passes (B and C) should be made deeper and across the previous pass.

TILLING

Rotary tillers combine the traditional cultivation practices of plowing, disking and harrowing into one operation. This convenience has made tillers a boon to gardeners. As a bonus, tilling is an excellent way of incorporating organic matter into the soil. Tillers are normally thought of as hand-guided equipment, but tiller attachments for the backs of small garden tractors are also available.

When preparing a garden with a tiller there are a few things to take into account.

● On soils poor in organic matter, make as few passes through the soil as possible to avoid harming the tilth of the soil. A soil pulverized into extremely fine particles by a tiller will lose much of its granulation. Poor granulation results in a soil which packs too tightly for good aeration and drainage.

● Make sure the soil has proper moisture content for cultivation before tilling. The same rules that apply to other methods of cultivation also apply to rototilling.

● On poor soils use the slowest tilling speed possible.

● Keep tiller blades sharp to reduce wear and tear on the machine and yourself.

When tilling sod for a garden make a pass over the area with the depth gauge set on shallow to break up the sod and make subsequent passes easier (Fig. 2-3). Allow the ground to set for a day after breaking up the sod, so the soil can dry a little and make the next pass more effective.

For the second pass, set the depth at a middle setting. Re-till the ground by making passes at a right angle to the previous tilling direction (Fig. 2-4). Do not fight the machine; let it do as much of the work as possible. Rear-tine rotary tillers tend to be easier to handle than front-tine ones.

If the second pass does not produce satisfactory results, make one more pass at right angles to the second pass, in the same direction as the original pass. Set the depth gauge as deep as it will go for this pass. By now, your soil should be crumbly. Rake the soil to form smooth seedbeds prior to planting.

Although the rotory action of tillers is less likely to form a hardpan than moldboard plows, frequent tilling at the same depth can produce compacted soil. Therefore, vary the maximum tilling depth from year to year and you should not be faced with a hardpan problem.

When turning organic matter under with a tiller, the first pass should mix the material to a depth of three inches. The next pass should be deeper, turning the material all the way under. Again, do not overwork your machine. Let it work at its own pace.

TRENCHING

In small gardens trenching is the most common form of soil cultivation. This method involves turning the soil with a shovel or spading fork in order to loosen it, to add organic material or to fertilize it.

To trench a garden, mark off the boundaries of where you plan to dig. Next, dig a trench as deep as your spade or spading fork along either of the short sides of the area. The soil removed from this trench should be moved by wheelbarrow to the opposite

Fig. 2-4. Work across previous tiller passes in order to mix the soil as thoroughly as possible.

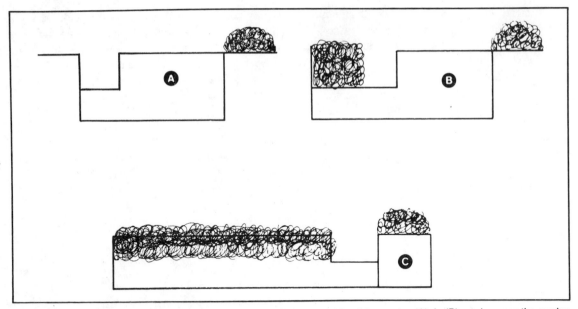

Fig. 2-5. The first step in trenching is digging a trench across the short side of the garden (A). In (B), work across the garden until the dirt from the original trench is filled into the last trench (C).

end of the garden—it will be used to fill in the final trench (Fig. 2-5).

When the first trench is completed, start a second next to the first. Turn each shovel-load of dirt into the first trench. Bury any plant residues, fertilizers, compost or mulch that was on top of the soil. If you tip each shovelful on its side rather than completely upside down, the plant residues will be buried at all depths of the soil instead of at one level.

Work across the garden, one trench at a time, until the entire garden is completed. Fill in the last trench with the dirt removed from the first trench.

Although you will be tempted to take as big a bite of dirt as possible each time you dig into the soil, don't do it. You will only tire faster. Instead, take moderate bites. Try to keep the side of the most recent trench as straight up and down as possible. After tipping each shovelful of soil into place, stick the shovel into the clod and give it a twist. This will loosen the soil and make the next step, hoeing or raking, easier.

The tool you choose for trenching will depend to a large extent on the soil. Soils presently in sod are easier to dig with a shovel since the blade cuts through the sod and makes removal easier. Spading forks, on the other hand, work best in loose soils since they offer less resistance going into the soil. You will also get better leverage with a long handled shovel or fork than with a short D-handled one.

DOUBLE DIGGING

In tight soils where plant roots have a difficult time growing down very far, double digging is the recommended cultivation method. The advantages of double digging include deepening the soil, improving drainage, making subsoil minerals available, allowing deep root growth and increasing your soil's resistance to drought.

Like trenching, this method loosens the soil one shovelful at a time. Unlike trenching, double digging works the soil to at least two shovels deep. Double digging is the hardest task you will encounter in the garden, but if you are willing to tackle the problem and see it through to the finish you will be well rewarded by abundant plant growth.

Since double digging is a time consuming job, I would recommend doing it in a garden laid out in beds. Working bed by bed will give you a sense of accomplishment as each bed is completed.

Before double digging you will need to gather a large quantity of compost, leaf mold or other organic material for incorporation into the soil. Also, you should know that a stout spading fork comes in handy.

To double dig, first mark off the area to be cultivated. Dig a trench along the short side of the area and remove the dirt to the opposite end of the bed. Next, take your spading fork and loosen the layer of soil in the bottom of the trench. Work the soil as deeply as you can, but do not remove it from the trench. When this soil is loose mix in a healthy amount of organic matter. See Fig. 2-6.

To begin the next step, start another trench right next to the first one. The dirt you remove from the second trench should be placed on top of the loosened subsoil in the first trench. Stick your shovel in each load of dirt and give it a twist to break it up. When the second trench is completed, break up the subsoil and mix in organic matter. Repeat these steps all the way across the bed. Do not walk on the bed once you have finished digging because your weight will compact the soil, undoing the loose structure you have just worked so hard to create.

The area you double dig will probably gain several inches of height over surrounding areas. This area will also do the best of any in your garden since roots will be able to reach deep into the soil for nutrients and water. Double digging is hard work, but well worth it. And each time you double dig the same area, the job becomes easier and easier.

RAISED BEDS

Raised beds are simply mounded-up garden soil. They can be any size and shape, although making them more than three feet wide is a mistake because it is difficult to reach the middle of the bed. Raised beds are a good idea on heavy soils where drainage is a problem (Fig. 2-7) because water collects in the lower paths around the beds instead of around plant roots. Additionally, you will not be tempted to walk on raised beds. Although benefits

are similar to double dug beds, raised beds are easier to make.

The first step in making raised beds is tilling or trench-digging your entire garden. Mark off the areas you want for beds. The remainder will be paths. Spread the soil in the paths on the marked off beds with a shovel or a tiller with a hiller-furrow attachment (Fig. 2-8). When removing soil from the paths do not dig deep enough to throw subsoil on the beds, but do remove as much of the topsoil as

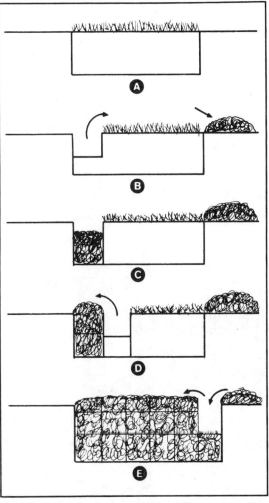

Fig. 2-6. To double dig, mark off area to be turned (A). Start with a trench along one side (B), work the soil in the bottom of the trench (C), and add organic matter. Dig the next trench filling the previous trench (D). Finish by filling in extra dirt (E).

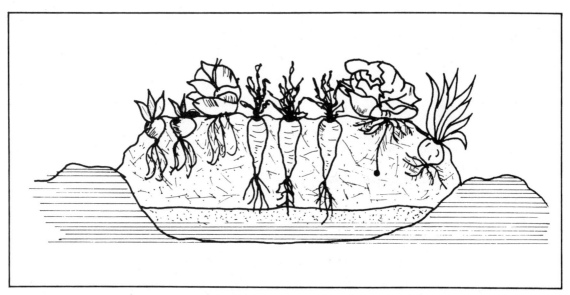

Fig. 2-7. Raised beds give plants plenty of root room while growing as many vegetables as soon as possible in a limited space.

Fig. 2-8. A hiller-furrow attachment for a tiller produces raised beds fast (courtesy of Troy Bilt Rototillers).

possible. Finally, rake the beds into mounded or flat-topped seedbeds. Mulch the paths to prevent weed growth or cover the paths with carpeting, boards, stones or whatever is available to keep weeds and mud to a minimum.

Here are a few things to remember when making raised beds:

● Do not make the beds too wide. You should be able to reach all the plants in a bed from the path.

● Work the soil as deeply as possible without disturbing the soil profile. This will give your plants more vertical root room and allow you to plant them closer together.

● When preparing the soil, work only the area you intend to plant. Do not worry about the paths once they are established, since they will not be supporting plants.

● As a general rule smaller plants—lettuce and cabbage for instance—do better in beds than big plants like corn and tomatoes; however, all plants will do better in beds than in rows.

LOWERED BEDS

In many parts of the arid Southwest, gardeners are faced with the opposite problems of Eastern gardeners. Instead of having a climate that keeps the soil so wet that raised beds are required to keep plants from drowning, lowered beds are required to keep enough moisture in the soil for good plant growth.

As if infrequent rains and drying winds were not enough of a problem, the soil is often a concrete-like calcium carbonate which will discourage even the strongest roots. The Indians, who have lived in the area for centuries, have found a way of overcoming these problems by developing what is known as a "waffle" garden. Instead of building the garden above ground, like raised beds, waffle gardens are made below ground (Fig. 2-9). The hard soil is broken up and removed to a depth of 3 feet, then replaced with organic material more suited to root growth. Having the bed lower than the surrounding ground ensures that any precipitation falling on the garden will collect in the growing area instead of running off. Although growing conditions remain far from ideal in lowered beds, they do allow the raising of vegetables in areas of the country where they would normally be impossible to grow.

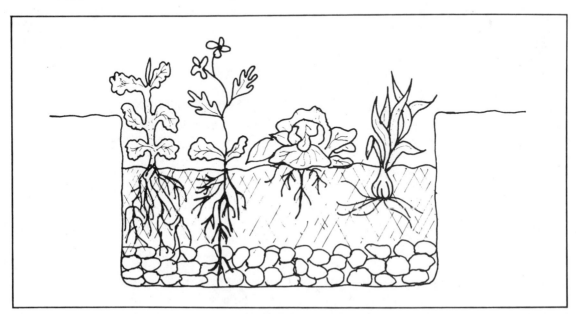

Fig. 2-9. Lowered beds are an attractive method of gardening in arid regions, since every last drop of rain is captured for vegetable plants.

To make a waffle garden, mark off the area where beds are to be made. The same rules that apply to raised beds apply to these lowered beds. Leave plenty of room between beds for paths and make sure the beds are narrow enough so that you can reach all parts of each bed from the walkways.

Once the beds are marked off, remove the topsoil and pile it nearby. Break up the subsoil to a depth of 2 to 3 feet and remove it. (Some of this material can be spread around the paths.) Next dig compost, leaves, food scraps and any other organic matter you can get your hands on into the beds. Each bed should be filled to within a foot of the path. Replace the topsoil and mix with the organic matter. Waffle beds settle quite a bit, so fresh organic matter needs to be added whenever it is available.

NO-TILL

No-till gardeners have thrown away the rototiller and shovel as a way of cultivation. Instead they leave a mulch on their garden year-round, which keeps the soil moist so that earthworms can dig around aerating and loosening the soil. Many people have adopted this method and it seems to work on loam and sandy-loam soils. These soils are loose to begin with and need minimal help. On tightly packed clay soils the no-till method can also be used, although it may take years for the soil to loosen up enough so you can completely quit tilling the soil. A better idea on clay soils is cultivating with some form of mechanical turning until the soil grows loose and crumbly with organic matter, and then begin the no-till method.

If you happen to have a good loam or silt sand soil and want to try the no-till method, here is how it is done. Simply mark off the area you wish to convert to no-till and cover it with between 8 inches and a foot of mulch. Most people who use this method prefer straw or hay as a mulch, although virtually any vegetable matter that decomposes readily can be used.

Cover the garden in the fall so that worms and other soil organisms can be kept working in the soil all winter. In the spring simply rake the mulch back from where you want to plant. Plant your seeds and, after they have established themselves, put the mulch around the plants. Whenever weeds appear, smother them with mulch. Rock fertilizers and other natural fertilizers can be broadcast on top of the mulch and then covered with a fresh layer of mulch. Slowly these nutrients will work their way down into the soil.

The no-till garden is never dug and fresh organic matter is always being added. Again, this method is not for everyone, especially those with heavy clay soils, but it will work on fertile soils rich in organic matter.

PLUG PLANTING

A variation of the no-till method which has gained popularity recently is plug planting. With this practice, a small plug is taken out of sod or a permanently-mulched bed with a small tool that resembles a large cookie cutter. Seeds or transplants are then placed in this cutout and covered with dirt. The sod and mulch keep the soil moist while eliminating weeds. Additionally, very little cultivation is required.

Like the permanent mulch system, the plug planting method works best in soils that are naturally loose. Do not try this practice in heavy clays because plant roots will not have enough strength to work their way through these tightly packed soils. Crop production using the plug planting method in sod is not as high as on cultivated land, but the savings in work are substantial.

CULTIVATING FOR WEED CONTROL

Cultivation for weed control should begin three or four days after crops are planted, long before most vegetable seeds germinate. Unfortunately, many weed seeds seem to germinate immediately after you have planted your vegetable seeds. If you look closely at the ground, you will notice weeds' tiny leaves a day or two after planting your vegetable seeds. If you put off weeding when the intruders are at this stage, the weeds will be much harder to kill by the time you get around to cultivating.

The best way to cultivate the first time after planting is with a hard rake. Run the rake gently over the entire seedbed. You can even go over the planted rows as long as you do not force the rake down into the soil to the level of your seeds. Cultivate again in a few days. By now, the seedlings should be up and can be cultivated with a hoe or cultivator. This little bit of preventative cultivation can reduce by hours the weeding you do later in the season.

Occasionally, you will manage to get your seeds in the ground right before a rain. This is great for the germination of both weed and vegetable seeds. If the wet weather persists, the ground will remain too wet to cultivate and weeds will begin to grow between the vegetables. When the ground finally dries enough to work, get out there with the hoe, rototiller or rake and knock down the weeds before they take over the garden.

When vegetable plants reach 4 to 6 inches in height, start your mulching program. Begin by laying a strip of mulch down the middle of each row. As the plants grow, move the mulch closer to the plants. The mulch should choke out most weeds so you will need to do no more than spot cultivate here and there the rest of the summer.

Hoeing

In addition to raking, hoeing is an effective cultivation method (Fig. 2-10). Hoeing can be hard work, but you can reduce the effort needed by using the correct technique. Avoid the temptation to chop with your hoe. Instead, hoeing should be a pulling effort.

Never raise the hoe blade higher than the top of your ankles. The slant of the blade on a good hoe is designed so that when you set the blade on the ground in front of you and pull it toward your feet with moderate pressure, the blade will naturally bite into the ground. A shallow furrow should result. Make 8- to 12-inch long furrows with the hoe for best results. Lift the hoe a couple of inches above the ground during the back stroke and return to the starting position 12 to 18 inches in front of you. Pull the hoe toward you scraping another furrow. Dirt spilling out of the second furrow should partially fill the first furrow. Practice this technique and you will soon be saving a lot of energy while gaining better control of your hoe.

Another technique that is useful for cutting weeds off at ground level is placing the hoe's blade on the ground in front of you and then pulling it toward you with little or no downward pressure. The blade will skim across the soil surface, cutting off weeds in its path. This hoeing method comes in handy when hoeing near shallow-rooted plants like lettuce and cabbage, where deep hoeing would hurt their roots.

Tilling

In addition to turning the soil, tillers are useful as a way of weeding the garden (Fig. 2-11). This is especially true in large gardens where gathering enough material to mulch between every row is prohibitively difficult.

Fig. 2-10. A long-handled hoe is the most popular cultivation method of all. You can knock down weeds, mix the soil, and incorporate compost all at once.

Fig. 2-11. Small tillers in large gardens make for easy weeding. Plant in rows far enough apart to allow a tiller between plants (courtesy of Troy Bilt Rototillers).

Gardens that are to be cultivated by the tiller should be planted with rows far enough apart that the tiller can pass easily between them. This means that if your tiller is 28 inches wide your rows need to be at least 40 inches wide. Using a tiller to cultivate weeds wastes a lot of space. Gardeners with limited space should steer away from this method of cultivation in order to achieve better production from the available space.

To till for weeds set the tiller at a very shallow depth. One or 2 inches is plenty, because you do not want to damage vegetable plant roots. Guide the tiller between the rows, churning the weeds out of the ground. As plants mature and occupy more of the space between rows you may want to remove the outside tines from the tiller. This will allow you to till a narrower space, reducing the chances of damaging your crops.

Your crops need you as much as you need them. Domesticated plants simply will not grow big and healthy without a helping hand from a gardener, and cultivation is that helping hand.

Regardless of which of the many cultivation methods you practice, vegetables need a good seedbed and minimal competition from weeds to grow their best. The method of cultivation you choose is guided by your soil type, climate, the tools you own, the amount of time and energy you have, and the crops you grow. You will need to experiment a few seasons to determine the cultivation method that works best for you. Once you have worked adequate amounts of organic matter into your soil, you will find that cultivation is no longer the chore it used to be. In fact, rich soil loaded with organic material may allow you to give up turning the soil altogether.

Chapter 3

What Makes
Plants Grow

*No creature of the soil stands alone—all
are interwoven, their pasts and futures,
in the economy of a piece of earth.*

—Peter Farb

You need certain amounts of food, shelter, and warmth to stay alive. The plants growing in your garden have similar minimum needs for good growth. Some factors affecting good plant growth include nutrients, air, water, sunshine, soil pH, and temperature. Each of these factors operates in a cycle that plants are adept at handling (Fig. 3-1). As an organic gardener, you want to mimic the cycles of nature as closely as possible in order to create a "natural environment" for your plants.

Most gardeners have a pretty good idea about the purpose of fertilizer. It is a plant's food, supplying the nutrients necessary for growth. Sadly, not everyone knows that the same nutrients are available in natural forms. In fact, nutrients are always being returned to the soil, replacing those that are used in the normal course of a plant's growth. Leaves, stems, and roots all decay, giving back to the soil the nutrients they removed during growth.

If you dig your fingers down into the soil of a mature forest, you will notice that the first few inches are organic materials from the decomposing parts of fallen trees. The top layer of soil consists of leaves and twigs from last year—this layer resembles very much the mulch that organic gardeners use. Below this layer is a zone of crumbly black leaf mold—the same thing organic gardeners make through composting. Next comes a layer of topsoil, and finally the subsoil. Tree roots bring up nutrients from these lower layers, which feed the tree. Rain constantly recycles nutrients by carrying nutrients down into the soil from the top layers. The goal of organic gardening is to mimic nature's nutrient-cycling process.

PLANT FOODS

The most important of all plant foods are the ones least often mentioned: hydrogen, oxygen, and carbon. Plants obtain these elements from the air and water available to roots and leaves. You cannot

Fig. 3-1. Many things are necessary for good plant growth. Each of them must be readily available for the plant to be healthy.

feed plants hydrogen, oxygen and carbon; plants must gather them for themselves. However, you can help plants gather these elements by keeping the soil adequately aerated, watered and rich in the other nutrients necessary for life.

In addition to these nutrients, plants draw a host of minerals from the soil. These minerals are what most gardeners mean when they say "fertilizer." Gardeners can, to some extent, control the amounts of these minerals available to plants.

A small number of these minerals are considered more important to plant growth than others. These are labeled macronutrients. Macronutrients are required in relatively large amounts by plants. Macronutrients include carbon, oxygen, nitrogen, phosphorus, potassium, calcium, and sulfur. Regrettably, most gardeners know only nitrogen, potassium and phosphorus as macronutrients. This shortsightedness is due to the influence chemical fertilizer manufacturers have

wielded in modern agriculture. Hydrogen, too, is needed in macro amounts—not as a nutrient, but as an ion to be traded by the plant to the soil in exchange for certain nutrients. (This process is called cation exchange.)

The dozens of other minerals which plants use in lesser quantities are called micronutrients. These include such little-thought-of elements as magnesium, copper, zinc, molybdenum, boron, chlorine, iron and various trace elements. The distinction between macro and micro nutrients is one of convenience and not an absolute. Plants cannot live without a full complement of nutrients—macro, micro, or otherwise.

Scientists cannot agree on what it takes to feed and maintain a plant in good health. Fifteen elements are commonly listed as essential, yet more than 56 elements have been detected in plant tissue. The best way to provide the vegetables and fruits growing in your garden with all the nutrients they need is by working as great a variety of plant and animal materials into your soil as possible. Nature will do the rest.

The elements that scientists say are absolutely essential include carbon (C), hydrogen (H) and oxygen (O), which come mainly from air; soil; and water. Nitrogen (N), phosphorus (P), potassium (K), sulfur (S), calcium (Ca), magnesium (Mg), and iron (Fe) are other well-known essential elements. More recently, boron (B), copper (Cu), manganese (Mn), molybdenum (Mo), and zinc (Zn) have been added to the list of essential nutrients.

Other elements such as silicon, chlorine, and sodium are found in plants, although their presence has not yet been shown to be essential. Plants also cycle small amounts of a group of elements that seems to be nonessential—at least for plant growth. These are aluminum, arsenic, lead, barium, mercury, bromine, tin, cobalt, gold, nickel and selenium. Although scientists claim that many of these elements are nonessential, don't be fooled. The fact that these trace elements are in a plant gives you a pretty good clue that they are necessary in some as-yet-unknown way.

The yield of a crop is controlled by and directly proportional to the limiting growth factors, including things such as water, air, temperature, sunlight, soil pH, and soil nutrient content. The limiting factors most gardeners are familiar with are nutrient deficiencies. Each nutrient must be present in sufficient quantities, or plants simply will not grow as they should. This is where you, the gardener comes into play.

You have the responsibility of keeping the nutrients in the soil in balance. This does not mean that there should be as much calcium, for instance, as nitrogen in your soil; however, these two elements do have an optimum ratio that encourages good plant growth. When we remove vegetables from the garden and carry them into our kitchens we are taking the nutrients in those vegetables out of the garden's ecosystem. These nutrients must be returned to keep the soil balanced. This is where fertilizers come into play. Think of them as a way of paying back the soil for the nutrients you remove as food.

The problem with chemical fertilizers is that they tend to concentrate on three nutrients— nitrogen, phosphorus, and potassium (the NPK listing on fertilizer packages). When huge additions of these materials are added to a soil the balance of soil nutrients is upset, not because the trace minerals are lacking, but because the excess of these major nutrients makes the trace mineral ratio too low. You can keep the ratio of nutrients in your soil fairly stable by adding only nutrients from natural sources. As a rule, these nutrients match fairly well the ratio of soil nutrients found in nature.

Although science has been able to identify and separate the various elements in a soil necessary for life, little attention has been given to the way in which these materials become available to plants. Chemical fertilizer manufacturers insist that simply adding a nutrient to soil in a form available to plants gives plants all the food they need. Chemical fertilizers fail to take into account the fact that events in nature are cyclic, and that nature is capable of using and reusing (recycling) the materials from which it is built.

Early in the nineteenth century a few of the chemical events that take place in soil were discovered. Scientists quickly came to the conclusion that these few chemical reactions were the whole story. The question "What causes these events?" was not asked. In fact, at that time it could not have been answered, because microorganisms had yet to be discovered.

Nowadays, soil scientists know that in nature the microorganisms in a soil are responsible for much of the work of converting dead plants and animals into new plant food. Humus is responsible for a large portion of the remaining conversion.

Most of mankind seems bent on improving nature. The old way of feeding the soil so that it will feed plants has given way to the idea of soil as a prop for holding up plants, into which the neat, simple applications of chemical fertilizers containing NPK (all that is needed to produce good crops) are introduced. Put in NPK and out comes food. Nature and soil have nothing to say in the matter.

Fortunately, things are changing as more and more gardeners realize that the only way to produce living food is to maintain a living soil. Farmers, too, are beginning to get the picture: the only way to keep soil from dying is to treat it as a living thing. Nature will do the rest.

Organic gardeners believe that what you do to the soil should be done to encourage nature's constant process of recycling. Careless exploitation by man has upset this delicate balance. Slowly, we have come to realize that once an animal or plant species has been destroyed no amount of wishful thinking or scientific research can bring it back. The soil as part of nature comes under the same restrictions, though not as permanently. Once it has been depleted and eroded away, soil cannot be brought back to life without tons of organic matter and an army of microorganisms.

NUTRIENT CYCLES

Organic matter and microbes hold the key to most of the nutrient cycles in nature. Let's look at a couple of nutrient cycles to get an idea of how elements that are vital to plant growth cycle through nature.

Nitrogen

There are three basic sources of nitrogen in mineral soils. Most of the nitrogen in a soil is associated with organic matter. Some nitrogen is also found in clay minerals. Soluble ammonia also provides a little nitrogen, although this form of nitrogen is especially subject to volitization and leaching. Nitrogen in a form usable to plants is derived almost exclusively from organic matter.

Although nearly 80 percent of the atmosphere is nitrogen, this element tends to be one of the major limiting factors of plant growth. The catch is that nitrogen must be fixed (combined) with one or more elements in the soil before it can be of use to a plant. Rain does a little fixing, perhaps 5 pounds of nitrogen per acre per year—hardly enough for all the plants growing on the acre. Lightning, too, fixes some nitrogen; however, most nitrogen is fixed by bacteria in the soil. Some of these little fellows are symbiotic, some are not. The former are those associated with legumes, and the latter grow independently in the soil. A natural nitrogen cycle depends on a healthy living soil and almost every cycle in the soil-nutrient process depends on the nitrogen cycle in one way or another.

A hasty sketch of the nitrogen cycle goes something like this: Atmospheric nitrogen is fixed by bacteria. One such bacterium is the rhizobium, which lives in the nodules on the roots of legume plants such as clover, peas and beans (Fig. 3-2). These bacteria are capable of combining the nitrogen from air in the soil with carbohydrates that they get from the legume. The result is an amino acid that is used by the plant and other bacteria for building tissue. The relationship between the bacteria and the plant is symbiotic. The process is of mutual advantage to both plant and microbe.

In addition to this symbiotic relationship,

Fig. 3-2. Nitrogen-fixing bacteria called rhizobia live in the nodules of legumes. These are the nodules on a bean plant.

there are free-living bacteria in the soil which can transform the carbohydrates found in decaying organic matter to proteins by combining atmospheric nitrogen with other nutrients. Other bacteria then break down these proteins into ammonia and then into nitrates, which plants take up as food.

The nitrogen from organic matter is released slowly in a process called mineralization. Nitrogen bound up in organic matter is protected from loss due to leaching. Although nitrogen in this form is unavailable to plants, microorganisms can and do feed on this nitrogen, transforming it into nitrates which plants can then use.

These nitrates are used by plants to build tissue and produce a crop. When the plant dies the nitrogen is locked in the plant's tissues. As the organic matter decays, some of the nitrogen is liberated in a process called denitrofication by bacteria and returned to the air. Once in the air, this nitrogen must be fixed in order to become available to plants. The nitrogen that is not released is used by microorganisms to make proteins which are converted to plant food. Some of the nitrogen is lost through leaching and erosion. What is lost must be replaced from the atmosphere or from fresh organic matter in order to keep the nitrogen cycle operating. Fortunately, when a plant dies (usually because of a killing frost in the fall) the nitrogen-releasing microorganisms in the soil are slowed by the low temperatures. The following spring they once again come to life, releasing nitrates as new plants start the growth cycle. This keeps much of the soil's nitrogen locked into a form nearly usable by plants.

Carbon

Carbon, which makes up nearly 50 percent of all organic matter, is often given short shrift by gardeners. However, next to the sun carbon is the major source of energy in a garden ecosystem. Every cell of every plant and animal uses carbon. It is constantly recycling through the organic processes of respiration, death, decay and tissue building.

The carbon cycle goes something like this. Carbon is present in the atmosphere, largely in the form of carbon dioxide (CO_2). Plants breathe in carbon dioxide and use it to build the carbohydrates

in their tissue. Plants return a portion of this carbon dioxide to the atmosphere through respiration. When a plant is eaten by an animal, the animal releases much of the carbon back into the atmosphere as carbon dioxide. The remainder is returned to nature as manure, or when the animal dies and its body is broken down by microorganisms. When the plant dies, it is eaten by microorganisms, which use the carbohydrates for food energy and release much of the carbon as carbon dioxide. This gas mixes into the atmosphere where it is once again available for plants.

MACRONUTRIENTS

In both nitrogen and carbon cycles, microorganisms play an important role in changing materials from a form unusable to plants to a form that plants can use. These microorganisms call the soil home. Soils rich in organic matter support large microbe populations—hence the nutrient cycles. In fact, microbes are merely looking out for their own good, but in the process they supply nearly all of a plant's nutrients. Soils that have been bombarded with a series of toxic chemicals such as salt-based fertilizers, pesticides, herbicides, and fungicides are low in microbal life, and the natural nutrient cycles do not work as they should. Feeding the plants growing in these soils becomes a major effort.

Which would you rather have, soil that feeds the plants almost by itself, or a soil you have to add expensive fertilizers to in order to feed the plants?

Microorganisms and organic matter in the soil will make the difference. A quick review of these major plant nutrients should convince you of that.

Nitrogen

Although nitrogen cycles continuously through the environment of your garden, it is available to plants at only one place in this cycle. Growing plants and then harvesting them, the purpose of every gardener, depletes the available nitrogen content of your soil. If you do not put back as much nitrogen as you take out of your garden, you are losing ground. When you put more organic matter into the soil than you remove through harvesting, you are building soil. You are also building nitrogen fertility. Soils rich in organic matter are seldom deficient in nitrogen, since nitrogen is produced during the decomposition of organic matter.

Nitrogen is one of the major nutrients involved in the production of leaves and stems on a plant. Plant growth is strong and plant maturity is reached rapidly when nitrogen is available in the correct amounts.

You can upset a plant's growth by providing either too little or too much nitrogen. Too little nitrogen in the soil and plants grow spindly and yellowish. Too much nitrogen and the plants produce lots of stem and leaf at the expense of fruit production. Excess nitrogen causes tissue to be spongy instead of stiff, which makes plants susceptible to wind and frost damage. Many diseases attack plants that are weakened by an excess of nitrogen. Nitrogen must be available in amounts that maintain the proper ratio among other nutrients.

Phosphorus

To most gardeners, the relationship between decomposing organic matter and the availability of nitrogen is common knowledge. What gardeners do not realize is that the decomposition of organic matter is equally important to the release of phosphorus.

In all soils short on organic matter, phosphorus tends to be locked up by the soil, unavailable for use by plants; however, nature has devised two methods by which phosphorus in the soil becomes available.

The first method depends on the decomposition of organic matter and on the microbes living on that material. These little workers excrete nitric and sulfuric acids which break phosphorus away from its relationship with other minerals, making it available for plant use. Many of these microorganisms produce more phosphorus than they need. This extra phosphorus is there for plants to use.

Plants do not depend entirely on the excess phosphorus released by microorganisms. They also have a strategy for gathering their own supply of this nutrient. Plant roots give off carbon dioxide and certain organic acids. When roots develop near a piece of phosphate in the soil, these root-produced acids make the phosphorus available for absorbtion by the root.

Phosphorus in many soils is bound with calcium. Root hairs coming in contact with this combination of particles can absorb the calcium. This frees the phosphorus, which is then absorbed. For this reason, lime, which is high in calcium, should not be added to soil at the same time as phosphate rock. Plant roots will absorb the calcium from the lime before the calcium bonds to the phosphate. A shortage of available phosphorus results.

All growing plants need phosphorus. It is a constituent of genetic materials and is important for proper seed development. Although the specific properties of phosphorus are not completely understood, a deficiency seems to cause stunted growth and seed sterility. Phosphorus is said to hasten maturity, increase seed yields, increase fruit development, increase resistance to winterkill and diseases, and increase the vitamin content of plants.

Potassium

Luckily, soil contains plenty of potassium—potash in fertilizer jargon. Unluckily, most of this potash is in an unavailable form.

Microbes must be present in the soil to make potassium available. When soils have few microbes, potassium is likely to leach from the soil or bind itself to other minerals in such a way that plants cannot use it. The acid secreted by microbes can break these potassium complexes down. Free potassium then attaches itself to clay or humus particles in the soil. The potassium then enters the plant.

Although potash is found in decaying organic matter and is free and available for plants, this supply is rarely enough to satisfy all of a plant's needs. So, plants also use their roots to free potassium locked to other minerals. The process is similar to the way roots unlock phosphorus, but involving different elements.

Potassium is one of the least-understood elements necessary for plant growth, but it is of major importance. Scientists have not discovered exactly what potassium does. It is not built into the structure of a plant, but it does seem to be required in all the functions of a plant. The most commonly-held belief is that potassium is an important plate in the armor of a plant's disease resistance.

Potassium protects plants from both cold and heat by reducing water loss. Plant sugars are also formed in the presence of potassium. It helps in the formation of carbohydrates, and it is necessary for protein synthesis. In addition, it promotes early growth, improves stem strength, contributes to stem hardness, and improves the keeping ability, color and flavor of fruit. Plants deficient in potassium are usually stunted and have poorly-developed root systems. Their leaves, particularly the older ones, are usually spotted, curled or mottled and may even appear burned around the edges. Even before these symptoms appear, plants deficient in potassium will produce lower yields.

Plant-available potassium appears to move around a lot in the soil. It is easily leached from soil and must be constantly resupplied. This is a strange condition, since in the top 6 inches of an acre of soil there may be up to 40,000 pounds of potassium, and only about 1 percent is available to plants. You can keep the maximum amount of potash available to plants through the frequent application of plant residues, mulch, manures, and compost. Natural mineral sources like granite dust are good long-term providers of this nutrient.

Calcium

Although calcium is not usually classed with nitrogen, phosphorus, and potassium as a macronutrient, this element plays a major role in plant nutrition. The reason calcium is frequently overlooked when discussing fertility is that it is abundant in all fertile soils.

Calcium acts as a middleman in the exchange of nutrients from the soil to plants. Many of the mineral elements in soil attach themselves to calcium during part of their cycles. In most cases, when these other nutrients are released from the cal-

cium, the nutrient is in a form available to plants.

Inside plants, calcium collects mainly in the leaf material. It is known to cleanse plants of many of the toxic acids formed during metabolism. Calcium is also integrated into the proteins and cell walls.

MICRONUTRIENTS

Most gardeners, and most of the agribusiness community, concentrate their fertilization efforts on the big three: nitrogen, phosphorus, and potassium. They often overlook the importance of a wide variety of micronutrients that must be present in the soil in available form in small quantities for plant growth. Some of the more notable micronutrients (or "trace minerals" as they are often called) are zinc, manganese, boron, iron, sulfur, copper, magnesium, molybdenum, and chlorine. There are others, such as barium, vanadium, strontium, silver and titanium, which may be necessary, though their functions are not yet entirely understood.

Some elements, although they're thought to be necessary for plant life, are necessary for the animal life that feeds on plants. Selenium, iodine, and cobalt are examples of such elements. The field of micronutrients is clouded in mystery; scientists do not know exactly how each trace element effects plant growth. Still, two general observations have been made. If there are no trace elements in a soil, plants have a hard time growing because of the deficiency. On the other side of the ledger, when too much of a trace element is present in the soil, plants also have a hard time growing because the soil is toxic. The question is how you can balance the micronutrients in the soil for best growth. The answer is quite simple: let nature do it.

Most soil scientists will agree that soils rich in organic matter seem thoroughly capable of supplying plants with all the micronutrients they need. Trace minerals become available to plants during the normal process of decomposition. Adding organic matter to the soil makes much more sense than trying to add micronutrients chemically, since a slip of the teaspoon can produce a toxic soil situation. The cure is often worse than the deficiency.

For instance, soils suffering a boron deficiency

may require the addition of only 5 pounds of boron per acre. If you add more, you could make the soil too toxic for good plant growth. The requirements for molybdenum are measured in *ounces* per acre. Add a single ounce to a small garden, and you render the soil unfit for plant growth for many years. The only sure way to keep your soil in the safe micronutrient range is through the use of organic matter and natural fertilizers.

Organic matter helps provide trace minerals to plants in two ways. First, organic matter can provide them directly from its humus—the end product of decomposition. Second, certain organic molecules will clamp onto trace minerals in the soil. This process is called chelation. Plants can normally take trace minerals from these organic molecules as they need them. Organic matter does more than simply put minerals back into the soil. It also provides the chelating agents that make the trace minerals available, something that cannot be said for most chemical fertilizers.

Here are short introductions to some trace minerals.

Zinc

The best way to maintain proper levels of zinc in a soil is through the application of manure. Raw phosphate rock fertilizer also contains small amounts of zinc. Chemical growers use zinc sulfate as a source of zinc, but the effects of the excess sulfur may outweigh the benefit of the zinc.

Boron

Boron and calcium influence each other noticeably in the soil. Boron becomes unavailable in soils with an excess of calcium (lime). The two elements must be kept in balance for proper soil fertility. The best way to keep this balance is by making sure soils are rich in organic matter. Soils with an organic content of more than 3 percent seldom show boron deficiencies. Granite dust is a good source of slowly-released boron.

Magnesium

Magnesium is a vital element in the formation of chlorophyll in plants. Magnesium is the central atom of every chlorophyll molecule, and without it photosynthesis would be impossible. Fortunately, few soils are deficient in magnesium since only very small amounts are necessary. The regular addition of raw rock phosphate or dolomitic limestone will provide all the magnesium your soil needs. The chlorophyll in decomposing green vegetable matter also supplies magnesium.

Iron

Iron is a rather common element in most soils. Unfortunately, it tends to be in the form of iron oxide, which is unavailable to plants. Iron is most available in a slightly acid soil. Neutral and alkaline soils tend to hold iron in forms unavailable to plants.

Although plants need very little iron, they cannot live without it. Like magnesium, iron is a necessary ingredient for chlorophyll. The organic acids formed during the decomposition of organic materials in the soil are able to provide enough iron for most plant needs. Glauconite or greensand is a good source of iron.

Sulfur

Sulfur is a nonmetallic element in the soil that is of major importance to fertility. Some plants contain more sulfur than phosphorus, which is a macronutrient.

Sulfur is oxidized in the soil and combined with other elements to form sulfates such as calcium sulfate, potassium sulfate, ammonium sulfate and zinc sulfate. These sulfates are then taken up by roots and transported to cell-building sites where they are incorporated into cycstine, a protein constituent. When a plant dies, proteins are broken down by microorganisms and sulfur reenters into the soil complex, where it once again becomes an available nutrient.

Sulfur is not chelated by particles in the soil, so it tends to leach through the root zone and into the deep subsoil out of the grasp of roots. This is especially true in sandy, quick-draining soils. Although all soils contain sulfur, it is not always in an available form. Rain carrying the smoke of sulfur-bearing fossil fuels should supply all the sulfur crops need.

Manganese

Inside plants, manganese acts as a guide for

other plant nutrients. It makes sure that other nutrients coming to the plant will arrive when they are needed for the plant's metabolism. Manganese is also an important assistant in the process of nitrogen fixation in legumes.

High organic content in a soil seems to have little direct effect on the availability of manganese. Instead, pH plays a major role. Soils high in alkalinity due to excess liming often have manganese deficiencies. The best correction is to stop liming and to add mildly acidic materials, such as oak leaves, cottonseed meal or pine needles, to the soil. This organic matter will acidify the soil and release manganese for plant use.

Copper

Soil organic matter cannot be depended on to provide adequate amounts of copper. Some soils which are extremely rich in organic matter, notably peat and muck, often lack sufficient copper. In soils where too much lime or phosphate has been used, resulting in an alkaline soil condition, plants may suffer copper deficiencies. Deficiencies of copper are usually not encountered in soils with a decent balance of organic matter, mineral content, and pH.

Although copper's function has not been entirely determined, it is recognized as essential to plant growth. This metal is thought to be active in many enzymes and as a catalyst for plant respiration. Some hardwood sawdusts and wood shavings contain significant amounts of copper.

Molybdenum

Molybdenum is rarely lacking in soils, yet soil with a pH below 5.2 often shows this deficiency among other problems. When this metal is a problem in the soil it is usually due to an overabundance. Excess molybdenum is a result of pollution from industrial smoke. It can easily be overabundant because plants need very little of it. Legumes are known to use it during nitrogen fixation, but its use in other plants is little known. You will not need to worry about this trace mineral as long as the soil's pH remains normal.

Cobalt

Although cobalt has not yet proved necessary for healthy plant growth, it is necessary for healthy animal growth. This metal is an essential component of vitamin B_{12} and is found in the tissue of living plants. A well-balanced program of adding a wide variety of organic material to your soil will prevent any chance of cobalt deficiency.

Chlorine

Chlorine is needed in very small amounts for optimum plant growth. Rainwater seems capable of supplying a sufficient quantity of this element for good fertility.

The nutrients available to a plant have a significant effect on the plant's growth. Adequate nutrition, however, is not enough to ensure healthy plant growth. Several other factors including soil pH, aeration, water, sunlight, and temperature affect the growth of plants.

pH

The acidity or alkalinity of a soil is measured in terms of pH, and is known as the soil's reaction. In most cases the soil's reaction is determined by the parent material and the decomposition of organic matter in this parent material.

All you need to know about pH is that it is a measure of the degree of acidity or alkalinity in a soil. Soils at a pH of 7 are neutral since acidity and alkalinity are in balance. When the pH of a soil is below 7 (6.5, for instance), the soil is acidic. The further away a number is from 7 (either up or down on the pH scale), the more acidic or alkaline the soil is. The pH scale ranges from 0 to 14 with 0 being the most acidic and 14 representing the most alkaline conditions. We will be talking mostly about the pH range of 5.0 to 8.0, since these are about the outer limits that most plants can tolerate.

Acidity and alkalinity are measured in units of pH (power of hydrogen). This is a scientific term used to describe the amount of hydrogen in a substance. Hydrogen content determines how well various mineral and organic compounds within a soil reacts with moisture in the soil. Most nutrients must be dissolved in water before they can be absorbed by plants. The pH of a soil will tell you, in a general way, how reactive your soil is, especially in terms of the minerals that are plant nutrients.

Every unit of pH represents 10 times more acidity or alkalinity. For example, soil with a pH of 5.8 is 10 times more acid than one at 6.8. A soil at 4.8 is 100 times as acid as soil at 6.8 and 10 times as acid as soil at 5.8. This helps explain why plants find it difficult to live outside of their optimum pH. Acidity and alkalinity increase far more rapidly than the numbers suggest.

Different plants have varying pH preferences, so pH is a rather imprecise measure of fertility. The parent material of a soil and the varying amounts of air, water and organic matter in the soil affect the fertility of soils that have the same pH in quite different ways.

Generally speaking, soils between 5.8 and 6.8 (slightly acidic) meet most plant needs, see Table 3-1. The more organic matter in a soil the less critical the pH becomes, because organic matter acts as a pH buffer. Soil with optimum organic content (4 to 6 percent) usually shows no signs of pH imbalance and almost all crops will do well in it. Rich organic soils are often able to grow plants with a variety of preferences in the same bed, right alongside each other. Beneficial bacteria in the soil which feed on organic matter adjust the soil pH to meet plant needs. The home gardener who tends a soil that is rich in organic material and is filled with bacteria can throw away the book on pH. Bacteria and humus act as a buffer, evening out the effects of a too-acidic or too-alkaline soil, so it has a pH more to the liking of individual plants.

Sadly, most soils are not organically rich and do not contain lots of microscopic critters. To achieve the best yields, know the pH of your soil. This will allow you to choose to grow plants which tolerate this pH, or to adjust the soil's pH for the plants you want to grow through the judicious use of lime.

Many plants do best in soil with a pH between 6.5 and 7.0. If the pH is lower than this, even by a little bit, the difference in yield can be tremendous. Corn, for example, will yield 100 bushels to the acre at a pH of 6.8, but will return only 83 bushels when the pH drops to 5.7. There are several reasons for this decrease in production. The microorganisms that fix nitrogen and decompose organic matter work best in the 6.5 to 7.0 pH range. All of the essential mineral nutrients are available within this range, and crumb structure and tilth are more likely to be good.

Why plants will not tolerate highly acidic conditions is not known. Several possible reasons may be: the slowing down of beneficial microorganism action; increased toxicity from certain trace elements like aluminum; and decreases in the availability of nutrients like calcium, magnesium and phosphorus which are locked up by acids in the soil.

On the other side of the scale, overly-alkaline soils have an equally harmful effect on plants. Alkaline soils have a slightly corrosive effect on roots causing them to shrink in a way that discourages water absorption. The salts present in alkaline soils also displace many vital nutrients, especially phosphorus, iron, and manganese. Alkaline conditions tend to break up soil structure, hinder water infiltration and root growth, and reduce aeration. Also, many of these soils are deficient in organic matter and nitrogen.

Curing Acidic Soils

Lime is the cheapest and easiest way to cure acid soil disorders. Do not use quick lime because it can destroy soil humus. Use either hydrated lime (which might also tend to limit soil organisms) or ground limestone.

Agricultural ground limestone is the commonest and safest liming material in use. There are two kinds of agricultural lime: calcic and dolomite. Dolomite is the best since it contains magnesium, an important plant nutrient. Another good liming material is hardwood ash. Do not use coal ash as it is of little value. As a rule-of-thumb, limestone should be applied at the following rates to increase pH by one unit on a 1,000 square foot patch of soil: very sandy soil, 30 pounds; sandy loam, 50 pounds; loam, 70 pounds; heavy clay, 80 pounds.

Spread lime on top of the soil in the fall after tilling or plowing. Do not turn lime under since it leaches down into the soil quickly on its own. Refer to Table 3-2 to determine a rate of application for your soil.

When using ground limestone do not expect a

Table 3-1. This Table Shows Which Plants Do Best in Various pH Ranges.

Outside most crops growing range

Favorable for asparagus beets, broccoli, cauliflower muskmelons, grapes

Favorable to lettuce, cabbage, beans, peas and most other garden crops

Favorable to corn, tomatoes, potatoes, cucumbers, raspberries, strawberries, watermelon, sweet potatoes

Favorable for cranberries blueberries, azaleas, rhododendrons, laurel

Injurious to most crops. Favorable to growth of harmful microbes

7.3

7

6.8

5.9

5.4

4.3

4.0

Alkaline

Neutral

Acidic

Table 3-2. Use This Table as a Handy Guide for Determining the Correct Rate of Lime Application for Acidic Soils.

	Pounds of lime needed to raise the pH of 100 sq. ft. of soil to 6.0pH.					
Original pH	Light Sandy Soil		Average Soil		Clay/Loam	
	Ground Limestone	Hydrated Lime	Ground Limestone	Hydrated Lime	Ground Limestone	Hydrated Lime
4.0	9	6	17.2	11.5	21.7	14.5
4.5	8.2	5.5	15.7	10.5	20.2	13.5
5.0	6.7	4.5	12.7	8.5	15	10
5.5	5.2	3.5	9.7	6.5	12	8

tremendous change in pH the first year. The second year will be better, and you only need to apply this material once every three to four years. Do not overdo it—a temptation on a small garden—since a pH over 7 is not beneficial for most plants.

Curing Alkaline Soils

If your soil is on the alkaline side on the pH scale (above 7.0), you may need to add acidic material to bring the soil within the range of optimum plant growth. Lowering the pH is a difficult proposition for the organic grower since the most common methods of lowering pH—borax and manganese, gypsum (calcium sulphate), and sulfur—are not really suited to the organic concept of soil improvement.

A better, but slower and longer-lasting, way to lower pH is through the use of acidic organic materials like swamp muck, oak leaves, oak sawdust, pine needles, ground oak bark, cottonseed meal, and acid peat moss. Almost any organic matter will work since these materials produce weak organic acids as they decompose. These acids go a long way toward neutralizing soil alkalinity.

Organic matter also builds tilth, often poor in alkaline soils, and acts as a buffer between plants and toxic conditions. Humus adds to the availability of nitrogen in the soil. As your soil becomes loaded with a good healthy amount of organic material, pH problems should decrease.

WATER

All plants need water, and lots of it. In fact, plants absorb more water during their lives than any other soil nutrient. Most of the water is given off by the plant during respiration, some is kept in plant tissue, and a little bit is broken down so the hydrogen and oxygen can be used by the plant. On the average, green plant tissues contain 75 percent water. Young growing tips often contain more than 90 percent water. Plant tissues must be full of water for vital functions to proceed at full pace. When water is lacking, leaf stomata close and the plant wilts to save water. Drought is the most common cause of crop failure.

Water is a largely colorless, odorless, and flavorless substance that is essential to all life for a host of reasons. The two most important reasons in terms of a plant's needs are that plants absorb nutrients when they are dissolved in water, and that plants need water to carry out photosynthesis and many other complex functions. Lack of water in the soil prevents plants from taking up the necessary nutrients. Too much water limits the amount of nitrogen, depletes mineral nutrients, and slows plant growth by suffocating roots. Roots need both water and air for optimum growth.

Soil water occurs in three forms: hydroscopic, capillary, and gravitational. Hydroscopic soil water is chemically bound to minerals in the soil and is unavailable to plants. Gravitational water normally drains out of the large pore spaces of soil shortly after a rain. Slow drainage causes the soil to be soggy and unproductive. Excessive drainage shortens the time when capillary water runs short and plants wilt from lack of soil moisture.

Capillary water is the water that plants depend on most heavily for their supply of moisture. This water is basically gravitational water trapped in microscopic pores between soil particles. The ability of the soil to hold capillary water against the pull of gravity is of great importance. Organic matter and good soil structure add to a soil's ability to hold capillary water for plants.

Plants cannot extract the last drop of water from soil. The attraction of soil materials is greater than the pull exerted by plant roots, and water remains unavailable in the soil. The point at which the pull of the soil and the pull of the plant is equal is called the wilting coefficient of soil. This term is used to express the percentage of water in the soil at the time when the transpiration of plants exceeds the removal of water from the soil by plant roots.

Medium-textured loams and silt loams are two soils that handle soil moisture very well. In addition to allowing water to percolate quickly into the soil after a rain, these soils also allow water below the root zone to move upward where plants can use it. These soils act more like sponges than any other soil.

In soil with proper moisture content, water films all of the soil particles and flows through the soil touching all the minerals, all the organisms, and carrying everything into solution that will dissolve. This soil water is slightly acid and more reactive than rainwater, which is nearly neutral. The reactivity of soil water makes it capable of aiding many chemical reactions, including the formation of minerals that are available to plants.

The minerals affected by water include silicate, phosphate, potassium, calcium compounds, magnesium salts, and dozens of others. Unfortunately, water's ability to dissolve many important minerals means those minerals can easily be leached from the soil. Organic materials, especially humus, will reduce this leaching process by holding water in place instead of allowing it to be carried off.

The best soils are approximately 25 percent water. Soil varies greatly as rain adds to the soil's moisture reservoir while plant uptake and evaporation draw moisture from the reservoir. The amount of soil moisture is ever-changing. The best method for keeping moisture in the soil while maintaining good aeration is through the addition of organic material and by mulching. When these methods fail to keep soil moisture above the wilting point, irrigation is necessary.

AIR

Good soil aeration is essential to almost all of the life in a soil. Among the myriad functions of soil air are the:

● Release of carbon dioxide during the respiration of plant roots.

● Carrying in of the atmosphere nitrogen necessary for bacterial conversion to plant available forms of nitrogen.

● Oxygen intake by plant roots and release of carbon dioxide. This is just the opposite process of that found in plant leaves where carbon dioxide is taken up and oxygen is given off.

● Presence of sulfur dioxide, carbon dioxide, and hydrogen necessary for some soil reactions.

● Decomposition of organic matter and the oxidation of minerals requires air.

● Release of some plant nutrients.

● Room given to roots to stretch out in their search for food by air chambers in soil.

Soil aeration is directly related to the porosity of the soil. Having different size particles—which fit together less perfectly than particles all of one size—is important for good soil structure. The spaces between soil particles allow both air and water to move through the soil and breathe life into it.

One way the soil breathes is through changes in atmospheric pressure (measured by the rising and falling of a barometer). See Fig. 3-3. When atmospheric pressure increases, air is forced down into the soil. In a crude way, the soil is inhaling. The soil exhales as atmospheric pressure drops and air moves out of the soil. Another way the soil breathes

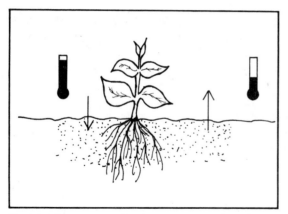

Fig. 3-3. When atmospheric pressure rises (left), air is forced into the soil. When the barometric pressure falls (right), air exits the soil.

is through the displacement of air as water percolates through the soil. When water is applied to the surface of a soil, the water runs down into the pore space displacing air. The water can either force the air deeper into the soil or cause it to escape back into the atmosphere. As the water is absorbed by the soil particles, taken up by plant roots, or evaporated back into the atmosphere, fresh air moves down into the soil.

The roots of plants need air in order to breathe, as do the microorganisms found in soil. This can lead to competition when not enough air is present. Soil with a good structure will have plenty of pore space and air will move around easily. Oxygen and carbon dioxide are exchanged and everyone is happy.

Problems develop as soon as the flow of air is interrupted. A carbon dioxide buildup begins. Roots can no longer take up the oxygen necessary for good health, but then neither can the aerobic microorganisms living in the soil. The result is an imbalance in the microbe population. Microbes that live in the absence of oxygen—anaerobic microbes—begin to multiply. Unfortunately, many of these types of microbes seem to be plant diseases. In normally-aerated soils, these diseases are held in check by the larger population of aerobic microbes; however, when oxygen is not present, the anaerobic microbes have the advantage. They begin attacking roots that are weakened by a lack of oxy-

gen, and trouble soon develops. To avoid this problem, make sure that soil gets plenty of air.

The best way to maintain good soil structure is by turning organic matter, green manures, animal manures, and compost into your soil. These materials form humus when broken down. Humus produces a soil structure noted for its pore space. The earthworms that feed on organic matter are also great soil aerators. These workhorses will burrow down 6 feet or more, leaving tunnels which enhance the movement of air. Tilling is also an excellent way of aerating the soil because the mixing action reduces the carbon dioxide content while raising the oxygen and nitrogen levels of the soil.

SUNLIGHT

The scientific name for the process by which green plants use light energy to synthesize carbohydrates is *photosynthesis*. Light supplies the energy needed to convert carbon dioxide, water, and minerals into plant tissue and oxygen. When light is absent, photosynthesis stops and plants absorb oxygen, giving off carbon dioxide.

The radiant energy your plants need does many things other than supply power for photosynthesis. The length and intensity of sunlight triggers growth processes that control stem length, flowering, and enzyme action. Although seed germination takes place in the dark of a soil, radiant energy is needed to keep the soil warm. In fact, all the energy used by plants and animals comes directly or indirectly from the sun.

Plants ripen to full maturity in full sunlight. When the amount of sunlight reaching a plant is adequate the nutrients in a plant are balanced, leading to optimum root growth, shoot formation, and leaf development. Without good light, some proteins do not fully develop, and many simple sugars do not develop into more complex forms. Plants receiving inadequate sunlight remain stunted and the quantity and quality of the crop suffers (Fig. 3-4).

When plants are grown near shade, they tend to reach out for light. Hormones in the plant stem on the side away from the most intense light, cause the cells on that side to elongate. This pushes the plant toward the light. Once stems grow spindly, they remain that way. A plant needs direct overhead light to keep this elongation to a minimum.

The intensity of light is not the only factor affecting plants. Plants also respond to the length of the daily period of illumination. This light/darkness rhythm influences the timing of blossoming, maturation, tuber and bulb formation, seed germination, root formation, leaf color, and branching of stems.

Plenty of light will also protect your garden from excessive dampness, slugs, snails, and earwigs. Shade encourages the growth of fungus and bacteria that will sap the vigor of young plants. Don't get discouraged if your garden does not re-ceive its fair share of direct sunlight—many plants will grow and produce in minimal light, because photosynthesis continues in almost any light—even moonlight!

You can use light-colored mulches or aluminum foil under plants to increase the intensity of light they receive. Painting a fence or nearby wall white will also increase light intensity.

TEMPERATURE

Temperature is another non-nutrient, which has a profound influence on the growth of plants. Temperature affects every single chemical and physical process involved with plants including solubility of nutrients, absorption of water, gas diffu-

Fig. 3-4. The shade of this tree is stunting the growth of the corn nearest to it. The farther away the corn is (left), the healthier it grows.

sion, and photosynthesis. In short, the entire life of a plant depends on the correct temperature. Most plants grow very slowly at temperatures below 40° F, and most are killed or damaged by temperatures of 100 to 130° F. Different plant species have temperature ranges below which growth is not possible. This is called the minimum growth temperature. There is also a maximum growth temperature above which growth stops. The ideal growth temperature is called the optimum growth temperature. See Table 3-3 for the specific temperature requirements of some common garden plants.

All of the cell activity within leaves is either fast or slow depending on how warm or cold it is. The colder it is, the slower cell life moves; the warmer it is, the faster it moves. Plants with plenty of sunlight, water, and nutrients will not grow when they are too cold because nutrient movement within the plant is so slow that photosynthesis takes place at a minimal level.

Tender annuals escape the freezing point by completing their life cycle—seed to seed—between frost dates. Perennials beat the cold by allowing their leaves and stems to die back while keeping life in their roots, bulbs, tubers, and rhizomes. When temperatures become more favorable, the roots fuel the growth of new above-ground foliage. Many cold-hardy plants (like spinach and

cabbage) can withstand ice on their leaves for a short time. Not many plants have such an advantage.

Extremes of temperature on the hot side are just as bad as cold for plants. When plants are pushed out of their natural temperature zones, production falters. Defoliation, premature fruit drop, and death often result. Plants grown in extreme heat will often produce vegetative matter like leaves and stems in place of fruit. Lettuce, spinach, and cole crops rush to produce seeds in order to beat the heat.

The absorption of water by plant roots is affected by soil temperature. Heat-loving plants will not absorb water when the temperature drops below 40° F. Plant root growth increases as soil temperature rises to a certain point. When that temperature is reached or surpassed, root growth slows. This may help explain why root growth is greatest during the early and latter parts of summer.

Most soil microorganisms (at least the good ones) seem to do best between 50° and 100° F. Some disease microbes grow well at temperatures beyond 100° F, especially when plants are weakened by the heat.

Temperature has a great affect on the germination of seeds. Peas, spinach, and lettuce seem to

Table 3-3. Every Plant Has Its Temperature Preference.
This Table Will Give You a Good Idea of the Temperature Requirements for Many Common Garden Plants.

Minimum Growing Temp F	Optimum Temp. F	Maximum Temp. F	Vegetables
30	75	85	Asparagus, rhubarb
35	75	85	Garlic, leek, lettuce, mustard onion, parsley, peas, spinach
40	85	90	Beet, broccoli, Brussels sprouts, cabbage, carrot, collard, kale, kohlrabi, parsnip, potato, radish, rutabaga, turnip
50	85	100	Corn
60	85-90	95-100	Bean, cucumber, eggplant, melon, okra, pepper, pumpkin, squash
65	80-85	95	Tomato

take forever to germinate in cold spring soils. Plantings of these same crops in late summer almost pop out of the ground overnight. The difference is the soil temperature. The warmer the soil, the quicker germination will be.

The temperature of soil fluctuates greatly to a depth of a few inches during a 24-hour period. The temperature of deeper soil remains more constant though substantially lower than at the surface. Nutrients are more readily available at the warmer temperatures in the top few inches of soil, which may explain why plants keep their feeder roots close to the soil's surface.

Many plants grow poorly as long as the soil fails to warm up. It is not necessarily true that the temperature is directly unfavorable to the plant; more often, the low temperatures are unfavorable to the microorganisms responsible for releasing nitrogen and other vital plant foods in the soil. When soil warms up to a certain temperature in the spring, presto! Microbes swing into action and plant nutrients quickly become available. Prior to this warming, the soil is rather low in fertility. This may help explain why grass can seemingly green-up overnight—the soil has reached the critical temperature for microorganisms and nutrients are suddenly available for the grass.

By now you are probably asking yourself how you can ever hope to keep all the things necessary for good plant growth balanced. You cannot, really—nature has to do it. But by feeding your garden organically you can be sure that you are helping instead of hindering.

Think of the various nutrient cycles in terms of decaying plants passing nutrients to microorganisms, and microbes feeding plants these nutrients when they are finished with them. The plants eventually decay, beginning the cycle anew. There is a lot more to it, of course, but if you make this connection and treat your soil accordingly you will have few problems maintaining a garden where plants are happy to live.

Chapter 4

Fertilizing Naturally

If I could play on Homer's lyre
and wing with true poetic fire
to what great theme would I aspire?
Barnyard manure!

—Alfred Virian

You already know that plants do not have stomachs, but depend on the soil to act as their digestive tract. When you add fertilizer to your garden you are really feeding the soil. In turn, the soil feeds the plants. Like a too-rich dessert which upsets your stomach, a too-rich fertilizer upsets the soil. A disturbed soil bothers the plants growing in it. On the other side of the coin, a soil lacking key nutrients will cause plants to suffer malnutrition.

In its broadest definition, fertilizer is any substance you add to your soil to improve the soil's fertility. As has been noted earlier, plants need a wide range of nutrients for ample growth. During this growth plants lock up nutrients in their leaves, stems, and roots. As nutrients are captured by the plant's tissues, the soil becomes less fertile. Fertilizer is added to the soil to try and replace missing nutrients. Chemical fertilizers concentrate on the major plant nutrients to the exclusion of the less noticeable, but equally important, micronutrients. Chemical fertilizers also tend to ignore the growth of soil microorganisms in favor of the plants. This short circuiting of nature's well-defined nutrient cycles is a mistake.

The highly-concentrated nature of chemical fertilizers and their immediate availability tends to give soil indigestion—especially soils low in organic material. Sadly, many gardeners who use chemical fertilizers also like to believe that the fertilizer bypasses the need for organic matter in the soil. This reduces the digestive ability of the soil even more, harming the soil's ability to handle large doses of fertilizer. A vicious circle develops as more fertilizer is added to a soil containing less humus. Eventually, the soil gets sick. Diseases, pests, erosion, poor tilth, and a host of other problems develop. The soil simply wears out. You can avoid over-feeding your soil by adding plenty of organic matter and using mild, natural fertilizers.

Organic fertilizers come in many forms including manures, green manures, composts, organic materials, rock powders, and commercially-available natural fertilizers (usually byproducts of a refining process of vegetable or animal matter). Barnyard manures, organic matter, green manures and composts should be thought of as entrees or main meals for your soil. One of these foods—compost—is so important to the health of your soil that the entire next chapter will be devoted to it. Right now, we are concerned with the rock powders and commercially-available fertilizers which are best thought of as vitamin supplements for your garden.

Although rich soils will provide most of the nutrients necessary for good plant growth, leaching, erosion, and crop harvesting remove nutrients from your garden's ecosystem. These nutrients must be replaced if your garden is to continue producing at an optimum level. Adding organic fertilizers and organic matter to your soil on a regular basis will replace these lost nutrients. Remember, though, that the object of fertilization is to feed the soil. The soil, in turn, will feed your vegetables.

This natural approach to garden fertility requires a long-range commitment to soil building. In this way, the organic approach varies sharply with the chemical gardener's idea of supplying only the minimum amount of nutrients necessary for a single season's crop.

One of the best reasons for gardening with organic and natural fertilizers instead of chemical fertilizers is that both major and minor nutrients are conserved and protected by organic fertilizers. Organic fertilizers release nutrients slowly in amounts that can be used by plants without too much going to waste. Chemical fertilizers, on the other hand, tend to release their nutrients all at one time, which floods the soil with nutrients that are quickly leached away by rain. Using organic fertilizers actually builds up a soil's structure to the point where fertilizer input can be reduced.

Which would you rather have: a soil that constantly needs more fertilizer, or one which requires less and less each year? I think you will agree that

the latter option makes the most sense. You can achieve this result by using natural and organic fertilizers.

Before you run down to the local garden center and buy a bag of natural fertilizer, you need to know which nutrients are deficient in your soil. The best way to do this is with a soil test, but the plants growing in your soil will also tell you a lot about the soil's fertility.

READING NUTRIENT DEFICIENCIES IN PLANTS

Although plant symptoms of nutritional deficiency are helpful indicators of what is missing in your soil, they do not always tell the whole story. Many conditions like excess water, insufficient soil aeration, and lack of light can cause symptoms similar to nutrient deficiencies. When you spot what you think is a nutrient deficiency, have your soil tested. If the test tells you that the soil is deficient in one or more nutrients you will need to add a fertilizer containing that nutrient. In most cases, a deficiency observed during the growing season cannot be corrected quickly enough to allow a plant to produce at its full potential the same season. The best you can hope to do is prevent the same deficiency from occurring next year.

Tomatoes are, by far, the favorite vegetable of American gardeners. Given a single square foot in which to grow the vegetable of their choice, most gardeners will choose a tomato. In fact, more than 95 percent of all gardeners list tomatoes as their favorite garden vegetable. Since tomatoes are so widely grown, we'll discuss the symptoms of 10 nutrient deficiencies and how they affect tomatoes.

Should you notice one of these deficiencies in your tomato patch, immediately add a lot of well-decomposed organic matter to the soil or pour manure and compost teas near the plants to help them through the crisis. Sadly, by the time you notice a nutrient deficiency it is usually too late to get the plant back to full potential. However, you can make a special effort to add materials containing the missing nutrients so that a shortage does not reoccur next year.

Nitrogen. Nitrogen deficiency exhibits the same symptoms in the tomato as it does in other plants. Leaves turn yellowish, especially the older ones, and they eventually drop off. Stems are often yellow and stiff. When fruit manages to form, it is usually small and hard. The fruit is light green when unripe, but quickly turns bright red during ripening.

Potassium. Potassium deficiencies show up in the leaf margins, which shrivel and die. The remainder of the leaf area is mottled and what is left of it curls downward.

Phosphorus. Phosphorus shortages show up as a dull purple tint in the leaves, especially along the central rib and veins.

Calcium. Calcium inadequacies are indicated when the youngest leaves turn brown at the edges and die back. These new leaves often show a purplish-brown tint, while older leaves remain intact.

Manganese. Manganese deficiency produces a yellowing of the tissue between leaf veins. This mottling shows up first on the young leaves, but can spread to the older leaves.

Magnesium. Magnesium shortages produce a yellowing between the leaf veins. Also, a green band often remains around the margins of these yellow leaves. Young leaves often curl upward, turn brittle and die.

Iron. Iron deficiency results in yellowing between the veins on young leaves, especially those at the base of leaflets.

Boron. Boron deficiencies show up as light, medium, and dark spots of purple, brown, and yellow on the leaves. The growing points of the plant will die, and stems become stiff and straight.

Zinc. Zinc deficiencies result in unusually small leaves and growth points. Stems often split after the stem hairs disappear.

Sulfur. Sulfur shortages result in leaves which turn light green. Spindly stems and poor growth also result. Here are some of the symptoms in other vegetables of common nutrient shortages that may be present in your garden.

Nitrogen

Sometimes you can spot a nitrogen deficiency in your garden by the color of your plants. Vegetables with the right amount of nitrogen are deep green and grow fast in warm humid weather. If growth slows and plants are yellowish-green, chances are your soil is short on nitrogen. The leaves of the plants yellow first, and then the stems. When a lack of nitrogen reaches the critical stage, the whole plant turns yellow, then brown, and dies.

Unfortunately, yellowing leaves can also be an indication of other problems. Too much water or not enough aeration are the two most common ones. When you see yellow leaves, a lack of nitrogen is not the only possible culprit.

Phosphorus

The best indication of phosphorus deficiency in plants is a reddish-purple discoloration in the leaves, leaf veins, and stems. Knee-high corn with purple-fringed leaves almost always indicates a phosphorus deficiency. Crooked and incomplete rows of kernels on an ear of corn, caused by the slow emergence of silk at pollination time, is another indication. Cole crops also turn reddish-purple on leaf edges. Before adding phosphorus to cole crops, especially cabbages, make sure you have not planted purple cabbage by mistake.

Potassium

Plants grown in soils lacking sufficient potassium grow slowly. The leaves may get yellow streaks and the edges and tips of the leaves become dry and scorched. Cabbage turns bronze along leaf borders and then scorches brown. Beets grow tapered roots instead of bulbs. Radishes show an abnormal deep green color in the center of their leaves before the edges develop a scorched appearance.

Calcium

Calcium deficiencies are rare, but when they occur the tips of young leaves curl and die.

Sulfur

The principal symptoms of sulfur deficiency in plants are light green leaves, leaf veins lighter in color than the surrounding area, upper leaves lighter in color than the bottom leaves, and, in severe cases, yellow leaves. Sulfur deficiency can be distinguished from nitrogen deficiency because leaves do not usually shrivel and die.

Magnesium

Small deficiencies of magnesium usually result in no visible symptoms at all. More severe deficiencies cause paling and streaking in leaves, curling leaf margins on lower leaves, and yellow spots with green veins on lower leaves. The symptoms appear very similar to those of other deficiencies. The only really effective way of spotting a magnesium shortage is through a soil test.

Zinc

Zinc shortages are most common in the alkaline soils west of the Mississippi River. Disturbed soils, perhaps where a bulldozer has scraped away the topsoil during construction, tend to show zinc deficiencies. Generally, zinc deficiencies result in yellowing and dead spots in older and lower leaves. Holes in the lower leaves and stunted plant growth are also indications of zinc shortage.

Corn that is suffering a zinc deficiency looks weak and pale, and often has white streaks on the leaves and a white color (or lack of color). In apple trees, zinc shortages create a symptom called "apple rosette." The new growth on branches form terminal whorls of small misshapen leaves. Leaves further down the branch may drop off. Peach trees suffering a lack of zinc may become crinkled and chlorotic; however, these problems may indicate other diseases as well. Squash is often prone to zinc deficiencies, indicated by brown spots on the leaves. Brown spots on potato skins also reveal·a zinc deficiency.

Boron

Vegetables often show signs of boron deficiency when very light or very heavy soils are limed excessively. New tip growth often dies and plants become brittle.

Beets, turnips and other root crops will show what is known as "brown heart" disease when a boron shortage exists. Brown heart disease can be found by cutting across the root of sickly looking plants. If the core is brown and watery, the disease is present. Cauliflower will show similar brown heart disease in the stems of the cauliflower head. Cabbage with hollow stems is likely to have a boron deficiency. Sweet potatoes suffering a boron deficiency develop a dark water-soaked area inside the tubers, and dark cankers may erupt at the surface. Symptoms of boron shortage in sweet potatoes are seen in gnarled and twisted vines, which normally grow straight. Apple trees suffering a boron deficiency often exhibit internal and external corking. Internal corking produces brown watery lesions inside the newly formed apples. Eventually, these lesions will dry out in a manner resembling cork. External cork appears as lesions on the outer skin of the fruit that crack and wrinkle. Corking diseases caused by boron deficiencies are often confused with apple scab.

Manganese

Manganese shortages are very difficult to spot in plants, since the symptoms look like many other problems. New and upper leaves often have yellow or dead spots, while veins remain green. These symptoms are similar to several other shortages, notably nitrogen and sulfur. Beets may take on a purplish-red hue when manganese is lacking in a soil.

Copper

Copper shortages result in young leaves that wilt prematurely and wither, while showing little if any yellowing.

Iron

The symptoms of iron deficiency are the yellowing of new and upper leaves. Also, the edges and tips of these leaves may die.

Detecting deficiencies through plant symptoms is a tricky proposition, and even the experts can be fooled. When you think you have a deficiency, the safest thing to do is have your soil tested by a lab that includes trace elements in its analysis. This will give you a pretty good idea of whether or not you have read the signs correctly. If you read the signs right, good for you. Now correct the problems with natural fertilizer and powdered mineral rocks. If you have not read the signs correctly, the soil test will help you plan corrective measures.

SUPPLYING MACRO-NUTRIENTS AND MICRONUTRIENTS

Nitrogen, phosphorus and potassium, the three macronutrients, are those that plants feed on most heavily. See Table 4-1 for the nutrient content of some common organic fertilizers. They are also the nutrients most often deficient in the soil. Here is how you can supply these nutrients naturally.

Nitrogen

Nitrogen is represented in fertilizer jargon as N. If you believe your soil is deficient in nitrogen, you can correct it by adding compost, manures, or other nitrogen-rich fertilizers such as dried blood, cottonseed meal, fish emulsion, feather meal, bone meal and sewage sludge. Returning weeds, grass clippings, and other kitchen and garden wastes to the soil will add to its humus structure and improve the nitrogen content.

Although the nitrogen content of organic sources are rarely as concentrated as those of chemical sources, they have a major advantage. Most natural fertilizers release nitrogen slowly, over a period of weeks or months, and do not have a tendency to burn plants like chemical fertilizers.

Natural nitrogen fertilizers should be applied by side-dressing or as a fertilizer tea when plants have established themselves in the garden. It is best to mix nitrogen fertilizers into the soil so that they come in contact with the soil microbes which break down the nitrogen into a plant usable form. Do not leave nitrogen-rich fertilizers on the soil's surface since the nitrogen will escape into the air where it is useless to plants.

Be careful not to add too much nitrogen to fruit-producing crops, or they will grow a lot of leaves at the expense of fruit production. Leafy vegetables like spinach and mustard greens love nitrogen.

Dried Blood. Dried blood is a rich source of nitrogen, but it is expensive. This material is best used in small gardens or around perennials. Dried blood meal is between 10 and 15 percent nitrogen. It should be side-dressed around plants and then worked into the top few inches of soil.

Bone Meal. Bone meal can be used as a side-dressing or tilled into the soil prior to planting. Bone meal is slow to break down and so provides nitrogen over a long period of time.

Cottonseed Meal. Cottonseed meal is applied like dried blood meal. This material is acidic and should not be used on alkaline-loving plants.

Feather Meal. Feather meal is a byproduct of the poultry industry and an excellent source of slow-release nitrogen. This material often contains up to 15 percent nitrogen. Turn it into the soil several weeks prior to planting, or use it as a mulch.

Manure and Compost. Manure and compost are good all-round fertilizers with a modest amount of nitrogen. However, these materials are important as sources of food and energy for the soil microbes which release nitrogen from organic materials. Rabbit droppings have a nitrogen content of about 2 percent, which is considered high among manures. Hog and cow manures have the lowest

Table 4-1. This Table Lists the Macronutrient Content of Some Popular Organic Fertilizers. Availability and Acidity Are Also Shown.

Organic Material	Percent			Availability	Acidity
	N	P	K		
Basic slag*	-	8	-	Quick	Alkaline
Bone meal	3.5	22	-	Slow	Alkaline
Castor pomace	5	2	1	Slow	Acid
Cocoa shells	2.5	1	2.5	Slow	Neutral
Cottonseed meal	6	2.5	1.5	Moderate	Acid
Dried blood	12	1.5	1	Moderate	Acid
Fish meal	10	4	-	Moderate	Acid
Greensand*	-	1	6	Slow	Neutral
Ground rock phosphate	-	33	-	Slow	Alkaline
Horn and hoof meal	12	2	-	Moderate	Neutral
Seaweed*	1	-	4-10	Moderate	Neutral
Sewage sludge	2-6	1-3	0-1	Slow	Acid
Wood ashes	-	2	4-10	Quick	Alkaline

* Also contains a wide variety of trace minerals, in varying amounts.

concentration of nitrogen among manures. Compost will vary in its nitrogen content, depending on what materials were used to make it.

Sewage Sludge. Sewage sludge can be used as a nitrogen-rich fertilizer on many crops. Activated sludge contains about 4 percent more nitrogen than digested sludge. Sludge is usually sterilized before being made into fertilizer. Sludge is not recommended for use near greens or root crops.

Phosphorus

Phosphorus, represented by a P, is the second major nutrient. A good soil, rich in organic matter, seldom shows phosphorus deficiency because decomposing organic matter makes the phosphorus in a soil available. Still, it is a good idea to add phosphorus-rich materials to the soil, especially if the soil is heavily cropped. The most common source of phosphorus is phosphate rock. Phosphate rock is not cheap, but you will only need to apply it once every three or four years.

Colloidal or raw phosphate rock powder is the best for organic gardens. Although unprocessed rock powder is not as soluble in water as superphosphate, modern mechanical crushing techniques are able to make a very fine powder which speeds up the release of nutrients. When a good amount of organic matter is present in the soil, there is hardly any difference in the release rates of phosphorus between raw phosphate and superphosphate.

There are a number of reasons not to use superphosphate rock. The most immediate is cost. The energy-intensive processing necessary to convert phosphate into superphosphate is expensive. You, the consumer, end up paying this cost. Additionally, sulfuric acid is used during part of the conversion process, which encourages the growth of certain bacteria that crowd out helpful soil microorganisms. Sulfuric acid also seems to make the boron and zinc in rock phosphates unavailable to plants.

Basic slag, bone meal, dried blood, cottonseed meal, and activated sludge are also good sources of phosphorus. Dried blood, which is about 3 percent

phosphorus, is noted for its high nitrogen content. It is still a good source of phosphorus, though. Bone meal is another material high in phosphorus. Bone meal is relatively expensive and works best in small gardens.

Potassium

Potassium represented by K in the N-P-K formula used to describe the strength of fertilizers. (K is this element's letter on the periodic table.)

Potassium is the most difficult fertilizer for organic gardeners to obtain in large amounts at a reasonable price. Potassium, often called potash, is available via two sources: natural mineral sources and organic matter. Mineral sources of potash hold potassium in a form that is not immediately available to plants. As these rocks get dissolved by the soil, the potassium in them becomes available to plants. The potash from plant residues is available more quickly, but it does not remain in the soil as long as potassium delivered by rock powders.

Muriate of potash is the most common source of potash in the United States. Although muriate of potash is mined from natural deposits left when ancient seas evaporated, using this source of potassium has a serious flaw. The potash in these deposits is in the form of salts of potassium chloride. These chlorine salts often remain in the soil, harming plant growth.

Granite dust and greensand are two natural sources of potash without the salt-producing side effects. Like all rock fertilizers, these materials do best when applied in conjunction with an organic material.

Wood ashes, hay, leaves, and compost are also good sources of potash. Seaweed and seaweed extracts are being used more widely to raise the potash level of soil. Since potash is leached quickly from soil, it is necessary to frequently add organic material that is rich in potash. Use one of the long-lasting powdered rock sources in conjunction with the quick-release sources.

Micronutrients

One of the benefits of adding natural fertilizers to your soil to keep the macronutrients up to par is that these fertilizers often contain all the trace elements that plants need. Frequent additions of organic material will also help provide all the micronutrients plants normally require.

The objective of the organic method of gardening is to feed the soil a balanced diet for long-term good health, not to supply the minimum amount of nutrients needed for raising a single crop in one season.

Since most organic fertilizers release their nutrients slowly, your soil will be improved for many years following application. Do not be afraid to use relatively large amounts of natural fertilizers on your garden. In most cases, they will not harm your plants.

Below are a dozen basic organic fertilizers. Many must be purchased from garden centers, but some you will be able to find free in your community. A quick look at this list reveals that many major organic materials are missing. Bulky items like leaves, grass clippings, and sawdust, which are more often used in compost or as mulches, will be discussed in more detail in later chapters.

ROCK POWDERS

The various rocks found in the earth's crust are capable of supplying all the nutrients necessary for plant growth, except nitrogen. Many of these rocks are rich in different plant nutrients and occur in easily-mined deposits. This makes them an attractive way to correct soil deficiencies.

After you add a rock fertilizer to your soil it breaks down slowly, supplying nutrients in a way that does not disturb soil microorganisms. Since rock fertilizers do not contain nitrogen, they should be added to the soil with nitrogen-rich materials. In fact, adding rock powders to the soil at the same time manures are added will coax more nutrients from these two materials than if either one was added separately. The organic acids in manures and other decomposing organic materials release nutrients from the rock powders, then the rock nutrients feed the microbes producing organic acids, which release more nutrients from the rocks—all to the benefit of your soil and plants.

Rock fertilizers should never be applied with lime, and many rocks should be plowed or disked under following application to prevent leaching.

Granite Dust

Granite dust is an important source of slow-release potassium. Its potash content varies between 3 and 5 percent. Granite dust also contains a wide range of trace minerals. It is less expensive than commercial chemical sources of potassium and leaves behind no chemical residues.

Although other sources of potassium—notably wood ashes—are alkaline, granite dust has no affect on soil pH. This allows granite dust to be used as a fertilizer around all plants and in all soils without worry.

In the garden, the suggested rate of granite dust application is 10 pounds per 100 square feet. The powder should be applied in the fall and turned under so that soil acids have a chance to work on it and release nutrients for the following spring. Applications of granite dust are needed only every four or five years.

Greensand

Greensand is not really a powdered rock, although it is mined and used in much the same way. Greensand, sometimes called glauconite or glauconite potash, is mined from deposits left by ancient seas. It contains approximately 7 percent potash, all of it in available form. In fact, greensand has a higher potash content then granite dust and generally provides more potash than wood ash does. Greensand also contains many, if not all, of the minerals found in sea water, including silica, iron, lime, phosphorus, plus traces of about three dozen other minerals.

Actually, greensand is made of a clay, not a sand, which explains why it is so good at holding water. Soil containing greensand will hold water just below the soil surface where the roots of a plant can utilize it. This water tends to carry many nutrients dissolved from the greensand. Greensand also conditions soil by binding sandy soil and loosening clay soils.

The recommended application rate for greensand is 10 pounds per 100 square feet. Greensand is used as a side-dressing around plants, tilled in or added to compost heaps. In fact, greensand can be added to the soil at any time during the growing season.

Limestone

Limestone is seldom thought of as a fertilizer since most soils contain enough of its main ingredient, calcium, to supply all of this nutrient that plants need. Lime and limestones, however, are commonly used to reduce the acidity of soils. By reducing the acidity of a soil and bringing the pH near to neutral, many of the nutrients already in a soil can be made available to plants.

Ground limestone is the best source of lime for the organic garden. There are two basic types of limestone: calcic and dolomitic. Dolomitic limestone is particularly valuable because it contains magnesium, a trace element important to plant growth.

One function of lime is to release phosphorus and potash from their insoluble mineral compounds, making them available for plant use. Thus, though lime is not itself a fertilizer, it increases the fertility of acid soils.

Fall or spring applications, well in advance of planting, are best. Liming is done on freshly-cultivated soil. Water will quickly wash lime down into the soil. Therefore, this is one rock fertilizer which should not be turned under. When turned under, lime leaches quickly out of the root zone and is wasted.

Phosphate Rock

Phosphate rock, a natural rock product containing from 28 to 30 percent phosphorus, is the organic gardener's best source of this macronutrient. When phosphate rock is finely-ground, the phosphate becomes easily available to the soil. The bacteria that thrive in soils rich in organic material secrete organic acids that promote the breakdown and availability of phosphorus. These organic acids release rock phosphate nutrients slowly so that they are available to plants for a long time.

Phosphate rock is most effective when applied in combination with manure—about 25 pounds of manure for every 10 pounds of phosphate. In late fall or early spring, spread manure on your garden, then work the manure into the soil. Add phosphate rock a month or two later. Sprinkle the ground phosphate on the soil just as you would lime, then work it into the top inch of soil , or simply leave the mineral on the soil and rain will wash it into the root zone.

OTHER FERTILIZERS

You may be able to find some of the fertilizers listed below for free in your community. Others you will be able to buy at garden centers, feed stores, or through the mail.

Basic Slag

Basic slag is a byproduct of the iron ore smelting process. Large amounts of limestone and dolomite are used during smelting. These minerals eventually end up in the slag. Slag contains many other trace minerals, including magnesium, silicon, aluminum, and manganese. Although slag is hard and rock-like, when ground it makes an excellent mineral fertilizer.

Since slag is alkaline it can be used to bring acid soils closer to neutral. It works best on moist clays and loam, and on peaty soils deficient in lime. Slag should be added to light soils, such as sand, along with a potassium supplement.

The best time to apply slag is during the late fall or early winter. Slag is especially helpful to legume crops such as beans, peas, clovers, vetches and alfalfa, many of which are cover crops.

Try to avoid slag with a high sulfur content since too much of this mineral can have a toxic effect on soil and plants.

Bone Meal

Bone meal is just what its name implies— ground bones. Bone meal is generally rich in nitrogen and phosphorus. The exact content of these nutrients varies according to the animal from which the bones came and the animal's age.

Bone meal fertilizers come in three varieties: raw bone meal, steamed bone meal, and bone black.

Although bone meal takes a long time to release its nutrients, the wait is well worth it.

Young bones normally contain less phosphorus and more nitrogen than old bones. Raw bone meal averages between 2 and 4 percent nitrogen and 15 to 20 percent phosphorus. Raw bone meal contains some fat which slows the rate of decomposition.

Most of the bone meal now on the market has been steamed. It is made by steaming or boiling green bones under high pressure to remove their fat. This practice increases the speed at which the nutrients in this material can be absorbed by the soil. Steamed bones have a slightly lower nitrogen content—1 to 2 percent—than raw bone meal. Steamed bone meal's phosphorus content remains high—20 to 30 percent.

Bone meal works best when applied with other organic materials. Because of its lime content, bone meal tends to reduce acidity. The high nitrogen content of this material makes it a valuable addition to compost heaps. Almost all garden centers carry bone meal in one form or another.

Compost

Compost is such an important part of the organic concept that the next chapter of this book is devoted entirely to it. Still, it is worth mentioning here.

Commercial composts are available, but they tend to be expensive. A smarter move is to make your compost a part of the operation of your garden.

The nutrient value of compost depends in large part on the parent material and what has been added during decomposition. As a general rule, compost has good trace mineral content. Nitrogen content will be higher when dried blood, cottonseed meal, bone meal, or activated sludge is added to the mixture. Phosphorus content is increased when rock phosphate, basic slag, bone meal, or sludge is added. Greensand, granite dust, manure, or wood ash will increase compost's potash content.

Well-decomposed compost, in which you cannot distinguish plant parts, can be added to the garden at any time. It is especially useful in seedbeds and as a side-dressing. Compost that is not as decomposed can be spread on the garden in the fall or spring prior to turning the soil.

Cottonseed Meal

Cottonseed meal is the flour-like remains of cottonseed after it is removed from lint and hulls and then pressed for oil. This reminder is rich in protein and is often used as an animal feed. Little of it finds its way into organic fertilizers. For this reason, cottonseed meal may be relatively expensive when bought as a fertilizer. However, if you buy cottonseed meal as a livestock feed supplement, the price is usually less.

A word of warning about cottonseed meal. This material may contain high concentrations of pesticides. Since cotton is not an edible crop, farmers are allowed to use larger doses of more potent pesticides on cotton than on edible crops. A measure of these pesticides remain on the cotton boles as they are processed. Cottonseed meal is part of the trash left over from the ginning of cotton boles. Some of this gin trash will be carrying pesticides and you may not want to use it in your garden. On the other hand, the benefits of added nitrogen and soil acidity, which cottonseed meal contributes to your soil, should outweigh the pesticide problem.

Cottonseed is rich in nitrogen (around 7 percent), phosphorus (2 to 3 percent) and potash (near 1 percent). This material is of special value on alkaline soils since it has an acid reaction. Use it liberally around acid-loving plants.

Cottonseed meal should be used as a side-dressing on leafy green vegetables (Fig. 4-1). Work it slightly into the soil so that microorganisms can release the nutrients for plant use.

Dried Blood

Dried blood is a byproduct of slaughterhouses where it is collected, dried and ground into a powder or meal. Much dried blood goes right back into animal feed, while only a small portion is used as garden fertilizer. Therefore, dried blood is expensive. Sources of dried blood include mail-order, garden centers, and feed stores.

For the home gardener, dried blood is an ex-

Fig. 4-1. Side-dress leafy vegetables like spinach with cottonseed meal when these plants have established themselves.

cellent source of quickly-available nitrogen. Dried blood contains 12 to 15 percent nitrogen by weight, a rather high nitrogen content. It should be used carefully around plants which might produce excess foliage at the expense of fruit, or excess root growth in the presence of too much nitrogen. However, dried blood is an excellent side-dressing for quick-growing, leafy greens like spinach and lettuce.

Dried blood has a pungent odor that attracts dogs and carnivorous wild creatures. It should always be dug or tilled into the soil immediately after application.

Seaweed

Unless you live on the coast and can gather seaweed directly, you will have to settle for processed seaweed products. Seaweed extracts are available commercially in two basic forms: powder and liquid. Seaborn, Maxicrop, and Sea Crop seaweed extracts are some of the brand names you are likely to see advertised.

Powdered seaweed is dissolved in water and then fed to plants as a tea or sprayed on leaves as a foliar fertilizer. Liquid seaweed is also diluted with water and used in the same ways.

Liquid seaweed is very useful when you are growing your own seedlings. Regular waterings with this fertilizer will keep plants from getting spindly. As a bonus, seaweed has an amazing ability to keep the fungus that causes damping-off under control.

Seaweed products have many of the same chelating properties of humus and clay particles. In addition to seaweed's ability to act as a middleman during soil-to-plant nutrient exchanges, this fertilizer also contains a healthy quantity of many trace minerals. Barium, chromium, lead, lithium, nickel, silver, strontium, tin and zinc are found in seaweed products. Arsenic, boron, cobalt, molybdenum, vanadium, and about 60 other trace minerals are found in seaweed. In fact, seaweed will supply virtually every trace mineral required for plant life. The nitrogen, phosphorus and potassium content of seaweed varies widely from season to season. The chlorophyll content of seaweed is almost as high as that of alfalfa.

Seaweeds normally contain healthy quantities of potash, twice as much as barnyard manure. Growth hormones found in seaweed encourage healthy plant growth. Plants grown with seaweed products also tend to stand light frosts better than their untreated counterparts.

While there is no question about the organic nature of seaweed products, they are expensive. When you need only a small amount for a small garden the cost is not steep. For example, a bottle of undiluted liquid seaweed will last several years since you mix only one or two tablespoons of the concentrate with each gallon of water. In large gardens, the frequent use of seaweed extracts may become prohibitively expensive.

Sewage Sludge

Sewage sludge is made up of the solids removed from sewage during treatment. This sludge is removed from waste water in a variety of ways, including screening, sedimentation, chemical precipitation, and bacterial digestion. There are several forms of sewage sludge available. The two most important types are activated and unactivated.

Activated sludge is made when sewage is agitated by bubbling air rapidly through it. Active bacteria coagulate the organic matter and it settles out. This material is then generally heat-treated and dried before being made available to gardeners and farmers. Activated sludge has a nitrogen content of between 5 and 6 percent, and a phosphorus content of from 3 to 6 percent.

Unactivated sludge is that which settles naturally without the aid of bubbling air. This type of sludge has a foul odor and may contain pathogens. The odor problem is often eliminated through an anaerobic fermentation in a digester. The resulting sludge is called digested sludge, which is then dried. Pathogens may persist, to some extent, but they will be overpowered by good soil microorganisms when added to the soil.

Digested sludge has about the same fertilizer value of barnyard manure. Nitrogen content is around 2 percent, with phosphorus content less than 1 percent. Sludge also contains many trace elements and it improves the moisture-holding capacity of a soil.

Sludge comes in two forms: dried and liquid. Dried sludge can be spread over your entire garden and then worked into the soil. It can also be used as a specific fertilizer by incorporating it into the soil around certain plants. Dried sludge may also be applied as a mulch, since its nitrogen content is not high enough to burn most plants. Liquid sludge should be applied to the garden on a one-shot basis and then worked into the top six inches of soil immediately. Such handling reduces odor problems and leads to a quick release of nutrients.

Regrettably, many sewage sludges contain heavy metals from industrial wastes, which can create serious problems for the soil, plants and eventually you. The heavy metal you need to be most concerned about is cadium, since this metal affects animals before it affects plants. The maximum permissible amount of cadium in sludge to be spread on agricultural land is 50 parts per million. Sludge with 15 ppm or less is better. Before gathering sludge at a nearby sewage treatment plant, ask for a heavy metal analysis of the sludge.

Composting sludge before applying it slows the uptake of heavy metals by plants. Organic matter in the soil will do the same.

Pathogens and parasites present in human excrement represent a potential health problem when raw or undigested sludge is used on open soil. Composting sludge aerobically kills many of these harmful organisms.

Uncooked root crops and other vegetables which are eaten raw, especially leafy vegetables, should not be grown on sludge-treated soil for one year following sludge application. Sludge is still a good fertilizer to apply when taking part of your garden out of production as part of a rotation scheme.

Wood Ashes

Wood ashes are a rich source of potassium for your garden. They contain calcium, phosphorus, magnesium, and a little sulfur in addition to potash. The potash, calcium, and magnesium in wood ashes are in an alkaline form which can be used in place of ground limestone to counter soil acidity. Because of this, don't use wood ashes around blueberries, raspberries and other acid-loving plants.

Hardwood ashes are the best for garden application. Ash from hardwood trees contains from 1 to 10 percent potash and up to 2 percent phosphorus. Since nutrients in wood ashes dissolve readily in water, ashes are a good way of applying nutrients that will become available quickly.

Wood ashes should be side-dressed around plants. Avoid spreading wood ash where it can contact plant roots and seedlings. Five to 10 pounds of wood ash spread over each 100 square feet of garden will supply sufficient potash for most gardens. However, you must keep an eye on the soil's pH, since ashes make the soil alkaline.

The quick-dissolving characteristics of wood

ashes can make storing them a problem. They should be stored where they will not get wet, or the water will carry away valuable nutrients.

Only wood ashes should be used in your garden; coal ashes do more harm than good.

COMMERCIAL BALANCED FERTILIZERS

There are many commercially-available organic fertilizers which claim to be balanced. The fertilizer is blended to be about equal in nitrogen, phosphorus and potassium content, or at least close enough to supply the needs of plants growing in most soils.

Balanced organic fertilizer mixtures usually consist of composted animal manures, powdered rock minerals, organic residues, natural byproducts such as cottonseed meal, dried blood, peanut shells, seaweed products, and other organic materials. When these organic fertilizers are combined with a soil building program that includes lots of green manure, compost, and decomposing mulch, nutrient deficiency problems become a thing of the past.

What the people who make balanced organic fertilizers have done is mix the various materials mentioned above into a single-application fertilizer. They have taken different materials, most of them rich in one or two nutrients, and mixed them together in a way that will most effectively help heal any imbalance in the soil. Although organic fertilizers usually list their nutrient values in terms of nitrogen, phosphorus, and potash content, since they are made from so many materials they also tend to supply all of the trace elements needed by plants. See Table 4-1 for the macronutrient content of some popular organic fertilizers.

When buying organic fertilizers read the label carefully to make sure that what you are getting is a natural fertilizer. Many of the "organic-based" fertilizers are nothing more than dry manures or composts laced with chemical fertilizers. While these types of fertilizer are better for your soil than straight chemical fertilizers, they are not really natural. It is much better in the long run to buy the real thing.

If you have ever investigated a bag of chemical fertilizer, you will notice that there are usually three numbers in the front and sides of the bag. These numbers tell you, in percentages, the availability of three macronutrients: nitrogen, phosphorus, and potassium (N-P-K). The numbers 12-12-12, for instance, mean that this fertilizer contains 12 percent available nitrogen, 12 percent available phosphorus and 12 percent available potash. Unfortunately, these fertilizers are leached from the soil within months of application, leaving behind only salts which deter both the growth of microorganisms in the soil and the growth of crop plants.

It is difficult to play the N-P-K numbers game with natural fertilizers. The percentage of immediately-available nutrients looks rather low in organic materials. Cottonseed meal, for instance, has an available nitrogen content of 7 percent. However, the nitrogen in cottonseed meal is available much longer than nitrogen applied through a chemical fertilizer.

Although organic fertilizers do not release a lot of nutrients immediately, after a year these materials—especially the rock powders—are hitting their stride and releasing more nutrients than they did when first put into the soil. This presents a problem, because nutrients that become available a year after application will not help this year's plants very much. For this reason, fertilizers should contain both a quick-release and a long-term source of each of the major nutrients. Such a combination will feed plants now and next season with one application of fertilizer. For example, seaweed and granite dust in the same fertilizer will provide both slow-release and quick-release potassium.

MIXING AND MATCHING FERTILIZERS

You do not always have to buy balanced organic fertilizers. You can make them yourself by mixing several individual organic fertilizers together in a way that provides about equal amounts of the major nutrients (Table 4-2). In most cases you will not need to worry about micronutrients, because they will be present in many of the materials you add to your homemade balanced fertilizer.

As a general rule, most fertilizer materials

Table 4-2. Homemade Balanced Organic Fertilizers.

2-2-2

3 parts cottonseed meal
2 parts rock phosphate
2 parts greensand

1 part blood meal
1 part bone meal
3 parts granite dust

2-4-2

2 parts activated sludge
1 part bone meal
2 parts wood ashes

1 part leather dust
1 part bone meal
3 parts granite dust

0-5-4

1 part phosphate rock
3 parts greensand
2 parts wood ash

4-5-4

4 parts dried blood
2 parts rock phosphate
4 parts wood ashes
4 parts granite dust

weigh about one pound per pint. The ground rocks may be a little heavier and materials like cottonseed meal may weigh a little less, but one pound per pint is a good measuring standard for most gardens.

When mixing your own fertilizers, you will need some way of estimating an application rate. The measurements for many fertilizers, especially rock fertilizers, is usually given in tons per acre. One acre contains 43,650 square feet, although most gardeners are content to round this off to 43,000 square feet. For each ton (2,000 pounds) per acre a similar rate of application for 1,000 square feet would be 50 pounds, and 100 square feet would require only five pounds. One of the beauties of natural fertilizers is that over-application is difficult since the nutrients are released evenly and they make up a balanced percentage of the total fertilizer material.

You can use the above suggestion to determine how much fertilizer you will need to make for your garden. If your garden is 1,000 square feet, then the recommended rate of application for rock phosphate will be 50 pounds. Let us say you need to apply a balanced 2-2-2 fertilizer. Look under the 2-2-2 heading of Table 4-2 and choose the fertilizer mixture with rock phosphate. Substituting 50 pounds for 2 parts, you will then need 50 pounds of greensand and 75 pounds of cottonseed meal to make a balanced fertilizer. You can adjust your fertilizer to fit the recommendations of a soil test by adding more or less of a material rich in one of the three major nutrients.

For instance, if your soil test suggested adding more phosphorus than the other major nutrients, double the amount of rock phosphate in your mixture. This requires making a mixture of 100 pounds rock phosphate, 50 pounds of greensand and 75 pounds of cottonseed meal. Alternatively, you could make a batch of fertilizer from the 2-4-2 section of the table.

FERTILIZER APPLICATION

Now that you have mixed your fertilizer, you need to apply it so that it helps your garden the most. There are several ways to apply organic fertilizers, depending on the type of garden you are growing, the season, and the materials in the fertilizer.

Broadcasting

This is one of the most popular methods of fertilizer application, probably because it is one of the easiest. To broadcast an organic fertilizer, simply sprinkle it over the entire area of your garden and then turn it under with green manure, compost, mulch, or other organic material. Fertilizer can be added efficiently during spring or fall while you are cultivating the soil.

Using the broadcasting method may mean that plants do not get the full strength of the fertilizer since some of the fertilizer ends up between rows or under paths and out of the reach of roots. Because organic fertilizers are slow-release, most will still be active the following year when rows are put in different places. What is wasted this year may be right where it is needed next year.

Fertilizers which contain raw or undecomposed organic matter should be turned under several weeks prior to planting. The earlier it is turned under the better since soil bacteria has a longer time to work on the organic material before plant roots arrive. Later, when plant roots finger out in the soil, soil microbes and plant roots will not begin a tug-of-war over the nutrients since the microbes will be finished using them.

Broadcasting is a good method for spreading rock fertilizers, but things like dried blood and wood ashes that tend to break down rapidly in the soil should be applied around plants as a side-dressing.

Side-Dressing

Once plants have established themselves in the garden you will not want to dig fertilizers into the soil near plants. Such major disruptions of the soil are dangerous to plant roots. Instead, fertilizers can be applied as a side-dressing (Fig. 4-1). To side-dress, sprinkle fertilizers right along the row of vegetables 1 to 2 inches from the base of the plants. Be careful though, because some materials like activated sludge and wood ashes may have harmful effects on seedlings.

It is a good idea to work the soil along the row with a hoe before side-dressing. This allows the fertilizer to fall into the loose soil. Not only will this keep the wind from blowing the fertilizer away, but the next rain will wash it even deeper into the soil. A rough soil also allows the fertilizer to contact the soil organisms which are responsible for making nutrients available to plant roots.

Side-dressed fertilizer leaches down into the soil when it rains, delivering nutrients that are dissolved in water, which is just the way plants take their nutrients. If you apply a mulch over a side-dressing, weeds will be prevented from growing and your plants will get the full benefit instead of sharing the nutrients with greedy weeds. A mulch will also keep the wind from blowing your fertilizer into the neighbor's garden.

Fertilizer in the Plant Row

Since organic fertilizers are slow-release, they can be added right to the seed trench without fear of harming germination. This allows seedling roots to tap the fertilizer's nutrients immediately with a minimum effort, and you do not have to worry about burning the plants.

To add fertilizer to a seed row, sprinkle the fertilizer in the seed trench. Go back over the trench lightly with a hoe to mix the soil and fertilizer at the bottom of the trench. This will put soil microbes in contact with the fertilizer, and microorganisms will begin breaking down the nutrients for your plants. Spread the seeds in the row and cover them with soil.

Fig. 4-2. Since most balanced organic fertilizers are slow-release, you can add them directly to the hole you have dug for heavy-feeding transplants.

59

A variation of this method is useful when transplanting heavy-feeding plants like tomatoes, eggplants, cucumbers, melons, squash and peppers. After you have dug the hole for the plant, throw in a shovelful of compost and a handful of a balanced fertilizer (Fig. 4-2). Mix the compost and fertilizer with soil in the hole, and then put in the plant. Fill with dirt and water. The nutrients from the compost and fertilizer will feed each plant through the growing season.

Compost and Manure Tea

Plants drink their food. Plants take nutrients from the soil only when the nutrients are suspended in water. Because of this fact, feeding your plants with a liquid fertilizer or "tea" makes a lot of sense. This is especially true during hot summer days when water and nutrients are likely to be lacking in the soil. Compost and manure teas are just the thing for putting nutrients into the root zone where plants can make the most use of them.

Most of the nutrients in compost and manure leach readily into water. Instead of placing manure or compost on the soil and hoping for a rain to wash nutrients into the root zone, a fertilizer tea makes sure the nutrients arrive where they are needed.

Making a compost tea is not difficult. Place a shovelful of compost in a 5-gallon bucket, swirl it around with a stick a few times, then pour off the water directly at the base of your plants. The same compost can be used several times, since one soaking will not wash out all the nutrients. After three or four waterings, replace the compost with fresh material. Add the old stuff to your compost heap, use it as a side-dressing, or mulch with it.

Gardeners with large gardens may want to make batches of tea in a 55-gallon drum. Put 1 or 2 bushel baskets of compost in the drum. Add water, then stir and let stand overnight. In the morning, dip out the tea-colored water and use it on plants.

Manure teas take a little longer than compost teas to make, but the wait is well worth it. To make manure tea, combine as many different types of livestock manure as you can get your hands on. Put a shovelful of each into the same burlap bag, and hang the bag in a 55-gallon drum of water. You can

Fig. 4-3. Compost or manure in a burlap bag dunked in a 5-gallon bucket of water is a good way to make small batches of fertilizer tea.

make manure tea on a smaller scale in a 5-gallon bucket, (Fig. 4-3). Try to keep the ratio of manure to water at about 1 part manure to 3 parts water. Let the manure steep for a month and you should have a nice strong manure tea. This tea can be diluted to make it stretch. One part tea to 3 parts water is about right.

As a general rule most rock fertilizers and other commercially available fertilizers, like cottonseed meal, do not work too well as teas. Seaweed and fish emulsion are two notable exceptions. These materials can be mixed at a rate of about 2 tablespoons per gallon and poured around the base of plants or sprayed on leaves as a foliar fertilizer.

Foliar Feeding

No one will argue with the idea that fertile soil

is the best way of providing all the nutrients a plant needs; however, under certain conditions, like drought, soil deficiency, insect attack, and when a plant's growth pattern is changing—a plant may not be getting the nutrients it needs from the soil. At these stressful times you may want to give your plants a nutrient boost with a foliar spray.

Research has shown that it is eight times more efficient for plants to absorb fertilizers through their leaves than through their roots. All three of the major nutrients (nitrogen, phosphorus and potassium) as well as a host of trace minerals can be absorbed through a plant's leaves.

Foliar sprays can be made from any fertilizer which is water soluble. The four most often used leaf-sprays are fish emulsion, seaweed, manure tea and compost tea. Regrettably, none of the leaf-sprays provide a totally balanced diet for plants, although manure and compost teas do come close.

Liquid seaweed contains very little of the major nutrients, but it does contain traces of the 70 elements found in the oceans. Therefore, seaweed leaf-sprays are an excellent way to correct minor mineral deficiencies during times of stress.

Fish emulsion, manure tea, and compost tea are more often used to supply the major nutrients. These solutions contain many trace minerals, but not as many as liquid seaweed.

To make a fish emulsion or seaweed leaf-spray, mix 1 or 2 tablespoons of the fertilizer in a gallon of water (Fig. 4-4). Add a squirt of biodegradable soap so that the spray so that the spray will stick to the plants. Spray the solution on your plants early in the morning when the stomata are open.

Compost and manure teas should be strained through a fine mesh cloth so that they do not clog your sprayer. Dilute tea with water until it is the color of pale tea. Spray on plants.

Midsummer is the best time to consider foliar spraying. Temperatures are high, the soil is dry and fruiting crops like tomatoes, peppers and cucumbers can lose their blossoms because of the stress. Insect and disease pressures will also be high at this time and your plants will respond favorably to a nutrient boost.

Another good time to give plants a dose of leaf-spray is when they are changing their growing patterns—for instance, when a vine starts sending out runners, forming flowers or setting fruit.

Foliar feeding can also help enhance the flavor of some fruits. Cantaloupe, for example, tastes flat when cultivated in soils low in magnesium. A foliar spray of seaweed or Epsom salt (magnesium sulfate) immediately after fruit set and again when fruits are 2 inches in diameter will make melons sweeter.

Despite all the good things to be said about foliar feeding plants, do not depend on this method as the main source of nourishment for your crops. A rich soil should be a plant's major source of nourishment, but leaf-sprays can be used as a supplement to help your plants through their growing pains.

Fig. 4-4. Pour a mixture of fish emulsion and water into a sprayer for foliar feeding of your plants.

Chapter 5

Compost

The best compost for the lands is the wise master's feet and hands.

—Robert Harrick

If you were asked to choose the one organic material that would do your soil the most good, what would you choose? Compost, of course.

Compost, or decomposed vegetable and animal matter, is the best organic material you can add to your soil. Pound for pound, compost is the finest soil conditioner to be had. In terms of nutrient content, compost contains nitrogen, phosphorus, potassium, and a laundry list of essential trace minerals. But the best part of compost is the abundance of microorganisms found in it.

When you apply compost to your soil, you are adding a living material—not a dead weight. Since the life in a compost heap is almost identical to that in the soil, except in a concentrated form, the benefits of compost are tremendous. Compost is no more than a speeded-up version of what goes on in nature—the cycle of life, death, decay and new life. The nutrient content of compost is not its only claim

to fame. Compost also loosens the soil, improving its structure and allowing water and air to penetrate rather than run off.

Although it is not necessary to compost all organic materials, many gardeners prefer to compost as much of these materials as they can gather. The compost heap becomes a stopping point for leaves, weeds, grass clippings, garbage, and other compostable material on its way to the garden's soil. In this way, compost heaps are an extension of the nutrient recycling process that goes on almost everywhere in nature. The leaves, stems, branches and twigs of all types of plants fall to the ground where they decompose into plant nutrients. Gardening disrupts the natural pattern by not returning plant matter to the soil. Composting is the link between what happens in nature and in a domesticated garden. It's simply an extension of nature's soil-building process. Through your compost heap you can return the accumulation of organic trash to your soil where it will do your plants some good.

In addition to returning organic material to the soil, there are two other major reasons to make compost. First, composting reduces materials such as garbage and manure to a substance that is pleasent to handle. Second, composting increases the nitrogen content of many materials. When microoroganisms feed on organic matter, they burn off much of the carbon in the material. This both reduces the bulk of the material and increases the nitrogen content. There are two types of bacterial activity: anaerobic (without oxygen) and aerobic (with oxygen).

Anaerobic composting was developed largely as an industrial process for decaying large quantities of organic waste. The organic material is kept in airtight tanks during the decomposition process. Since air encourages oxidation which in turn releases nitrogen, decomposition in the absence of air reduces the loss of nitrogen. In fact, in a perfect anaerobic decomposition process no nitrogen is lost at all. During aerobic decomposition as much as 40 percent of the nitrogen in organic material is lost to the atmosphere.

Unfortunately, home gardeners will find anaerobic decomposition a difficult task to accomplish. Most gardeners do not have the large airtight containers necessary for this process. Instead, most gardeners opt for aerobic composting.

Aerobic decomposition is accomplished by microorganisms which live in the presence of air. These organisms use the oxygen in the air to convert the carbon in the organic material to energy. This creates heat and explains why an active compost heap may reach a temperature of 160° F. Aerobic decomposition is the most widely used type of composting method, and is the process found in most compost bins and heaps.

An active compost heap requires oxygen, moisture, nitrogen, phosphorus, potassium, carbon, and a host of trace minerals. The critical factor for good aerobic composting is the relationship between carbon and nitrogen in the heap.

CARBON/NITROGEN RATIO

The relationship between the amount of carbon and nitrogen in a compost material is called the carbon/nitrogen ratio—C/N ratio for short. The bacteria, fungi, and other microscopic critters found in a compost heap need both carbon and nitrogen to survive. Microbes have a definite preference for the amount of these two materials in the compost heap. These decomposing microbes use the carbon in organic matter for energy, and nitrogen as a body-building material. When the C/N ratio is out of whack, the compost heap simply does not deteriorate correctly.

When too little carbon is present, a large amount of nitrogen is lost because the microbes do not have enough energy to convert the nitrogen in the organic material into their own body tissue. The nitrogen escapes into the air and is lost to your soil. Materials too high in carbon also make composting inefficient. When not enough nitrogen is present in the decomposing material, the composting process takes an extremely long time. When this incomplete compost is added to the soil, the microorganisms in the compost rob nitrogen from the soil in order to complete the decomposition process. As a consequence your plants suffer a nitrogen deficiency.

Most experts agree that the proper C/N ratio for compost is 30 to 1, or simply 30 (Fig. 5-1). Raw garbage, for example, has 25 times as much carbon as nitrogen. Its C/N ratio is 25. Farmyard manure, which is much higher in nitrogen, has a C/N of 14. The higher the number the more carbon is present. Sawdust, for instance, is generally stated at a C/N of 400. Sawdust left to rot on its own, without the addition of nitrogen, may require up to three years to decompose. When a nitrogen-rich material is added to sawdust so that the C/N ratio begins to approach 30, decomposition takes place.

As you can see, the relationship between carbon and nitrogen in a compost heap determines how quickly the material will break down. It is a good idea to mix materials with a low C/N ratio with materials that have a high C/N ratio. For most home gardeners, a rough estimate of a material's C/N ratio is all that is needed.

You can use Table 5-1 as a guideline for determining whether the materials you plan to use for compost fall into the high or low categories. The materials listed in the "low" section of the table have a C/N ratio low enough for these materials to

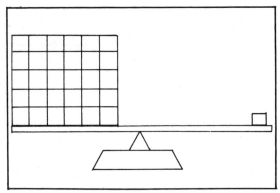

Fig. 5-1. The optimum carbon/nitrogen ratio for good composting is 30 parts carbon (left) to 1 part nitrogen (right).

compost without the addition of nitrogen. Materials in the "high" section of the table will require the addition of nitrogen for good decomposition.

Since a lack of nitrogen can keep the pile from heating properly, it is important to know which materials lower the C/N ratio of a compost heap. Dried blood is a good nitrogen-rich material which should be added to high carbon organic matter at the rate of 3 pounds per 30 pounds of compost pile. Manure is the best addition since it contains bacteria capable of starting off the decomposition process. When manure makes up one-fifth of a compost pile, success is virtually guaranteed. Cottonseed meal, grass clippings and weeds are also good sources of nitrogen.

In addition to the C/N ratio, other factors which influence the action of a compost heap include moisture, air temperature, pH, pile size, aeration, and the materials from which the pile is made. With all these variables, it stands to reason that no two compost heaps will ever be exactly alike. By keeping these variables within the range suitable for microbe growth, however, you can achieve good compost every time you try.

MOISTURE

Moisture has an important affect on the compost heap. Moisture can cause problems when there is too much or not enough. The best moisture content for a compost pile is between 45 and 60 percent by weight. When the moisture content

drops below 45 to 50 percent, microbial action slows. The minimum moisture content at which microorganisms can live is around 12 to 15 percent. At the other extreme, a pile with a moisture content of more than 55 to 60 percent will also have a slow rate of decomposition. Soggy piles smother aerobic microorganisms by preventing air from entering the pile.

The ideal heap is moist, and about 50 percent water. You should not be able to squeeze water out of the composting material. If you can, it is too wet. On the other hand, compost should leave a moist feeling in your hand when you squeeze it. In dry areas you may want to cover the heap with a moisture-retaining material like plastic to keep water in. In wet areas you may need to cover the pile with plastic for the opposite reason: you want to keep excess moisture out of the pile. In fact, too much water is often worse than not enough water since water tends to leach valuable nutrients from compost. The more water there is, the more leaching will occur.

AIR

Since aerobic microorganisms are the most efficient composting organisms, compost heaps should be well supplied with air. Turning is the primary way to do this (Fig. 5-2). Even when a pile is turned, parts of it may become shut off from air. Anaerobic decomposition sets in at the expense of

**Table 5-1. Compost Materials with
Low Carbon/Nitrogen Ratios (Left) Should
Be Mixed with Materials High in Nitrogen (Right)
for Good Compost Action. A C/N Ratio of 30 Is Appropriate.**

Carbon/Nitrogen Ratios			
Low: 6 to 30		High: 30 to 400	
Sewage sludge, activated	6	Fruit wastes	35
Humus	10	Leaves	50
Alfalfa hay	12	Sugar cane residues	50
Young sweet clover	12	Corn stalks	60
Alfalfa	13	Oat straw	80
Food wastes (table scraps)	15	Straw	80
Sewage sludge, digested	16	Timothy hay	80
Grass clippings	19	Paper	170
Rotted manure	20	Sawdust	400
Mature sweet clover	23		

Fig. 5-2. Turning is an important part of the aeration process for compost. Turning also keeps the pile loose for good water penetration.

the quicker aerobic process. As a general rule, the more a compost pile is turned the quicker it will decompose.

Shredding or grinding all materials prior to adding them to the compost heap is a good way to increase aeration (Fig. 5-3). Additionally, the smaller pieces facilitate turning. Layering compost heaps with coarse materials also tends to produce air channels for the pile. Keeping a compost pile's moisture content near optimum will also encourage adequate aeration.

TEMPERATURE

Working compost heaps often heat to 160° F. This is hot enough to destroy weed seeds and harmful microorganisms, but perfect for the beneficial microbes. A hot compost heap also breaks down quickly, preventing the loss of many nutrients.

Air temperature has a lot to do with how quickly your compost pile decomposes. Although the microbes in a compost heap are capable of producing heat, they cannot overcome the coldness of most winter weather. Instead, your compost heap will lay dormant until warming spring temperatures arrive. Once the weather has warmed enough for the microbes to live, they quickly generate enough heat to keep going strong until the organic matter is thoroughly decomposed. You can speed the warming of your pile in the spring by covering it with black plastic or a dark material such as dirt. In the fall, the same heat-retaining practices will help your heap work a few extra weeks into cold weather.

pH

The acidity or alkalinity of most organic materials is not much different than the optimum pH for most microbes. Most microbes like acid conditions, and in fact, they produce acid as part of their digestive process. Most finished composts are nearly neutral by the time you spread them on the ground. However, you can alter the final pH of compost by carefully juggling the materials you add to the pile.

When making a compost to be added to an acidic soil, it is a good idea to add limestone to each level of the heap during construction. The limestone will neutralize the acids produced in the compost heap. As a result the finished compost will have a slightly alkaline pH which will help neutralize the acid condition of the soil. Unfortunately,

Fig. 5-3. Shredding leaves is a must for this organic material to break down quickly in the compost heap (courtesy of Amerind MacKissic).

limestone tends to promote the loss of nitrogen. Make sure you add an extra helping of nitrogen to any heap to which you have added limestone. Do not use composts made with limestone around acid-loving plants like blueberries.

Where soils are alkaline, you should not add limestone to your compost heap. Instead, you should add materials which will increase the acidity of the finished compost. Cottonseed meal and pine needles are two acidic materials that work well in this regard.

When your soil tests show deficiencies in certain trace minerals, make sure you add materials to the compost which contain these minerals. By the time the compost is added to your soil, the minerals will be in a form available to plants.

COMPOST ACTIVATORS

Many companies sell materials labeled as compost activators. These materials are said to supply nutrients and bacteria necessary for good compost action. Most tests show that these materials are only marginally effective, when they work at all. In most cases the manure, soil, and organic matter you add to a compost heap will contain all the microorganisms necessary for good compost action. If the C/N ratio is correct, native microorganisms will multiply so quickly that there is little difference between compost piles with activators and those without. You will probably do much better to buy a bag of nitrogen-rich cottonseed or dried blood for your compost instead of an activator.

COMPOSTABLE MATERIALS

Compost can be made from virtually anything that was once living, since composting is a part of the natural cycle of life, death, decay, and new life. You will find many sources of compost in your own backyard and around the community in which you live (Table 5-2). From your yard and garden you can gather grass clippings, leaves, weeds, garbage, and animal hair. After you have exhausted the sources of compostable material in your own yard you can go out looking for more compostable material in your community.

Around town you will be able to find many

Table 5-2. The Macronutrient Levels of Some Common Compostable Materials Are Listed Here.

Percent Macronutrients of Various Compostable Materials			
Material	N	P	K
Alfalfa hay	2.45	.5	2.1
Apple leaves	1	.15	.35
Coffee grounds	2	.32	.28
Corn (green)	.3	.13	.33
Cotton factory wastes	1.3	.45	.36
Eggshells	1.1	.38	.14
Feathers	15	-	-
Fish scraps (fresh)	2-7.5	1.5-6	-
Greensand	-	1-2	5
Hair	12-16	-	-
Hoof meal and hair dust	10-15	1.5-2	-
Kentucky blue grass	.66	.19	.71
Leather dust	10-12	-	-
Lobster shells	4.6	3.5	-
Oak leaves	.8	.35	.15
Orange culls	.2	.13	.21
Peanut shells	.8	.15	.5
Pine needles	.46	.12	.03
Potato leaves and stalks	.6	.15	.45
Red clover hay	2.1	.5	2
Salt marsh hay	1.1	.25	.75
Seaweed	1.68	.75	4.93
Shrimp wastes	2.7	9.95	-
Spanish moss	.6	.1	.55
Tea grounds	4.15	.62	.4
Timothy hay	1.25	.55	1
Tomato (leaves and stalks)	.35	.1	.45
Wheat straw	.5	.15	.6
White clover (green)	.5	.2	.3
Wood ashes	-	1-2	4-10

different sources of organic matter. The specific type of material will depend, of course, on where you live. But, canning factories, stables, city clean-up crews, sawmills, wineries, restaurants, sea shores—in short, any place where plants or animals grow—is likely to be a good foraging ground for compostable material.

Many people, especially non-gardeners, consider things like leaves, grass clippings and stable manure as trash and in many instances they will give it away for the hauling. All you have to do is ask and you may find that you have more sources of more compost fodder than you can possibly use. Do not return to the same place again and again to gather materials. A compost heap needs a wide variety of materials, and so does your soil. The wider the number of materials you incorporate into compost, the better chance you have of assuring that all the nutrients essential to good soil and plant health will be available in your garden.

Finding compost is not all that hard. Farms and orchards are good places to gather manure, spoiled hay, corn silage, spoiled fruit, and a variety of other organic materials. Factories and mills are good places to gather cannery and food processing wastes of all kinds. Often, woodshavings and sawdust, felt wastes, cotton gin trash, spent hops, wood chips, and a host of other materials are also available. A quick look in the Yellow Pages will give you many clues as to where you can gather all the free organic material you need.

A few cities around the country supply dried sewage sludge, leaf mold and leaf dumps, and wood chips from tree trimming operations (Fig. 5-4).

Stables and feed lots are ideal places to gather manure. Choose places where livestock is confined and manure is likely to be a problem instead of working farms as likely candidates. Many restaurant and vegetable wholesalers produce tremendous amounts of vegetable scraps. These materials are as high in nutrients as the table scraps generated in your kitchen. Do not overlook them!

Rock powders and organic fertilizers can also be added to compost heaps in order to increase the nutrient content of the finished product or to correct pH or C/N ratio problems. These materials were discussed in detail in Chapter 4. Their action in the compost heap is basically the same as in the soil.

Here are a dozen likely candidates for the compost heap.

Coffee Grounds

Coffee grounds contain up to 2 percent nitrogen, smaller amounts of phosphorus, and potassium.

Fig. 5-4. City leaf dumps are a valuable place for mining compostable leaves and leaf mold.

As a rule, drip coffee grounds are richer in nitrogen than boiled grounds. Coffee grounds absorb moisture and encourage acid-forming bacteria in the compost heap. They should not be used in composts destined for plants that do not like acid soils.

Corncobs

Whole corncobs are a good compost material. Corncobs are even better when shredded. Since corncobs are relatively small, they make turning the compost heap easier. Their bulk will prevent materials like leaves from matting together. Corncobs hold a lot of moisture. They are high in carbon and should be mixed with a high-nitrogen material when added to the compost pile.

In many parts of the country, you can find a ready supply of corncobs at local corn mills and feed lots. Corncobs will also make an excellent mulch since they stay in place and their water holding capacity is high. Do not turn corncobs into the soil or your soil is likely to suffer a nitrogen deficiency.

Food Processing Wastes

The wastes from all food processing plants and breweries are valuable additions to your compost heap. A word of caution though: do not use only one type of waste, or decomposition will be slow. Instead, try to mix the wastes with other materials.

In sugar beet regions where sugar beets are grown, you may be able to find a ready supply of beet wastes. This material contains nearly equal amounts of potash, nitrogen, and phosphorus, in addition to calcium and magnesium. Castor pomace, the residue remaining when oil has been pressed from castor beans, is rich in nitrogen. In some cases, this material can be used in place of manure as the main source of nitrogen in a compost heap.

There is some danger in using citrus wastes for composting because these fruits receive heavy applications of pesticides. It is best to compost citrus wastes from organic growers. When such citrus wastes are available, they should be shredded and mixed with a bacteria-rich material such as manure in the compost pile. Cotton gin, the material left over from the processing of cotton, is read-

ily compostable when mixed with other wastes. Manures are especially suited to getting cotton wastes off to a quick start.

Spent hops, the residue of hops in the brewing process, can contain up to 75 percent water. Dry hops have a higher content of nitrogen and phosphorus. Wet hops heat quickly in the compost pile. This makes them a good activator for slower-decomposing materials.

Molasses residues are rich in sugars and therefore quick to break down in the compost heap. Sugar cane trash has a C/N ratio of 50. Pea wastes are rich in nitrogen and are a good addition to compost heaps with a lot of carbon-rich materials. Rice hulls are rich in potash and decompose quickly. Since rice hulls are small, they prevent matting and are easy to turn. Sugar wastes are a quick-energy source for the microorganisms in a compost pile. Some sugar wastes contain large amounts of phosphorus. Peanut hulls are rich in nitrogen, and the stiffness of this material will help the aeration of a compost heap.

Garden Wastes

Garden wastes of all kinds, from ground fruit tree trimmings to beet tops, should be added to the compost pile. These materials contain many minerals and nutrients that you have added to your garden as fertilizer. By returning them to the soil through the compost heap, you can reduce future investments in fertilizer.

Garden trash should be considered part of the green matter of a compost heap (Fig. 5-5). Do not add diseased or insect-infested plants to the compost heap, since the problem may not be destroyed by the composting process. (It is smarter to burn such problem materials.) Tough vines and stems should be chopped or shredded prior to incorporation into the compost heap. This precaution will speed their breakdown.

Garbage

Kitchen wastes and wastes from restaurants are a prized addition to compost heaps. Most garbage is high in nitrogen and contains a wide range of other minerals. Raw garbage has a C/N ratio of 25.

Fig. 5-5. As crops go out of production, their debris should be removed from the garden and added to the compost pile.

Because of this low C/N ratio, kitchen wastes should be counted as part of the green matter of a compost heap. In most cases, garbage will help heat the pile.

Avoid using soapy water and animal fats since the former adds harmful salts to the finished compost and the latter attracts varmints. Do not be afraid to include bones and cooked foods to the compost heap.

Grass Clippings

Grass clippings are an excellent addition to the compost heap. Rich in nitrogen with a C/N ratio of 19, quick to break down, and widely available, grass clippings should be used whenever you can find

them. The nitrogen in this material will get most compost heaps off to a good start.

Beware of grass clippings from yards without weeds. Chances are such immaculate lawns have been sprayed with potent herbicides.

Leaves

Next to manure, leaves are the best material you can add to a compost heap. Leaves are loaded with minerals, usually more than manure, easy to get and easy to handle when chopped or shredded (Fig. 5-6). Leaves have a low C/N ratio, varying from 40 to 80, so nitrogen must be added to a compost heap containing a lot of leaves. Leaves are important for the large amount of fiber they add to compost.

To ensure proper composting of leaves, you need to do two things: First, shred or chop them so that they do not mat together and reduce air and water circulation in the pile. (You can add rough materials like corncobs to whole leaves to achieve the same effect.) Second, a high nitrogen material must be added to leaves in compost. Manures are best, but fertilizers like cottonseed meal and dried blood also work well.

Leaves piled up and left to decay on their own for a couple of years will make a fine, black humus known as leaf mold. Although this material is not as rich in nutrients as composted leaves, it has excellent soil-building properties. The water-holding ability of leaf mold is impressive. Leaf mold will hold 300 to 500 times its own weight in water—excellent drought insurance.

Manure

Although you can make compost successfully (quickly and with the proper heating action) without manure, the excrement from common livestock is one of the best composting materials around. There are several reasons for this: manure tends to contain a plethora of bacteria, it is already partially broken down, and manure's C/N ratio is such that it will compost easily. Most rotted manure has a C/N ratio of about 20.

Horse, cow, goat, sheep, pig, rabbit, and poultry manures are all excellent for the compost

Fig. 5-6. Nongardeners bag leaves for disposal. You can collect these leaves and use them for composting or for mulch.

heap (Table 5-3). Even better is manure mixed with bedding materials soaked in the animals' urine. Urine is high in nitrogen and will prevent many of the problems associated with compost heaps too low in this nutrient. Although the nutrient value of manure varies according to which animal it came from and what that animal ate, all manures contain digestive enzymes which enhance the activity of your compost heap.

The age and manner in which manure is handled will affect its nutrient value. Manure that has been stacked outside in the weather will not be as rich as fresh manure because some of the nutrients, nitrogen and potassium in particular, will leach from the manure. Therefore, when collecting manure for composting try to get the freshest manure possible. When you plan to turn manure directly into the soil, rotted manure is better since it has

less chance of burning plants.

Chicken manure is the hottest manure. "Hot" means that it is rich in nitrogen, phosphorus, and

Table 5-3. All of These Animal Manures Make Excellent Additions to the Compost Pile.

NPK Composition of Animal Manures (Percent)			
Manure	**N**	**P**	**K**
Cattle (fresh)	.53	.29	.48
Cattle (dried)	2	1.8	2.2
Chicken (fresh)	.89	.48	.83
Duck (fresh)	.6	1.4	.5
Goat (fresh)	1.5	1	.2
Horse (fresh)	.55	.27	.57
Hog (fresh)	.63	.46	.41
Pigeon (fresh)	4.2	2.2	1.4
Rabbit (fresh)	.2	1.4	.5
Sheep (fresh)	.89	.48	.83
Sheep (dried)	1.4	1	3

potassium. A compost heap with its fair share of chicken manure will heat quickly and thoroughly. This manure must be composted before being added to your soil.

Cow manure is considered a cold manure because it has a relatively low nitrogen level. Cow manure contains a lot of water. When used in the compost heap it will not heat as efficiently as other kinds of manure, but the large amounts of minerals and bacteria it contains makes it a valuable addition all the same.

Horse manure is another hot manure, although not as hot as chicken manure. Horse manure should be added to the compost heap with a large quantity of high-carbon material. This precaution will prevent the escape of nitrogen and prevent the compost from reaching too high of a temperature. Horse manures leach nutrients easily and should not be watered excessively.

Pig manure is a highly concentrated source of nutrients for the compost heap. Pig manure is cold and tends to work rather slowly.

Rabbit manure is another hot manure. In fact, it is hotter than some poultry manures. Do not use too much of this material in the compost heap without adding a carbon-rich material.

Pine Needles

Although the tough outer layer on pine needles makes them slow to decompose, they are a useful addition to compost piles. The loose structure of pine needles fluffs up the pile, allowing good air and water circulation. For this reason, pine needles are good when added to compost piles containing a large amount of leaves or other material that mats easily. Pine needles are acidic, and a large helping of them in a compost pile will make the finished compost slightly acidic.

Sawdust and Wood Chips

The byproducts of sawmills and tree-trimming operations are useful additives to the compost heap. Although these materials have a low C/N ratio of 400, when mixed with high nitrogen materials they break down rather well in the compost heap. Additionally, sawdust is easy to turn.

Many sawmills give sawdust away. When collecting sawdust, try to get material that has weathered as much as possible. You will usually find the oldest sawdust at the back and bottom of the waste pile. This older sawdust will be dark instead of white in color. Aged sawdust will not require as much nitrogen for decomposition as fresh sawdust does.

Seaweed

If you happen to live along a coast with a lot of seaweed, you have an excellent supply of compost material. Seaweed breaks down rapidly in the compost heap and adds a variety of minerals to the finished compost. In order to save as many of the minerals as possible, compost seaweed when green. Since seaweed is generally rich in potassium it should be a major source of this nutrient for your garden.

Straw

Straw is relatively low in the major nutrients, but it is a valuable addition to compost heaps since it will supply much of the carbon energy needed for good action in the pile. Straw will also add a decent measure of mineral nutrients to compost. It is generally better when used as a mulch. When straw is added to a compost heap, it should be accompanied by a nitrogen-rich substance like manure. The C/N ratio for straw is 80. Straw is bulky, providing the space necessary to keep air and water moving through an active compost heap.

Other Compost Materials

Of course, there are many more materials suited for composting. There are also a few which should not be used for composting, including human feces and urine. Grease, oil and animal fat or meats should not be used in compost. Not only do these materials attract animals and insects, but they also slow bacterial action. Large objects like tree limbs, corn stalks, clam shells, and bones will not break down readily and they make turning the pile difficult. These materials can be used in compost piles only if they are shredded. Dog droppings can be used, in moderation, as long as the dogs are not diseased. Do not use materials that have been treated with chemical-based insecticides or herbicides, as both of these chemicals inhibit microbial activity. Besides, inclusion of these materials in the compost heap leads, eventually, to their incorporation into the soil.

COMPOST-MAKING METHODS

There are as many different ways of making compost as there are gardeners. In fact, every time the same gardener makes compost it will be different since you will never be able to get exactly the same amount of the same materials for each batch. Don't worry, though. As long as you keep the materials in the pile moist, aerated and at a C/N ratio near 30 your compost-making should be successful.

Making compost is not really difficult. All you need to do is combine organic materials and then let nature's bacterial action take over. Below you will find a few of the more popular methods of compost making. These methods are merely guidelines to help you get off to a good start making compost. Any or all of them can be adapted to the materials, time and space limitations you have without fear of failure.

Grinding and shredding have several affects on materials added to compost. First, the surface area of the material is increased, which means that the microorganisms responsible for decomposition will multiply rapidly. Second, aeration is improved since fine material tends to be looser than large pieces. Third, like air, water is more evenly distributed in the heap. Finally, shredding and grinding make turning the pile much easier.

There are a number of shredders and grinders available for home use. Lawn mowers can also be used. Weeds, leaves, straw, hay, manure, and crop residues can be shredded by spreading them on the ground and then running over them with the mower. Do this near a wall or into a grass catching bag so that gathering the chopped material will be easier. Additionally, many lawn mowers now come with mulching attachments. These work quite well and are an inexpensive alternative to garden shredders.

Indore Method

The Indore method of composting was de-veloped by Sir Albert Howard. This is the first scientifically designed method of composting. The Indore method ensures a correct C/N ratio while keeping various materials spread evenly throughout the pile. These factors almost guarantee successful decomposition.

The Indore method can be used in open piles or bins. Although open piles work well, bins will reduce the unsightliness of the pile. Bins also tend to provide better moisture and temperature control for your pile.

Compost piles should be at least 6 feet wide, 6 feet long, and 4 to 5 feet tall in order for proper heating to take place. Piles smaller than this lose too much heat to reach the 150° to 160° F temperature required for finished compost.

The Indore method uses a series of layers of different materials to ensure that the pile has all the nutrients necessary for proper decomposition (Fig. 5-7). First, start with a layer of plant wastes spread over the area to be covered by the pile. This layer should be 6 inches deep and may include materials like straw, hay, leaves, sawdust, wood chips, peanut hulls or ground corncobs. Next, add a 2-inch layer of manure. Include the bedding material. A layer of topsoil should be sprinkled on this layer to a ¼-inch depth. Finally, sprinkle lime, phosphate rock, greensand, granite dust, or wood ashes on the topsoil. Water the pile and then begin again with

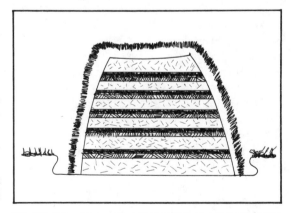

Fig. 5-7. This cross-section of an Indore compost pile shows the alternating layers of loose organic materials, dirt, manure, and rock minerals. The whole pile is covered with dirt or straw to keep excess water out.

another layer of coarse organic material. The end result is a pile with about 4 parts vegetable matter to 1 part manure.

The outside of the pile should be covered with a layer of soil. This will reduce flies and other pest problems. The top of the pile should be slightly concave so that water runs into the pile instead of away from it. Do not walk or step on the heap once it has been made or you will compact it and reduce the flow of air and water through it.

Within a few days, the pile should begin to heat. Turn the pile after about six weeks, making sure to place the material on the outside of the pile on the inside. This will ensure that the pile decomposes evenly. The pile should heat up again, but not as hot as the first heating. After a month turn the pile again. At the end of three months, the pile should be cool and ready to use on your garden.

Fourteen-Day Method

For those of you who need compost now instead of several months from now, the 14-day method is a good choice. Although you will get your compost quicker, you will have to invest some extra time and energy to make the process work. This investment is worth it since 14-day compost is often higher in nutrient value than compost that has been outside in the weather for months.

With this method, all material to be used in the heap must be shredded or ground. You do not need to layer materials; simply mix them together before or after shredding and make a pile about 5 feet tall. Water the pile until water begins running out of the bottom. Make sure that manure is added at the rate of about 1 part manure to 4 parts vegetable matter, and the pile should heat rapidly.

Two or three days after the pile heats it should be turned. Turn it again at regular intervals every two to three days until two weeks have passed. By this time, the material will drop in temperature and be sufficiently decomposed for use on your garden.

Sheet Composting

If your garden is large enough so that a section of it is taken out of production each year for green manure cropping or to lay fallow, sheet composting

may be an attractive alternative to building a compost heap. Sheet composting is not as attractive for small gardens because gardens with limited space cannot afford to have a section out of production for an extended time.

The best way to sheet compost is to combine this practice with green manuring. Plant a green manure crop. When the green manure has grown sufficiently, lay a 1- or 2-inch layer of organic matter over the green manure. The organic material should be ground or shredded prior to spreading. Do not be afraid to use low-nitrogen materials like sawdust or straw since by the time you plant another crop in this area plenty of nitrogen will be available—likewise, you can use materials rich in nitrogen, manure or sludge, because you do not need to worry about burning following crops.

After spreading the organic matter, work it into the soil. When this is done in the fall the area can be planted to vegetables the following spring. When turning is done in the spring, you will have to wait at least three months before planting vegetables. The microbes breaking down the vegetable matter will prevent nitrogen from being available for plant use if crops are planted immediately after incorporating this compost.

Rock fertilizer can be added along with the sheet compost. The decay of the organic matter will release these minerals for plant use.

Winter Compost

Many people build compost heaps in the fall using the residues gathered from their garden. This debris is combined with leaves, grass clippings, manure and any other compostable material they can get their hands on.

A winter pile should be protected in some way against precipitation, wind and coldness. If you have a compost bin, placing a piece of plastic over the top is enough. For exposed piles, cover the whole thing with plastic, or with a layer of leaves held in place with boards or rocks. The idea is to keep wind from scattering your pile all over the yard. A covering will also prevent rain and meltwater from leaching nutrients out of the heap. There will not be much decomposition in the pile during the winter. The following spring the pile will begin to heat. After a few turnings, you should have a batch of compost ready for the garden.

Now that you have heard about a few compost-making methods, it is time to choose a spot for your compost pile.

WHERE TO BUILD THE HEAP

A compost bin or heap should be placed on a flat area so that water will not carry away nutrients. The heap should be near enough to the garden so that you will not feel like a pack mule carrying compost from the heap to your garden. (One cubic yard of compost weighs about 1,000 pounds.) The compost heap should also be close enough to the driveway so that you can unload materials without having to carry them too far. A site within reach of your hose is also advisable. This last point is especially necessary in arid regions where supplementary waterings are a must for keeping your pile moist enough to work. A shady, sheltered spot that meets all the above requirements is perfect. If such a location is not possible work out the best compromise you can.

If you do not feel comfortable with an exposed compost pile in your yard, you can hide it by building a compost bin. Bins come in about as many shapes, sizes and materials as there are gardeners. However, as a general rule bins should be easy to shovel material into and out of, they should allow circulation of air, and they should be made of materials that do not decompose along with the organic matter you place in the bin. Most bins have an open or removable front so that working the pile is easy.

It is a good idea to build bins with two or three compartments so that you can keep a fairly continuous supply of compost coming of age during the year. When one heap is built and begins to heat start in on a new one. The normal dimensions for a compost heap are 6 feet wide by 6 feet long and 5 feet tall. Do not make your heaps or bins too small since a cubic yard (3 feet by 3 feet by 3 feet) of material is required to make the pile heat properly.

Here are some bin styles you may be interested in copying, or adapting to the materials and craftsmanship you possess.

Picket Fence Bin

A compost bin made from picket fence is an easy-to-make bin which can be moved from place to place. To make a square bin, simply place four stakes in a square and wrap snow fence around them. Have the ends of the fence meet at a corner, or in the middle of one side, and this will form a door. You can use this door to work the pile. A simpler method is to form the fence into a circle. This round bin works the same as a square one, but may sag if the diameter is too great. Use stakes at intervals around the bin to prevent sagging.

Board Bins

A permanent bin can be made from boards or poles. Four corner posts are set into the ground and then boards are nailed up around the outside of the posts. Leave an inch or two between boards to allow air and water circulation. Use rot-resistant boards like cedar, cypress and locust for your bin, or use a rot-resistant treatment like linseed oil on less-resistant boards. Painting also works, but creosote should be avoided since it is harmful to the bacteria trying to live in your bin.

When you make a wooden board bin, a good front is a must. Fronts with individual slats that can be removed by sliding them upward so that they become free of the bin are common (Fig. 5-8). This type of front is called a New Zealand box. The key is to have two channels on either side of the bin slightly wider than the boards which slide down into the channel. This arrangement allows you to build up the door by adding slats as you add materials to the bin. The door is opened by sliding slats up and out of the channels. When the compost is completed, all the boards are removed and the compost is easily shoveled out.

If you go to the trouble to make a board bin, build at least two of them. The best arrangement is side-by-side so that you will be able to start a fresh pile while the first bin is decomposing. An effective method of turning the pile is shoveling the composting material from one bin to the other.

Hay Bale Bins

Temporary compost bins can be made by ar-

Fig. 5-8. Board bins are very popular. Make sure to leave an inch of air space between boards. The front should be easily removable for working the compost.

ranging baled hay into a "U" or "W" shape and then making your compost within the curves of this construction. Of course, the hay will decompose along with the compost, but when the compost is finished the bin can be torn down, the compost dug into the soil, and the undecayed hay used as a mulch. Set the hay bales on their ends, where the hay has been cut, in order to prevent the baling twine from contacting the ground and rotting.

Concrete Block Bins

Concrete blocks, both new and old, make good compost bins. There is no worry about them rotting away, and when you use them without mortar they can be moved around when the need arises. To make a concrete block bin, lay out a "U" or "W" of blocks on the ground to act as the foundation. It is a

good idea to lay this first row of blocks on their sides—this gives the next row of blocks a wider surface to rest while allowing ventilation for the bottom of the pile. Next, build up the rest of the courses, leaving room between blocks here and there for air and water circulation. Although a door is not really necessary for this type of bin, you can place a row or two of blocks along the front to hold the compost in. These front blocks will make working the compost in the bin a little difficult.

Stones or solid concrete blocks can also be used to make this type of bin. If you want to make a permanent bin, you can pour a concrete slab as a floor and mortar the blocks together.

Barrel Bins

Simple and effective compost bins can be made

from discarded 55-gallon drums, metal garbage cans, or other large decay-resistant containers. The container you choose should have holes cut in the bottom and at various places around the sides. The barrel can rest on the ground, be dug into the ground, or be set up on concrete blocks.

When the drum is positioned add organic material, soil, manure, and water. Stirring this type of bin is difficult, but if you have two of them you can fill one and let it work until compost is finished. Meanwhile, the second drum can be filled and allowed to decay. Since you will not be able to turn the compost, it will take longer to break down than in loose piles.

More elaborate bins can be made by removing the bottom of the barrel and adding a grate. The whole affair is then set on blocks or a wooden support. Thoroughly-composted material will fall through the grate and you can shovel it onto the garden.

Some manufacturers make barrel-type compost bins with sides made from slats that slide up and down (Fig. 5-9). Compostable materials are placed in the top of these bins. After decomposition several of the side slats are raised, and the finished compost is shoveled out of this opening.

Fig. 5-9. Commercial compost bins with sides made of sliding slats provide a pleasing appearance while continuously making compost (courtesy of Kinsman Co.).

Rotating Barrels

Several manufacturers make barrels that are supported on a metal or wooden frame. The barrels are suspended on an axle through each end of the barrel so that it rotates horizontally. Organic matter is added through a door and then the bin is turned every two or three days. This is a quick compost method, and works best with shredded or chopped organic matter.

Wire Bins

A variation of the picket fence bins are those made from hardware or fence wire. Like the picket fence bins, these compost containers are easy to move and can be adjusted to the size of pile you want to make. The easiest method for making a wire bin is simply buying a length of wire with 4-inch-or-smaller holes so that material will not fall through the wire, and shaping it into a circle (Fig. 5-10). The seam between ends acts as a door. Layer in the organic material and away you go. Nature will do the rest.

Since wire is flexible, it can be made into a square simply by putting stakes in a square and wrapping the wire around them. Use heavy wire, not chicken wire, since the latter material will last only a few years. Steel reinforcing wire, used in poured concrete, is a good wire for this type of compost bin, although it is somewhat difficult to handle.

WHEN TO APPLY COMPOST

The main influences on the timing, the rate of application, and the method of applying compost are its condition, age and the degree to which the composting process is completed. Fully mature compost, resembling light loam, can be added at any time to any part of your garden. Unfinished compost will not be as uniform in texture as finished compost. You will still be able to identify individual plant parts in the mix. This type of compost will continue to break down and produce heat when added to your soil. It should not be used near growing plants. However, unfinished compost can be safely applied in the fall so that it will release nutrients the following spring.

Fig. 5-10. Compost bins made from fence wire can be moved from place to place when empty. When full, aeration and water movement are good, although turning compost in such bins is difficult.

The best time to apply finished compost is a month before planting time. You can add it to the soil just before planting, but it needs to be finely shredded and mixed well with the soil.

Compost that is finished in the fall should be stored in a protected place away from rain and snow. Precipitation will leach valuable nutrients from the compost. Storage during the summer should also abide by the same conditions, except that the compost should be watered occasionally to keep it moist.

HOW TO APPLY COMPOST

Compost is the best fertilizer and soil-improver around. Although compost will not burn plants as chemical fertilizers do, and compost will not rob the soil of nitrogen as undecayed organic materials are likely to do, there are a few applica-

tion methods which will make compost work at its best in your soil.

Generally, soil should be hoed or tilled thoroughly prior to application of compost. Compost should then be added and mixed with the top few inches of soil. Apply from 1 to 3 inches a year for best results.

When plants are already established and compost is to be added, do not dig the soil. Instead, side-dress with the compost. First, loosen the soil with a hoe. Then spread 1 to 3 inches of compost around plants. The compost will provide food for the plants as water washes nutrients out of it and into the root zone. Side-dressing will also moderate soil temperatures and moisture content. You can add another mulch material, like leaves or corncobs, over the compost to help keep weeds down.

Around fruit trees, compost should be applied

78

in a ring surrounding each tree. Begin about 2 feet from the trunk of the tree and spread compost in a circle out to the tree's drip-line. You can work the compost into the soil slightly, no deeper than 2 inches, and then cover with a mulch in order to hold moisture and reduce weeds.

Grapes, strawberries, and cane berries have shallow root systems. Compost should be spread on the ground around these plants and worked in little, if at all. Apply a 3-inch layer of compost in the early spring in order to feed the plants all summer. Mulch after composting.

Compost is the backbone of the organic garden. When you know how to make good compost you will be imitating nature's way of supplying soil with the nutrients to produce healthy vegetables.

Chapter 6

Tools:

Garden Workhorses

Handle your tools without mittens.
—Benjamin Franklin

Many gardeners fall into the trap of buying a new garden tool each year whether they need one or not. This purchase occurs during their first trip to the garden center around seed-buying time. They end up loitering near the rack where tools of unique materials and design promise to do jobs they have never heard of with less than half the effort. These tools are hard to resist as they sit gleaming in the rack, begging to be bought and taken home. Resist, no matter how seductive the tool may be, or you will end up with a shed full of seldom-used tools.

Harsh advice while visions of your biggest and best garden ever dance in your head? You bet, but when you stop and think for a moment garden chores fall into four basic categories: digging, planting and transplanting, moving stuff from one place to another, raking, and weeding and cultivating. Like any job, gardening is easier when you use tools designed for the work at hand. Shovels, spades, spading forks, and trowels will meet the

requirements for the first chores. Pitch forks, spading forks, and shovels will move stuff from place to place. Rakes are the only tool for raking, and hoes and cultivators will take care of weeding and cultivation. As you can see, it does not really require a wide variety of tools to do these jobs, and many tools can be used for several tasks.

Many gardeners with small plots say they can handle the jobs which arise in each of the categories with a minimum number of tools (Fig. 6-1). They often mention shovels, trowels, rakes, hoes, and carts or wheelbarrows as enough tools to do about anything that needs to be done.

Gardeners with more land under cultivation often add wheel-cultivators, tillers, and shredders to the list. Tools that are nice to have, but not absolutely essential, include spading forks, pitch forks, spades, and small hand tools like three-pronged cultivators. Beyond these basic tools, there are hundreds of implements which manufacturers claim are essential to the well-kept garden. Most of these tools usually end up collecting dust in the tool shed.

Fig. 6-1. This selection of tools is adequate for most small to medium-size gardens: From the left, spade, trowel, shovel, three-pronged cultivator, rake, hoe, turning fork and garden cart.

The first question you need to answer in regard to the number and type of tools you will need is: How large a garden are you planning to work? Regardless of the size of your garden you will need some hand tools, but the use of hand tools is limited by the amount of time you have for your garden, and by the size of the garden. A garden of 3,000 square feet is about the most area one adult can work by hand with basic tools like shovels, rakes, hoes and hand-powered cultivators. By way of comparison, ⅛ of an acre equals 5,700 square feet. Gardens bigger than 3,000 square feet will require a helper or some type of rotary tiller for working the soil. In order to make the large amounts of compost required for a large garden, a shredder might also come in handy.

Another important consideration in buying tools is quality and price. In most cases, what you get is proportional to how much you spend. Low-price tools are low in quality, and high-price tools are usually high in quality—but not always.

A well-made tool will last and last—more than a lifetime, if you take care of it. Good tools rise in value through the years, while cheap or inferior tools will need to be replaced frequently. Additionally, high-quality tools are strong and firm in your hands, making them work with ease. Using loose and wobbly cheap tools means you will have a struggle in your garden.

So, buy the best tools you can afford, and then take good care of them so you can consider your money well-spent. Look for quality craftsmanship and design in your tools and you cannot go wrong.

Most tool makers turn out three grades of tools: cheap; mediocre; and professional-quality. The majority of tool sections in garden stores stock the cheap and mediocre varieties for their mass trade. As a minimum, buy the best of the mid-range tools you can find. Better yet, go to a store that caters to professional nurserymen or lawn care specialists. These stores usually carry top-of-the-line models. You might also consider ordering top-line tools directly from the manufacturer. You will end up paying a premium price for these premium tools, but you will get a premium performance for your investment.

In order to help you select the right tool for the job, make sure you get a tool that will last, and keep your tools up to par. The rest of this chapter is divided into four sections: hand tools, power tools, shredders, and tool maintenance.

HAND TOOLS

The idea that one tool is just as good as the next is simply not true, as anyone who has had a shovel handle break in their hands, a trowel bend, or a hoe head fall off will tell you. Here are a few things you should look for when buying hand tools. More specific suggestions will be given in each section.

A quality tool is made from as few pieces as possible so that the number of joints to bend, break,

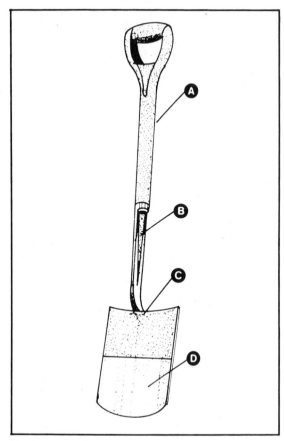

Fig. 6-2. Quality hand tools have these features: (A) straight, strong handles: (B) secure handle blade connection: (C) smooth strong welds or one piece construction: (D) quality steel blades (courtesy of Smith Hawken Tools).

Shovels and Spades

Although many people use the words shovel and spade interchangeably, they are not one and the same. The word *shovel* comes from the same root word as *shove* and *scoop*. The rounded blade on this tool makes sense for scooping and digging jobs. The word *spade*, on the other hand, comes from the root words for *sword* or *blade*. These tools are designed with straight blades in order to cut the ground more than to move it.

Still, the confusion is justifiable, since spades look like shovels except that the blades are flat. These tools are designed to cut rather than scoop. The handles of spades come in the long straight variety or the short D-handled style. They are usually mounted with less angle than shovels, in order to deliver more force for cutting. Spades are good for tasks like cutting straight wall trenches, breaking up sod, and digging trees from the ground.

The rounded-blade shovel is considered the garden workhorse by many people. If you only have money for one digging implement, the best bet is a long-handled, curved-blade shovel. This tool will handle most digging, scooping, and shoveling jobs without problem provided you keep a few points in mind. Rounded-blade shovels are useful for digging into the ground, while straight-blade shovels are designed to scoop up loose materials. The blade should be set at a slight angle to the handle to increase leverage, and the back edge of the shovel face should have a step, or foot rest, which is usually made by turning a flat of metal forward or backward, or rolling it into a smooth step. The wider this step is the better, since less pressure will be felt by your foot. The handles on shovels come in two varieties: the long straight type which allows you to really lean into the work, and the D-handled variety which provides better control for scooping and digging in tight areas. Beyond these major points, there are a few finer things to consider.

or wear are kept to a minimum (Fig. 6-2).

Metal tools should look smooth with no irregularities such as pits or gouges. A tin-looking stamped-out metal piece is sure not to last as long as a forged metal piece. Tempered steel is the best tool metal around. Welds should be smooth. If they are not, it is an indication of poor craftsmanship. When craftsmanship is poor, materials should also be suspect.

Wooden handles should be made from hardwoods like hickory and ash. The handles should be smooth and straight. Rough, poorly-finished wood is another sign of inferior material and craftsmanship. Cracked and split handles will be murder on your hands.

Shovels and spades with handles fitted into a partially-closed tube on the blade are inferior. It is only a matter of time and use before the handle manages to work itself loose. The best-quality shovels and spades have closed or solid sockets.

These seamless sockets are forged from a single piece of steel, and the handle fits snugly and deeply into the blade.

There are three basic classes of D-handles. The worst are thin metal and are attached to the shaft with rivets. These handles will probably have a seam with a gap in them. They will fall apart after a few seasons. A better handle is one made from heavier gauge metal with a good tight seam. Many of these handles have wooden cross handles. The best D-handles are those made entirely of wood (Fig. 6-3). The wood has been shaped in a special mold and is formed from the same piece of wood as the shank. There is little chance of this type of handle falling off.

Hoes

Next to a shovel, a hoe is the most important tool you will own. It certainly gets used the most.

The best buy in a hoe is one of the old-fashioned rectangular hoes with a wide blade. There are many V-shaped warren hoes, scuffling hoes, and serrated-tooth hoes to temp you away from the simpler standby, but resist buying them, especially when purchasing your first hoe. Those other hoes are smaller than a standard hoe, so they will not cover as much ground. Additionally, many are made for one job and only one job. You cannot use them for several tasks. The rectangular hoe, on the other hand, is very versatile. Why buy a warren hoe when simply tilting your rectangular hoe 45° will produce the same affect?

The handle on a hoe should be straight and long—long enough so that when you grab it near the end and place the blade out in operating position 18 to 24 inches from your feet, your back is still straight. Remember, though, that the longer the handle the less pressure you can put on the blade.

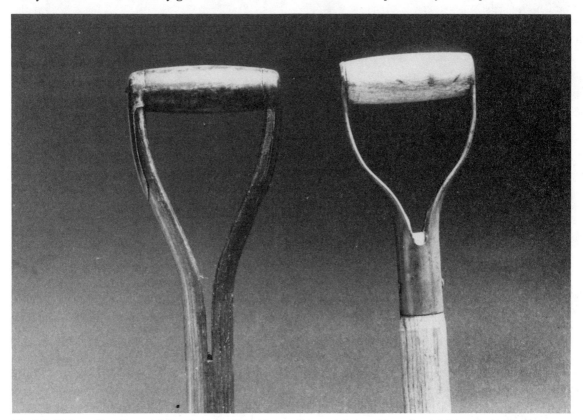

Fig. 6-3. High-quality, all-wood D-handle (left) will last longer than an inferior, stamped-metal D-handle (right).

Most hoe blades are attached to the handle using what is known as the *tang and ferrule* method. A thick wire is welded to the hoe blade and inserted into the end of the wooden handle. A metal collar, called a *ferrule*, is then wrapped around the handle to hold the tang in place. This attaching method is inherently weak, so shop around for the best looking connection you can find. Remember that open seams in the ferrule can lead to a loose connection, especially when the hoe is used heavily. Seamless forged cups into which the handle is forced are the best method of attachment, but they are hard to find.

Trowels

Trowels are the small hand-size shovels used in the garden for delicate tasks like transplanting seedlings. Trowels come in two basic blade sizes; narrow and wide. Most gardeners will find a place for both tools in their garden. The narrow trowel is handy for making deep narrow holes for transplants and bulbs. The broad ones work better for scooping out large amounts of dirt during transplanting chores.

Avoid cheap trowels. Since expensive ones are only a few dollars more than the cheap ones, it makes sense to buy the better tool. The solid one-piece trowels that are all of one material are the best (Fig. 6-4). There is very little chance of these tools bending, breaking, or rusting out. The single-piece-cast aluminum alloy trowels usually have few places for dirt to stick and cause rusting, but many of these tools are not as strong as the tempered steel tools.

Cheap trowels have cracks and crevices where moist dirt can lodge and cause rusting. Most of these cheap tools are stamped from a piece of sheet metal and have a wrap-around tube where a wooden or metal handle is inserted. These tools bend easily. Like shovels, trowels with a solid forged cup into which the handle is inserted are best. Many of the tang and ferrule construction trowels are also well made.

Rakes

Typical garden rakes have stiff steel tines

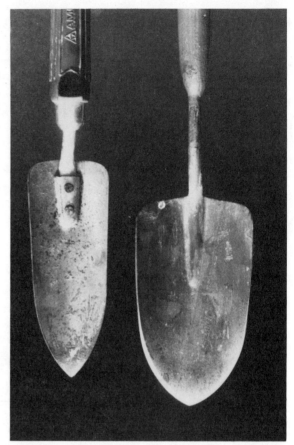

Fig. 6-4. A cheap trowel (left), with a stamped-metal blade riveted onto a handle, is inferior to the one-piece or welded trowel (right). Notice the difference in width.

about 2 inches long. These rakes are used to pulverize clods and remove stones and other debris from loose dirt. There are three basic types of hard rakes: those with straight tines, curved tines, and thatching rakes with moon-shaped metal blades instead of tines. Each tine has its own function in the garden, but you will not really need all three.

Most hard rakes come with 10 to 16 tines across the head, each about 1 inch apart. The more tines a rake has, the wider and heavier it will be and the more energy it will take to use. Choose one that fits your garden and your strength. The length of a rake's handle is also important. The handle should reach at least to your ear when you stand it up beside you. A shorter handle will mean more bending and a greater strain on your back. Additionally, curved tines tend to dig straight into the ground while the straight tines dig in at an angle.

Thatching rakes are designed to pull thatch out of a lawn, but they can be used to good effect in the garden, especially on seed beds. Most hard rakes leave ping-pong size clods. The narrowly spaced knife-like blades on the thatching rake will cut up these clods into fine granules. These rakes are designed to be pushed and pulled across the ground. You do not need to lift them after each stroke, which makes using them easier.

Many manufacturers use the tang and ferrule arrangement to join handle and head. Rakes with this arrangement have the same shortcomings as hoes put together in this fashion. It is better to buy a rake with a handle that fits into a solid socket. You may have to order such a high-quality tool, but it is worth the wait and price. Rakes with bolts through the ferrule and handle are also good, since you can tighten the bolts to keep the head in place.

Spading or Digging Forks

These tools usually have 4 square or rectangular tines made of strong steel. They resemble an overgrown kitchen fork. Most come with short D-handles, but a few have long, straight, shovel-like handles.

Spading forks have several uses around the garden. They are used primarily to loosen dirt prior to shoveling. They are almost worthless for moving dirt from one place to another, but come in handy for turning compost and carrying organic materials like manure. These tools are also good for digging out roots since they do not stop cold when they hit unforgiving obstructions. Spading forks also dig up below-ground crops like potatoes, carrots, beets, and turnips with a minimum of damage to the vegetables (Fig. 6-5).

Digging forks should be strong enough to match your strength. Do not buy a lightweight tool for heavy work since you are likely to bend one of the tines. Once a tine is bent, you can straighten it by placing a piece of pipe over the tine and applying pressure, but the tine will never be as strong as it was originally.

Before buying a spading fork, check it over carefully. You should expect to find the same quality craftsmanship and materials that you find in a good shovel.

Hand Cultivators

For removing weeds close in to the stem of plants, few tools beat the hand cultivator in efficiency. These 3 or 4-tined claw-like tools look like a metal hand (Fig. 6-6). These fingers break up the ground around plants without disturbing the roots as much as a hoe. Most hand cultivators have rigid tines, but a few of the better models have spring steel tines which give, and tend to work somewhat independently of each other. There are both short-handled and long-handled cultivators on the market. The short ones require you to bend or stoop to get at the ground, while the long-handled ones are used much as a hoe.

Most hand cultivators use the tang and ferrule method of attaching the tool's head to the handle. Solid socket attachments are better, but hard to find. Consider the same criteria for other hand tools when selecting a hand cultivator.

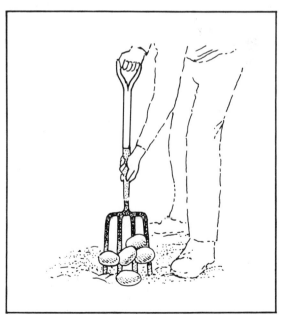

Fig. 6-5. A spading fork has many uses in the garden, including digging root crops (courtesy of Smith Hawken Tools).

Fig. 6-6. Hand cultivators break up the ground close to the base of plants without danger to the plants.

Wheel-Cultivator

Wheel-cultivators are the answer for ecologically-conscious gardeners with big gardens. In fact, wheel-cultivators blur the distinctive line between hand tools and power tools, not because these tools use petroleum, but because they are mechanical in nature, magnifying the effects of your muscle power and allowing you to place more area under cultivation.

There are two basic types of wheel-cultivators: high-wheel and low-wheel. High-wheel cultivators have a single wheel of approximately 24 inches. Low-wheel cultivators have two wheels of half that size. Wheel-cultivators are not as efficient as motor-powered cultivators, but they are effective in larger vegetable gardens with straight rows.

Both cultivators work in a similar manner: you get behind it and push as you walk down the row (Fig. 6-7). Most people find the low-wheeled variety more stable and easier to use.

Both types of cultivators are made so that many different attachments can be used throughout the season. Most have at least the following options: cultivator-weeders which resemble the tines on hand cultivators, moldboard plows, furrowers, and seed box attachment for planting. When considering buying one of these machines, make sure to get one that has several attachments. Again, choosing the right tool for the job at hand is important.

Buy only cultivators of sturdy construction and take a close look at welds and wooden parts. Any abnormalities will show up quickly if you use this tool much. Many of the all-steel constructions are

Fig. 6-7. Wheel-cultivators magnify your muscle power, allowing you to place more land under cultivation.

sturdy, but much heavier than those with wooden parts.

Wheelbarrows and Carts

When it comes time to move a lot of compost from your bins to the far end of the garden, it's hard to beat the convenience of a wheelbarrow or a garden cart. Unfortunately, many wheelbarrows and carts are priced so high that they are considered a luxury by many gardeners.

The shallow, least-expensive wheelbarrows have small solid-core tires and metal parts that bend under heavy use. They are suitable for light garden work, but don't expect to haul much more than a bale of hay in them. These wheelbarrows simply do not have the sturdiness or stability of the bigger balloon-tire wheelbarrows. They do not come with inflated price tags either.

More expensive, but much easier for handling large loads, are the bicycle-tire wheeled carts. The two wheels on these carts are positioned close to the cart's balance point, so very little exertion is required for lifting. The dual wheels also add stability so hauling large loads is easy (Fig. 6-8). Garden carts, designed specifically for around home jobs instead of construction work, have taken over where the wheelbarrow left off. Take a close look at any equipment you are planning to buy. Make sure the cart's construction and materials are up to the job you will be asking it to do.

Fig. 6-8. Garden carts with two bicycle-like wheels are able to carry large loads with a minimum of effort (courtesy of Garden Way).

POWER TOOLS

With the proper power tools, a gardener can effectively manage a garden three to four times as large as is possible with hand tools. There are two power machines that the home gardener might be interested in: tillers and shredders.

Tillers

You will need to consider buying a tiller when the amount of ground you work exceeds the energy and time you have to work in your garden. This means having a big garden, since buying a tiller for a small backyard garden is about as inefficient as trying to cultivate an extra-large garden by hand.

Tillers provide a quick way to break up the soil, and they also encourage the incorporation of organic matter into the soil. Turning organic matter into the soil by hand can be an exhausting job and impossible if you have back problems, but a tiller will do all the hard work for you.

There is wide variation among tillers in horse-power, engines, speed, size, tines, tilling width and depth and the accessories that can be used on the tiller. Like other tools, there is no such thing as an inexpensive, high-quality tiller. Good engineering and materials cost money, but if you are willing to pay for it, you will be rewarded with a machine that lasts a lifetime.

The best way to determine what size and style tiller you will need is to rent or borrow several different types and sizes. Then when you think you have a pretty good idea of what you will need, get the literature for that style of tiller and study it. There are three main points to consider before buying: the amount and nature of the work you plan to do, the quality of the machine, and repairability.

Tillers are basically a combination of engine and tiller blades, mounted on a frame with wheels and handles. The engine powers the blades, causing them to cut down into the soil and then pull back out of the soil in a circular motion. The engine's power is delivered to the blades through a transmission of some sort; either gears, belts or chains. The action of the blades should leave the soil loose and fluffy, ready for seeds. In addition to conditioning the soil, tillers should also be able to chop up organic matter and turn it into the soil. The ability of a tiller to do these tasks depend on its design, weight, strength, the shape of its tines, and the condition of the soil.

When it comes to tines you have three basic choices: spring steel, bolo, and slasher. Each has a different use. Spring steel tines are the all-purpose variety. Made from heat-treated steel which absorbs stone and rock impact, these tines penetrate hard soil, dig in organic matter, and cultivate without much problem. Bolo tines are narrow and curved—more like blades—and are good on loose soils for deep tilling and shallow weed control. Slasher tines are the heavyweights. Their thick steel construction enables them to chew through tough soil and roots.

The type of soil you have has a lot to do with the size of the tiller you need. Tight-packed clay requires a tiller with enough strength to bite into the soil. Rocky soils also make tilling difficult, since each rock slows down the blades. You will need a rather large and strong tiller on these soils. On the other hand, light loose soils will be much easier to work, and can usually be cared for with a smaller, lightweight tiller.

Although most tiller manufacturers claim that their machines will chop organic matter like leaves, green manures, and crop residues and then turn them into the soil all in one operation, it pays to be skeptical. Long-stemmed, stringy, and fibrous material tends to wrap itself around the tiller tines and shaft mounts, straining the machine and slowing its progress. A simple test to see if the material you plan to turn under can be easily handled by a tiller is to chop the ground with a hoe. If the hoe breaks up the material easily, so will your tiller. Material that cannot be chopped with a hoe will give your tiller problems too. As a general rule, the more powerful the tiller and the sharper the blades, the easier incorporating organic material will be.

The better tillers are heavy and made of strong materials like cast iron. They have thick steel plating, heavy tubing, powerful engines, tough bearings and controls that are easy to reach and operate. Even the best machines contain some parts that will wear out through normal use. Therefore, parts like tines, gears, and grease seals should be easy to remove and replace. Good tillers come with clear, well-labeled parts diagrams and replacement procedures. Parts and service centers should be nearby.

Front-Tine Tillers Versus Rear-Tine Tillers

The debate about whether front-tined or rear-tined tillers are best has raged among gardeners for years, and there is no way to resolve it. Both types of tillers have advantages and disadvantages (Table 6-1). The one you pick depends on personal preference, which will develop after you try models of each design. Still, there are a few generalizations that will help you make a knowledgeable decision.

Front-Tine Tillers

Front-tined tillers are generally less expensive than rear-tined tillers because they are more simply engineered, requiring less material (Fig. 6-9). The weight of the engine is used to help push the tines into the soil, propelling the tiller forward.

Table 6-1. Use This Chart to Help You Decide Whether a Front- or Rear-Tine Tiller Is Best for You.

FRONT-TINE TILLERS

Advantages

Lighter and less expensive than rear-tine tillers.
Easier to turn.
Dig deeper than rear-tine tillers.
Require fewer passes to turn soil.

Disadvantages

Compaction of soil occurs because wheels and operator follow machine.
Harder to control than rear-tine tillers.
Rarely self-propelled.

REAR-TINE TILLERS

Advantages

Easy to operate.
Better on heavy soils and large areas.
Often self-propelled

Disadvantages

Usually more expensive than front-tine tillers.
Harder to maneuver than front-tine tillers.
Do not dig as deeply as front-tine tillers.
Heavier than front-tine tillers and have more moving parts.

You will need to work to keep a front-tine tiller upright and digging in a straight line. On hard ground, the tiller is liable to walk away from you and you will have to pull back on it to get the tiller to dig deeply in one spot. Many front-tine tillers come with brakes—which are steel shafts that drag into the ground behind the tiller—to help you control the machine. Despite these disadvantages, front-tine tillers are very easy to turn, making them good in tight-cornered small gardens. Additionally, these tillers are not as complicated as rear-tined tillers, so service and repair is easier.

Rear-Tined Tillers

Rear-tined tillers have more moving parts than front-tined tillers; consequently, they tend to cost more. A shaft usually powers the tines, and many have their wheels geared in order to propel the extra weight of the tiller. A few of the more complex models are reversible. Rear-tine tillers tend to dig in better in hard ground and they have a smoother operation (Fig. 6-10). You do not have to keep pulling back on these machines to slow down their forward progress. Although tilling in a straight line with a rear-tined tiller is easier than with a front-tine machine, turning is usually more difficult. You will have to lift the machine's tines clear of the ground and guide or push the tiller around. Because these machines are larger than most front-tine tillers they will not do as well in smaller gardens with tight corners.

Counter Revolving-Tine Tillers

Tillers with two sets of tines that turn in opposite directions have appeared recently. The theory behind these tillers is that the forces produced by the tines work against each other instead of against you. Lifting the handle causes the front tines to dig in more and the tiller moves forward. Pushing down on the handles makes the rear tines dig in and the tiller moves backward. Most of these tillers are of the lightweight variety and are suited for working in high quality, loose soils. These tillers are still relatively new, so the verdict is not in yet on how they stack up to the standard models. Think long and hard before buying one of these new machines since the technology has not been tested over time.

Fig. 6-9. Front-tine tillers are generally lighter and of simpler construction than rear-tine tillers. (courtesy of Amerind MacKissic).

Fig. 6-10. Although rear-tine tillers are easy to operate, they have more moving parts and are bulkier than front-tine tillers (courtesy of Troy Bilt Rototillers).

SHREDDERS

Shredders are pieces of machinery that spell a step up into big-time gardening. Garden shredders can be one of the most valuable composting tools you own or they can be one of the least-used garden tools you own. It all boils down to how much woody and fibrous material your yard produces each year and how much compost you like to make.

Shredders are power-operated machines that chop up and tear apart fibrous and woody organic material for composting (Fig. 6-11). You feed it things like small tree branches, leaves, and tomato vines, and out comes a pile of shredded organic matter. The reduced size of this shredded material speeds up its action in compost and produces a wonderful mulch. If and when you decide to add a shredder to your tool shed, you will have many

manufacturers, styles and price ranges to choose from. The field is almost as mixed as the tiller field. Size is the most important consideration for buying a shredder. You want one large enough to handle the material you plan to feed it, but not so large that much of its capacity goes to waste.

The most common engines for garden shredders are one cylinder, four-stroke, gasoline engines with power ratings of from 3 to 10 horsepower. Electric motors are sometimes mounted on shredders, but these are rare because a gasoline engine will run virtually anywhere—miles from the nearest electricity. On the other hand, noise, fumes, and starting problems may make you opt for an electric motor.

Shredders are potentially the most dangerous piece of gardening machinery you can own. They

Fig. 6-11. Shredders come in handy for chopping large fibrous materials for mulch or composting (courtesy of Amerind MacKissic).

are designed to reduce tough organic matter to a pulp and this can include fingers! Common sense and strict adherence to the operating rules accompanying a shredder will prevent many mishaps.

Shredders come in three basic styles, differing mostly by size. Additionally, the two smaller sizes use blades to chop up organic matter while the bigger models use cutting devices called hammers.

Leaf Mills

Some of the smaller shredders are called leaf mills. These machines are designed to chew up leaves, small twigs, and lawn clippings (Fig. 6-12). Although these machines work well on the small stuff, they will not handle much of the heavier organic material headed for the compost bin. This type of shredder is adequate for small yards and gardens. Make sure your shredder has a manually operated clutch between the engine and the shredder's blades. This will make starting easier as well as providing safer operation.

Some lawn mowers come with "mulching" at-

Fig. 6-12. Small leaf mills are capable of shredding light organic materials. Many of these models are electrically powered (courtesy of Kinsman Co.).

tachments. These attachments prevent grass clippings, leaves, and weeds from spraying out of the mower by blocking the exit port. They work fine for loose materials like leaves, but have problems on large stuff like corn stalks. Rake material into a long narrow pile and run the mower back and forth across the pile. The volume of the pile will be reduced substantially. Rake up and add the material to compost bin or use as a mulch.

Shredder/Chippers

The next step up from the lightweight leaf mills is the direct-drive and belt-drive shredders and chippers. These machines are similar in design to the leaf mills, but their blades and engines are larger, enabling them to shred coarser materials. Although these machines will handle more than leaves, they still do not have enough muscle to grind a damp batch of compost. Wet materials often pack into the shredding chamber until the blades stop.

The two main types of shredders this size are direct-drive and belt-drive. There are advantages and disadvantages to each type.

Direct-drive models have the engine's shaft attached directly to the blades, although most good units have a shear key which breaks when the unit is overloaded, preventing damage to the engine. This reduces the number of moving parts, maintenance and overall cost of the machine. In most cases, stopping the blade with too large a load means killing the engine, which can damage the machine. In those machines with shear pins, stopping the blade usually means breaking the shear pin. Replacing this part may be both costly and time-consuming. Since direct-drives do not have a clutch, you must turn the blade when you turn the engine to start it. This can make starting difficult. Additionally, direct-drive shredders have no way of cutting power to the blades short of stopping the engine. This could prove dangerous during emergencies.

Belt-drive shredders have a few maintenance disadvantages. Because of their many moving parts, wear and slippage are problems. The belts also need shielding to protect the operator from entanglement. Belt-driven machines also have an advantage over direct-drive machines. When the cutting blades jam to a stop, the belt normally slips, taking up the majority of the shock. This reduces the likelihood of engine damage, but may fray the belt. Still, it is better to replace a $10.00 belt than a $200.00 engine.

Hammer Mills

Heavy-duty shredders are called hammer mills. Instead of having blades that cut up the refuse fed into the cutting chamber, these machines have a revolving drum or spindle with attached hammers. The drum is turned at high speed and the hammers move through the shredding chamber beating coarse materials into small pieces. Most of the hammer mills are belt-driven with a manual clutch. These machines are true workhorses, and will do the best job of preparing virtually any yard refuse

for the compost heap.

A nice feature on most of these machines is various sizing devices which determine the coarseness of the shredded material. Rods, bars, or screens hold material in the shredding chamber until it is small enough to pass through the sizing device. Another plus for these shredders is that many can be adapted to a garden tractor's power take-off.

There are two basic types of hammer mills: those with swinging hammers and those with rigid hammers.

Rigid-hammer machines have a central rotating drum or spindle to which blunt metal blades are bolted (Fig. 6-13). As the spindle turns, the blades are moved through the shredding chamber. All the power of the shaft is used to tear up the material being shredded.

The swinging hammer machines also have a

Fig. 6-13. This example of the hammers on a stationary hammer mill show how hammers are bolted to the central shaft (courtesy of W-W Grinders Inc.).

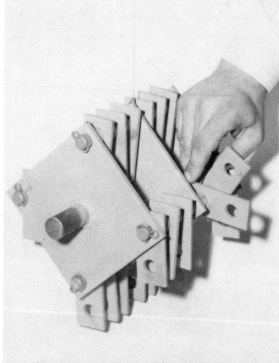

Fig. 6-14. The hammers in a swinging hammer mill are attached to a pivot instead of being bolted directly to the central shaft (courtesy of Amerind MacKissic).

central cylinder or shaft that spins. Instead of being bolted directly to this piece, the hammers hang on a pivot (Fig. 6-14). When the central shaft is not spinning, they hang down from their pivots. When the cylinder is spinning centrifugal force pulls them outward so that they shred the material in the chamber. Theoretically, these hammers give when they hit a hard object, reducing the strain on the machine. However, extreme vibrations occur during start-up and slow-down. These vibrations can cause excessive wear on the shredder's bearings.

TOOL MAINTENANCE

In order to get the most out of your tools you must take care of them. The instruction sheet that comes with power tools will give you step-by-step instructions for winter storage, belt tightening and access to oil and grease points. Hand tools do not usually come with instructions for maintenance, although they need proper care if you expect them to work efficiently.

It only takes a few minutes to bring your hoe, cultivator, shovel and tiller up to snuff. A snowy winter's afternoon of preventative maintenance will save you loads of time and energy when the hectic spring planting season rolls around.

The most important aspect of hand tool maintenance is keeping your tools sharp. Two methods of sharpening hand tools, grinding and filing, are used to restore a tool's bevel and to remove nicks.

The equipment necessary for sharpening your tools is simple, and you probably already have most of them around the house. You will need a file (8-inch flat mill) or a grinding wheel; a wire brush; crocus cloth; steel wool; an oily rag; and a vise to hold your implements steady.

A grinding wheel—hand-or electric-powered—is used to rough-in a new edge on very dull or broken tools. A file also works on soft metal tools like hoes, spades and tiller tines. The idea behind grinding and filing is to reproduce the original factory bevel. This blade shape was designed to suit the specific function of your tool. Altering it could ruin the effectiveness of the tool.

The final sharpening, which follows the rough-

ing in stage, removes metal on round and dull edges. Blades should resemble a wedge when you are finished. It is the point of this wedge that does the cutting. The sharper the leading edge, the less muscle you will need to get the tool to do its work.

It is best to practice the basic sharpening techniques on your hoe. Mistakes are hard to make on this garden mainstay.

Hoes are sharpened on the back side—that is, the side facing away from you when the hoe is in use. Secure the hoe in a vise, blade up, and with the back side easily accessible. Clean the tool with steel wool or a wire brush before sharpening.

Lay your file across the edge at an angle. Then raise the back of the file—the end with the tang—to a bevel of 45° (Fig. 6-15). Push the file down and away while sliding it along the edge to remove metal. Your file should attack the cutting edge of the hoe head-on. Use even strokes, pushing down with a steady force.

Remember that files cut only on the push or downward stroke. You should never drag a file back to the starting position in contact with the metal. This habit will ruin your file and tends to round the edge you are sharpening.

Lift and return to the original position and repeat the process until you are satisfied with the edge. Twenty to 30 strokes should give you a fairly sharp blade.

A blade bevel of 45° is standard for hoes that will be used in clay soils, but you might consider experimenting by adjusting your hoe's edge to your gardening needs (Fig. 6-16). A 60° bevel works best in loamy soils. Chopping grass and weeds is easier if your hoe has a sharper bevel, say, 30°.

To sharpen a lawn mower blade, or other straight edge like a tiller tine, secure the blade in a vise and follow the same side-to-side, back-to-front stroking motion you used on your hoe. Strive for steady strokes since jerky, lopsided movements will leave dull spots in the blade.

Do not ignore the rounded blades on tools like shovels and cultivator attachments. You will find their bevel on the inside of the blade. When filing a curved blade, let the file slide sideways from the back, or heel, of the blade to the point as the stroke

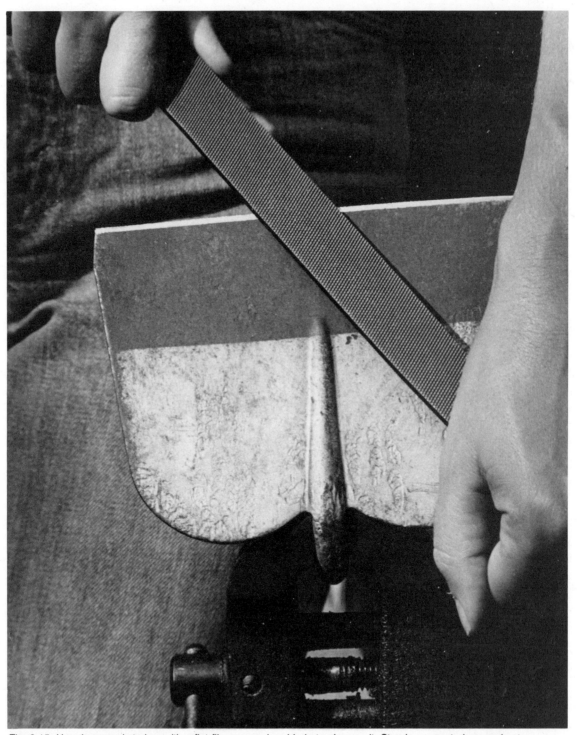

Fig. 6-15. Use downward strokes with a flat file on your hoe blade to sharpen it. Steady, even strokes are best.

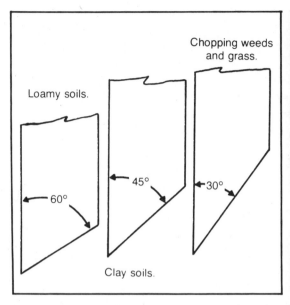

Fig. 6-16. A little experimentation with the angle of your hoe blade will result in easier use. The blade's angle is adjusted to meet soil conditions.

is completed. Sharpen an equal number of strokes on the right and left sides of the blade.

It is a good idea to wipe your tools with oil after sharpening to prevent rust. While you have the rag handy, why not oil your tool's wooden handles? See Fig. 6-17. Not only will you get less splinters, but the handles will regain some of the flexibility of new wood.

Linseed oil works best for this job, although the poor man's preservative (used crankcase oil) does a satisfactory job. Sand rough handles with 200- to 400-grit sandpaper until smooth, and then work in a generous amount of oil with a rag. Two to three minutes of rubbing should do it. The same

Fig. 6-17. Oiling tool handles will keep them smooth and flexible, reducing the chance of splintering and cracking.

cloth can be used to apply oil to both metal and wooden tool parts.

Choosing and using garden tools is not difficult as long as you choose high quality tools that are right for your gardening jobs. Keeping your tools in tiptop shape will also make gardening chores easier. In fact, there is no reason to dread working in your garden since your tools will become old friends as your gardening skills multiply.

Chapter 7

Productive Garden Planning

As is the Gardener, so is the Garden.
—Thomas Fuller

Ask a gardener with an efficient and productive garden what the secret is. You are likely to be told that planning made it all possible. Most successful gardeners plan their gardens on paper each year. This way they can make the best use of their garden. You should do the same for your garden.

You will want to keep your garden plans from year to year as a permanent record of your garden for as long as you have a garden. Old garden plans will jog your memory about varieties that grew well in your garden. Past mistakes can be avoided and planning for the future is easier. Drawing up a garden plan will also allow you to fit all the organic methods together into a tight unit. Working out the hitches on paper, before the hectic planting season arrives, will save time and energy. You will also be able to know how many of which seeds to order and their expected yields.

Some of the more important things you will need to consider in drawing up a garden plan are:

- Location of the garden.
- Size of the garden.
- Crop spacing.
- Succession planting.
- Interplanting.
- Companion planting.
- Crop rotation.
- Seed requirements.

LOCATING THE GARDEN

The first step in planning a garden is selecting its location. Choose a garden spot that receives at least 6 hours of direct sunlight a day (10 to 12 hours is even better). Few garden sites are completely untouched by the shade cast by walls, fences or trees, so choosing shade-free spots becomes an exercise in compromise. Often you must learn to live with site-imposed restrictions and settle for a little less than optimum light conditions.

One good way of avoiding light restrictions is by looking beyond the traditional concept of a single

Fig. 7-1. By looking beyond the traditional idea of one large garden, you can turn many smaller sections of your property into productive gardens. Here vegetables are growing successfully in cramped quarters.

plot for a vegetable garden. Two or more small plots can be located around your house and yard in sunny places where a single large garden would be impossible. Consider carefully the area between sidewalks and around the base of buildings as possible garden sites (Fig. 7-1). If part of your garden ends up in a little more shade than you would have liked, do not be afraid to plant vegetables in it since some vegetables like lettuce, spinach, green beans, and cucumbers do not mind a little shade.

Although there are shade-tolerant vegetables, there are no truly shade-loving vegetables. All plants respond to shade by growing slower and taller and then maturing later than plants grown in full sun. A plant's performance increases in direct relationship to the amount of sunlight it receives. A simple but often-overlooked fact about sunlight and shade is that in addition to their obvious effect on photosynthesis, sunlight and shade also influence the relative warmth of the soil. Seeds sprout and grow quicker in soils exposed to sunlight because the soil is generally warmer.

As a rule, it is a waste to garden in any part of the yard where less than six hours of direct sunlight is received. This includes areas close to the north wall of most homes. The east and west sides are usually okay because they get full morning or afternoon sun. A garden to the south of your house is best (Fig. 7-2).

A second major consideration for the location of your garden is the soil. It is easier to work with loamy or sandy loam soils than with clays. Most home construction requires the removal of topsoil for 15 to 20 feet in all directions around the base of a house. This soil will be harder to work into a fertile state than undisturbed soil. Unfortunately, most gardens will not be able to start with a perfect soil. The chapters on soil, compost and fertilizers will help you enrich your soil.

Your garden should be located away from low or soggy areas where water stands in puddles after rain. Vegetables are very sensitive to waterlogged soil. It is better to place the garden on a gentle slope to ensure good drainage. In addition to warming slowly in the spring, low spots are also subject to early frosts. A garden on higher ground will often miss the frost that settles into low areas.

Ideally, your garden should slope gently toward the east or south. A south-facing slope warms faster in the spring and cools slower in the fall than flat or north-facing slopes. When cold frames are used on south-facing slopes, you can begin and end the garden season many weeks before and after the last and first frost dates for your area.

Here are some other things to consider when choosing a garden site:

● Do not plant your garden near trees since they compete with vegetables for light, water and nutrients. As a rule, trees take food and water from the soil several feet beyond the drip line of their leaves.

● Avoid planting your garden in a windy location. Try to shelter it from the prevailing winds with buildings, trees or hills. Most objects will break the wind for a distance equal to four times their height. A 20-foot-tall house will be an effective wind screen out to 80 feet.

● Your garden should be close to a water supply. Tool sheds and compost bins should be built close to your garden. It might also be a good idea to make the garden close to a driveway so that unloading organic material for compost making or for mulching chores will be easier.

● Your garden should also be located fairly close to your house. This makes it easier to reach for weeding, watering, planting and picking chores. If your vegetable garden cannot be located close to the house, a supplemental herb and salad garden,

often called a kitchen garden, should be planted near the house. This way often-used plants like lettuce, radishes, spinach, parsley, and other herbs are more convenient.

You will seldom, if ever, be able to make your garden in a place that meets all of the best conditions mentioned above. You will have to make the best compromises possible. But try to at least get sufficient sun and to keep your garden out of low areas where water and frost collect.

If you do not have enough room in your own yard to grow all the vegetables you want, then you might try to find a nearby community garden. Community gardens are a growing phenomenon in this country. In the city they have given millions of

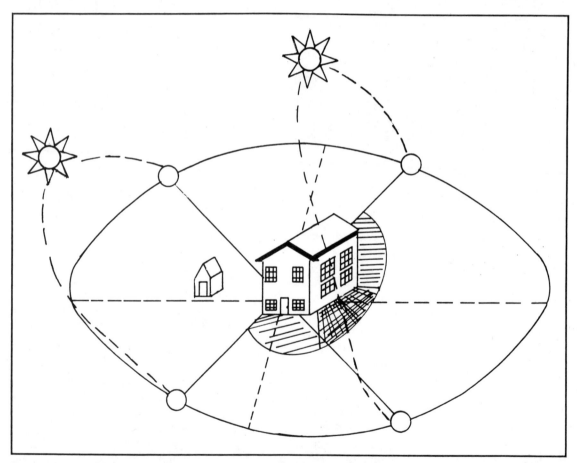

Fig. 7-2. The dark area on the north side of this house is the least desirable location for a garden. The gray areas on the east and west sides of the house are a little better. The south side is the best for gardens.

apartment dwellers a chance to grow some of their own food. The best places to look for information about local community gardens are at local extension service offices, community service organizations, horticultural clubs, and the bulletin boards in garden centers. If you happen to see what looks like a community garden in your neighborhood, stop by and chat with some of the gardeners. Chances are you will be able to find some ground to call your own. The fees for most community gardens are minimal. Many allow only organic gardening.

SIZING THE GARDEN

The best time to plan your garden is in December or January. The best way to begin your garden is by laying it out on paper. Begin, first of all, by deciding which vegetables you want to grow. While leafing through the seed catalogs make notes of such things as each crop's space requirements, time to maturity, companions and how tall the crop grows. Information like heavy, moderate, or light feeding habits is also nice to have. Your notes may end up looking something like Table 7-1.

Figuring the yield for crops which are harvested at one time—for instance, carrots, beets and onions—is relatively easy. When the plant matures, you remove the plant by harvesting it. Your yield will be in direct relation to how many of these single-harvest plants you put out. Most seed catalogs will tell you how many feet of a planted row yield a certain amount of each crop. Most catalogs also suggest the number of plants a package of seed will produce. Some will also tell you the expected yield for that package of seed.

Crops such as tomatoes, beans, and squash which produce fruits or pods over a period of time are more difficult to plan yields for. The yield from these crops occurs over a period of time since you do not remove the plant during harvest. These crops produce in relation to soil fertility, rainfall, temperature, and specific growing practices. After a few years of growing them, you will know how many of each plant is right for your family. First-time gardeners should follow package instructions closely, adjusting their cultivation practices in later years.

The size of your vegetable garden is determined by what you expect it to yield. Use the amount of food your family expects to eat from the garden as a base figure. Do not forget to estimate how much time you will have to tend the garden.

Beginning gardeners usually set aside more space than they know how to handle. Often they overestimate the amount of space a mature plant will occupy, or they tend to underestimate how much a short row will produce. These problems are easy to understand because most novices have not seen a plant grow to maturity first-hand.

A 40-by-30-foot garden does not sound very big, but that is 1,200 square feet—a big garden even for some experienced gardeners. Better to start small, say 200 or 300 square feet, and work your way up in succeeding years. Besides, a smaller garden will reduce your initial investment in fertilizers, rock powders, seeds, tools and energy. Nothing turns people off to gardening faster than laying out a large garden, working on it like a demon for two months, then watching the weeds take over. A much smarter approach is to begin with small intensive plots and work your way up to larger gardens as your gardening experience grows.

Gardens of about 100 square feet (10 by 10 feet) will provide enough room to grow many types of vegetables, including tomatoes, lettuce, onions, beets, beans, cucumbers, and squash. Where the room is available, a garden of 1,250 square feet (25 by 50 feet) will provide most of the in-season fresh vegetables that a family of five can eat. Gardens which produce food for storage will require increasingly larger amounts of space.

By calculating the number of plants needed to supply your family with vegetables, you will have a rough idea of how large a space each crop will occupy. By adding together the space requirements for individual vegetable crops and the distance to be left between rows and individual plants you will be able to calculate the size of your garden. If the calculated area is larger than the actual area you have to garden, you will need to cut back on the amount of some of the vegetables you plan to grow.

Do not try to condense your garden too much by moving rows and individual plants closer to-

Table 7-1. Vegetable Planning Chart.

Vegetable	When to Plant	For 50 Feet of Row	Distance Between Rows	Distance Between Plants	Average Days to Maturity	Yield Per 50 Feet of Row
Plants that Withstand Sharp Frost						
Beets	2-4 weeks prior to last spring frost	½ oz.	18 inches	3 inches	65 days	3/4 bushel
Broccoli	4-6*weeks prior to last spring frost	25 plants	24 inches	24 inches	100 days	15 bunches
	4-6 weeks prior to first fall freeze	25 plants	24 inches	24 inches	100 days	15 bunches
Cabbage	4-6 weeks prior to last spring frost	25 plants	24 inches	24 inches	100 days	25 heads
	90 days prior to first fall freeze	25 plants	24 inches	24 inches	100 days	25 heads
Carrots	2-4 weeks prior to last spring frost	½ oz.	12 inches	3 inches	70 days	3/4 bushel
	100 days prior to first fall freeze	½ oz.	12 inches	3 inches	70 days	3/4 bushel
Endive	2 weeks prior to last spring frost	1/8 oz.	24 inches	12 inches	90 days	40 plants
	10 weeks prior to first fall frost	1/8 oz.	24 inches	12 inches	90 days	40 plants

Vegetable	When to Plant	Amount	Spacing	Spacing	Days to Maturity	Yield
Kale	4-6 weeks prior to last spring frost	1/8 oz.	2 feet	16 inches	70 days	60 bunches
	60 days prior to first fall freeze	1/8 oz.	2 feet	16 inches	70 days	60 bunches
Lettuce, Head	4-5 weeks prior to last spring frost	1/2 packet	12-18 inches	6-12 inches	75 days	35 heads
	2 months prior to first fall freeze	1/2 packet	12-18 inches	6-12 inches	75 days	35 heads
Lettuce, Leaf	Same as above	1 packet	12-18 inches	6 inches	60 days	85 plants
Onions, Sets	4-6 weeks prior to last spring frost	1 pound	12 inches	3 inches	50-100 days	3/4 bushel
Parsnips	2-4 weeks prior to last spring frost	1/4 oz.	18 inches	6 inches	110 days	1 bushel
Peas	4-6 weeks prior to last spring frost	1/2 pound	18 inches	1 inch	65 days	1 bushel
	2 months prior to first fall freeze	1/2 pound	18 inches	1 inch	65 days	1 bushel
Radishes	4 weeks prior to last spring frost	1 packet	12 inches	1 inch	30 days	50 bunches
	1 month prior to first fall freeze	1 packet	12 inches	1 inch	30 days	50 bunches

Vegetable	When to Plant	For 50 Feet of Row	Distance Between Rows	Distance Between Plants	Average Days to Maturity	Yield Per 50 Feet of Row
Rutabaga	3 months prior to first fall freeze	1 packet	18 inches	10 inches	90 days	1 bushel
Spinach	4-6 weeks prior to last spring frost	1/4 oz.	16 inches	6 inches	50 days	1 bushel
	4-6 weeks prior to first fall freeze	1/4 oz.	16 inches	6 inches	50 days	1 bushel
Swiss Chard	1 month prior to last spring frost	1/2 oz.	14 inches	12 inches	65 days	30 plants
	2 months prior to first fall freeze	1/2 oz.	14 inches	12 inches	65 days	30 plants
Turnip	4 weeks prior to last frost in spring	1 package	18 inches	3 inches	60 days	3/4 bushel
	4-6 weeks prior to first fall frost	1 package	18 inches	3 inches	60 days	3/4 bushel
Plants that Withstand Light Frost						
Corn	Last frost-free date	1/8 pound	24 inches	18 inches	90 days	30 ears
Pole Beans	1-8 weeks after last spring frost	1/2 pound	2 feet	3 inches	80 days	1 bushel
Potatoes	4 weeks prior to last spring frost	3-5 pounds	24 inches	18 inches	90 days	40 pounds

Vegetable	Planting Time	Amount to Plant	Space Between Rows	Space Between Plants	Time to Harvest	Yield per 100 ft.
Snap Beans, Bush	1-8 weeks after last spring frost	½ pound	18 inches	4 inches	60 days	3/4 bushel
Summer Squash	On frost-free date	½ oz.	4 feet	3 feet	60 days	70 fruits
Sweet Potato	1-2 weeks after last spring frost	25 plants	30 inches	18 inches	120 days	50 pounds
Winter Squash	2 weeks after frost-free date	½ oz.	6 feet	3 feet	120 days	25 fruits
Plants that Cannot Withstand Frost						
Cucumber	1 week after last spring frost	¼ oz.	4 feet	3 feet	60 days	1 bushel
Eggplant	1 week after last spring frost	25 plants	2 feet	4 feet	75 days	2 bushels
Lima Beans, Bush	2-6 weeks after last spring frost	½ pound	2 feet	3 feet	85 days	3/4 bushel
Lima Beans, Pole	2-6 weeks after last spring frost	½ pound	18 inches	6 inches	85 days	3/4 bushel
Melons	1-2 weeks after last spring frost	¼ oz.	4 feet	4 feet	90 days	25 fruits
Peppers	Set out plants one week after last spring frost	25 plants	3 feet	2 feet	90 days	1½ bushel
Tomatoes	After last frost date	25 plants	3 feet	2 feet	80 days	2 bushels

gether. When plants are crowded they do not produce at their optimum rate. Still, many plants perform near optimum when barely touching another plant. Do not forget that some crops can share the same space through interplanting and succession-cropping techniques. Other crops use their assigned space the whole season.

Perennial crops are the most noted members of the latter group. Asparagus, chives, horseradish, Egyptian onions, rhubarb, some herbs, and berries all fall into this category. The areas where these crops are planted should be out of the way of annual tilling. In most cases they are planted in beds separate from the rest of the garden.

Annual vegetables that require sole possession of their assigned space during the entire summer include lima beans, Swiss chard, eggplants, okra, onions, parsley, parsnips, peppers, sweet potatoes, late white potatoes, salsify, squash, New Zealand spinach, corn, tomatoes, and melons.

The size of your garden will also be affected by the cultivation method you choose. A new method of garden cultivation is slowly making itself felt in this country. The idea is minimum work for maximum production. The way gardeners—especially those with limited space—are achieving such efficient gardens is by planting in permanent beds instead of by the more traditional row method. The city or suburban dweller with limited space should consider the intensive bed garden. These small flowerbed-size gardens produce heavily and make caring for the vegetables easier (Fig. 7-3).

There are two major differences between the bed method and the row method. The first is that once paths are established in a bed garden they remain permanent. This reduces soil compaction, one of the most overlooked reasons for limited plant growth. The second is that, instead of planting in long, drawn out rows which is a real space waster, plants are sown in blocks. This sowing pattern has many advantages including increased production, less work, and more efficient use of compost and rock fertilizers.

By way of comparison, traditional gardens have rows with a path on at least one side of each crop row. The path is necessary for getting to the plants in order to take care of them. Unfortunately, the soil beneath the paths is compacted each time they are walked on. This reduces the growing area for roots. In a bed, vegetables are scattered in an area where human feet seldom, if ever, tred. In a bed the proper size you can reach all the plants from the permanent paths, and soil compaction becomes a thing of the past. Consider how far you can reach when diagramming the expected size of your beds. Three feet across by 10 feet long is a fairly common bed size.

Another advantage to growing vegetables in a bed is that they form a living mulch. The leaves of the growing plants move closer and closer together during growth, until at maturity they overlap slightly. The closeness of the plants makes

Fig. 7-3. Bed gardens allow plants to be closely spaced, a space-saving strategy for gardens of limited size.

Fig. 7-4. Training vines to grow up instead of out, like the cucumbers pictured here, is a significant space-saver in a small garden.

maximum use of available sunlight since none is wasted on the soil. This reduces evaporation and the rate of weed seed germination. The affect is similar to that in a mature forest where very few plants survive below the forest's canopy.

In a traditional row garden, where every plant stands alone, sunlight penetrates to the soil. Your vegetables cannot use this sunlight since it has already passed them by. Weeds can and do use this light to compete with your vegetables for food and water. Additionally, the sun heats the soil and evaporation increases. Row gardens need more weeding and irrigation than bed gardens.

In small gardens you can get a lot of extra room by mulching between rows instead of cultivating. In a row garden space must be left between rows for hoe or tiller cultivation. This is more room than the plant really needs and it goes to waste. By moving the rows closer together, say 6 inches apart instead of the recommended 12 inches, and then mulching between the plants to eliminate cultivation, you can grow more in less space.

Another space-saver in a small garden are fences, trellises, and wire cages. If your garden is only 20 feet by 20 feet and surrounded by a fence, there are 80 feet of cropable row along the fence, Most people let the weeds take over the fence row, but by planting climbing crops like beans, melons, squashes, cucumbers, or even training your tomatoes to climb the fence, you can save considerable space. Stakes, trellises and frames that climbing plants will grow up can be scattered throughout the garden (Fig. 7-4). By getting these crops off the ground, you will be able to grow other crops in the space the raised crops would normally require as room to spread their vines. Besides, picking waist-high is easier than picking from the ground. Gardeners with limited space should consider growing vegetables up instead of out whenever possible in order to coax more food out of the same space.

If you own a tiller and plan to cultivate your vegetables with it you will need to leave considerable space (2 to 3 feet, or the width of the cultivator plus the width of the plants) in order to prevent damaging the crops during cultivation. Hand weeding will require less space between rows, usually 1 foot between the outermost leaves of mature plants. Substituting a mulch for cultivation will allow you to move the plants even closer: so close, that when mature, plant leaves will actually touch the leaves of plants in rows around them. Bed gardens will allow you to pack plants in at the closest possible distances.

CROP SPACING

While planning your garden you need to consider how much room different vegetable crops require. A single tomato plant, for instance, needs a lot more room than a dozen carrots because of the way they grow. If you tried to plant tomatoes as close together as carrots, severe overcrowding would result. This problem can be prevented by drawing the area occupied by plants in your garden to scale on your garden plan. You can scale down the size of your garden by drawing your paper plan on grid paper with ¼-inch squares. Each of these squares then becomes 1 square foot of actual space in the garden. One of the plots that makes up part of my garden happens to be 9 feet wide at the front, 11 feet wide at the rear, and 22 feet long. Last year my plan for this area looked like Fig. 7-5.

You should begin your plan by drawing a line around the number and shape of grid squares in a way that outlines your garden. Make sure that this outline has the correct orientation to north. This information will come in useful later when deciding where tall plants should be planted.

The main advantage to having a well-designed paper plan ready when planting time rolls around is that it will save you a lot of time. You will not have to take time out during the actual planting of your garden to figure out where everything goes. This is especially important in terms of how much room to leave between individual plants within each crop.

Tomatoes, for instance, require 4 square feet of room when staked, and up to 8 square feet when allowed to sprawl. A box where tomato plants go is made by drawing a line (using pencil so that mistakes can be corrected) around four of the ¼-inch squares on your plan. You can draw circles if you like, as long as they take up four squares. Leave one square empty between tomato plants. This represents a foot of maneuvering room between the plants. You might also consider planting basil between the tomato plants since this is a good companion crop and does not compete with the tomato for food or sunlight. The basil plants need a foot of room, so the distance between tomato plants would become 2 feet, represented by two squares on your plan.

Row crops can be shown by drawing a line around an area one block wide and as many blocks long as there are feet in the row. Beds are represented by drawing a line around the number and shape of squares representing the beds in your garden. A box four squares wide on the graph paper will represent a bed 4 feet wide. You do not want

beds much wider than 6 feet, since reaching into the center of a bed this size is difficult.

Place the name of the vegetable to be planted in or near each box you draw. Where late crops are to follow early ones, beans after radishes, for example, the late crop should be put in parentheses with the word *late*.

The late crop planning is useful, but you will often find that it is the most flexible part of your plan. By the time midsummer rolls around you probably will not have much time to consult your plan. Instead, you should be filling in open spaces in your garden as soon as they become available. If a tomato or cucumber plant dies suddenly, remove it and fill the empty space with a late planting of some other vegetable. Having already planned late crops, selecting a replacement should be easy. Keeping all of your garden productive all season long is especially important in small gardens where every pound of food you can harvest from the limited area is a delight.

Gardeners blessed with large gardens should try this too. They will soon find that they do not need such a large garden. Less time spent cultivating, fewer fertilizers used, and a neater appearance are but few of the benefits to cutting back the actual size of your garden while increasing its output. Careful planning is the key to high production.

Vegetables that last all summer and that you use a lot of, especially herbs like parsley and oregano, should be planted near the ends or edges of the garden. This way you do not have to tromp through the garden each time you need a few leaves for seasoning.

When planning a garden, an almost invariable rule is that the tallest vegetables go to the north of the garden. However, when you take crop rotation into account this rule is often bent. You do not want to grow the same crop in the same spot two years in a row. To get around this problem, you may want to plant only across half of the north side of your garden in a single tall crop, say corn, and plant the other half in another tall crop like pole beans. You can then alternate their positions each year and accomplish crop rotation while keeping the tall crops from shading shorter crops.

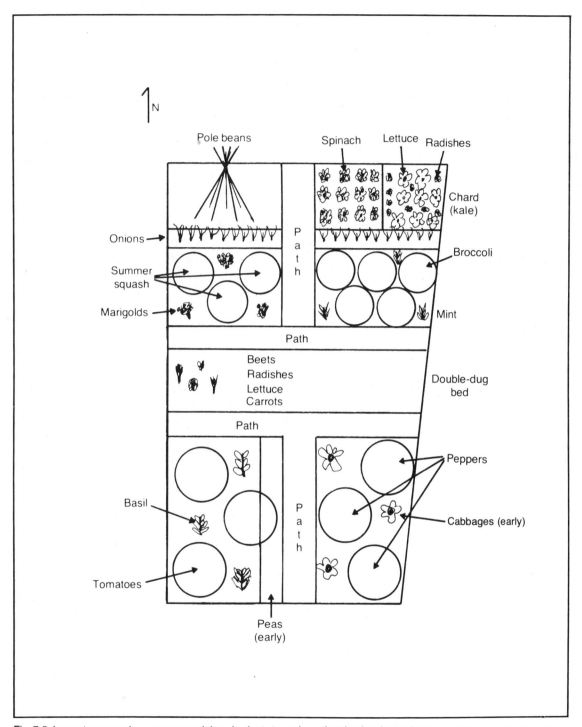

Fig. 7-5. Lay out your garden on paper and draw in plants to scale so that the drawings take up as much room on your plan as they would in the garden.

Another solution to this problem is using the tall crops as a sun screen for crops which can withstand some shade. Shade-tolerant crops include lettuce, peas, cucumbers, kohlrabi, scallions, and bush beans. Plant the tall crops in the middle of the garden and place the shade-tolerant crops to the north and the sun-loving crops to the south of the tall crop.

When laying out paths for the garden make sure they are wide enough so that carts, wheelbarrows, tillers and other equipment can be moved along them. Carts and tillers may require paths up to 4 feet wide. If only hand tools are to be carried along the paths, then paths 2 feet wide are about right. Do not make the paths narrower than this because as plants mature they will reach out over the path and make moving along the path difficult.

SUCCESSION PLANTING

One way to measure the success of your garden is by the length of time each year you are able to harvest from it. Many new gardeners fall into the trap of planting all their seeds early in the spring. When each vegetable crop matures the old picked-over plants are left standing, taking that area of the garden out of production. A better method, which actually requires less space under cultivation, involves succession planting. Succession planting simply means that when one crop is finished with an area, another is planted to take its place.

Your success with succession planting will depend in large part on the length of the growing season in your area. If you do not receive your last frost until Memorial Day then succession planting may not be possible. Following a crop of beets with tomatoes may cut the season so short that the tomatoes do not have enough time to mature before the fall's first killing frost. On the other hand, those gardeners who live in Florida or Texas, where it might freeze once or twice a year, can plant and harvest crops year-round. Of course, hot weather crops like corn may not make it through the winter, but they can be planted months ahead of the northern states.

Planting times for the garden should be planned in three general time frames. Each revolves around the last average frost date for your area (Fig. 7-6). Some plants will withstand a sharp frost. These plants should be planted as soon as the ground can be worked in the spring. The second category contains plants that can withstand a light frost. These crops should be planted no earlier than a week prior to the last average frost date. Finally, there are plants which cannot withstand frost. These crops are planted a week or two after the last average frost date. In many areas of the country, nearly all of the earliest crops will be harvested about the time the late crops are planted.

At the other end of the season you can also work around fall's first killing frost. Many of the hot weather crops will be slowing down their production as the weather turns cool. They can be replaced by quick-maturing cool-weather crops for one last harvest prior to winter. All it takes to extend the season at both ends is a little planning.

Some of the fast-maturing crops like lettuce, radishes, beets, turnips, and peas should be planted two or three times each spring and fall in order to increase the length of time the vegetable is harvestable. As a general rule, these crops are sowed at two-week intervals. This way, just as the first sowing is beginning to taper off, the second sowing is coming into production. Likewise, as the second planting begins to fade the third crop takes its place.

Short-season, cool-weather crops can be followed by later midsummer crops. The cool-weather crops can follow midseason crops for a fall harvest. To figure a planting date for crops expected to mature at the first fall frost, note the days to maturity on the seed package, count back that number from the first expected frost date, and mark this planting time on your calender (Fig. 7-7).

Vegetables for winter storage should not be sown first in the spring. Instead, they should be sown as late as possible so that they keep better. Crops that you can sow in the summer and have at top-quality for a fall harvest include turnips, carrots, beets, cauliflower, cabbage, rutabaga, broccoli, kohlrabi, onion sets, chicory, winter squash, pumpkins, potatoes, beans, and peas.

Many seed companies offer hot-weather varieties of the short, cool-season crops. Planting

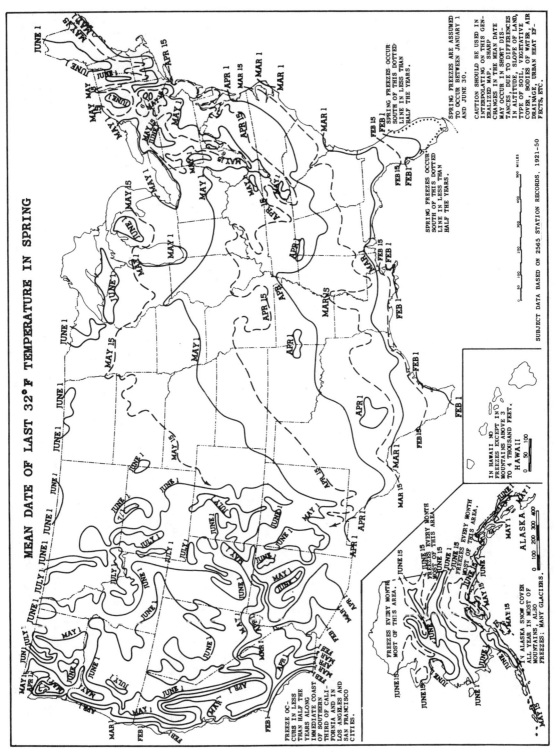

Fig. 7-6. The last average days of 32° F in spring are represented on this map.

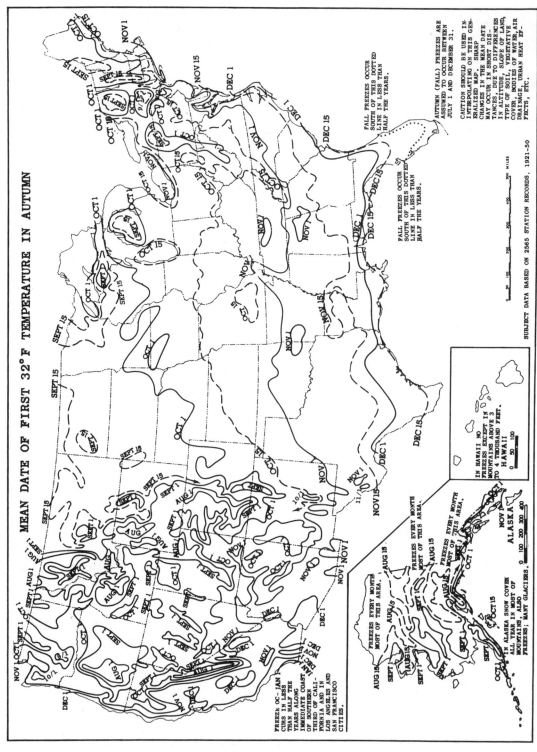

MEAN DATE OF FIRST 32°F TEMPERATURE IN AUTUMN

SUBJECT DATA BASED ON 2565 STATION RECORDS, 1921-50

Fig. 7-7. Autumn frost dates. To calculate a planting date for late-season crops count back from the dates on this map the number of days to maturity listed on seed packets.

these varieties will allow you to make later plantings in the spring so that they mature during the
heat of summer. These selected varieties also ensure good germination during sowings made at midsummer. These vegetables also work well as catch
crops which are planted in various places around the
garden as the space becomes available.

Plants which take a long time to mature, over
100 days, are difficult to succession plant. These
crops include Brussels sprouts, celery, leeks, onions (from seed), parsnips, and rutabaga. Slightly
quicker crops that mature in 80 to 100 days include
onions (from sets or plants), pole lima beans,
eggplant, carrots, winter squash, pumpkins, tomatoes, and corn. Seed companies are constantly
trying to reduce the time that it takes these vegetables to mature. Look for them in your seed catalog,
but the first time you order an untried variety also
plan on planting a variety that you know does well in
your area. This will help ease the sting should the
new variety not work out like you hoped it would.

COMPANION PLANTING

Companion planting is a term used to describe the sowing of plants in your garden in such a
way that they help each other grow instead of com-
peting against one another. Companion planting is a
step beyond the monoculture practices that have
permeated the gardening community for many
years. There are two basic types of companion
planting: interplanting and intercropping. *Interplanting* is a term used to describe mixing the
types of plants growing in the same row or bed.
Intercropping is a term used to describe planting
alternating rows or beds of plants that are beneficial
to each other.

Although scientifically very little is known
about companion planting, most organic gardeners
swear by it. I do, but there are still skeptics.

Very few gardeners will attempt to explain
why carrots dislike dill, or why tomatoes and basil
grow so well together. However, there are a few
theories about why plants like and dislike each
other. Most of these theories revolve around
smells, root excretions, and feeding patterns.
Some gardeners claim that stressed plants are more

susceptible to attack by insects and disease, and
that growing certain plants with friendly plants
helps reduce stress. Another theory says that companion plants often make compatible demands on
the environment. For example, leeks and celery do
well together because they both love potash and
both are tall growers. Another possible reason is
that the root systems of different plants occupy
different strata of the soil (Fig. 7-8). For instance,
carrots have deep-probing roots while lettuce roots
stay near the surface (Table 7-2). Many herbs have
very deep roots. It is believed that these deep root
systems enlarge the feeding area of plants with
shallow roots by working through the compacted
soil and loosening it so that shallow roots can grow
deeper.

When planting a companion garden, it is a good
idea to put friendly plants together. One way to do
this is to broadcast your seed in mixed beds instead
of planting in neat rows. Another is to zigzag your
rows. A third method is intercropping, and a fourth
is interplanting.

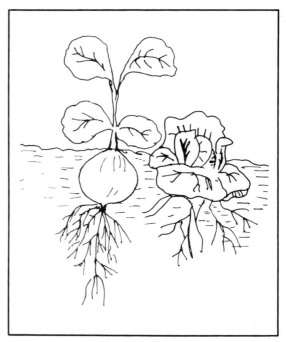

Fig. 7-8. The roots of various vegetables grow to different
depths in the soil. Though planted close together, there is
little competition between these roots for nutrients.

Table 7-2. Rooting Depth of Common Garden Vegetables.

Shallow
18 to 24 Inches

broccoli	garlic
Brussels sprouts	leek
cabbage	lettuce
cauliflower	onion
celery	parsley
Chinese cabbage	potato
corn	radish
endive	spinach

Medium
36 to 48 Inches

bush bean	mustard
beet	pea
carrot	pepper
chard	pole beans
cucumber	rutabaga
eggplant	summer squash
muskmelon	turnip

Deep
More than 48 Inches

artichoke	sweet potato
asparagus	tomato
lima bean	watermelon
parsnip	winter squash
pumpkin	

Companion planting may also operate on the succession principle. When early- and late-maturing vegetables are planted in the same row or bed at the same time, two crops can be grown in the space of one. Planting radishes with carrots, for example, means that you will be harvesting the radishes within weeks, while the carrots will take 2 to 3 months to mature. As the radishes are harvested, room is made for the carrots.

There are many herbs and flowers that you can plant in your garden to deter insects, act as trap-plants, or to add a generally good influence to the garden. Herbs with good characteristics should be scattered around the garden here and there. Plants that go well with specific crops should be planted right in the row or bed with their friends.

Herbs that are a good influence include borage, lavender, blue hyssop, sage, parsley, cherival, marjoram, tarragon, dill, chives, camomile and lov-age. Marigolds, petunias, and zinnias also fall into this category, although they are not edible.

Other herbs have pest-trapping, pest-confusing, growth-stimulating and insect-repelling characteristics which make them valuable additions to the garden. Not only will they add spice to your favorite dishes, but these herbs reduce pest problems. Trap plants attract insects to themselves instead of to your vegetable plants. Repellent plants turn bugs away before they have a chance to find their host plants. Some herbs exude substances from their roots which chase away underground pests, benefiting all nearby plants. Many herbs can be whizzed in a blender and then sprayed on plants to help confuse pests even more. Plan to add herbs to your garden not only for their food value, but also as alies in the war with bugs.

Tables 7-3 and 7-4 will give you some ideas about companion planting. Remember that just because pole beans like corn, and corn likes potatoes, and potatoes like cabbage, cabbage does not really like pole beans.

The best way to incorporate companion planting into your garden scheme is to list the vegetables you want to grow and then look up their companions. When you draw your garden plan try to keep the companion vegetables as close together as possible. Then go back through the plan and add companion herbs to your vegetable plantings wherever you can. The idea is to get those plants which grow best together as close to each other as possible. On the other side of the coin, you should also try to keep enemies separated.

CROP ROTATION

Crop rotation in its simplest form means planting a specific crop in a different place this year than you did last year. Crop rotation is another good reason to keep an accurate sketch of your garden plan from year to year. By keeping such a record, you can look at last year's plan while drawing this year's plan and avoid planting crops in the same spot. Disease control, insect control, and giving the soil a rest are the three most important reasons for crop rotation.

Disease Control

Soil is basically stationary, while plants (except perennials) can move from year to year. By planting crops in a different place than they grew in last year, you can control many root-related diseases. In many instances the disease perishes in the soil, and three or four years later, when you plant the host crop in that place again, the disease will be long gone.

Bean blight, black rot, fusarium wilt, fusarium root rot, and verticillium wilt can often be controlled by 3- or 4-year rotations. Nematode infestations can also be reduced through proper rotation.

Insect Control

Crop rotation is a valuable tool in thwarting pests that specialize in devouring one family of vegetables. Rotations are especially effective against those pests which overwinter in the ground. When you move the crop and the insect emerges in the spring, it has to search over your garden to find a host plant. Many of the pests do not survive their journey. Planting a crop in the same place year after year produces conditions favorable to increased pest populations.

Resting the Soil

Since each of the crops you grow will make a different demand on the soil in terms of nitrogen, phosphorus, potassium, and trace minerals, growing the same crop in the same place year after year can deplete your soil of certain nutrients. Crop rotation allows the soil to rest, or at least catch its breath, by having crops with different feeding habits grow in the same soil each year. This rotation can be broken down according to whether a plant is a heavy feeder, moderate feeder, or light feeder.

Heavy-feeding crops include corn, tomatoes, eggplant, and cole crops. These plants need a lot of nutrients, and they can exact a heavy toll on the soil's fertility. Heavy feeders should be followed by a moderate-feeding or preferably a light-feeding, crop. Moderate feeders include legumes, peppers, squash, and many leafy crops. The light feeders are root crops, bulbs, and herbs. Beets, carrots, on-

ions, leeks and herbs are included in this group.

In general, a rotation built around how plants feed should work like this: First, the heavy feeders are grown in a particular area; next, the moderate feeders; and finally the light feeders. Additional rest can be granted to the soil by planting a cover crop the fourth year, before planting heavy feeders again. Once the soil has been improved by judicious use of rock fertilizers and cartloads of organic matter, the light and moderate feeders can change places in the rotation without affecting yields.

The simplest rule for garden rotation is not to plant the same vegetable in the same place you planted it the previous year; but most crop rotations are planned in four year cycles. A typical rotation may start off with corn, followed by peas, then squash, and then corn again. Many farmers place a cover crop in their rotations. A rotation including a cover crop might go something like this: corn, peas, squash, cover crop, and corn again. Cover crops are added to the rotation to provide green manure (organic matter) for the soil, and to break the cycle of pests.

Maintaining an effective rotation scheme requires knowing where each crop was planted last year and in previous years in different areas of your garden. Although it may take a few years to get a feel for crop rotation, once it is established it becomes second nature. Besides, proper crop rotation moves the plants around in a way that gives the appearance of having a brand new garden each year.

The first step in determining a crop rotation schedule is dividing your garden area into three, four, or five parts. (There should be one area for each year of your rotation schedule.) If you have beds, these are perfect dividing lines. For row crops, you will have to superimpose the divisions on the plan and then implement them when you plant. Plants make good dividing lines in row gardens.

Next, decide which plants go in which sections. In most cases you will want to plant vegetables with their companions in each section of the garden. Keep crops like the cabbage family scattered, but still in one section. This way you can move the whole plot as a unit without worrying that

Table 7-3. Vegetables and Their Companions.

Vegetable	Likes	Dislikes
Asparagus	Tomatoes, parsley, basil	
Beans	Marigolds, nasturtiums, rosemary, potatoes, carrots, cucumbers, cauliflower, cabbage, summer savory, celery, chard, corn, radish, strawberry, eggplant	Onions, garlic, shallot
Beet	Onions, kohlrabi, bush beans, cabbage, lettuce, garlic	Pole beans
Bush beans	Potatoes, cucumbers, corn, sunflowers, strawberries, celery, savory	Onions, garlic, shallot
Cabbage family	Aromatic herbs, potatoes, cucumbers, lettuce, garlic, catnip, hyssop, mint, nasturtium, tansy, celery, dill, camomile, chard, peppermint, sage, rosemary, beets, onions	Strawberries, tomatoes, pole beans
Carrots	Beans, peppers, radish peas, lettuce, chives, onions, leeks, rosemary, sage, tomatoes	Dill
Celery	Leeks, tomatoes, bush beans, chives, garlic, nasturtium, cabbage family	
Chard	Beans, cabbage family, onions	
Chives	Carrots	Peas, beans
Corn	Potatoes, peas, bush beans, cucumbers, pumpkins, squash, melons, parsley, pigweed	Tomatoes
Cucumbers	Beans, corn, peas, radishes, sunflowers, cabbage family, tomatoes, marigold, nasturtium, oregano, tansy	Potatoes, sage
Eggplant	Beans, peppers, marigolds	
Leeks	Onions, celery, carrots	

Lettuce	Carrots, radishes, beets, strawberries, chives, cucumbers, garlic, cabbage family	
Melons	Corn, pumpkins, radishes, squash, marigold, oregano, nasturtium	
Onions (Garlic)	Beets, strawberries, chard, tomatoes, lettuce, savory, camomile, cabbage family	Peas, beans
Peas	Carrots, turnips, radishes, cucumbers, corn, beans, squash, chives, mint	Onions, garlic, potato
Parsley	Tomato, asparagus, corn	
Peppers	Carrots, eggplant, onion, tomatoes	
Pole Beans	Corn, summer savory	Onions, beets, kohlrabi, sunflower
Potato	Beans, corn, cabbage, horseradish, peas, marigold, eggplant lima beans	Pumpkin, squash, cucumber, sunflower, tomato, raspberry
Pumpkins	Corn, melons, squash, marigold, nasturtium, oregano	Potato
Soybean	Helps all vegetables	
Spinach	Strawberries, cabbage family	
Summer Squash	nasturtium, corn, radishes, melons, pumpkin, borage, marigolds, oregano	
Strawberries	Bush beans, spinach, borage, lettuce, onion, thyme	Cabbage
Sunflower	Cucumbers	Potato
Tomato	Chives, onions, parsley, asparagus, marigold, basil, bee balm, borage, dill, nasturtium, carrot, lima beans, wormwood, celery, cucumber, pepper	Kohlrabi, potato, corn, fennel, cabbage
Turnip	Peas	

Table 7-4. Herbs and Their Companions.

Herb	Likes	Dislikes
Basil	Tomatoes	Rue
Bee balm	Tomatoes	
Borage	Tomatoes, squash, strawberries	
Caraway	All-round herb, deep roots	
Camomile	Cabbage family, onion	
Catnip	All-round herb, deters flea beetle	
Chervil	Radishes	
Chives	Carrots, fruit trees	Peas, beans
Dill	Cabbage family, carrots	
Fennel		Most vegetables; plant away from vegetable garden
Flax	Carrots, potatoes	
Garlic	Beets, strawberries, tomato, lettuce, savory, camomile	Peas, beans
Henbit	All-round herb, repellent	
Horseradish	Potatoes	
Hyssop	Cabbage family, grapes	Radishes
Lamb's Quarters	All-round weed, deep roots	
Lemon Balm	All-round herb, aromatic	
Lovage	All-round herb	
Marigolds	All-round flower, deters Mexican bean beetles, nematodes	
Mint	Cabbage, tomatoes	
Marjoram	All-round herb	
Nasturtium	Tomatoes, radishes, fruit trees, cabbage, cucumbers	
Peppermint	Cabbage family	
Petunia	Beans	

Vegetables	Likes	Dislikes
Pigweed	Potatoes, onions, corn; Deep-rooted	
Purslane	Corn	
Rosemary	Cabbage family, beans, carrots, sage	
Rue	Raspberries	Basil
Sage	Rosemary, cabbage family, carrots, peas, beans	Cucumbers
Savory	Beans, onions	
Southernwood	Cabbage	
Sow Thistle	Tomatoes, onions, corn	
Tansy	Fruit trees, squash, cucumbers, raspberries	
Tarragon	All-round herb	
Thyme	Cabbage	
Yarrow	All-round herb, deep roots	

you are moving into a location where cole crops were grown the previous year.

Typical divisions for crop rotation might go something like this: plot A: tomatoes, peppers, onions, parsley, and eggplants; plot B: beans, peas, celery, radishes, endive, and kale; plot C: potatoes, carrots, cabbage, lettuce, and spinach; plot D: corn, squash, cucumbers, and melons.

These are the crudest of divisions, and you will soon discover that by practicing succession planting, intercropping, and companion planting a galaxy of variations can be introduced into the rotation plan. The two important considerations are keeping crops that suffer the same diseases and pests from following each other, and having light and moderate feeders following heavy feeders.

Introducing a cover crop such as wheat, clover, rye, or alfalfa into the rotation gives even more variation. Unfortunately, most vegetable gardeners do not have enough room to take a section of their garden out of production for a cover crop each sea-

son. That is okay, as long as you rotate your crops in a systematic manner.

Now that your plots have been labeled it is a simple matter to set up a rotation plan. Plot A of Year 1 occupies area D the following year, and each of the other plots is shifted accordingly. Following this pattern, the second year will find plot B where plot A was the first year, and so on down the line. The third year plot C will occupy where plot A was the first year. After four years, plot A is back where it started (Fig. 7-9).

Remember that it is important to know where plots are planted from year to year. Do not throw away your yearly plans.

SEED ORDERING

An important step of planning your garden is ordering seeds. Although you can buy many seeds locally, most gardeners prefer to buy seeds by mail. If you are not already on seed company mailing lists, send in a few of the forms found in gardening

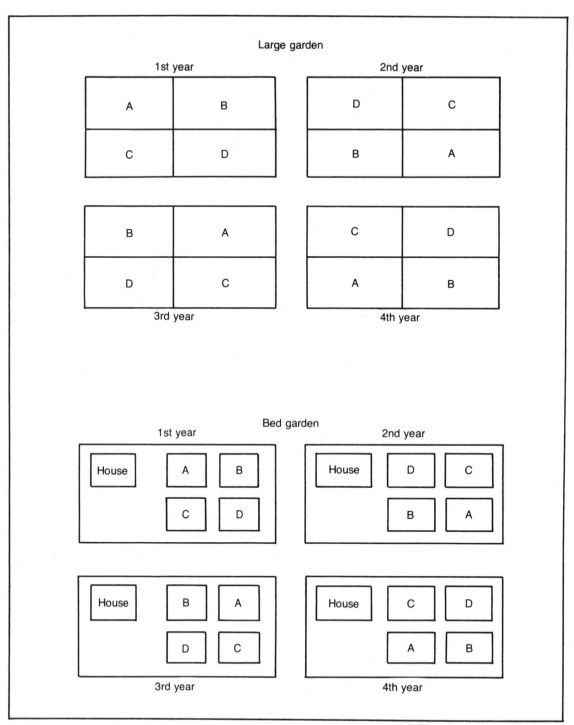

Fig. 7-9. Follow the top rotation scheme for a vegetable garden divided into sections. The bottom rotation plan will work for a garden divided into individual beds.

magazines to put your name on these lists. If you have ordered seeds by mail previously or subscribe to a gardening magazine, chances are you are already on a seed company mailing list. Sometime during December the catalogs begin arriving, bringing with them pictures of beautiful vegetables, berries, and fruit.

Besides the seeds and plants they offer, many catalogs also sell fertilizers, garden implements, and many other gardening aids. Some of these extras are worth your money, and others are not. Seed companies, especially the family-run businesses, which cater to the organic gardener provide a lot of advice about gardening through their catalogs. These seed catalogs make for some mighty fine reading while winter winds howl outside your window.

Most seed companies will tell you the cultural methods used to produce certain seeds. Reputable dealers will also tell you which of their seeds are treated with fungicides or other chemicals; that is, if you ask. You can feel good about seed companies that are not afraid to tell you how they handle their seeds. Additional assurance about the philosophy of the seed company can be discovered by flipping to the fertilizer section. Those that advertise only organic fertilizers and natural pesticides will be as equally conscientious about their seed cultivation methods.

Whenever possible, try to order seeds from regional companies that have growing conditions similar to your local climate. Although plant breeders try to grow varieties that do well in most parts of the country the process of natural selection will, through the years, favor one or two varieties for their area. Since the seed companies are getting their best return on these varieties they will concentrate on producing these seeds. What may result is seed that does well in their area, soil, and growing conditions, but may not be up to par in your area. If you live in Minnesota, for instance, do not order seeds from a company with its seed farms in Florida. Chances are those seeds will not do as well as seeds ordered from a company in Minnesota or in a neighboring state.

If you are a first-time gardener, consult seed catalogs and read seed packets, or ask friends and your county extension agent for suggestions about the best varieties to grow in your area. Of course, many of these suggestions will be based on the personal tastes of those making the judgments, but their advice is usually sound.

Most seed companies build their reputations through the continuously high quality of their seed. Avoid catalogs that make lavish promises or claim that their plants will grow to impossible proportions. Instead, look for catalogs that give such useful information as "bears well for several weeks, when picked," "frost tolerant," and "heavy crop." These low-key statements allow you to make sensible judgments about the seeds you order without a blizzard of hype.

Many of the better catalogs also give planting advice such as plant spacing, planting dates, planting hints, how much one packet will plant, and the areas where certain varieties may be difficult to grow. Like everything else, cheap seeds from a less than reputable seed company usually give poor results. Pay for quality and that is usually the type of seed you will get.

The first time you look through a catalog simply flip through it. Notice new varieties, planting instructions, recommendations, and the gadgets and fertilizers offered. This preview will give you a feel for the company. When you finally decide to draw up a list, go through the catalog vegetable by vegetable and pick a favorite, or one that sounds like it will do well in your climate. Write down the variety, price, maturity date, space requirement and the company. Do this for each catalog and you will have a handy way to compare the seeds you plan to buy. This list will also come in handy when it is time to lay out your garden on grid paper.

An advantage to having such a definite garden plan is that you will know exactly how much of each type of seed to order. Without a plan chances are that you will order too much of some seed and not enough of another.

Buy the best seed you can afford. Cheap seed is hardly ever the bargain your pocketbook says it is. Do not use seeds over from previous years unless you have stored them properly. Year-old seeds on a store rack usually have not been stored properly and poor germination will result. When buying seed locally it is imperative to check the freshness date on the package. Most people who sell seeds are conscientious about rotating their seed and offering only seed intended for this year's sales. However they do slip up occasionally and you do not want to get stuck with seed that is past its prime.

Between the time your seeds arrive and planting time store them in a cool, dry, dark place.

SEED CATALOG GLOSSARY

Below is a short glossary of some terms used frequently by seed companies which may be confusing when left unexplained.

All-America Selections

All-America Selections is a nonprofit organization which awards bronze, silver, and gold medals to outstanding new vegetable and flower varieties. This organization is allied with the National Garden Bureau, Inc., and has been active since 1932. The All-America Selections judges grow varieties to be rated in trial gardens in order to make their selections and awards. Not all All-America Selections garner immediate public acceptance. Many of the Gold Medal winners are more novelties than true horticultural advances. Still, approval by All-America Selections is prestigious, so most good seed companies feature several All-America Selections in their catalogs.

Determinate

Determinate means that plants grow to a certain size, set fruit, mature the fruit, and then die. Determinate tomatoes, for instance, have flower clusters at the ends of their stems (Fig. 7-10). These plants grow bushy and rarely need staking. Many early and main crop tomatoes are determinate.

Gynoecious Cucumbers

This term describes a hybrid cucumber that has been bred to produce an unusual number of female flowers. The result is a plant that produces more cucumbers than standard vines. A gynoecious cucumber is also likely to produce earlier crops of cucumbers than standard varieties.

Hybrid

The hybrid seed sold through catalogs is the seed produced by cross-pollination of two plants of known characteristics. These parents produce hybrid seed with superior growing habits. Gynoecious cucumbers are an example of hybridization. A major disadvantage of hybrids is that their seeds do not run true to their type. Seed from a hybrid plant will not produce the same quality vegetable as the original hybrid seed.

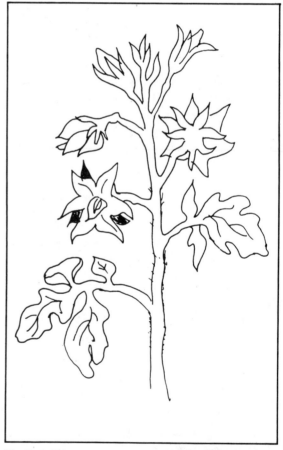

Fig. 7-10. This drawing of a determinate tomato shows how blossoms grow on the ends of branches.

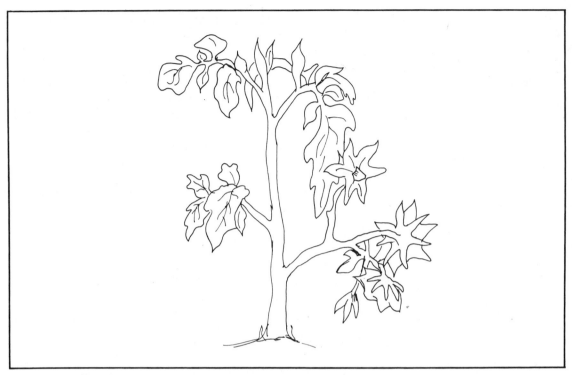

Fig. 7-11. This drawing of an indeterminate tomato shows how the blossoms form on side shoots, allowing the termination of the branch to continue growing.

Indeterminate

Indeterminate vegetables grow all season producing flowers and setting fruit until killed by frost. Indeterminate tomatoes, for example, continue setting fruit until the vines are killed by frost. Indeterminate plants usually grow larger than determinate plants (Fig. 7-11). Fruit from indeterminate plants is produced later in the season, but often reaches impressive size.

Mosaic Indexed

This term describes a plant that has been bred to be resistant to the mosaic virus. Mosaic is spread from plant to plant by vectors such as insects, tools, hands, clothes, and tobacco smoke. This disease stunts plants and mottles foliage. If this disease is a problem in your garden, buy resistant seed.

Open Pollination

Open pollination means that the fertilization of vegetable blooms is accomplished by wind and insects. The seeds produced by open pollination plants are usually true to their type as long as two types do not mix. Home seed savers will do well to look for good open pollination plants.

Rhizome

This describes a stem-like structure on plants that lies just beneath the surface of the dirt and sends up leaf shoots from its upper surface while sending roots down from its lower surface. This is a method of asexual reproduction common in vegetables like asparagus and Jerusalem artichokes.

Special Selections

Many seed companies put together packages of different varieties of vegetable seed that they think home gardeners will be interested in. The selection is often based on ease of growing, taste, variety, or season-long production. Most special selections are priced lower than if you bought each variety included in the selection individually. These collections allow many gardeners a chance to compare the growing habits and success of different varieties at minimal expense.

VF, VFN, VFNT

These code letters describe various disease resistances bred into tomatoes, cucumbers, and other susceptible vegetables. V stands for verticillium wilt, F for fusarium wilt, N for nematodes, and T for tobacco mosaic. If these diseases have been a problem in your garden, it is wise to grow resistance varieties.

TYING IT ALL TOGETHER

There are a lot of things to consider when drawing up a garden plan, but each variable must be included if you expect your garden to run smoothly.

Run through the following checklist with your completed garden plan to make sure you have not forgotten anything.

- Are perennials planted where they will not be disturbed by cultivation of your main garden?
- Are tall growing crops at the north side of the garden? If not, are shade-tolerant crops planted to the north of tall crops?
- Have you made the proper companion planting combinations?
- Have you considered possible succession and interplanting combinations?
- Are often-used vegetables near the edge of the garden?
- Are the early-planted and quick-maturing crops planted together?
- Have you over-planted untried varieties? How about vegetables your family is not particularly fond of?
- Are rows placed across the slope of hills?
- Is there adequate spacing between rows and beds? Between plants? (This will vary according to the cultivation method you choose.)
- Remember, long rows save time and energy. Several crops may be planted in different sections of the same row. Beds are an even better idea since there is less wasted space.
- Will shade from surrounding trees affect your garden?
- Has your plan been drawn up in a way that makes crop rotation easy?

Chapter 8

Growing Your Own Seedlings

A plant is like a self-willed man, out of whom we can obtain all which we desire, if we will only treat him his own way.

—Goethe

Many novice gardeners take a major step toward becoming advanced gardeners when they master the art of growing their own seedlings from scratch. Gardeners who grow their own transplants save money. Often a single transplant from a nursery will cost half the price of a whole packet of seed. Gardeners who grow their own also have greater control over the variety of plants they grow. Most nurseries usually limit themselves to varieties that sell well, not necessarily the ones that will grow best in their area. Gardeners who choose to start their own seedlings are also able to raise plants already acclimated to their locality, thereby exercising greater control over disease and pest problems. Finally, when you grow your own transplants you can order varieties from around the world and experiment with growing them in your garden.

Why are seedlings or transplants grown in the first place? Many plants like tomatoes, peppers, eggplants, and some squashes and melons must be started inside and set out in the garden in order to provide a long enough growing season to mature. This is especially true in the northern states where summers are short. Others like cabbage, broccoli and cauliflower require short, but cool growing seasons, and must be set out as seedlings so that they have a chance to mature prior to the onset of the hot days of summer. You can obtain seedlings from two sources: at the local greenhouse or by growing your own.

At first glance growing your own seedlings appears to be a difficult proposition, especially if you have never grown them before. It is not, really. Seeds need warmth, light, air and food in order to germinate and then grow into garden-ready seedlings. The trick to growing healthy seedlings is providing the correct amounts of these life-giving necessities. If you do not have the room or patience to grow your own seedlings, you can always buy them, but you will be missing out on the pride that comes with nurturing the vegetables in your garden from seed until they are dinner on your plate. If you must purchase already-grown seedlings, here are a few things to remember.

Plants cooked in the sun on the asphalt out front of the local supermarket or dime store are not worth buying. The people responsible for these plants do not really care about them, so the plants are often weak from over or under-watering. Besides, these plants have often been trucked in hundreds or thousands of miles for sale in your area. Chances are they are not adapted to your climate. Many of these transplants are also sprayed with pesticides. Those that escape the pesticide treatment usually carry insect pests which will quickly multiply in your garden.

A much better place to buy seedlings is at a local nursery, or through the mail. Most of the people at a nursery care about their plants. After all, they want you to return year after year. Greenhouse plants are generally healthy and grown under ideal conditions. The little extra you pay for this service is worth it in the long run.

Be careful when ordering from magazines and newspapers. You cannot always tell from an advertisement how healthy the seedlings are. Buying seeds by mail is a pretty safe bet, but buying a living plant is an entirely different matter. Additionally, traveling plants are subject to overheating, freezing and drying during delivery. Although the plastic bags and boxes that many plants are now shipped in provide excellent protection against rough handling, they are also good breeding grounds for disease and insect pests. Better to buy locally, where you can inspect the plants thoroughly before carrying them home.

While you are at the greenhouse, take a close look at the plants you have an interest in buying (Fig. 8-1). They should be large and sturdy with good root systems. The size of the root system can be judged by the size of the container in which the plant is growing. The larger the container, the bigger the root system. Vegetable plants should have the same look as a house plant in its proper size pot. Seedlings in flats should be adequately spaced,

stocky (not tall and spindly), crisp, of good color, and have straight unblemished stems. Keep an eye open for flea beetles and whiteflies which will propagate rapidly in your garden.

Avoid stunted plants, plants with drooping leaves, and those with holes in the leaves. If there are only one or two specimens of the variety you want left on the sales table, do not buy them. Chances are these plants are the only ones left from a much bigger selection. They are probably plants no one else wanted because they did not measure up to the plants that have already been sold. Previous gardeners did not want them and neither do you. Ask the greenhouse help if they have any more of that variety in the back room. Finally, when you get your newly-purchased seedlings home, harden

Fig. 8-1. Inspect greenhouse transplants closely, checking for insects, disease, and the overall health of the plants.

them off for a week before setting them out in your garden.

SEEDLING BASICS

Before moving into the specific methods for growing seedlings at home, you need to be familiar with a few of the basic terms, culture requirements, and the equipment you will use for growing your own seedlings.

Soil

The texture and water-holding capacity of a soil is more important to getting seedlings off to a good start than the nutrient content of the soil (Fig. 8-2). However, small plants need a full complement of nutrients just like their parents. In most cases, mixing one of the potting mixes listed below will provide all the nutrients small plants need.

Soil for seedlings should not be overly fertile since you want the seedling's roots to grow outward in search of food. When the soil is extremely rich, the plant will be lazy and will not develop an extensive root system. Excessive amounts of certain nutrients can also weaken small plants. Too much nitrogen, for instance, will cause a lot of leaf and stem growth at the expense of root expansion. When seedlings are transplanted into the garden, there will be more plant above ground than the shocked roots can support. On the other hand, should you think your seedlings are developing signs of a nutrient deficiency during growth, you can water them with a weak solution of compost or manure tea as a supplement. Regular waterings with diluted liquid seaweed will also provide nutrients. Do not water seedlings with fish emulsion since this fertilizer contains a lot of nitrogen.

Fig. 8-2. Soil for starting seeds should be loose with a light mixture capable of holding a lot of moisture.

Two good potting mixtures are: 1 part sand, 1 part peat moss or compost and 2 parts garden soil (pasteurized); or a mixture of 1/3 sand, 1/3 peat moss or vermiculite and 1/3 garden soil or compost. The garden soil and compost used in potting mixtures should be pasteurized to prevent the spread of damping-off disease. Pasteurization will not kill all of the microbes in the soil, but it will take care of most of the harmful ones. See the damping-off section below for pasteurization techniques.

Vermiculite is a heat-expanded mica. Mica is a rock with many thin layers. When mica is heated, these layers puff up, much like a pop corn kernel expands when heated. This heating process sterilizes the vermiculite, creating a good, trouble-free addition to potting mixes. Vermiculite will hold several times its weight in water, provides good aeration, and adds a light crumbly structure to the soil—allowing lots of room for growth by plant roots. Unfortunately, vermiculite does not supply plant nutrients, so it cannot be used as a substitute for compost or garden soil, both of which supply nutrients to seedling roots.

Peat moss is the partially-decomposed residue which accumulates over several centuries under the moist cool conditions found in peat bogs. Peat acts much like vermiculite in a potting soil. It holds a lot of water (up to 15 times its own weight), increases aeration, aids root development by keeping soil loose, and prevents nutrients from leaching away with water. Although peat is a broken-down plant material, it contains no weed seed, no plant pathogens and no insect eggs or larva. This makes it a trouble-free additive to potting soil.

Light

Most plants are extremely sensitive to light. This sensitivity begins the moment a seed swells with water and comes to life. Although germination takes place in the darkness of the soil, the stem of the seedling immediately begins reaching for the light beyond the soil surface. Seedlings grown in the presence of intense light are short and sturdy, while those grown in less light become spindly as they reach farther and farther for light.

Within a week or two after germination, the stored food in a seed is exhausted. The plant needs ample light at this time in order to make its own food through photosynthesis. Plants without adequate light can actually starve during the transition from feeding on seed-stored energy to photosynthesis.

Artificial lighting is usually necessary for good seedling growth, unless you are lucky enough to have a greenhouse. Artificial light has an advantage over the sun in that you can control the duration of light that plants receive each day. You can also control the intensity of the light by altering its distance from the plant.

As soon as seeds germinate and break through the soil, they should be placed under artificial lights or in a south-facing window that receives at least 8 hours of direct sunlight per day. The more light the better. Artificial light should be positioned 2 to 3 inches above plants, and turned on for 10 to 12 hours per day (Fig. 8-3). Do not leave lights on 24 hours a day, because seedlings need rest just as humans do. You can increase the intensity of artificial lights and the sunlight in south-facing windows with aluminum foil or mirrors. Seedlings grown in windows should be rotated daily to prevent them from becoming lopsided by being forced to reach in a single direction for light.

It is a good idea to hang light fixtures on chains or ropes above seedling flats so that the lights can be raised as the plants grow. Another good idea is to buy a timer so that the plants are sure to get the correct amount of light each day even when you are not home. A timer is not really necessary if you get in the habit of turning on the light just after waking and then turning it off right before bed each evening.

Generally speaking, fluorescent lights are better for growing plants than the incandescent type of light because the former produces blue, short-wave light while the latter produces a red, long-wave light. Although the red light is good for top growth and seed germination, the blue light encourages root growth and greener leaves.

There are many "grow lights" on the market. These lights produce a wide spectrum of wave-

Fig. 8-3. Artificial light, in the form of fluorescent lights, is a must for sturdy seedlings.

lengths (combining short- and long-wave light) which simulates sunshine. Unfortunately, these lights are about twice as expensive as regular flourescent lights. The short time that your plants will be under artificial light calls for no more than standard fluorescent lights.

Water

Watering your seedlings is a ticklish operation. Too little water causes seedlings to wither and die. Seedlings do not have enough mass to store water so they tend to show the affects of drought quickly. Adult plants have enough size to store water and can withstand some drought. Too much water will also cause problems. Damping-off is one. Another is the suffocation of a plant when water forces air from around the roots for a day or more. A regular watering schedule is a must; not necessar-

ily every day, but often enough to keep the soil moist.

After seeds have been covered with soil and lightly watered, the flats should not be watered again until the seeds germinate. You can keep adequate moisture in the flat by stretching a sheet of plastic over the flat (Fig. 8-4). After the seeds break through the soil, they have very shallow roots. You should not wait until the surface of the soil dries before watering. Instead, plants and soil should be misted each day or every other day to keep the soil moist. Some people set their flats into trays of water twice a week and allow the water to soak up into the flat through the bottom. Do not pour water on the flats from a single nozzle watering can or hose because the stream of water will wash seedlings right out of the soil. When you water, make sure the water is at room temperature

129

Fig. 8-4. Plastic stretched over seedling flats will ensure enough moisture for proper germination. Remove plastic when seeds poke through the soil.

Lower temperatures may result in poor germination and higher temperatures may kill off the seedlings as they emerge. Once germination has been completed the temperature of the flats can be reduced somewhat.

Generally, cool-season crops such as broccoli, cabbage, cauliflower, endive, kale, and lettuce should have night temperatures of about 50° to 55° F with day temperatures ranging from 60° to 65° F. Warm weather crops like cucumbers, eggplants, muskmelons, peppers, tomatoes, and squash prefer night temperatures that do not dip below 60° F with day temperatures ranging from 65° to 75° F.

The best way to heat seedling flats is from the bottom. Placing them on a radiator or other heat-producing appliance in the house is a good idea, but do not allow the temperature to pass 75° to 80° F at any time. Many companies also sell heat cables that can be placed in the bottoms of seed flats to provide a nice even heat for the seedlings. Do not set flats in front of space heaters or the register of a forced air heating system because the seedlings will quickly dry out and perish.

When to Start Seeds

One of the secrets to having your home-grown seedlings do well in the garden is transplanting them outside when they are at the proper stage of

in order to prevent shocking the seedlings.

Do not allow the soil to become soggy or damping-off disease will raise its ugly head. A once-a-week watering with a solution of 1 tablespoon of liquid seaweed in a gallon of water will reduce the chances of this disease. Seaweed will also slow down the leggy growth of plants that are forced to develop in less-than-optimum levels of light.

Temperature

The temperature at which you keep your seedlings is flexible to a certain extent. Most seeds germinate best at temperatures ranging from 65° to 85° F. 75° F is a safe middle ground (Table 8-1).

Table 8-1. The Temperature Range Required for the Germination of Commonly-Transplanted Seeds.

Vegetable	Minimum Temp. F	Optimum Range F
Cabbage	40	45-90
Cauliflower	40	45-85
Celery	40	60-70
Cucumber	60	60-90
Eggplant	60	75-90
Lettuce	35	40-80
Muskmelon	60	75-90
Onion	35	50-90
Parsley	40	50-85
Pepper	60	65-95
Pumpkin	60	70-90
Squash	60	70-95
Tomato	50	60-85
Watermelon	60	70-95

their development. This stage of growth should correspond with the proper weather conditions and soil temperatures in your garden. Most plants are grouped loosely together in two categories: cold-tolerant (hardy) varieties and heat-loving (tender) varieties. The cold-tolerant plants can be transplanted outside a week or two before the average date of the last spring frost. Heat-loving plants cannot be transplanted until after this average last frost date has passed and the soil has warmed up sufficiently.

The best way to determine when you should start your seeds indoors is by determining when the last expected frost is for your area. From this date, decide when cold weather crops can be successfully planted and when hot weather crops can be planted. Then read the seed packet carefully to find out how much time is required for growing the seeds to the correct size plant for transplanting into the garden. Count back from your estimated planting date and you will arrive at a date when you should start seeds indoors. Follow this projection closely. If you start seeds too early, the plants will probably grow too large for their containers by the time you are able to plant them outside. This oversize condition will cause them to become rootbound, weakening them so that they are more susceptible to shock during transplanting. When you plant the seeds too late, the seedlings will not be mature enough to transplant easily. They will often be too small and fragile to survive long in the garden.

Here is an example of how I determine when to start tomato seed. In my area the average day of last frost is May 10. Each year I use this day as the day to aim for to transplant tomatoes into the garden. Tomatoes need about eight weeks of growth before they are planted outside. Counting back eight weeks from May 10, I arrive at a starting date sometime around mid March. You can do the same calculation for any plant as long as you know when they can be safely planted into the garden and how old they should be at transplanting time.

Damping-Off

Damping-off is a fungus disease that attacks the stems of small plants. This disease is also known as "black root" and "wire stem." Its symptoms include seedlings with very thin and fragile stems which cannot support the plant's leaves. The plant falls over and dies.

Although the disease is caused by several types of fungi, they all have similar growth characteristics. These fungi tend to grow near the surface of the soil and enter plants where the stem emerges from the soil. An early indication of this problem is a white fuzz on the surface of the soil in your seedling flats. All of these fungi require a high moisture level in the soil and the air just above the soil in order to do their damage.

You can reduce the chance of damping-off by pasteurizing your soil before planting seeds and then not over-watering once the seeds have germinated. Another line of attack is to water growing seedlings with a mixture of liquid seaweed and water. Whenever I notice a fungus growth on my seed flats, I mix a solution of 1 tablespoon of liquid seaweed in 1 quart of water and then water the bed with this infusion immediately. The fungus disappears and damping-off is prevented.

As you have probably guessed, the damping-off disease is carried by the soil or compost you add to your potting mixture. You can reduce damping-off by pasteurizing the soil or compost you add to your potting mixture. There are several ways to pasteurize your soil. One is to bake these materials in an oven at 160° F for two hours. Stir the material every 15 minutes. This treatment will kill most of the harmful critters in your soil or compost without damaging the helpful ones to any great extent.

You can also rid your soil of harmful pests and disease by pouring boiling water through it. One gallon is usually sufficient for a standard size flat. Another method is pouring water laced with vinegar through the soil. Mix 1 cup of vinegar in a quart of water and pour this slowly through the soil in a single flat. Allow the soil to rest at least 24 hours after either of these treatments before planting seeds.

Flats and Pots

Flat is the term used to describe the tray-like container in which seedlings are grown (Fig. 8-5).

131

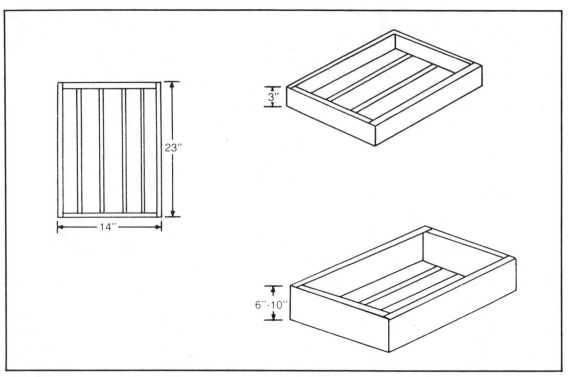

Fig. 8-5. Top view (left) and side views (right) of common seed flats.

Standard-size flats are 3 inches deep by 14 inches wide and 24 inches long. Although the width and length of flats is not critical, they should be easy to handle when loaded with moist soil. The depth of a flat is its most important dimension.

Flats with a depth of less than 3 inches can spell trouble for seedlings. When the roots of some seedlings hit bottom, they think that they have reached the limit of their growth. Many will shift to their seed-formation stage. Plants that have reached this stage are useless for transplanting. Other plants will simply bend their tap root along the bottom of the flat. This weakens them so that later when they are transplanted, they do not do as well as transplants grown in deeper flats. Flats that are 6 inches deep should be used for plants that will grow for more than 6 weeks in the same flat without transplanting.

Flats should be made from a nonrotting wood like cedar or redwood. These woods are expensive, and you may want to opt for a cheaper alternative

such as pine. These lesser woods will last a long time when properly cleaned and dried at the end of the seedling growing season. Under no circumstance should you use wood treated with preservatives for flat construction. When a wood preservative is desired, use linseed oil. There is also a wide variety of plastic flats on the market. The thicker the plastic and the heavier the construction, the better.

When making your own flats, the ends can be made from a single piece of wood of the desired width. The long sides and bottom are made from lathing. Leave ⅛ inch of space between lathing strips to allow adequate drainage.

There are several varieties of natural planting pots on the market. These range from pressed sphagnum moss pots to those made from pressed dried manure. These pots are planted with the seedling in the garden and so minimize root damage during transplanting. They come in round, square and multiple-compartment shapes that resemble an ice cube tray. Some have chemical fertilizers blended right into the pot material, and others are held together with plastic netting. The type of pot you choose depends largely on what you can purchase conveniently in your area. If you keep the pots in flats while the plants are growing, the square ones will fit into the flat better and reduce the chance of tipping over the plants.

In addition to the natural material pots there are planting pots made of plastic and clay. These pots cannot be planted with the seedling, so some root damage is likely to occur during transplanting. These pots can, however, be used again and again, reducing your cost. In fact, anything from cutoff milk cartons to yogurt containers can be used as planting pots as long as they are at least 3 inches deep and have water drainage holes in the bottom. Remember: the bigger the pot the more room roots have for growth. The bigger the root system is at transplanting time the better the seedling will do.

Hardening-Off

The idea behind hardening-off seedlings is to affect a smooth transition from the growing conditions found inside your home or greenhouse to the harsh realities of life in the garden. The hardening-off process exposes seedlings to garden conditions for a short time at first, increasing the length of exposure time each day until after about 2 weeks the plants are fully adjusted to life outside.

The hardening-off process should be timed so that at the end of the 2-week acclimation period (beginning when the plants are first brought out and ending when they are transplanted into the ground) the plants are fully used to life outside. The best way to harden-off seedlings is to reduce their water

Fig. 8-6. Harden-off seedlings by placing them in a sheltered location for increasing periods of time until they can withstand full days and nights outside.

and fertilizer ration a week prior to taking them outside for the first time. The plants should not be allowed to wilt, but the top of the soil should be relatively dry to the touch. Then carry them, still in their flats, to a cold frame.

Place the flats in the cold frame and leave the lid shut for the first few days. Be careful not to allow the seedlings to get too hot during the day, and do not allow the sun to scald their tender leaves. After the first few days, leave the lid open slightly day and night. Gradually expand the size of the opening until the plants can withstand having the lids removed entirely. For the earliest crops, where days are warm enough for growth but nights still freeze, the lid can be closed shortly before sunset to keep heat in through the night. The lid should be opened before sunlight falls on the cold frame in the morning.

If you do not have a cold frame yet (everyone who is serious about starting their own seedlings has one), you can harden-off plants simply by carrying them outside during the warmest part of the day 2 weeks prior to the time you expect to set them out. Place the plants in a sheltered shady location (Fig. 8-6). Bring them inside at night the first week. Gradually increase the time they spend outside and their exposure to the sun. At the end of the two-week period, they should be able to stand full sun through the day as well as remaining outside 24 hours a day. The plants are now ready to be planted in the garden.

Cold Frames

A cold frame is a garden structure designed like a bottomless box with a clear lid. It traps the sun's warming rays while protecting plants against cold air, wind and other unfavorable growing conditions. You can use cold frames to harden-off seedlings prior to transplanting or for starting cold weather crops when unprotected ground is still too cold to work.

You can make a cold frame from plywood or other scrap lumber, old window sashes, or a wooden frame over which plastic is stretched. The ends of the cold frame are usually 10 to 12 inches tall in the front, 18 to 24 inches tall at the back, and

wide enough so that the angled top edge (from front to back) matches the width of the window sash or plastic-covered frame you use as a top. The front and back pieces are long enough so that they accommodate the length of the clear top used to cover the frame. The sides, front, and back can be screwed, nailed, or held in place with hook and eyes (Fig. 8-7). The latter is best, since it allows the cold frame to be taken apart and folded for storage. Two strips of wood should be nailed or screwed to the front and back edges of the sides so that they form a channel. The front and back pieces are then slid down into this channel in order to make the cold frame stand on its own. The wood on a cold frame should be painted to prevent water damage. Do not use treated wood since the preservatives will dam-

Fig. 8-7. Hook and eye latches at the corners of a cold frame allow the frame to be folded up and stored when not in use.

age plants inside the bed. The sashes can be secured on the back of the frame with hinges or left unattached for easy removal and access to the bed.

A cold frame is used to control three growing conditions: temperature, light and humidity. Temperature control is its major function. During the day, the glass on a cold frame taps the sun's radiation and turns it into heat. This heat is then stored by the mass of the soil. A thermometer is handy for controlling the temperature within the cold frame. On bright sunny days when the inside temperature soars above 85° F, crack the lid to allow ventilation. At night, when temperatures drop, the lid can be closed to retain heat. Usually, the cold frame will keep temperatures inside a few degrees warmer than the outside temperature at night. During the day the temperature difference may be from 30° to 60°F.

Light is important to plant growth and to make the cold frame work effectively. You should locate the cold frame where it will get maximum light. This usually means facing south. You can increase the amount of reflected light the frame receives by placing its back wall against the south wall of your house or another structure. In southern regions where light intensity may be too much for the plants in the frame, you can filter the sunlight by draping cheese cloth over the frame, or by whitewashing the glass so that the light is diffused.

The humidity requirements for most seedlings is rather high—around 80 percent. A heavy condensation on the glass means that the moisture level in your cold frame is too high. To eliminate this problem simply raise the lid of the cold frame for a few minutes each morning.

When using a cold frame to start seedlings or to harden off different types of plants, it is a good idea to divide the frame into two sections. One section will be planted with cold-tolerant plants such as the cole crops. A few weeks later when the soil has warmed sufficiently, you can plant heat-loving plants like tomatoes, peppers, and cucumbers in the second section.

Most plants, regardless of whether they are cold-tolerant or heat-loving, do best at air temperatures around 70° (Table 8-2). You can regulate the

Table 8-2. Selected Cold Frame Temperatures of Some Common Garden Plants.

65° F day - 55° F night	
Broccoli	Cauliflower
Brussels sprouts	Lettuce
Cabbage	Spinach
75° F day - 65° F night	
Tomato	Squash
Eggplant	Melons
Pepper	

temperature by adjusting the cold frame's lid. Be careful when opening the frame that cold winds do not swoop down on the seedlings. After a night of nice warm air, a cold blast will upset even the hardiest of plants. It is better to open the cold frame a little at a time, say at 5-minute intervals, to create a smooth transition of temperatures.

Cold frames can also be used to extend the growing season well into late fall. Make a sowing of lettuce, endive, and turnips (for greens) a week or two after the first frost. Close the cold frame and allow seeds to germinate. Keep the temperature regulated near 65° F and you should be harvesting greens well past Thanksgiving.

Another way to use the cold frame is to make a sowing of your late crop of spinach in a block of ground slightly smaller than the size of your cold frame. When night time temperatures begin dipping below freezing, place the cold frame over this planting. The protection afforded by the cold frame will keep spinach going strong several weeks later than usual.

If plants in a cold frame freeze at night, sprinkle them with cold water and cover the frame so that it is dark for half an hour. Uncover it, and plants should recover from the freeze.

When nights begin to grow very cold, surround the cold frame with bales of straw or bagged leaves to act as insulation. You may want to cover the glass with a blanket to hold in more heat. Remove blanket during the day and open the frame on sunny days. On overcast days you will want to leave the frame closed to conserve heat.

The cold frame should be closed several hours before sunset to allow enough heat to build up inside the frame to keep it above freezing through the night. There are no hard and fast guidelines for this procedure, so you will have to experiment to find out what is best for your area.

Hot Beds

Hot beds are nothing more than cold frames with a source of heat. There are two methods for keeping a hot frame warm: electricity and natural heat.

Electric warming cables are available for keeping the soil in hot frames at the perfect temperature for good seedling growth. Unfortunately, electricity is getting more expensive each year. Natural heating methods utilize the heat produced by the decay of organic matter to warm the seedbed. Although this method is a little trickier than burying a cable in the hot bed's soil, it is a virtually free source of heat.

Hot beds heated naturally are made by making a small compost heap in a pit over which a cold frame is placed. As the material in the compost breaks down, heat is created. This heat filters upward through the soil placed over the compost to warm the seedlings (Fig. 8-8). To make your own hot bed, follow these simple instructions.

The first step in preparing a hot bed is getting the compost material ready. You will need a hot (rich in nitrogen and biologically-active) material like horse or chicken manure mixed with about twice its own volume of straw, leaves, or other litter. Insufficient litter will result in a compost that heats quickly, but also loses its heat quickly. The idea is to get a good even temperature from this heat source for as long a time as possible.

About 10 days to 2 weeks before the manure is to be placed in the pit, shovel the manure into a pile and water it. The material should heat up within 3 to 4 days. Turn it and allow it to reheat. After the second heating, the manure is ready to place in the pit. The pit should be 2½ feet deep and the same size as the frame to be placed over it. Fill the pit until manure reaches to within 6 inches of the top of the pit. Tamp the manure so that heating is more

uniform and excess settling does not occur. Sift 6 inches of rich garden soil or potting mix over the manure so that the bed is level.

The material in the pit should heat up again. This is fine, since the heat will kill many weed seeds and pathogens in the soil above it. The bed is ready to use when the temperature has dropped to about 85° F. Do not plant seeds when bed is first made because they will suffer, the same as weed seeds do, from the excess heat.

Many seedlings can be started directly in the hot bed and then transplanted to other areas of the garden when weather conditions are correct. Heat-loving plants like eggplant, peppers, tomatoes, squash, and cucumbers do best when grown in a hot bed. If you make the hot bed in the garden, the space should be planted to a plant that

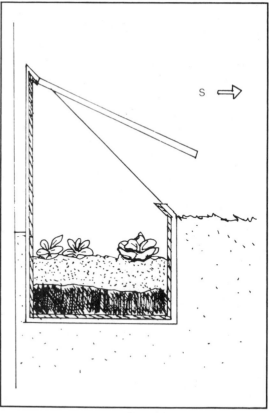

Fig. 8-8. A hot bed is no more than a cold frame with a source of heat—in this case, decomposing manure in the bottom of the frame.

Fig. 8-9. You can make cloches for tender garden plants from a variety of materials, cut-off beverage containers, up-turned cottage cheese containers, paper bags, and buckets are used, as well as a hat made of newspaper.

requires rich soil after the frame has served its purpose.

Cloches

Cloches or hot caps are widely used in Europe in place of the cold and hot frames used in America. A cloche is anything you can place over a plant after it has been planted in the garden to protect the plant against the weather. This way, instead of bringing the plant inside, it remains outside in the garden. Cloches create a more-or-less constant environment by protecting plants from wind, rain and pests.

Commercial cloches come in all shapes and sizes, but most are made from translucent plastic. Many fold up for easy storage. You can also make our own from virtually any material except metal

that will fit over your plants (Fig. 8-9). Cloches made from opaque materials should be removed from plants each morning so that they get their full share of sunlight. Replace the caps each evening to protect the plants against falling night temperatures.

TWO METHODS

There are two basic methods for growing your own seedlings. The first is called the two-step method, and the second is called the one-step method. The two-step method involves sowing seeds in flats and then transferring them to peat pots or deeper flats for continued growth prior to transplanting into the garden. In the one-step method, seeds are sown directly into the container in which they will live until planted into the garden.

Two-Step Method

To plant seeds using the two-step method, fill flats with a commercial or homemade soil mix. Prior to putting soil in your flats, it should be sieved through a screen with 1/4- to 1/6-inch holes. Then the soil should be moistened with water until it forms a ball when squeezed, but is still sufficiently dry so that it falls apart easily when poked with a finger. Seeding soils containing dry sphagnum or peat moss are hard to wet. You will probably have to work the water into the soil with your fingers or chop the water in a little at a time with a trowel. Wet soil in a 5-gallon bucket or wheelbarrow, depending on the amount of soil you need.

Scoop the soil into the flats. Soil should be level with the top of the flat and completely filled into the corners. Scrape soil off level with the top of the flat with a straightedge. At this point, the soil

should be resilient and showing a tendency to spring back into place after being pressed lightly. Pack the soil lightly to ensure a firm seedbed.

Using a pencil, dowel rod, or your finger, make shallow furrows in the seedbed. Furrows should be 2 to 3 inches apart and can run lengthwise or across the flat. When more than one kind of seed is to be sown in a flat, choose seeds that mature at the same rate for the same flat. This way the entire flat can be transplated at the same time.

Water the flat with a fine mist spray until water runs out the bottom of the flat, or place the flat in a shallow tray of water until the surface becomes quite moist. As a preventative measure against damping-off, you can add a teaspoon of liquid seaweed to each quart of watering solution.

When the soil is moist, sow seed directly from the package into the furrows. Where more than one

Fig. 8-10. A fine mist spray does a dandy job of watering small seedlings without washing them out of the soil.

to retain moisture and to keep temperatures near 75° F. While seed flats are covered, the cover should be removed at least once a day in order to inspect the seedbed and to allow air to circulate. Keep a sharp eye out for fungus or mold on the soil. Remove the covering completely and leave it off if this problem arises.

When the first few seeds have germinated and poked through the soil, remove the cover and expose the flats to light—the more the better. Keep soil moist, but not waterlogged (Fig. 8-10). If seedlings were planted too thickly they need to be thinned by trimming unwanted sprouts with scissors. Do not jerk unwanted seedlings from the bed or you will disturb the roots of nearby plants.

When the first true leaves have formed on your plants dig the strongest plants out of the flat and transfer to individual peat pots, clay pots, or a 6-inch-deep flat (Fig. 8-11). Seedlings should be spaced at least 2 inches apart in the flat, and they should be buried slightly deeper than they were in the original flat (Fig. 8-12). Handle these tender seedlings only by their leaves and try to damage roots as little as possible. By the time plants reach 6 inches in height, they will be ready to harden-off and then transplant into the garden.

One-Step Method

The one-step method of seedling production requires the same considered care as the two-step method. The major advantage of the one-step method is that it allows plants to grow without suffering the root shock associated with transplanting. Additionally, this method saves time by eliminating one transplanting.

In the one-step method, instead of planting seeds in a flat they are sown directly into peat pots filled with moist potting mix. Place two seeds in each pot and cover with a sprinkling of potting soil. After the first true leaves have formed, the weaker of the two plants is snipped off with scissors. Make sure to label each pot so that you know what is growing in it.

Large-seeded plants such as cucumbers, squash, and melons prefer this planting method since their roots do not like to be disturbed once

Fig. 8-11. When seedlings have developed their first set of true leaves, transfer them to individual containers or deeper flats.

type of seed is sown in a flat, label each furrow so that you know what is growing there. Labels can be made from a lot of things; for instance, popsicle sticks, or cut-up cottage cheese containers. Mark these labels with a waterproof marker such as a grease pencil. If you do not use a waterproof marking material, a few waterings will wash the label off.

Cover seeds in furrows with a thin layer of potting soil, sand, peat moss, or vermiculite. Firm the soil lightly and water with a fine mist spray or by soaking from below. Be careful not to wash seeds out of the soil.

The freshly planted seed flats should be covered with newspaper, plastic bags, or glass in order

Fig. 8-12. Top, a properly-buried seedling has plenty of support for its stem. Bottom, a shallowly-buried seedling is likely to fall over and not grow well.

they begin to grow. When plants are 6 inches tall, they can be hardened-off and transplanted into the garden.

TRANSPLANTING INTO THE GARDEN

Transplanting seedlings into the garden is one of the most important, yet hazardous, stages of a plant's life. It is hazardous because you are taking a plant out of a protected and pampered environment and sticking it into the open, often cruel, environment of your garden. This change in growing condi-

tions can produce a shock capable of killing your seedlings. Proper hardening-off prior to transplanting is a must. Another precaution is transplanting on cloudy days, early in the morning, or late in the evening so that the sun will not damage tender plant roots.

Some plants suffer more from transplanting than others (Table 8-3). The easiest plants to set out are broccoli, cabbage, cauliflower, lettuce, onions, and tomatoes. Slightly more difficult to transplant are beans, eggplants, peppers, and celery. Difficult, but not impossible, plants to set out are corn, cucumbers, melons, and squash. Those plants not worth starting in flats include the tap root plants like beets, carrots, and turnips.

During transplanting, it is important to handle seedlings as little as possible and to handle them properly. Hold them by the tips of their leaves, or by the soil ball around their roots. Never lift them by the stem as this is the most sensitive part of the plant. Also, plants should never be removed from their pots or flats before a hole is prepared for them in the garden. The roots cannot stand even a little sun and allowing your seedlings to lay exposed to the sun while you dig a hole is a very dangerous practice.

The holes you dig in the garden for transplants should be wide and deep enough to allow good root spread. After you dig the hole for a seedling throw in a handful of compost and some balanced organic fertilizer (Fig. 8-3). Mix the compost and fertilizer with the garden dirt at the bottom of the hole, then water (Fig. 8-14). When water has drained from the hole it is ready for the seedling. Make sure the hole is deep enough so that the plant can be buried up to its first set of true leaves. This way as the soil is packed down during watering all of the roots will remain underground. An additional reason for planting seedlings up to their first set of leaves is to provide support for the plant. When planted too shallowly the plants become top heavy and fall over from the wind.

When you transplant seedlings into the garden from flats, some of the plant's roots will be torn away as they are lifted from the flat. You can reduce this damage by watering the flat heavily an hour or

Table 8-3. Use This Table to Decide Which Plants Are Worth Growing as Transplants and Which Are Not.

Easily Transplanted	Somewhat Difficult	Not Successfully Transplanted
Broccoli	Celery	Bean
Brussels sprouts	Cucumber	Carrot
Cabbage	Eggplant	Corn
Cauliflower	Muskmelon	Lima beans
Chard	Onion	Peas
Lettuce	Pepper	Turnip
Tomato	Salsify	
	Squash	
	Watermelon	

Fig. 8-13. Add a handful of compost and organic soil to holes for transplants.

Fig. 8-14. Water transplant hole after compost and fertilizer are in place. Allow water to drain from hole.

141

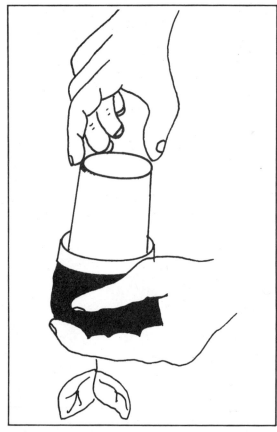

Fig. 8-15. Turn permanent pots upside down and tap out transplant. Handle by the root ball to prevent damaging stems.

Fig. 8-16. Even peat pots, which are supposed to allow root growth, should be torn up a little prior to planting to encourage good root growth.

two before transplanting. Then, when you remove the seedling from the flat, take as big a root ball as possible with the plant. Many people find that a regular kitchen fork is one of the best plant-looseners around.

When transplanting seedlings grown in clay or plastic pots, removing the plant from the pot must be accomplished with minimal root damage. The proper way to remove the plant is to slip the plant stem between your second and third fingers so that your palm rests on the lip of the pot (Fig. 8-15). Grasp the pot with this hand and turn it upside down. Tap the bottom of the pot with a trowel or tap the edge of the pot on a solid object until you feel the root ball loosen. Slip the pot off and cradle the plant

Fig. 8-17. An improperly-buried peat pot will wick water away from plant roots.

Fig. 8-18. A properly-buried peat pot will not present the evaporation problems associated with an improperly-buried peat pot.

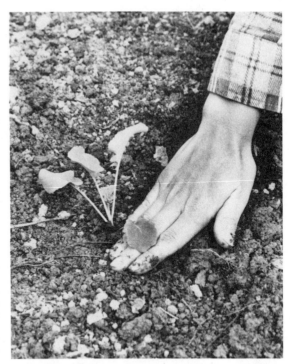

Fig. 8-19. Pack dirt around transplants to remove air pockets, which slow root growth.

Fig. 8-20. Tender transplants need protection against cutworms. A cutworm collar pushed 1 inch into the soil works well.

in your hand. Place it into the hole you have prepared for it.

Root damage can be almost entirely eliminated by planting seedlings grown in peat or pressed manure pots. During transplanting the whole pot is simply buried. It is, however, a good idea to break the pot a little or tear the bottom off in order to encourage the growth of roots out of the pot and into the surrounding soil (Fig. 8-16). When plants in peat pots are buried in the garden make sure to cover the top edges of the peat pot with soil (Fig. 8-17 and Fig. 8-18). If you do not, the pot will act as a wick through which water can evaporate, reducing the amount available to the plant.

When you are satisfied with the way the plant

looks in the garden, pack the soil loosely around the plant (Fig. 8-19). This will ensure that roots contact the soil. Do not pack too tightly as this will reduce the inflow of water and air. Not packing the soil at all will allow air pockets to form, inhibiting root growth. You should water plants after transplanting to help settle the soil, to eliminate excess air, and to provide water for growth. You can use a dilute solution of manure or compost tea or a solution of fish emulsion and seaweed for this initial watering. Plants should be kept moist after planting until they have established themselves in the garden.

Also, place a collar around the new transplants to prevent cutworm damage (Fig. 8-20). A cutworm collar can be made from stiff cardboard or plastic rings cut from the top of drinking cups. Push the collar 1 inch into the ground and leave 2 inches or more exposed above ground.

Growing your own transplants from seed will be rewarding and save you money. There is nothing mysterious or difficult about it if you take the time and effort to do the job right.

Chapter 9

Planting

God Almighty first planted a garden.
—Francis Bacon

Like a journey of a thousand miles that begins with a single step, an abundant harvest begins with the proper sowing of a single seed. Although planting seeds is not the most difficult aspect of gardening, it is an important one. The manner in which you plant your seeds will determine how and where each plant in your garden grows.

When you plant a seed, you are putting a tiny, dormant plant into the ground in hopes that it will break dormancy, grow to adulthood, and mature into food for your table. A seed's life is a perilous one since there are many hazards in a garden that can prevent a seed from growing to its full potential. Among these obstacles are disease, insects, drought, excess moisture, temperature extremes, lack of light, wind, and other plants that fight root and leaf for their share of a garden's life giving properties. It is you, the gardener, who must orchestrate the growth of your vegetable plants to achieve the maximum yield from your garden.

Seeds are pretty tough. They can withstand environmental extremes that would kill a plant, but during the first few weeks after a seed's germination, every plant is extremely vulnerable. The new seedling needs a proper combination of water, warmth, air, light, and nutrients to survive. For instance, once moisture has been added to a seed, it cannot be cut off without destroying the seedling. Air, too, is needed so that the seedling can transpire carbon dioxide and take up oxygen. Temperature is equally important, and a seedling without light and nutrients will not be able to manufacture its own food and will quickly die. That is what this chapter is all about: how to get the seeds you plant in your garden off to a good start, so that you will be able to harvest their rewards throughout the growing season.

THE FROST FACTOR

After a long cold winter there is nothing most gardeners would rather do than plant vegetable seeds. Getting the earliest start possible is the goal of virtually every gardener for a couple of very good reasons. Diseases and pests are the least trouble-some early in the season. Getting a crop into the ground as early as possible provides less chance for insects and diseases to do their damage. Planting too early can mean trouble.

Planting your seeds in season, when they will grow during the weather conditions they prefer, is the best way to ensure that the plants spend their energy producing food. When plants are forced to grow out of season through planting at the improper time, they spend all their energy battling excesses of heat or cold, drought, or inadequate amounts of light. In addition to not being able to produce well, plants in this state of imbalance are susceptible to disease and insect attack. In most cases the result is that your vegetables spend all their energy simply trying to survive instead of producing food for your table.

The time for spring seed planting revolves around the last frost date for your area. Many seeds can be sown prior to the average date of last spring frost. Others should not be planted until all danger of frost is past. A good natural indicator of the last

freeze date—after which frost will occur, but cold-hardy plants will survive—are oak trees. Oak trees usually leaf out about the time of the last spring freeze.

If you do not have any oak trees in your neighborhood, you can use the map in Fig. 7-6 to get a good idea of the average last frost date for your area. Unfortunately, no two places in each of these zones has exactly the same last frost date. If you live in a valley, chances are that you will experience frost later than someone who lives on a hill. You can ask your county extension agent, other gardeners, or the employees of nearby garden shops for more precise estimates of the last average frost date for your area.

Vegetables fall into two rough categories in relation to their ability to withstand cold or hot weather. Some plants are hardy (cold-tolerant); others are tender (heat-loving). Most of the cold-tolerant crops thrive in cool spring and fall weather. Their growth is hindered by the hot days of summer. On the other hand, the heat-loving crops are damaged by the cool weather of spring and fall,

Table 9-1. This Table Shows Cold and Heat Tolerances of Many Common Garden Vegetables.

Hardiness of Crops (Grouped According to Planting Times)				
Very Hardy Plant 6 Weeks Prior to Last Spring Frost	**Hardy** Plant 2 Weeks Prior to Last Spring Frost	**Not Hardy** Plant on Last Frost Date	**Heat-Loving** Plant 1 to 2 Weeks After Last Frost	**Hardy** Plant 2 Months Prior to First Fall Freeze
Broccoli	Beets	Cucumbers	Cantaloupe	Beets
Cabbage	Carrots	New Zealand spinach	Chard	Broccoli
Collards	Chard	Okra	Eggplant	Cabbage
Garlic	Chinese cabbage	Pumpkins	Lima beans	Cauliflower
Kale	Green manure crops	Soybeans	Peppers	Chard
Lettuce	Jerusalem artichokes	Snap beans	Sweet potatoes	Chinese cabbage
Onions	Kohlrabi	Summer squash	Watermelon	Collards
Peas	Mustard	Sweet corn	Winter squash	Cover crops (winter)
Potatoes	Parsnips	Tomatoes		Kale
Spinach	Radishes			Lettuce
Turnips				Mustard
				Peas (edible pod)
				Radishes
				Rutabaga
				Spinach
				Turnips

146

though they thrive in the hot days of summer. Table 9-1 should help clear up which plants are which and when they can be planted for best results.

PLANTING DEPTH

Seeds are very particular about how deeply they are planted. Generally, small seeds (carrots, lettuce and radishes, for example) should not be planted more than ¼ of an inch deep. Larger seeds (beans, peas and corn) should be planted ½ inch to 1 inch deep. These guidelines are far from hard and fast rules. A better way to gauge planting depth is to look at the size of a seed. Most vegetable seeds should be planted deep enough so that when you rake dirt over them the dirt layer is as deep as the seeds are wide. The condition of your soil (texture and temperature), however, may call for adjusting the planting depth of your seeds. When the soil is heavy and soil temperature is low, seeds may be planted slightly shallower than normal. In light soils or during warm weather, the seeds should be planted slightly deeper than normal.

A good way to make sure that larger seeds get off to a good fast start in your garden is to soak them overnight before planting. The seeds will soak up water and swell to almost twice their dry size. In addition to providing ample moisture for the first stages of germination, this pre-planting soak also softens the shell of the seed allowing it to split and send forth the plant's first tiny root (radical) and seed leaves (cotyledon).

Too much of a good thing, even moisture, can cause problems. When seeds are to be planted in wet, cold ground they should not be soaked overnight. The excess moisture will allow various fungi and seed rots a chance to put the seed out of commission before it can break ground. Pre-planting soaking is, however, a good practice for seeds to be sown in dry soils, or for seeds sown in midsummer.

For midsummer sowings, make sure to water the seedbed thoroughly after planting in addition to soaking seeds, so that the seeds will have enough moisture for germination. Unfortunately, clay soils will often form a crust that hinders seedlings by keeping them from pushing up through the soil's surface. You can prevent this in one of two ways.

First, you can cover seeds with compost instead of garden soil. Compost will not crust and it will act as a mulch, keeping the seeds moist throughout germination. Second, you can cover the seeds with boards, newspapers, or a light mulch of grass clippings. This will prevent the soil from crusting and will retain moisture. Check the seedbed daily. When the first seed sprout appears, remove the boards or newspaper mulches. Seeds will be able to push their way through light grass clipping or compost mulches.

GERMINATION TIMES

Some seeds germinate faster than others. These different germination rates are a natural part of the growing habits of seeds. Soil temperature and moisture content have a lot to do with the speed at which different seeds germinate. As a rule, the lower the moisture content or temperature of a soil, the slower a seed will germinate. Table 9-2 shows how long various seeds take to germinate under

Table 9-2. Not All Seeds Are Created Equal. Some Germinate Faster than Others. 10-15

Germination Times			
0-5 days			
Chinese Cabbage	4-5	Turnip	4-7
Radish	4-6		
5-10 days			
Beets	8-10	Lettuce	6-8
Broccoli	6-10	Lima beans	7-10
Brussels sprouts	6-10	Mustard	6-8
Cabbage	6-10	Okra	8-10
Cauliflower	5-10	Onion	8-10
Celery	5-10	Parsley	8-10
Chard	8-10	Peas	7-10
Chives	5-10	Pumpkin	8-10
Collard	5-10	Rutabaga	5-8
Corn	5-9	Snap beans	7-10
Cucumber	8-10	Spinach	5-9
Endive	8-10	Squash	8-10
Kale	6-10	Tomato	8-10
Kohlrabi	7-10	Watermelon	8-10
Leek	8-10		
10-15 days			
Carrots	10-15	Parsnips	12-15
Eggplant	10-12	Peppers	12-15
20 or More Days			
Potatoes (sprouting)	21-28		

ideal conditions. If for some reason your seeds do not germinate within their allotted time, allow an extra week before digging up the seedbed and starting over. When you do dig up the seedbed, check closely for indications of fungus, disease, or underground pests which may have destroyed the seeds.

THINNING

One of the common mistakes gardeners make is sowing seeds too thickly. The reason this is often done is that in the early stages of growth, when seeds have just peeked through the soil, there are often gaps between the seedings. A 3- to 4-inch gap when plants are this small looks a lot bigger than a 3- to 4-inch gap between mature plants. Most gardeners tend to sow thickly to prevent gaps between seedlings. The result is a row or bed of seedlings that comes up cotyledon to cotyledon. This close spacing looks great during the early stages of growth but before long the plants are crowding each other (Fig. 9-1). They must be thinned for proper growth.

Not thinning crowded seedlings will result in weak plants that are susceptible to damping-off diseases and insect attack. Additionally, plants that are crowded become spindly instead of stocky during their early growth, which makes them weaker later in the season. You can save both time and seeds by sowing seeds thinly so that little thinning is required later on.

Invariably, some sowings will be too thick. This is especially true for small seeds which are difficult to spread evenly during planting. Thinning will be necessary to give the plants enough growing room. Here are a few thinning tips.

● Thin when plants are small.
● Thin when soil is moist so that plants can be pulled out easily without harming the roots of those plants left behind. (Better yet, snip off plants to be removed from the row or bed with scissors. This prevents disturbing surrounding roots.)
● Thin stunted or misshapen plants first.
● Thin bug-eaten or diseased plants first.
● Remove thinned plants from the garden so that they do not attract pests or encourage disease.

Fig. 9-1. This spinach is too close together. As the plants grow, crowding will result. Thinning is necessary to give plants room to spread during growth.

● Thin plants with taproots (carrots, beets, turnips) before taproots become fleshy.
● Radishes can be left in the ground until those to be thinned are large enough to eat.
● Carrots should be thinned when 2 to 3 inches tall. After thinning, remaining plants should be 1 inch apart. When carrots reach finger size, pull every other carrot, leaving room for those left behind.
● Cucumbers and melons in hills should be thinned to the two or three strongest plants per hill when 4 to 6 inches tall.
● Beans and corn should be sown far enough apart so that thinning is unnecessary.
● Lettuce should be allowed to grow until big enough to eat before thinning.

• Beets should be thinned when 4 to 5 inches tall and their leaves eaten for greens. Thin to 3 inches between plants.

FIVE WAYS TO PLANT SEEDS

There are many ways to sow seed. Here are five common methods which can be adopted to your garden design and cultivation methods.

Rows

Row planting is the most common method of seed planting. This method is necessary for crops to be cultivated with tillers or wheel cultivators.

After the seedbed has been tilled and raked smooth, put stakes in at the ends of the bed so that the line between the stakes corresponds to where rows are drawn on your garden plan. Most people prefer to run their rows north to south, but east to west rows are just as effective. The only real problem arises when tall plants are grown to the south of short plants because the taller plants reduce the light reaching the shorter plants. This problem should be considered and worked out when planning your garden on paper.

When stakes are in place, tie a stout cord to one stake and wrap the loose end around the stake at the opposite end of the seedbed. Pull the cord tight enough to be lifted free of the ground. This will ensure that the row is straight. When the string is in place, make a seed furrow beneath it. For fine seeds, your hoe handle will probably make a sufficiently deep furrow. Larger seeds require a deeper furrow, and the corner of your hoe blade can be used for this job. In either case, the depth of the furrow should be about twice as deep as your seed is wide. If you desire, a balanced organic fertilizer can be sprinkled into the furrow at this point.

Sow small seeds by shaking them out of the package. Tearing a corner off of the seed packet will make a good spout. Larger seeds should be placed one by one in the row (Fig. 9-2). When the row is seeded, rake or hoe soil over the seeds. In cloddy soils, try to rake only the finest dirt over the seeds. In sandy soils the dirt can be tamped lightly to help hold the soil in place against wind and rain. In heavy soil, do not tamp the dirt over the seed because crusting is likely to result and the seeds will have a difficult time pushing their way through this barrier.

Finally, mark each row with a waterproof marker or the empty seed packet. You may want to water the row after planting. (This will not be necessary when the soil is cool and moist.) Watering will increase the germination success of mid-summer plantings in hot dry soils.

Broadcasting

With the increasing popularity of bed gardening and planting crops in blocks instead of rows, broadcasting seed has gained prominence. This

Fig. 9-2. Large seeds should be placed one at a time into a furrow. Space seeds so that later thinning is not required.

Fig. 9-3. Mix small seeds with coffee grounds, sand, or sifted compost prior to broadcasting to keep seeds from clumping together.

Hills

The seeds of vining plants are often sown in hills when the vines are to be allowed to run across the ground. To make a hill, dig a hole about 1 foot across and 1 foot deep. Put a 6-inch-deep layer of well-rotted manure or compost in the bottom of the hole. A balanced organic fertilizer can also be added. Replace the dirt, pack slightly, and plant seeds in the hill at their desired depth. Water the hill if soil is dry. Sow about six seeds per hill, and thin to the three strongest plants when first or second set of leaves appear.

The advantage of planting in hills is that the raised areas indicate where the roots of the sprawling plants are located. The organic matter and fertilizer placed in each hill also provides a ready source of food for these heavy feeding vines.

The distance between hills is determined by the length of the vines. Hills for watermelon and squash vines are usually made 10 to 12 feet apart. Shorter vines, like cucumbers, need only 5 feet between hills. Corn can also be planted in hills when you do not have enough room to plant it in rows.

Drills

The drill method of planting is a variation of the row planting method. Instead of digging a furrow

method is an effective way of sowing small seeds. After the seedbed has been prepared, the seeds are simply scattered over the area and then a thin layer of soil, compost, or peat moss is sprinkled over the seeds. To help reduce clumping of seeds during sowing, mix the seeds with two or three times their own volume of sand, dried coffee grounds, or fine dirt, and then broadcast this mixture over the seedbed with your hands (Fig. 9-3).

Planting seeds with the broadcast method will necessitate hand weeding during the early stages of the crop's growth since the plants will not be uniformly spaced and hoeing will be difficult. Mulch around plants once they are established to help reduce the amount of weeding needed.

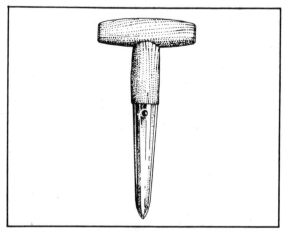

Fig. 9-4. This tool, called a dibble, is designed to punch a hole in the soil. A seed is placed in each hole and then covered with soil (courtesy of Smith Hawken Tool Co.).

with your hoe, make a hole in the soil where each seed is to go. A sharp stick or a tool called a dibble—designed specifically for this job—can be used to make the drills (Fig. 9-4). Make the hole the proper depth for the seed. Drop a seed in each hole and then fill the holes with soil or compost.

A variation of this method is to push individual seeds to their desired depth with your finger. This is an effective method for planting peas in the early spring when the soil may be too wet to work. Small seeds are very difficult to handle using the drill method. Plant smaller seeds by broadcasting or in shallow furrows.

Pattern Planting

This method is also known as *diagonally offset* or *equidistant pattern planting*. It is similar to the broadcast method of planting, except that instead of letting the seeds fall where they may (and hoping that they are evenly spaced), you sow each seed at an equal distance from surrounding seeds. The idea is to plant individual seeds far enough apart so that when they are mature the outer leaves of the adult plants touch. Plants in this configuration act as a living mulch that shades the soil, cutting down on weeding and water loss through evaporation. With this method, you can plant more plants in a given area than by using the row method.

For crops like carrots, onions, and beets that require only 1 to 2 inches between plants, you can stretch a piece of chicken wire over a frame, lay the frame over the seedbed, and then push a single seed down into the soil at the center of each hole. This will provide the proper spacing for early growth. As the plants mature, they can be thinned by pulling the immature plants for greens.

Fig. 9-5. A template will ensure correct distance between seeds when planting them in a bed. A seed is planted at each corner of the triangle.

Larger plants like cabbage and broccoli can also be planted in a similar pattern. Simply cut a stick so that it is equal in length to the desired distance between plants and then use this measuring device to mark off the distance between plants. Work in triangles, planting three plants at a time so that the bed keeps a uniform spacing. A triangular template made of wood or cardboard can also be used as a guide for spacing plants or seeds (Fig. 9-5). Each edge of the triangle should be as long as the desired distance between plants. One seed or plant is put in the ground at each point of the triangle.

SPECIAL TREATMENT FOR LEGUME SEEDS

The term *legume* comes from the Latin meaning "to gather," and that is just what properly inoculated legumes do in your vegetable patch. Legumes are unique because of their ability, in conjunction with certain bacteria that grow on their roots, to gather atmospheric nitrogen for their own use. This ability to capture nitrogen gives legumes an advantage since nitrogen is often one of the limiting nutrients in soil. Properly-inoculated legumes make more nitrogen than they use, adding this nutrient to the soil instead of depleting it as a majority of plants do. By inoculating each and every legume seed you plant, you can turn your garden into a solar-powered fertilizer factory. You can do it cheaply and easily by putting nature's best known method of nitrogen-fixation, the legume-rhizobia symbiosis, into action.

Scientists have found that some rhizobia bacteria work better than others on certain legumes. Seed stores sell these different strains so that they can be matched with particular legumes to ensure the best nitrogen production possible. The result is that legumes inoculated with good nitrogen-fixing rhizobia will out-perform uninoculated seed. Some gardeners report increases of up to 25 percent in their legume harvest after inoculating seed for the first time.

If you inoculate every legume seed you plant each spring with scientifically selected nitrogen-fixing bacteria, you will increase the quality and quantity of these crops. Also, the nitrogen-rich crop residues will fertilize future crops when turned back into your garden's soil.

Green beans, peas, soybeans, lentils, and other legumes make up about one-quarter of the crops planted in most gardens. Only by inoculating every last one of these fertilizer factories will your garden collect its fair share of the 75 million tons of nitrogen over every acre of land.

One of the bargains of fixing nitrogen right in your garden is its low cost. As the price of fertilizers (even from organic sources) skyrocket, inoculation is becoming an inexpensive alternative source for the all-important plant-available nitrogen.

Garden inoculants are available at most seed stores and farm co-ops for a dollar or two per package. Garden inoculants are mixtures blended to work on many different peas and beans. The 1- to 2-ounce packages come as an easy-to-use powder and will inoculate several hundred feet of row.

Inoculants are sold as a matter of course with seed for green manure crops. You may have to ask for the garden variety inoculants. Buy separate inoculants for beans and peas and green manures.

Although most states have laws regulating the quality of inoculants, when buying yours make sure to:

● Get the correct strain for your specific seed.

● Check the culture expiration date.

● Store the inoculant in a cool place until you are ready to use it. Refrigeration does not harm the microbes, but beware of heat and sunlight as they will kill the bacteria.

Inoculants are so easy to use that once you have bought your seed and an inoculant the job is one-third complete. Next, you must decide on a method of inoculation.

The three most common methods of inoculation are spreading the inoculants directly on the seedbed with the seeds; mixing a slurry of water, seed and inoculant; and pelleting. Pelleting delivers the most bacteria to the tender seedling roots, thereby increasing nodulation. In fact, some studies have shown that pelleting increases nodulation (root nodules are responsible for nitrogen-fixation) by up to 60 percent over the slurry method.

Spreading the powdered inoculant directly on the prepared seedbed is the quickest and easiest way of inoculating legumes, but it is also the least effective. Exposure to sunlight and the drying affect of wind work against a good "take." The distance between the bacteria and the legume roots also reduces the chance of nodulation. The few minutes saved by using the broadcast method is not worth the erratic nodulation which often results. A better choice is the slurry.

The slurry operation incorporates a water and molasses or corn syrup mixture to hold the inoculant to the seed during planting. This method keeps the rhizobia close to the seed, increasing the chance of effective nodulation.

The steps for the slurry method are:

● Moisten seed. (You can soak seed overnight to speed germination.)
● Place wet seeds in a mixing bowl or jar.
● Stir molasses or corn syrup into seed and mix thoroughly until seed is uniformly coated (Fig. 9-6).
● Stir inoculant into seed with a stick until thoroughly mixed.
● Plant immediately. Re-inoculate any seed that has been left overnight before planting.

This slurry method is effective for small seeds like alfalfa and clover. Since large seeds are notorious for their inability to carry bacteria, pelleting should be used on all peas, beans, and peanuts.

Pelleting involves nothing more than applying an additional protective coating, usually powdered limestone or powdered rock phosphate, over the inoculated seed. Ground lime is often suggested as a pellet coating, but this powder could be toxic to some acid-loving rhizobia. To be safe, use the less potent limestone and rock phosphate powders. This pill enhances rhizobia's survival rate and is the most effective way of achieving maximum nodulation.

To pellet seed you will need this simple equipment: two containers, one for wet mixing and one for dry mixing (the dry container should have a tight-fitting lid—a 2-pound coffee can works well); a stirring stick; powdered rock phosphate or finely ground limestone; molasses or corn syrup; and a package of inoculant. Then:

● Soak-seed overnight before applying this pellet coating.
● Thoroughly mix inoculant with wet seed (Fig. 9-7).
● Stir molasses into seed so that inoculant and molasses get the seed wet and sticky without becoming a soggy mess.
● Sift the rock phosphate (about 25 percent of the seed weight) through a window screen into the dry container.
● Scoop the wet seed into the dry bucket. Snap on the lid and roll or tumble the container (Fig. 9-8). Remove the lid to check the pellets, adding more powder and breaking up clods when neces-

Fig. 9-6. Pour molasses or corn syrup over seeds to stick inoculant to seeds. Stir thoroughly.

153

Fig. 9-7. Sprinkle inoculant over wet seed and mix thoroughly.

sary. Do not over-agitate the seed. Agitating the seed too much breaks the coating off. Just roll the container back and forth a few times until coated.

● Plant the pelleted seeds immediately.

The best time to plant inoculated seed is just before a rain. The moisture lifts rhizobia's survival rate beyond that of seeds planted in dry soil. Water if necessary.

Although the sun is harmful to rhizobia during spring planting time, by midspring the little workhorses are busy producing nitrogen for your growing legumes as nature's solar-powered fertilizer factories.

PLANTING BY THE PHASES OF THE MOON

Perhaps you have noticed that one planting of

peas comes up 3 or 4 days after sowing. Another planting may take up to 2 weeks to sprout. Why?

The difference may be in your soil's nutrient, moisture, pH, or humus content, but the next time you see a difference check your calendar. Determine which phase the moon was in when you sowed the seeds, and you may be pleasantly surprised to find that the moon had an influence.

Through the years certain general rules have been established for planting by the phases of the moon. The first is avoiding planting on the days on which the new moon, full moon, and the first and last quarters fall. The second is planting leafy and fruiting crops during the first week of the waxing (getting-larger) moon. Root crops should be planted during the first week of the waning (getting-smaller) moon. Everyone knows that Good Friday is the traditional potato-planting day.

Many gardeners believe that the phases of the moon affect plant growth. They always consult their almanacs before planting. If you plan to try this method, be sure to get a current almanac listing your area's lunar cycles.

The reasons behind planting by the phases of the moon are not as mysterious as they at first appear. Varying gravitational, magnetic, and light forces from the ever-changing position of the moon influence plant growth in different ways during the 28-day lunar cycle. Sometimes these forces work against one another, and at other times they reinforce each other. The lunar cycle can be divided into four phases: new moon, waxing moon, full moon and waning moon (Fig. 9-9).

At the new moon, when the moon is dark in the sky, the sum of magnetic and gravitational lunar forces is the greatest. These forces help seeds soak up water, burst their seed coatings, and begin new growth. The earth's gravity is counteracted during the new moon and seedlings find it easy to pop out of the ground.

During the second 7 days, after the moon has passed the first quarter and is moving toward full, leaf growth is stimulated by the increasing moonlight. Increasing gravitational attraction slows root growth during this phase.

In the third 7-day period, after the moon pass-

Fig. 9-8. Roll seeds coated with inoculant and molasses in a container holding powdered rock phosphate or limestone. Tumble them just enough to pick up a good coating of powder.

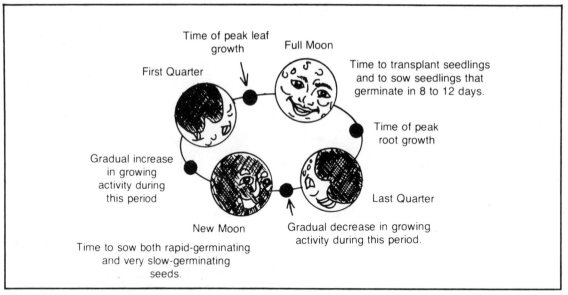

Fig. 9-9. Some gardeners believe that planting by the phases of the moon affects seeds' germination. Different seeds should be planted at different phases of the moon.

es full and begins to wane, the amount of moonlight decreases along with the lunar gravitational pull. During this period, leaf growth slows down and the increasing effects of the earth's gravity cause root growth to increase.

The phase following full moon is the time to sow seeds that require 2 weeks or more for germination. By the time these long-germination seeds break ground, the moon will be new and passing into a phase of maximum leaf growth.

This third phase is also the best time for transplanting chores. This period is conducive to strong root growth. Root shock will be minimized by this period of root growth, and the plants will be ready 2 weeks later when a phase of increasing leaf growth arrives.

In the last 7 days of the lunar month, between the last quarter and the new moon, lunar gravitation begins to increase while moonlight lessens. This combination slows both root and leaf growth. This period is believed to be a time of rest for plants. The almanacs suggest that this phase of the lunar cycle is a good time to leave the vegetable patch alone and to catch up on other chores.

To sum up: a seed planted just before the dark of the moon goes through a cycle of balanced root and leaf growth; proceeds to a period of stimulated leaf growth (full moon); passes into a period of increased root growth; and winds down with a phase of rest. This 28-day cycle repeats itself throughout the growing season so you can make succession plantings 28 days apart. Do not fail to figure the proper phase for planting during fall and summer.

The effects of the moon reach beyond your seed. Many weather patterns are associated with moon phases. Rain, for instance, seems to be most plentiful during the week of the full moon. If you plant a day or two before the full moon, your seeds will benefit from the moisture.

Although planting by the phases of the moon may seem a little far out to some gardeners, others swear by it. You will have to try it for yourself to see if it works.

Chapter 10

Successful Perennials

Perennial vegetables and herbs, as well as fruit trees and vines, have an important role to play in the home garden. Every gardener with the room for perennials should consider incorporating them into the yard. Not only do perennials supply fresh food each year, but they become old friends as they take on a personality in the space you provide for them.

Working perennial vegetables and fruits into your garden plan involves more than simply planting them in or near the garden. Many of the taller perennials, like fruit trees and berry bushes, can be used as informal screens along property lines or around buildings. Others, such as strawberries, rhubarb, and asparagus, can occupy beds all of their own. Despite the fact that most perennials seem to grow on their own after planting, you need to consider carefully where they are placed in your yard so that they have adequate growing conditions.

Most perennials require full sunlight, a well-drained and rich soil, good air drainage, and a place where they will not be disturbed during growth. This latter point is an important consideration when planning placement of your perennials. If you want to place them in the regular vegetable garden, perennials should be set out along the edges of the garden or in a section reserved for permanent plants. This placement will allow you to work around perennials without disturbing the extensive root systems they send out. If it is at all possible, perennials should be located in beds separate from the annual vegetable pitch. This will allow you to work up the soil to each perennials liking without having to worry about digging or tilling too close to the plants.

Perennials have a wide range of cultural preferences. The following sections will give you a capsule description of how to handle some common perennial vegetables, herbs, cane fruits, and fruit trees.

Remember that many perennials require quite a bit of room for top growth. Table 10-1 will give you a good idea of the space requirements of various

**Table 10-1. Use This Chart
to Plan the Spacing of Your Perennial Beds.**

Fruit/Veg.	Between Plants (feet)	Between Row (Feet)
Aspararus	1½	4
Blackberries	4	2-3
Blueberries	5	7
Grapes	8	3-4
Horseradish	1½	3
Raspberries	4	3-4
Rhubarb	3	5
Strawberries	1	2-3

perennials. Bed planting can provide this extra room efficiently.

ASPARAGUS

Asparagus is one of the earliest crops you will harvest each spring. The spears, which are actually immature ferns, make a welcome fresh addition to early spring diets. Mary Washington and Martha Washington are two favorite varieties that have rust-resistant characteristics. Roberts Strain is also rust-resistant and a heavy producer.

Although asparagus can be grown from seed, it produces much quicker when grown from one-year-old roots. Asparagus roots suitable for transplanting are often called crowns. Crowns should be planted in permanent beds of deep, rich, well-drained soil, in a location that receives full sun. Asparagus ferns grow to 5 feet in height, so the bed must be positioned where it will not shade other plants.

Asparagus roots should be set out as soon as the ground can be worked in the spring. Dig a trench 12 inches deep, 12 inches wide, and long enough to accommodate the number of roots you want to set out (Fig. 10-1). Plan on placing crowns 18 inches apart in the trench. Place 3- to 4-inch thick layer of compost or well-rotted manure in the bottom of this trench and then mix it with the soil at the bottom of the trench. Shape the soil/compost mixture into cones every 18 inches. On these cones set the crowns and spread the roots (Fig. 10-2). Roots should be trimmed so that they are about 6 inches

long prior to being set in place (Fig. 10-3). The crowns should be 10 inches below the surface of the soil. Sift 2 inches of fine compost over the crowns. During the first summer, as the spears grow upward, fill in around them with compost and fine garden soil until the bed is level. Do not cover crowns with all the soil removed from the trench at one time, or the spears will not be able to push up through the soil.

Take care when planting asparagus. Hasty planting will set back the plants, and they may never recover to produce the fine spears you desire. Asparagus roots search deep and wide for the food they need—reaching downward and outward from their crowns some 6 to 8 feet. Thorough and deep bed preparation is essential for good growth. Once you get your asparagus off to a good start, you will need to care for it little, beyond a yearly

Fig. 10-1. Place crowns in the trench on 18-inch centers.

Fig. 10-2. Make sure to spread the roots of asparagus crowns to help them off to a good quick start.

growth during the first summer, then the next spring the bed can be cut lightly, say, one or two spears from each crown. An even better practice is to allow the bed to grow another year before cutting. By the third year the asparagus should be in high gear and you can cut moderately.

When cutting asparagus spears, be careful not to damage the crown. A better way to harvest the spears is to grasp the spear and pull it over toward the ground until it snaps. Spears will usually snap between the tender and toughest section of the stalk.

Asparagus should be mulched lightly in the fall with a loose material like straw or hay to protect the crowns against severe freezes. Do not remove ferns until the following spring when the ground is

mulching with compost or well-rotted manure. These organic materials should be piled on the bed each spring before shoots appear. The compost will blanch the base of the spears and leach valuable nutrients down to the root zone. Additionally, this mulch adds slightly to the height of the bed, an important consideration since asparagus crowns tend to move toward the surface through the addition of fleshy deposits on the top of the crown. A crown near to the surface will produce a short spear that begins to open soon after it pokes through the soil. This characteristic will reduce your harvest.

Asparagus shoots should not be harvested the first season. This will allow the plants to produce a more extensive root system which will lead to increased yields in later years. If there is good shoot

Fig. 10-3. Usually the last 6 inches of asparagus crown roots are dead. Trim this off to encourage new root growth.

lightly cultivated and a new layer of compost or well-rotted manure is added to the bed.

The asparagus beetle is the most common insect pest for this plant. Proper garden sanitation and late fall cultivation of the soil should help reduce this pest. The most harmful disease of asparagus is asparagus rust. The first signs of this disease are small reddish pustules on the main stalks. These pustules burst, releasing a rust colored cloud of spores. The spores require dampness for germination and where heavy dews or mists are present they can quickly infect the entire plant and kill it. Buying rust resistant varieties should prevent rust problems.

BLUEBERRIES

This shrub grows 6 to 10 feet in height and bears heavily with little pruning in acidic (5 to 5.6 pH) soils. Blueberries prefer soft, humus-type soils, heavily mulched to resemble the forest soil they normally grow in. Peat soils also provide good growing conditions. Although blueberries like lots of moisture, they should not be grown in areas where water stands in or on the soil.

Blueberries usually arrive as rooted shrubs and are very fragile in this condition. They should be planted immediately. When this is not possible, great care must be taken to keep roots moist and away from exposure to wind and sun. Wrap roots in moist burlap and place plants in a cool, moist cellar or deep shade until planted. Blueberries should be planted in early spring in the north and late fall in the south.

The hole to receive each plant should be large enough to accept roots without bending. Hard subsoils should be worked deeply and thoroughly with a maddox or spading fork. Ample amounts of peat moss or well-decomposed compost (made without lime or limestone) should be worked into the soil. When subsoil is prepared, set the plant in the hole so that it will be 1 or 2 inches deeper than it was at the nursery. You should be able to see the soil ring indicating the nursery planting depth.

Spread roots naturally and fill in with good soil mixed with peat moss. As each layer of dirt is added, tamp the soil to remove air pockets. When hole is full, tamp the soil to form a depression which will catch rainwater. If manure or compost is used during planting, make sure it is well-rotted and mixed thoroughly with the fill dirt to ensure that roots are not burned. New bushes should be spaced 5 to 7 feet apart.

Blueberries are not self-pollinating, so several varieties should be planted together. Blueberries are somewhat finicky about where they grow, but several varieties are available for different areas of the country. Michigan varieties include Earliblue, Blue Ray, Bluecrop, Jersey, and Coville. New Jersey varieties include Earliblue, Blue Ray, Ivanhoe, Bluecrop, Herbert, and Darrow. Some varieties that do well on the East Coast and the northern Midwest are Concord, Rancocas, Waymouth, and Stanley. Look closely at varieties before buying and consult your local county extension agent about the prospects of growing these berries in your area.

GRAPES

Grapes are one of the easiest fruits to grow. There are thousands of varieties, and most are capable of growing just about anywhere in the United States.

One of the major reasons grapes are so easy to grow is that they do well in almost any soil, as long as it is well-drained and fairly deep. In fact, soils of average fertility are best since overly-rich soils tend to encourage excessive cane growth at the expense of fruit production. Grapes should be located in a section of your yard that receives full sun and has good air and water drainage. Protection from icy winter winds is also nice, but not absolutely necessary in most parts of the United States.

Grapes are usually trained to grow along trellises. Although the shape of the trellis is not really important, grapes need ample room in which to spread their vines. Most gardeners prefer to grow grapes on double wires that are parallel to the ground at heights of 2 and 5½ feet. The wires should be stretched between posts about 15 feet apart.

One-year-old grape vines, also called whips, can be planted in late fall or early spring. In the northern reaches of the United States, where win-

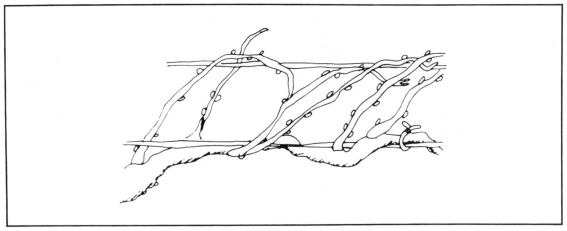

Fig. 10-4. A grape cane prior to pruning. The canes coming out of the main branch (tied to the wire) are branches produced during the past growing season.

ters are severe, spring planting is preferred. Vines should be planted as soon as the ground can be worked. In the south, vines should be planted after frost but before the ground freezes.

Holes for grapes should be 12 to 18 inches deep, 7 to 10 feet apart. Mix some organic matter in the soil as it is replaced around roots. When the whip is in place, prune back to a single cane and cut back this cane so that only one or two buds remain.

If a trellis is in place, the first year's growth can be trained upward by tying the canes to this support. If a trellis is not in place, vines can be allowed to run across the ground. After the first year the main stem must be trained into a trellis. Most gardeners pull the stem up to the top wire and tie it in place. This main stem is then cut off parallel to the top wire. The strongest canes, near to each of the four wires running away from the main stem, should then be tied to the parallel wires. Prune off all other growth, except that which occurs on the canes tied to the wires (Fig. 10-4). When this pruning is accomplished, it is time to think about the next few pruning cuts as they will make or break the shape and productivity of the plant.

Grapes develop on the growth which occurs during the current year. This growth is commonly called "new growth." New growth from one-year-old canes tends to produce the most heavily. During the first pruning, trim back the canes tied to the wire so that four or five buds remain. These buds will produce new growth and maybe a few grapes during this, the second season, for the vine.

Pruning for the following years involves cutting off the branch that produced fruit last year. Since this is year-old wood, you want to leave one or two canes which will produce new wood and fruit this year (Fig. 10-5). In addition to this one-year-old vine, choose another vine near the trunk of the plant, usually growing from older wood, and trim it back to two or three buds. This spur will act as a replacement should the stronger cane die off. This spur will also serve as a year-old growth for fruit production the following year.

Favorite grape varieties include:

● Purple jam and jelly grapes: Concord, Fredonia, Wardon, Beta, Van Buren, and Steuben.

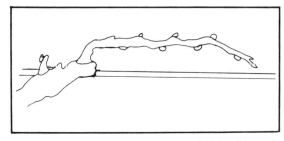

Fig. 10-5. Trim back all but one cane and all but five or six buds on that one cane. Notice the extra spur with one or two buds at the lower left. This will produce an extra cane in case the main cane fails.

Fig. 10-6. Wrapping grapes in newspaper will discourage many grape pests.

- Red: Delaware, Caco, and Catawba.
- White: (seeds) Niagra, (seedless) Interlaken, Himrod, Lakemont, and Romulus.

Although grapes suffer less from pest and disease than most other fruits, they do have a few problems. Birds can be discouraged by wrapping each grape cluster in paper after fruit has set (Fig. 10-6) or by spreading netting over the vines. Milky spore sprayed on the ground around grapes will reduce Japanese beetle populations. Adult beetles can be hand picked. Black rot can be controlled through pruning that allows adequate air and light to reach all parts of the vine. Resistant varieties will also help reduce this problem. Additionally, removing diseased fruit and leaves as they appear will slow the spread of this disease.

HORSERADISH

This perennial member of the mustard family is grown for its thick fleshy taproot. When left undisturbed, horseradish will spread by producing many fleshy side roots in the top foot of soil. The following year these roots will then sprout new growth. This plant grows best in deep, well-drained, and fertile soil. Deep cultivation and good light soil will allow well-formed roots to be produced. Hard packed and tight soils will produce twisted and unsightly roots.

To plant horseradish, dig the bed and work the soil well, adding lots of organic matter. Horseradish is planted as a root cutting. Place the top of the cutting 3 to 4 inches beneath the soil and pack dirt securely around the root. Fill in soil and mulch lightly to keep weeds down. Roots should be set out 18 inches apart in rows three feet apart.

Horseradish fills out its roots late in the season, around the time of first frost, and should be kept well-watered then. Dig roots as you need them. Those roots that are not dug will send up new growth in the following spring.

RASPBERRIES

Raspberries are a fruiting cane that is often overlooked by gardeners. This is really too bad, since raspberries are relatively easy to grow and their fruit is expensive at the supermarket.

Raspberries prefer an acidic, light soil. Soil preparation should include plenty of compost made without limestone or lime. Birds can be kept away by covering brambles with netting during the ripening season.

Red raspberries are cold-hardy and heavy producers. They grow throughout the northern half of North America. Most red raspberries are not heat-tolerant. They may not do too well in the southern states.

Latham is the most widely adopted raspberry variety. Others that do well in particular regions of the United States are Newburgh, Taylor, and Early Red in the New England and Great Lake states; Canby, Buckeye, September Red, Durham, and Willamette are suggested for the Pacific Northwest. Black cap or black raspberries are generally less hardy than the red and yellow varieties. They do not usually do well in the extreme north, but they do perform better than the red varieties in the southern states.

Each year raspberries send up new shoots that overwinter and then produce fruit on short side stems the following season. After fruiting, these canes begin to die back. They should be removed in order to allow new canes (next year's producers) ample room for growth. It is best to cut old canes off at ground level. They are easy to recognize because they are usually bigger and darker in color than the new shoots. They also have the spurs or side shoots on which this year's fruit was produced. It is recommended that pruned canes be hauled away from the berry patch and burned to destroy diseases and pests which may be in them. The ashes can be used as fertilizer elsewhere in the garden.

RHUBARB

Rhubarb grows just about anywhere in the United States. It is a hardy plant that likes long, cool seasons and freezing winters. MacDonald and Ruby varieties produce bright red stalks with a tender texture. Valentine is the sweet variety and requires little sugar for cooking. Victoria is an old-fashioned variety that produces thick stalks with a somewhat tart flavor. Canada Red is a tender and sweet variety preferred by many.

Rhubarb is propagated by division of its fleshy root. These roots are also known as corms, and each should have a vigorous eye for adequate growth. Rhubarb is usually planted in early spring, but in warmer regions of the country it can be set out in late autumn.

Select a well-drained, rich, loamy soil for rhubarb. Where this is not possible, dig in a bushel basket of compost or humus for each corm you set out. The roots should be planted 3 to 4 inches deep so that the top of the eye is 2 inches below the soil's surface. Plants should be fed yearly by heaping compost or well-rotted manure around the plant in the fall. This dressing should be incorporated into the soil the following spring.

Rhubarb should not be pulled from first-year plants. The plant needs this foliage during its first year in order to establish a strong root system. When stalks are pulled the first year, the plant spends its energy producing more stalks and leaves instead of more roots. Whenever flower stalks appear, remove them. They rob the plant of vitality that would normally be used to produce a thicker stand of stalks. Rhubarb patches produce for many years, but should be divided each 6 to 10 years after planting. Rhubarb is relatively pest-free, although crown rots may develop. When a plant begins to appear sickly with limp yellow stalks or drooping leaves, dig it up and remove it from the patch or the other plants may become infected. Leave soil exposed and open to air and sunlight (turning once a month or so to keep weeds down) for a summer before replacing with a new corm.

STRAWBERRIES

Strawberries are low-growing herbs which can be raised throughout the United States and Canada. Nursery and seed catalogs are full of different strawberry varieties. You will want to consider each variety's insect and disease resistance, season, fruit size, growing characteristics, and hardiness when making your selection. Of course, the northern states and Canada need the hardiest varieties. Among these are Catskill, Dunlap, Royalty, Totem, Trumpeter, and Vibrant. Good Northeastern varieties include Catskill, Dunlap, Empire, Fletcher, Midland, Midway, Premier, Sparkle, and Surcrop. Atlas, Gaurdian, Midway, and Surcrop do well in the Midwest. Special varieties for the Northwest and California include Northwest, Olympus, Salinas, and Tioga. Southern states do well with Apollo, Blakemore, Daybreak, Florida Ninety, Pocohontas, Sunrise, and Tennessee Beauty.

Strawberries are propagated by planting crowns in the early spring. As soon as the soil can be worked, prepare strawberry beds by digging in lots of organic matter cottonseed meal or dried blood, ground phosphate rock and bone meal. Do not add limestone because strawberries prefer an acid soil with a pH between 5 and 6. Strawberries prefer light, loamy soils with good air and water drainage. Planting on a slight slope is a good idea.

When a bed for a strawberry patch has been

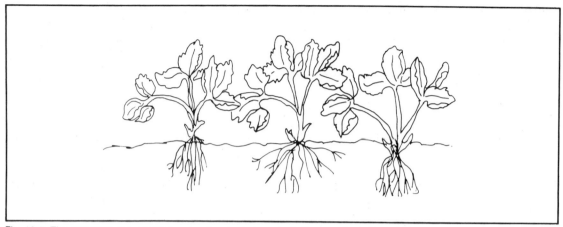

Fig. 10-7. The proper planting depth for strawberries is important. Crowns planted too shallow (left) will fall over. The proper depth (center) allows good root and crown growth. Crowns planted too deep (right) will develop crown rot among other problems.

prepared for planting you will need to dig holes for the individual plants. Each hole should be large enough to hold the plant without overly crowding its roots. The spacing between plants depends on the cultural method you plan to use. Usually, rows are 2 to 3 feet apart and plants are placed 12 to 18 inches apart within the row.

When holes are dug, shape a small cone of dirt at the bottom of each hole. Individual plants are set on the cones and their roots pressed firmly but gently into the dirt around the bottom of the cone. It is important to trim off the dead root ends of each plant before planting. (Cut back roots until they are only 6 inches long.) Each plant should be positioned in its hole so that when the hole is filled with dirt the roots are covered, but the small leaf buds in the crown are left exposed (Fig. 10-7). This is important since a strawberry plant with its crown buried too deeply will often develop crown rot and die. A crown that is too far above the soil will be weak and will not develop fruit or runners effectively.

When a plant is in place, the hole should be half-filled with soil. Pour enough water into the hole to thoroughly wet the soil. This will eliminate air pockets and give the roots enough moisture to get off to a good start. Fill in the remainder of the hole and firm the soil around plants. Beds should be kept moist for several days following transplanting.

Like other transplants, strawberries are best set out on cloudy days. This will prevent roots from being damaged by the sun. When this is not possible, the plants should be protected from the sun and wind with burlap, an inverted bushel basket, or cardboard.

There are many cultural possibilities for growing strawberries. Some of the more common cultural practices are the row method, the hill method, and the alternating-row method.

The row method is used by many commercial growers. Plants are set out in rows 3 to 4 feet apart with 18 to 36 inches between plants. During the first year of growth the plants are not allowed to set fruit. This is accomplished by pinching off any blooms that appear. All runners are allowed to root in the space between the original rows. In the fall, the bed is mulched. The following spring all plants are allowed to flower and set fruit. When the fruiting season is over, the bed, plants and all, is turned under and a new crop is planted. This method produces heavy yields every other year from each planting area. Two beds, planted with new plants on alternate years, are necessary for yearly crops.

The hill method is often used in gardens with limited space. Plants are spaced in rows or hills 2 feet apart with 12 inches between plants. When runners appear, they are pinched off so that fruit production is dependent on the original plants. Individual plants will become large and bear more heavily in relation to plants allowed to send out runners, because as strawberry crowns grow they store food by producing new crowns around the original. Each of these crowns then sets fruit.

The alternating row method is a variation of the above methods. Plants are set out in 3- to 4-foot-wide rows with 18 to 30 inches between plants. The first-year flowers on the original plants are pinched back to encourage runners. The following year the new plants will begin producing fruit. The heaviest bearing plants in this group should be marked with stakes. When fruiting is finished but before the plants begin forming runners, the original row of plants is tilled under. The plants not marked for saving are also removed from the bed. As runners form on the marked plants, they are trained into the rows left open by the removal of the original plants. The following year the best producers of this batch are saved and allowed to send out runners that fill in the rows left open by removal of the previous year's plants.

A few strawberry tips are:

● Strawberries like a lot of water, especially when they are producing fruit, but the soil should not be allowed to become waterlogged. Strawberries should also be heavily watered late in the season when runners are rooting.

● Strawberries should be mulched for winter production. Wait until after the tops of the plants have died back and the soil is frozen to a depth of about 1 inch before mulching. This will ensure that the plants remain dormant during the winter. Mulch with a light material such as straw or pine needles. Pine needles are preferred since they are acidic and strawberries like acid soil.

● Strawberries should be fed heavily in late summer so that they can store up energy for next season's growth. Use cottonseed meal, dried blood and compost, or well-rotted manure as a side-dressing around plants.

● As the weather begins to warm in the spring, loosen mulch and remove it a little at a time so plants can adjust to the open environment gradually.

● Strawberries may suffer from insect pests including leaf aphids, spider mites, root weevils,

and crown borers. The best control for these pests is rotation of the beds every two or three years. Do not plant strawberries where tomatoes, potatoes, or other crops suffering from virus or fungal diseases were grown. Strawberries are susceptible to these diseases.

● Red Stele is a comon fungus disease. Symptoms include the wilting of the plant and death just before fruits starts to ripen. This disease is often caused by excessive moisture in the bed, and can be prevented by planting where there is adequate drainage, by removing affected plants, and by planting resistant varieties.

● Verticillum wilt is another fungus disease which attacks strawberries. Its symptoms include the drying out of the outer leaf edges of the plants. Eventually, the whole plant is affected and it takes on a dry flattened appearance. Again, planting resistant varieties will cut down on the problem, as will planting strawberries in beds not previously used to grow tomatoes, potatoes, and cucumbers.

FRUIT TREES

Growing fruit trees is one of the most rewarding activities you can undertake as a gardener. It is also one of the most challenging. Although fruit trees can and should be used to enliven the landscape of your yard, this should not be the only consideration for tree placement. Fruit trees also need hospitable growing conditions. Some of the important considerations to be made when deciding on a place for fruit trees are climatic conditions, light exposure, soil quality, water and air drainage, and exposure to prevailing winds.

Temperature is the most important weather factor affecting a fruit tree's survival. Unfortunately, it is also the condition over which a gardener has the least control. Careful study of nursery catalogs is necessary in order to select varieties that will survive in your climate. Check with local county extension agents when questions about which varieties will survive your climate arise.

Extremely cold winters with temperatures that dip to −30° or −40° F can be murderous for all types of fruit trees. Winters where temperatures bounce back and fourth between freezing and thawing will also be hard on trees. Warming temperatures often tempt trees into breaking dormancy, and then falling temperatures force them to become dormant again. This condition quickly saps the strength of the trees. Trees need a period of uninterrupted rest each winter in order to produce well the following year.

Late frosts in the spring will also prevent trees from setting fruit. This is especially true for peaches and apricots which blossom early, often before their leaves emerge.

Light is another factor which greatly influences a fruit tree's ability to produce. The more direct sunlight a tree receives the greater is its fruit production. Southern exposures, proper pruning, and planting trees away from shade-producing objects such as buildings and native trees is a must.

Although fruit trees can survive in a wide range of soil types and conditions, they do require deep soils with good structure so that root growth is not impaired. Any tree you plant will produce a root system matching the above-ground growth of limbs and branches. Figure on the roots being as wide and deep as the tree's above-ground structure. Soil should be fertile with an emphasis on nutrients such as phosphorus, potassium, and the trace minerals. Too much nitrogen results in excessive leaf growth at the expense of fruit production. Organic matter should be added to the soil whenever possible, especially during planting. Permanent mulches of straw, leaves, and other organic materials placed around trees will continue adding humus to the soil year after year.

Air drainage is important to the successful growing of fruit trees. Trees planted on gentle slopes often escape late spring frosts because cold air moves down the hill and away from the trees. For this reason, river bottoms or valley floors where cold air may settle during still nights are undesirable places for fruit trees. Many orchardists suggest not planting trees within 50 feet of the bottom of a slope in order to avoid frost pockets. Windswept hills where the winter wind chill factor may plunge below −40° F should also be avoided.

Fruit trees will not grow in areas where the water table remains high after a rain or late into the spring. Avoid planting trees in areas where water remains on the soil's surface for several days after a heavy rain. As a general rule, when trees are planted on a slope so that they benefit from good air drainage, water drainage will be no problem.

Fruit trees come in three basic sizes, allowing some flexibility in fitting trees into the available spaces in your yard or garden. The sizes range from standard size trees to semidwarfs, to dwarfs. Table 10-2 should help you decide which size tree is right for your yard.

Standard trees do best when planted in orchards where plenty of room is available. These trees produce heavily, but require substantially more care than dwarf and semidwarf varieties. Standard size trees are not worth growing unless you have an outlet for the extra fruit you will have on your hands come harvest time.

Semidwarf trees are made by grafting a standard size top section onto semidwarf root stock. These trees will not grow as large as standard trees, but are considerably larger and more productive than dwarf trees. Semidwarf trees can be used in yards that have ample space, but not enough for a full fledged orchard.

Dwarf fruit trees produce fruit that is of the same size, taste, and quality of standard size trees. The only difference is that these trees do not reach the same size as semidwarf or standard trees at maturity. Dwarf fruit trees, when properly cared for, can yield 50 to 100 pounds of fruit per year, making them an attractive alternative for those gardeners with limited space.

Table 10-2. Use This Chart to Plant Which Trees Are the Right Size to Fit the Space Available in Your Yard.

Tree	Height (Feet)	Between Trees	Varieties
Dwarf	8	8	Apple, cherry, peach, pear, apricot nectarine
Semidwarf	15-20	15-20	Most types
Standard	20-25	35-40	All types

Dwarf trees have several traits that make them especially suited for use in or near a home garden. They are compact enough to be picked and pruned from the ground, sprays can be more thoroughly applied, and they produce soon after planting—often within two to three years.

Dwarfing of most fruit trees is accomplished by budding common tree varieties onto dwarf root stock. The root stock prevents the above-ground part of the tree from developing to full size. Problems can develop when the budded tree is planted too deep and the top budded section is allowed to form roots. These roots effectively bypass the dwarfing characteristics of the root stock, allowing the tree to grow to full size. When planting dwarf or semidwarf trees, it is imperative to make sure that the graft (the place where root stock and main part of the tree are joined) remains above ground.

Although most methods of creating a dwarf fruit tree involve grafting a slip or stem of a standard tree onto a root stock of a dwarf variety, nowadays smallness can be bred into several types of trees. Apples, peaches, nectarines, cherries, and plums have been genetically dwarfed. This is a welcome improvement over the grafted dwarfs since the grafted trees require careful planting to prevent these trees from rooting and reverting back to standard size. Genetically-developed dwarf trees require no such precaution since they are programmed by their genes to grow small, regardless of how deeply they are planted.

Buying Trees

The quality of the fruit trees you buy is a critical factor in how well your trees produce. Inferior trees produce poorly even when properly cared for. Good trees give outstanding results when properly cared for and often produce admirably when neglected. Study nursery catalogs carefully before buying even if you plan to buy locally, since catalogs contain much information about varieties and planting tips. Medium sized one-year-old trees are preferred to two- or three-year-old trees, since younger trees withstand transplanting better.

Do not attempt to grow fruit trees from seed, since they usually do not produce true to their variety because of cross-pollination. In most cases, trees from seed produce small, misshapen fruit.

When ordering fruit trees by mail, order only from reputable nurseries. Avoid those that make lavish claims about the quality of their stock and advertise exotic varieties that cannot be obtained anywhere else. Many times nurseries in your geographic area handle stock that is especially suited to your climate. These trees will normally do better than those shipped halfway across the country. When buying trees from a local nursery, the stock you select should have the following characteristics:

● A tree should have an ample spread of branches, which shows that the plant has had enough space during previous growth.

● When leaves are present, they should be of normal size and color. Leaves should feel supple—not dry and brittle.

● Look for strong straight trunks and good structure showing correct pruning practices.

● Limbs and twigs should be smooth, glossy, and firm. Buds should be plump. You can tell if the tree is alive by the greenness of its cambium layer (just under the bark). A sick or dying tree will often be dry under the bark.

● The tree should have an adequate root ball, which reaches nearly as wide as the branches do. Trees should look like a plant does when it's in a flower pot the correct size.

Do not accept:

● Trees that have withered, wilted, mildewed, or dried-out roots, stems, or foilage.

● Trees and shrubs with dried-out root balls. Even bare-root stock must be kept moist in damp spaghnum moss.

● Any tree that shows signs of disease or pest damage.

Pollination

Another important consideration for buying and setting out your own orchard are various fruits' pollination requirements. Many would-be orchardists have labored hard and long setting out and caring for their trees only to discover that the flowers on their trees are not setting fruit. The problem usually revolves around improper pollination.

Pollination is the term used to describe the transfer of pollen from the male part of a flower to the female part. Trees will not set fruit without pollination. Pollination can occur between male and female parts of the same flower, among flowers on the same tree, among flowers on different trees of the same variety, or among flowers of different trees of differing varieties. There are two basic types of trees in terms of pollination, those that are self-sterile and those that are self-pollinating.

Self-pollinating trees have the ability to fertilize the female part of their flowers with pollen from the same flower or another flower on the same tree. Many of these types of trees will produce fruit when planted alone.

Self-sterile trees require the presence of another tree of the same or a compatible variety in order to be pollinated to set fruit. This transfer of pollen from one tree to another is commonly called cross-pollination. There are several factors which must be met for proper cross-pollination.

● The two (or more) trees must be compatible. That is, the polen from one must be able to fertilize the other.
● The trees must be close enough together to allow insects (usually bees) or wind to transfer pollen effectively. (A distance of less than 100 feet between trees is normally considered adequate.)
● Blossoms on both trees must be in bloom at the same time to ensure the transfer of pollen.

Here is a list of fruit trees and their pollination requirements:

Apples. Most apples need cross-pollination to produce heavily.

Apricots. Most are self-pollinating.

Peaches. Most are self-pollinating, although better results are obtained when trees of more than one variety are planted together.

Pears. Most varieties are self-sterile. At least two trees of different types are required for good pollination.

Plums. A few of the European varieties are self-pollinating. The remainder of the European, American and Japanese varieties require cross-pollination with other varieties.

Sour Cherries. Most are self-pollinating. Sour cherries are often used to pollinate sweet cherries.

Sweet Cherries. Most are self-sterile and must be grown near compatible varieties for good results.

As you can see, careful study of each fruit type and variety you plant is required to assure proper pollination. The better nursery catalogs will recommend suitable cross-pollinators for self-sterile varieties. Local nurseries and your county extension agent can also help you choose suitable cross-pollinators for your area.

Choosing Varieties

Orchardists and nursery researchers are coming up with new fruit varieties every year. The list of types from which you can choose seems almost endless. In addition to choosing varieties that do well in your climate, you will also want to choose fruits that appeal to your taste. Although the following description of the same common varieties is by no means comprehensive, it will familiarize you with a few of the more widely-known fruit varieties.

Apples. There are more than 6,000 apple varieties. Usually they are classified according to the time of harvest, color, size, and texture of the fruit. The size of the tree used to be a strong criteria, but is less so now that dwarfing is gaining in popularity. Some of the varieties are also scab-resistant. Local county extension agents and nurseries will be able to help you guide you toward those that are resistant to diseases common to your area.

Some of the better-known apple varieties (in order of their harvest dates) are mid-July: Lodi, Vista Bella, July Red, Jerseymac, Viking, Tydeman Early; mid-August through late September: Gravenstein, Paulared, Prima, McIntosh, Cortland, Macoun, Spartan, Jonathan, Rhode Island Greening, Empire; late September through October: Delicious, Grimes Golden, Priscilla, Jonagold, Golden Delicious, Spigold, Northern

Spy, Stayman, Winesap, Granny Smith, Idared, Red Rome, Mutsu and Melrose. As a general rule, gold and transparent apples do not keep as well as red apples.

Some scab-resistant varieties include Prima, Priscilla Macfree, Nova Easygro, Priam, and Sir Prize.

The above varieties are relatively new to the apple scene. They have been selected recently for their size, color, and ease of care. Many people prefer the old-time varieties and claim that they taste like a real apple should. Old-time varieties (when you can find them) include: American Beauty, Rhode Island Greening, Blue Pearmain, Esopus Spitzenburg, Maiden's Flush, Pound Sweet, Twenty Ounce, and Fameuse.

Apricots. This member of the peach family comes in many varieties. The most common are Perfection, Goldrich, Alfred, Curtis, Blenheim, Moorpark, Scout, Early Golden, Kok-pshar, Manchu, and Zard. The last three are recent imports from China.

Cherries. Sour cherry trees (also known as pie cherries) are one of the hardiest fruit trees in the United States. Sweet cherries, while hardier than most other fruit trees, often suffer from late spring frosts.

Common cherry varieties include Bing, Emperor, Francis, Lambert, Napoleon, and Duke. Duke is a hybrid cross between sour and sweet cherries and is a favorite of many home gardeners and orchardists. It is an effective pollinator tree for many varieties of both sweet and sour cherries.

Peaches. Peaches and apricots are the least hardy of the stone fruits. Most varieties of this fruit cannot withstand winter temperatures below −10° F.

Common peach varieties hardy enough for most sections of the United States include Glo Haven, Elberta Reliance, and Golden Jubilee. The latter two are more suited to cooler areas.

Pears. Some common pear varieties include Bartlett, Spartlett, Moonglow, Seckel, Clapps Favorite, Aurora, Corham, Magness, and Highland. Magness and Moonglow have some resistance to fire blight, which is a severe disease problem for pears.

Plums. Plums are grouped according to the region of the world from which they originate. The three basic divisions are American, European, and Japanese. Common American varieties include Surprise, Wolf, De Sota, Hawkeye, Wild Goose, French, and Damson. European varieties include Stanley, Italian Prune, Imperial Epineuse, and Iroquois. Japanese varieties are Formosa, Burbank, Satsuma, Inca, Stanta Rose, and Abundance.

Planting Fruit Trees

When your trees arrive in the mail, or when you carry them home from the nursery, unwrap them from their packaging. The roots should be kept moist and above freezing. If the planting site is not ready, the trees should be heeled-in.

Heeling-in is a term used to describe placing a tree in a temporary shallow hole in the ground. Choose a shady spot with moist ground and make sure all roots are covered with dirt to prevent damage due to drying. Trees should be planted while still dormant, or at least before much leaf growth occurs.

Prior to planting prune off damaged, broken, diseased, or dead roots and limbs. Cut off tips of excessively long roots so that roots are no more than 15 to 18 inches long.

In the milder climates of the southern part of the United States, fall is a good time to plant fruit trees. The warm soil gives roots a chance to establish themselves, so spring growth will be much more vigorousm. In the north, where severe winters would kill fall-planted trees, planting should be done as early in the spring as soil can be worked. You can move up the planting date in the spring by performing some planting chores in the fall. Digging the holes and gathering compost for the holes are two such jobs.

The hole for fruit trees should be about twice as large as the root ball. If you buy bare-root stock, the hole should be deep enough so that the main taproot will not be bent when the tree is held at proper depth in hole. The hole should be wide enough so that roots can be spread adequately (Fig. 10-8).

Fig. 10-8. Do not skimp when it comes to digging planting holes for fruit trees. Holes should be wide enough for ample root spread and deep enough so the tap root remains straight.

The hole size is not the only factor for getting fruit trees off to a good start. The soil that goes back into the hole should be rich and of a texture suitable for good growth. When you dig the hole, keep the dirt from the top half of the hole on one side of the hole and the dirt from the bottom half on the opposite side. Fill the hole with water and allow the water to soak into the soil before placing the tree in the hole.

Next, mix the topsoil with compost, aged manure, peat moss, or a mixture of all three. You can mix a portion of this right in the hole (Fig. 10-9) then add the rest as you fill in around the tree's roots (Fig. 10-10). Make sure to pack soil lightly around roots to remove air pockets (Fig. 10-11).

Finally, spread the soil that you removed from the bottom of the hole around the base of the tree so that it forms a rim that will make rainwater run toward the trunk and soak into the ground instead of running off. Water it well to help force air out from around the roots. A tree guard can be wrapped around the tree to prevent sun scald and to keep rodents from gnawing tender bark.

The tree can be staked if necessary. This is especially important for dwarf trees that usually do not produce a strong root system their first season. Support is also necessary in windy areas. Stakes should be driven into the ground about 6 inches from the trunk. Twine or strips of rag or wire threaded through an old section of garden hose can be used to tie the tree to the stakes. Do not wrap the ties too tightly around the tree, or as the tree grows

Fig. 10-9. Pour compost and other organic matter in the fruit tree's hole and mix with soil before planting the tree.

characteristics and by keeping the tree open to ample sunlight and air.

At planting time and during the first years of a tree's growth, pruning is used to train the tree. The idea is to establish a strong framework which will support later growth. During the third through sixth years, little pruning will be necessary if the tree has been shaped properly during its first few years. In fact, over-pruning between the second and third years of the tree's growth may delay fruit production. Once the tree has begun bearing, pruning should be limited to removing dead wood, repairing damaged or weak branches, controlling the shape of the tree, and maintaining the tree's proper size and shape.

During the first 2 years of pruning, save

Fig. 10-10. Add well-rotted compost and other organic matter to soil as you fill in around roots.

the tie will girdle it and choke off the flow of sap.

Mulch around the tree with compost and leaves or straw once the tree is established and has leafed out. Mulch should form a ring from the edge of the drip line to within 6 inches of the trunk. Do not mulch right up to the trunk, or gnawing pests may use the mulch for cover while chewing on the tree's trunk.

Pruning

The pruning of fruit trees should be thought of as a form of maintenance necessary to coax peak production from the trees by directing their energy into fruit production. Increased production is accomplished by removing limbs with weak growing

Fig. 10-11. Make sure to tamp soil firmly around roots to remove air pockets which slow the growth of the tree.

Fig. 10-12. Branches which meet the main trunk or major branches of the tree at a wide angle (left) are stronger than narrow-crotch branches.

branches spaced at even intervals along and around the trunk. From the standpoint of strength, the best branches to keep are those that meet the main trunk or larger branches at right angles (90°) (Fig. 10-12). The weakest part of the union is where the upper part of the branch meets the trunk. Strange as it may seem, the smaller this angle (the narrower the crotch), the weaker the union is (Fig. 10-13). Therefore, by leaving the branches with the widest crotches and by spreading branches when necessary you can greatly improve the strength of the tree. During pruning at the tree's earliest stages of growth, remove branches with narrow crotches and save those with wide angles.

Saving branches that meet the main trunk at a wide angle will result in several other benefits. One is that snow and rain will have less chance of sticking in the wider crotches. This reduces the incidence of disease. Accumulating ice and snow can cause damage during fall and spring as freezing and thawing water contracts and expands in narrow crotches, often causing them to split. This is usually not the case in wide-crotch branch unions. Branches with wide angles also allow more air and sunlight to reach the interior of the tree. This is especially important on dwarf and semidwarf trees, which tend to set most of their fruit toward the inside of the tree. Finally, as mentioned earlier, wide-angled crotches are stronger than narrow crotches. This is not as important in the early stages of the tree's development as it is later when

Fig. 10-13. Narrow crotch branch/trunk unions are weaker than wide branch unions. They also invite damage due to freezing and thawing water, snow, and ice.

172

Fig. 10-14. Correct pruning is the key to producing trees which can withstand the weight of a full crop of fruit.

of the tree. From this main leader, several strong lateral or scaffold branches are allowed to develop. The result is a tree with a strong framework that is relatively open and easy to work with.

The open center method is slightly more radical than the modified leader method, but it is very successful with apple, peach, apricot, and necterine trees (Fig. 10-16). To achieve an open center, the main leader of the tree is trimmed back severely. At the end of the first year the main leader should be cut back so that only a few scaffold branches remain. Pruning a tree in this manner allows ample light and air to reach the center of the tree, leading to sustained fruit production.

Espalier pruning is the most radical pruning method. It is also the most time-consuming and

the tree begins bearing fruit. Wide-angle branches have more give than narrow branches, allowing them to bend and support fruit more effectively. In fact, many wide-angle branches can bend clear to the ground without suffering ill affects (Fig. 10-14). Narrow-crotch branches often split from the trunk under this condition, ruining the shape and productivity of the tree.

Most fruit trees grow in one of three shapes: the modified leader system, the open center, and espalier.

The modified leader system is the most common tree shape (Fig. 10-15). This shape most closely resembles the shape of trees growing naturally. As is suggested by the name, a strong leader or trunk is allowed to grow up in the middle

Fig. 10-15. A modified leader most closely resembles the natural shape of trees.

173

Fig. 10-16. Although radical in shape, open-center pruning is effective for many types of fruit trees.

difficult method. Espalier pruning is used on dwarf trees where space is limited. The idea is to train the tree to grow flat against a trellis or wall, similar to the way a grapevine grows. Dwarf varieties of apples, pears, plums, and peaches can be trained effectively with espalier pruning.

The general idea behind this method of pruning is to train the tree's branches along supports, and to have branches about equal in size and fruit production (Fig. 10-17). To accomplish this balance, you will have to hold back the strongest branches while allowing the weaker branches to grow longer. There are a couple of tricks you can employ to accomplish this quickly.

● Prune during the summer after leaves have fully emerged.
● When pruning, cut back the stronger branches more severely than the weak branches.
● Tie the strongest branches to the trellis early in the tree's growth, but hold back on the weak branches until they have caught up with the larger branches in terms of vigor.
● Allow the stronger branches to develop all

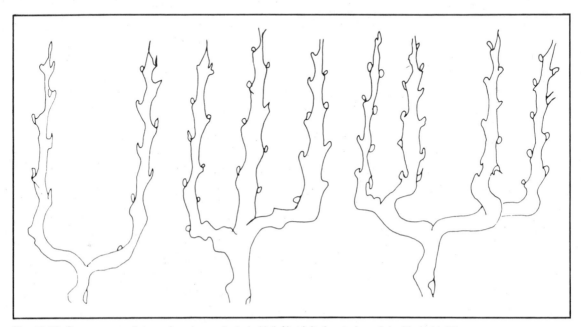

Fig. 10-17. Common espalier pruning shapes include U (left), triple (center), and double-U (right).

174

their fruit, but thin weak branches to one fruit every 6 inches.

Taken together these steps should allow the weaker branches to catch up with the stronger ones in a year or two. Eventually, all parts of the tree should achieve similar size and shape. At this point, only routine maintenance is necessary.

Here are a few other tips that will make pruning more effective.

● Cut out branches that cross each other or grow inward toward the center of a tree instead of outward. This will keep them from rubbing and producing open wounds. This problem can be serious during the fruit-bearing season when branches are pulled down by the weight of developing fruit.

● Pruning cuts should be made flush so that studs do not develop (Fig. 10-18). Stubs of dead or dying wood are perfect breeding places for insects and rot diseases.

● When pruning diseased wood, dip your pruning tool in denatured alcohol after each cut to prevent the spread of the disease.

● Suckers (shoots that emerge from a tree's root zone) and water sprouts (limbs that grow straight up from the top side of branches) should be cut off as soon as they appear (Fig. 10-19). These growths will drain much of the strength from a tree and they do not bear fruit.

● Many trees, especially those pruned to have a single leader, will attempt to develop a second leader. This condition will result in a forked tree if allowed to persist. Trim off the extra leader before the problem develops. When the tree is laden with fruit, the pressure on this fork may be enough to cause the tree to split.

Many trees develop a place on strong lateral branches where several small branches emerge at

Fig. 10-18. Pruning cuts should be flush with the branches and as nearly perpendicular to the ground as possible.

Fig. 10-19. Suckers such as this one should be pruned as soon as they are noticed. If not, they will compete with the main trunk and weaken the tree.

• Pruning a tree while it's young delays the time at which the tree will first set fruit. In order to have fruit as early as possible, as little wood as possible should be removed; however, branches that will later cause problems should be pruned. Small branches and short stubby spur growth on central branches should be allowed to remain since these are the fruit-bearing parts of the tree.

• Once a tree begins to bear, pruning should be limited to correcting problems such as forks or whorls, removing dead or broken branches, and removing suckers or water sprouts. Once bearing begins, the less you prune the better.

• When pruning branches over 2 inches in diameter, you will need to cut the branch in stages to prevent tearing the bark from the tree's trunk. Such wounds allow pests and disease to enter the tree. Most larger branches can be removed with three cuts.

The first cut is made about 1 foot from the trunk of the tree on the underside of the branch. This cut should go about halfway through the branch. Next, make a cut on the top of the branch. This cut should be about 1 inch farther out on the branch than the bottom cut. Saw here until the branch falls from the tree. Now that the pressure has been removed from the base of the branch, you can finish the job with a third cut beginning in the crotch of the branch. Saw down through the stub of limb until the cut is completed. This final cut should be made as close to the trunk as possible, yet do as little damage as possible. The face of the cut should be perpendicular to the ground, and it should be coated with tree wound dressing.

Following are some pruning tips for specific trees.

Apple. These trees do well with open centers. Prune only deadwood, misshapen branches, and water sprouts or suckers after trees are 3 years old.

Cherry. These trees grow best with a strong central leader which supports lateral branches spaced 6 to 8 inches apart. After first 2 years, prune only to remove water sprouts or suckers, crossed branches, and inward-growing branches.

Peach. Watch for sucker growth from the base

the same point. The result is multiple forks or a formation known as whorl. Remove all but the strongest branch from such a junction.

• Spreaders can be used to increase the crotch angles of limbs when the limbs are still young and supple. Spreaders (usually made by cutting lath boars to the proper length and then notching the ends) should be placed before pruning. The V on one end is placed against the central leader of the tree and the other against the branch in such a way that the branch forms an angle of more than 45°. Spreading can also be accomplished by driving stakes into the ground around the tree and pulling branches outward with rope tied to the stakes.

or the trunk. Cut suckers off flush with the trunk when they first appear. Prune off crossed limbs and those which grow out of line.

Pear. Once tree begins bearing, not much pruning is required. A little pruning is needed every year or two to induce new growth.

Plum. After trees begin bearing, pruning is limited to thinning dense top growth, crossing branches, and damaged, dead, or diseased wood. Some pruning should be done each year to encourage new growth, which in turn enhances fruit production in future years.

Pruning Tools

You should be able to accomplish most pruning jobs with three basic tools: hand pruning shears, long-handled lopping shears, and a pruning saw. Like all other tools, you pay for what you get. Buy the best tools you can afford and they will provide a lifetime of service.

Each pruning tool has a specific function. Which tool you use depends mainly on the size of the branch being cut. Branches thinner than ½ inch in diameter can be easily cut with hand shears (Fig. 10-20). Branches up to 1½ inches in diameter can be cut effectively with long-handled looping shears. These shears are also effective for cutting hard-to-reach branches—for instance, water sprouts in the center of a tree (Fig. 10-21). Anything larger than 1½ inches in diameter should be removed with a saw (Fig. 10-22).

Like all other cutting tools, pruning implements work best when they are kept sharp and in good working order. Dull pruning shears tend to chew and mash the wood instead of cutting it. This leaves a ragged wound that is more susceptible to

Fig. 10-20. Hand pruning shears will handle most small branches and fruit canes.

Fig. 10-21. Long-handle loping shears cut larger and hard-to-reach branches. Here they remove a water sprout.

Fig. 10-22. A pruning saw is necessary for large branch removal.

disease and insect attack than a clean cut.

To sharpen your pruning shears, secure a whetstone to a flat surface. This way both hands will be free to guide the tool across the stone. A rubber backing cemented to the stone's box or a small block of wood nailed to your workbench will hold the stone steady. Take the shears apart (most of the good ones are held together with a screw at the pivot) to give you better control during sharpening.

Grasp one section of the shears with the blade facing away. Hold the point with one hand and the handle with the other. Lay the base of the blade—closest to the handle—on the end of the stone nearest you. Then raise the back of the blade to a 20° angle from the surface of the stone. Push the blade away while sliding the cutting edge sideways so that the tip of the blade still makes contact at the far end of the stone. Follow the curve of the blade as closely as possible. Repeat an equal number of strokes on each side of the blade to prevent unevenness.

Bear down with a firm steady pressure when moving the blade on the stone. Imagine that you are trying to shave a thin layer off the top of the stone. Actually, the whetstone is removing a thin layer of steel from the blade.

After establishing the 20° bevel on each side of the blade, whet the very edge of the blade an additional 5°. Light strokes should be used to form this whetting angle. Variations of a few degrees do not matter as long as the whetting angle is about 5° greater than the bevel angle. Repeat the process with the other half of the shears and put them back together. Finally, wipe your shears with an oily rag to prevent rust.

Chapter 11

Fifty-four Vegetables and How to Grow Them

My garden will never make me famous,
I'm a horticultural ignoramus,
I can't tell a string bean from a soybean,
or even a girl bean from a boy bean.
— Ogden Nash

This chapter is all about helping you tell a string bean from a soybean and providing a few of the basic cultural requirements for these vegetables and 52 others. In this chapter you will find 54 common garden vegetables and herbs, each with its own section. The sections are arranged alphabetically so that looking up your favorite is easy. Each section lists the general traits of each vegetable, planting instructions, culture requirements, harvesting information, and a list of commonly-grown varieties.

BASIL

This easy-to-grow herb adds a pleasant odor to your garden and a savory taste to many cooked dishes. There are several types of basil available

through seed catalogs. They range from those with light green leaves through dark green and purple leaves. White and purple flowering varieties are also available.

Planting. Sow seeds in well-worked soil when all danger of frost is past. Basil makes an excellent companion to tomatoes.

Culture. Basil is one herb that likes a slightly rich soil with plenty of moisture. Basil will withstand partial shade. You may need to stake these plants when they reach over a foot in height to keep the mature plants (up to 18 inches in height) from blowing over in heavy winds (Fig. 11-1). Mulch heavily after soil has warmed to preserve moisture.

Harvest. Leaves can be picked and used green any time after plants are about 6 inches tall. Remove outer leaves so that the center of the plant will continue growing. For drying, cut plants just before flowering and hang upside down in a shady place with good air circulation. When leaves are dry, crumple into an airtight container for storage.

Varieties. Green Bush Basil, Large Leaved Italian Basil, Lebanon Basil, Lemon Basil, Lettuce

Fig. 11-1. Basil is a common garden herb that does well in most parts of the United States. Staking may be needed to keep these top heavy plants from blowing over.

Leaved Basil, Ornamental Dark Opal Basil, and Sweet Basil.

BEETS

Beets, which can be raised throughout the United States are a double-duty vegetable because their tops can be eaten as greens and their taproots eaten as a vegetable. There are four basic types of beets. Round beets produce a dark red and round root. Semiglobe beets have a slightly flattened top, and cylindrical beets produce long taproots similar in shape to a short stocky carrot. The fourth type of beet is grown mainly for its ample leaves that grow out of a flat, uneven taproot. Yellow or gold beets are also available. Most have orange skins with

yellow flesh and lighter leaves than red beets. Beets are relatively resistant to disease and insects.

Planting. Beet seeds are grouped three or four to a corky mass, which is really a dried fruit. Beet seeds should be soaked overnight prior to planting to increase the likelihood of germination. Plant sparsely in early spring making successive plantings 2 weeks apart. Thin regularly for good development. Beets are often used as an intercrop with carrots, lettuce, and radishes (Fig. 11-2).

Culture. Beets like loose, well-drained soil with plenty of room for their taproot to expand. Since beet taproots will go several feet into the soil, compost should be dug in to a good depth. The

Fig. 11-2. Beets grow well in beds, especially double dug beds. They should be harvested when they're 2 inches in diameter for tender, best-tasting roots.

deeper the compost, the better since beets draw few nutrients from close to the soil's surface. Beets do not tolerate acid soils and do best in soils that have been limed. Once plants have established themselves, the soil should be kept moist to encourage quick formation of the taproot. Quick root formation will keep the taproot from becoming woody.

Harvest. Greens can be harvested at any time, although the greens from the first thinnings are the most tender. Roots are best when they are 1 to 2 inches in diameter and have not yet reached maturity. Leave an inch or two of stem on the root to prevent bleeding. When beets are intended for winter storage, they should be left in the ground until just before the first fall frost. Leave an inch or two of stem on the root to increase storage ability.

Varieties. Round: Crimson (61 days) and Detroit Dark Red (60 days); Semiglobe: Crosby's Egyptian (50 days) and Golden Beet (55 days); Cylindrical: Cylindria Improved Formanova (58 days) and Tentersweet (55 days); Greens: Lutz Green Leaf (80 days).

BORAGE

This herb has woolly leaves with a cucumber-like flavor. It is used widely as a potherb in Europe and is beginning to find a place in many American gardens. This plant produces blue flowers that remain in bloom for a long time, making it a good flower for attracting bees.

Planting. Borage does not transplant well, so it should be started from seed in the garden. Sow seeds thinly in beds or rows after danger of frost has passed.

Culture. This plant likes sunny, dry locations. Average garden soil is enough for this skimpy eater. Water only when young and mulch when soil has warmed to reduce weed competition.

Harvest. Blossoms can be used as a garnish on plate or in drinks. Leaves can be used green in cooked dishes. Pick outside leaves so that the central section of the plant can continue growing. For drying, cut plants prior to blooming and hang in an airy, shaded place until leaves reach the crumbly stage. Crumble and store in airtight jars for winter use.

Varieties. Borage.

BROCCOLI

This member of the Brassica (cabbage) family can be grown anywhere in the United States where there is an extended period of cool weather. Broccoli is extremely heat-sensitive and will often bolt during the first hot spell of early summer. Although all broccoli plants grow in the same basic way (producing a main head on a central tall stem) there are several variations in the specific growth characteristics among the different varieties (Fig. 11-3). The most popular garden varieties produce a large central head with many side branches. Commercial growers prefer the varieties with one central head and few side branches. Purple varieties as well as varieties with a small central head and many side branches are also available.

Planting. Although broccoli is extremely heat-sensitive and cannot be grown through the summer except in the extreme north, it can be grown successfully in the spring and fall. Broccoli does best when transplanted into the garden as a seedling. Begin plants indoors by starting seeds in flats 5 to 6 weeks prior to the date of transplanting. Transplanting should be done as soon as the ground can be worked, usually several weeks prior to the date of last spring frost. Most greenhouses sell broccoli transplants, but when you buy these you may also be purchasing trouble if the plants are carrying diseases or insects. Planting for fall harvest follows the spring planting method, except that the plants are set out so that they will mature at about the time of the first fall frost. You can figure this date out by counting backward from your area's first frost date the number of days to maturity on the seed package.

Culture. Broccoli likes a loose rich soil. This heavy feeder needs plenty of calcium and nitrogen during its growth. Side-dress with cottonseed meal or dried blood about 2 weeks after transplanting and when heads begin to form. Add compost or well-rotted manure to the hole into which broccoli is transplanted. This plant requires a steady supply of

Fig. 11-3. Broccoli should be harvested while flowers are still immature and tightly-packed. As they open, they lose flavor.

moisture for optimum growth. Water frequently and mulch heavily to preserve moisture in the soil. This plant has shallow roots, so do not over cultivate or root damage may result.

Harvest. The central heads of broccoli are harvested when they have reached good size, but before the tiny flowers that make up these heads begin to open. Cut off the central head and about 5 to 6 inches of stem. Broccoli with side shoots will form smaller heads where the leaves intersect the main stem. The side shoots can be cut later for a continuing harvest. Broccoli freezes well, so consider this option when harvest exceeds your ability to eat fresh.

Varieties. Central head with side branches: Calabrese (85 days) and Green Umbrella Hybrid (50 days); Central head with few branches: Premium Crop (60 days) and Green Hornet (78 days); no

central head and many side branches: Raab or Rapa (100 days); and purple (turns green when cooked): King Robert Purple (57 days).

BRUSSELS SPROUTS

This member of the Brassica (cabbage) family produces tiny cabbage-like heads at the intersection of leaves and the central, tall stem. Although Brussels sprouts are easy to grow, they require a long, cool growing season. There are two basic types of Brussels sprouts: standard size plants which grow to 24 inches tall, and dwarf or semi-dwarf which average 12 to 15 inches in height.

Planting. Brussels sprouts do best when set out as transplants. These plants take nearly 2 months to grow from seed to transplanting size. Another 2 to 3 months is required to reach maturity, so count back from the date of the first expected fall

182

frost to determine seed planting date—usually in early- to mid-May for a fall harvest. In the northern United States where the summers are cool, these plants can be planted as soon as the ground can be worked for a late-summer harvest.

Culture. This plant likes a rich, loose soil with lots of nitrogen. Add compost to holes into which plants are set out and side-dress with dried blood, cottonseed meal, or fish meal a couple of weeks after planting. This plant is shallow-rooted, so do not over-cultivate. Mulch heavily to retain soil moisture, which Brussels sprouts require to thrive.

Harvest. Brussels sprouts should begin to be harvested when the bottom sprouts reach 1 inch in diameter. Pick from the bottom of the plant first, removing the leaves from beneath picked sprouts to encourage more growth of the sprouts at the top of the plant. Tightly-packed sprouts are the best.

Most gardeners contend that sprouts that have been frosted lightly a few times are superior in taste to those picked prior to frost. When growth begins to slow down because of cold weather, pinch back the top crown so that upward growth is retarded. This will encourage the plant to fill out remaining sprouts.

Varieties. Jade Cross Hybrid (90 days), Long Island Improved (90 days), and semidwarf: Semi-dwarf Paris Market (100 days).

CABBAGE

Cabbages are the best-known of the Brassica family and grow well throughout the United States, especially in regions with long cool springs and falls (Fig. 11-4). There are hundreds of cabbage varieties to choose from. They vary according to the size and shape of the head, color, and the time

Fig. 11-4. Long, cool growing seasons provide the perfect conditions for cabbage.

Fig. 11-5. When roots and stems are left in place after harvesting cabbage, smaller heads will grow out of the main stem.

during the growing season at which the heads are harvested—early, mid-season, or late. It is a good idea to experiment with different varieties and maturity times until you find those that do best in your area.

Planting. Like other Brassica crops, cabbages should be started in flats from seed and then transplanted into the garden as seedlings. Early cabbage should be started inside in flats 6 to 8 weeks prior to transplanting into the ground. Planting should be done as soon as the ground can be worked. For midsummer crops, seeds should be started later and transferred to the garden after 6 to 8 weeks. Count back from date of harvest to determine the time at which seeds should be planted. Fall crops of this vegetable can be started outside in open beds during the summer and transplanted to the growing area when plants reach transplanting size. Compost should be added to planting holes during transplanting.

Culture. Cabbages are heavy feeders and like rich, loose soils. Full sunlight is required for optimum growth as is adequate amounts of moisture. Water thoroughly during dry spells and mulch heavily.

Harvest. Cabbages should be cut from stems not long after full, solid heads have formed, since the core tends to expand inside the head until it eventually bursts through the top of the head and sends up a seed stalk. If you leave the roots and stem in the ground after harvesting the first big head, smaller secondary heads will be produced (Fig. 11-5). This means two harvests from a single plant. In the fall, harvest heads after they have been frosted a few times. This enhances their flavor and increases their storage ability.

184

Varieties. There are hundreds of cabbage varieties. Some of the more popular according to shape and time to harvest are early: Burpee's Copenhagen Market (72 days), Emerald Cross (69 days) and Golden Acre (64 days); mid-season: Stonehead (95 days) and Green Storage (100 days); late: Danish Ballhead (105 days), Eastern Ballhead (95 days) and Wisconsin Ballhead (100 days); red heads: Ruby Ball (70 days), Mammoth Red Rock (90 days), and Red Acre (75 days); flat heads: All Seasons (90 days) and Gurney's Giant (105 days).

CARROTS

Carrots do well in both cool and warm weather. Carrots come in a variety of shapes and sizes ranging from the long thick varieties most often found in supermarkets to the short round novelty carrots found only in the home garden (Fig. 11-6). There is a wide variety of carrots between these two extremes. The choice you make will depend largely on your growing conditions. Most gardeners tend to plant fewer carrots than they need, so plant more than you think you will use.

Planting. Carrots are planted as seed several times through the season to keep a fresh crop of these tasty roots coming on all season long. Since carrot seed is very fine, it is best to mix the seed with coffee grounds, sand, or finely-sifted compost to keep the seeds from clumping together during sowing. Carrot seeds are slow to germinate—3 to 4 weeks is not unusual. They can be planted as early in the spring as the ground is workable or in mid-summer for a fall crop. As mentioned earlier, sow heavily and then thin to stand about 4 inches apart. Inmature carrots can be eaten and often taste better than full-grown carrots.

Culture. Carrots send down deep roots so they like a soil that is loose and free of stones. Dig in plenty of compost or well-rotted manure several weeks prior to planting. Do not use fresh manure as this will burn the roots and produce oddly shaped carrots. Like most root crops, carrots need a constant supply of moisture during growth to produce fine-textured, nonwoody roots. Mulch when plants are 4 to 6 inches tall to conserve soil moisture. Hand weeding is recommended to prevent weeds from taking over these slow-germinating and slow-growing vegetables. The length of carrot you grow depends heavily on the type of soil you have. In deep sandy loams, the longer carrots can be grown. In the medium-textured heavier soils, the medium length carrots will do all right, but in

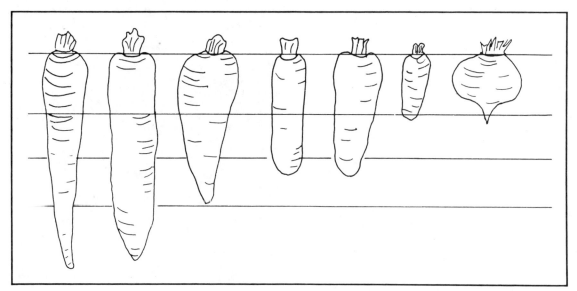

Fig. 11-6. Carrots come in a variety of shapes ranging from the long imperator (left) through the nates (center) to the baby finger and globe (right).

185

tightly-packed heavy soils only the short or round carrots should be attempted. Trying to grow a long carrot in a tight soil will result in misshapen and stunted growth.

Harvest. Carrots can be harvested at any time they are finger size or larger. The earlier you harvest, the better-tasting they tend to be. A good idea is to over-plant and thin at this stage, save the best thinned plants for eating. Fall carrots should be pulled after a few frosts to increase their storage capabilities. A nifty winter storage trick is to simply mulch heavily over the carrots after a few frosts. The mulch will keep the soil unfrozen through the winter and allow you to dig the carrots as needed through the winter. When dug and brought into a root cellar for storage, leave an inch or two of stem on each carrot to reduce shriveling. Overage carrots grow woody, so pick slightly before maturity for best flavor and texture.

Varieties. Long carrots: Gold Pack (75 days) and Imperator (77 days); medium: Danvers Half Long (80 days), Spartan Fancy (65 days) and Nates Half-Long (70 days); round: Golden Ball (58 days) and Planet (55 days); and small: Bunny Bite (70 days) and Little Finger (65 days).

CAULIFLOWER

This is perhaps the most finicky member of the Brassica (cabbage) family, but it is worth trying in areas with long cool springs and falls or cool summers. Hot summers prevent proper growth of this plant. Cauliflowers produce white, purple or green heads (similar to broccoli but tighter) at the crown of stalky stems.

Planting. Cauliflower, like other Brassica, does best when set out into the garden as a transplant. Start seeds indoors about 5 weeks prior to transplanting. Although these plants like cool weather, they are not very frost-tolerant and should be placed in the garden after all danger of heavy frost is past. Add a good helping of compost or well-rotted manure to each transplanting hole during planting and water thoroughly. Cauliflower does not like to have its roots disturbed during planting. The best method of starting seedlings is in individual peat pots. When grown in flats, cut around

root ball of each plant a week prior to transplanting. This will encourage the plant to start new roots closer to the stem, which are less likely to be disturbed during transplanting.

Culture. Cauliflower needs a rich, loose soil with a full complement of calcium for optimum growth. Water is also essential, and plants should be irrigated heavily during dry spells. Mulch will help conserve moisture while keeping soil cool. Cauliflower is shallow-rooted, so do not cultivate deeply.

Harvest. When cauliflower begins to form heads, blanching is required to keep white heads from turning green (Fig. 11-7). To blanch, pull a few leaves over the head and secure them in place with a loosely-tied string. Heads should fill out enough for

Fig. 11-7. Most cauliflower must be blanched by tying outer leaves around the central head to keep the head white.

186

picking within a week or two after blanching. Do not wait too long to pick them as heads quickly loose firmness. In the fall the entire plant can be pulled and hung in a cool place for up to a month prior to use.

Varieties. Early: Early Snowball (65 days), Daybreak (50 days) and White Horse (55 days); mid-maturing: Dry Weather (67 days), Ideal (60 days), and White Princess (60 days); green and purple: Chartreuse (115 days), Purple Giant (100 days), and Royal Purple Head (90 days).

CELERY

This vegetable prefers long, cool summers for growth, but can be raised in most parts of the United States with proper care. Celery is somewhat difficult to grow, but is well worth the effort (Fig. 11-8).

Planting. Celery is slow-growing and should be started indoors in flats or peat pots up to 10 weeks prior to planting into the garden. Although celery grows best during cool weather, it is not frost-hardy and should be transplanted into the garden a week or two after danger of frost has passed.

Culture. Celery plants are extremely heavy feeders, especially on potassium and phosphorus, and require loose soil with a high moisture content. Celery will not do well in acidic soils. It is best to grow celery in rows specially prepared by digging a trench up to 18 inches deep and then mixing compost or well-rotted manure into the soil throughout the entire depth of the trench. Water these plants heavily and often during growing season. Mulch will help reduce the need for irrigation, keep plants upright, and choke out weeds which may harbor virus carrying aphids. Damping-off is a common problem for young transplants in warm moist weather. To reduce this problem, keep celery well-weeded and spray occasionally with liquid seaweed.

Harvest. Celery should be harvested prior to the first fall frost. Before harvest, most gardeners like to blanch the stalks so that they take on a light green to white appearance. To blanch celery, place boards or other opaque materials around the stalks about 2 weeks before harvest. Six inches of the

Fig. 11-8. Celery is a garden crop often overlooked by gardeners. Although finicky, it is worth a try.

leaves should remain above the blanching material.

Varieties. Green: Clean Cut (125 days after transplanting) and Giant Pascal (135 days after transplanting); golden yellow: Golden Plume (100 days after transplanting) and Golden Tall Self-Blanching (110 days after transplanting).

CHINESE CABBAGE

This member of the Brassica family produces a loose head with curly leaves and thick leaf midribs. It is a cool weather crop that prefers to grow in the fall in the northern United States and the winter in the southern United States.

Planting. Plant seeds directly in prepared seedbeds in midsummer for fall crops. Dig compost into the soil about a month prior to planting. Although this plant will grow in the spring, the hotter the days get the more bitter the plant gets. This plant can also be started indoors in peat pots or flats for transplanting outside.

Culture. This plant, like all other Brassica, prefers a loose rich soil, with plenty of moisture. When soil is acidic, use lime to reduce acidity. When Chinese cabbage is planted in the summer for fall harvest, keep it well-watered to prevent wilting. Mulch heavily to save soil moisture.

Harvest. Cut heads off at soil line while centers are compact. This plant can be stored for up to a month in refrigeration, although it is much better when eaten fresh.

Varieties: Heading: Chihili (73 days), Michihili (70 days), and Wong Bok (70 days); loose head: Bok Choy (55 days) and Pack Choi (50 days).

CHIVES

This highly-productive member of the onion family has a delicate flavor that many gardeners prefer to onions. In most cases a 1-square-foot patch thickly sown with this vegetable will produce enough for an average family.

Planting. Sow only new seed. Chive seed remains viable for only 1 year, and older seeds will not germinate. Sow heavily in a small bed and allow all the plants that come up to grow. New sections of bed can be started by dividing clumps of chives and transplanting single plants to the new location.

Culture. Chives will grow just about anywhere in the United States. When allowed to grow tightly-spaced, they will choke out most weeds. Soil should be loose and rich. They need fertilization only when indications of nutrient deficiency appear.

Harvest. When chives are over 6 inches tall, they can be cut as needed. Leave about an inch or two of stem so that new top growth will be encouraged. The more you cut these plants, the better they will grow.

COLLARDS

Collards are one of the lesser-known members of the Brassica (cabbage) family and are not par-ticularly popular outside of the South. Collards produce leaves with a cabbage-like flavor. Unlike cabbage, collards are slow to bolt in hot weather—hence, their favor in southern gardens. Collard plants resemble a tall growing cabbage that refuses to form a head. The two basic types of collard are nonheading and those that form a very loose head.

Planting. In the north, collards are best when grown in the fall since a light frost seems to enhance their flavor. Midsummer planting is recommended. Although they can be planted in the spring as soon as the soil is workable, collards become tougher as the summer grows hotter. In the south, plant in spring and fall. Sow seeds in rows or beds and use thinnings as salad greens.

Culture. Collards do best with rapid growth. Therefore, loose, rich soils kept moist throughout the growing season are best. Mulch heavily to conserve moisture and to reduce cultivation which may harm this plant's shallow roots.

Harvest. The youngest, most tender leaves of this plant are the best. Early thinnings have such leaves. On older plants, leave the tough lower leaves and pick the uppermost or newest leaves. Plants will reproduce these leaves, allowing several pickings. Light frosts improve the flavor of this green.

Varieties. Georgia Green (80 days) and Vates Nonheading (65 days).

CORN

Although sweet corn is a favorite garden vegetable, it requires a lot of room and really does not produce as much food per plant as the size of the plant would indicate. Corn will grow in most parts of the United States where there is 3 to 4 months between frosts and a relatively warm growing season. There are hundreds of varieties of sweet corn, so experimentation with different varieties is necessary to find the one that does best in your soil and climate and appeals the most to your taste.

Planting. Corn can be planted in rows or hills (three to four plants to a hill) after all danger of frost is past and soil has warmed to between 50 to 60° F. Since corn is pollinated by wind-carried pollen, it is best to plant this crop in blocks of several rows or hills to ensure proper pollination. Make several plantings of corn 1 or 2 weeks apart early in the season so that harvest will occur over several weeks. When making multiple plantings, it is better to plant several short rows side by side than one long row of each variety. When planting in dry soil, soak seed overnight to increase the germination rate.

Culture. Corn likes loose, well-drained, and moderately-rich soil. Plant it where it will receive full sun, but will not shade lower-growing crops. Dig in a 1- to 2-inch layer of compost or well-rotted manure prior to planting to ensure adequate nutrients. Corn is not very picky about the alkalinity or acidity of the soil, but does require a full measure of calcium for proper growth. Water is required at a rate of about 1 inch per week. Mulch between rows to conserve moisture. Water is especially critical when kernels begin to fill out.

Harvest. Corn stays at its peak for less than a week, so proper timing of the harvest is important. Test corn by squeezing a kernel and checking the fluid that is released. When fluid is clear, the corn is not yet mature. When milky fluid squirts out, it is ready. A doughy consistency means that the corn has passed its prime, and the sugary fluids in the kernels are turning to starch. As soon as corn is picked, the sugars in the kernels begin turning to starch, so the shorter the period between picking and cooking, the better it will taste. Most corn eaters suggest having a pot of boiling water on the stove before going out to pick corn. Husk the corn quickly and slip it into the boiling water.

Varieties. Yellow: Early Sunglow (70 days), Early Golden Giant (70 days), Golden Cross Bantam (85 days), Iochief (85 days), and Jubilee (85 days); white: Country Gentleman (95 days), Silver Queen (95 days), and White Delight (85 days); extra sweet: Early Extra Sweet (70 days) and Illini Xtra-Sweet (85 days); bi-color: Butter and Sugar (80 days), Honey and Cream (78 days), and Bi-Queen (90 days); popcorn: Early White Hybrid (90 days), White Hull-less (105 days), Best Yellow (105 days), and Purdue 410 (105 days); ornamental: In-

dian Ornamental Corn (105 days) and Rainbow (110 days).

CRESS

This member of the mustard family is most commonly known to gardeners as garden cress or pepper grass. It is quick-growing and adds spice to salads and sandwiches.

Planting. Plant seed as soon as soil can be worked by broadcasting seed over a small square of soil. Cover with a thin layer of dirt. Plant in spring and fall during cool weather.

Culture. Cress grows best in rich soils with plenty of water. Fertilizer is rarely required. As summer heats up, cress becomes more bitter or hot-tasting.

Harvest. Cut as needed after cress is 6 to 8 inches tall. By cutting on several plants instead of cutting all the leaves off of one plant, harvest can be prolonged.

Varieties. American (60 days), Curlicress (45 days), and Salad Cress (10 days).

CUCUMBER

This member of the cucuberit family, which includes melons, squash, and pumpkins, is a favorite vegetable of many gardeners. Cucumbers are available in two basic types: pickling and slicing. Among these two types there are hundreds of varieties. In general, slicing cucumbers grow long, straight, and large while pickling cucumbers tend to be smaller and spindlier than their slicing counterparts.

Planting. Cucumbers are a warm-weather crop and cannot stand frost. They should be planted after all danger of frost is past and the soil has warmed to 60° F. Cucumbers are traditionally planted in hills 6 to 7 feet apart. Plant six seeds to a hill and thin to the three strongest plants when 3 inches tall. In rows, seeds should be spaced at least 6 inches apart. Make two or three plantings, 2 to 3 weeks apart, to increase the length of the harvest season. Seeds marked as polygameous have more cucumber-producing (female) flowers than other cucumbers. This makes them heavy producers.

Culture. Cucumbers like a really rich, very deep, loose soil. These plants prefer a warm, moist, slightly-shaded location. They do well when grown between corn rows. Cucumbers are very heavy feeders and drinkers. They need more water and fertilizer than most other plants in the garden. A weekly feeding of manure or compost tea is highly beneficial. During periods of drought, water them at least every other day. Soil should have ample amounts of compost and well-rotted manure worked in deeply prior to planting. Mulch heavily around plants to conserve soil moisture and to keep vines and fruit off the ground. Where space is limited, cucumbers can be trained to climb trellises or fences. They will grow 5 to 6 feet tall, and fruit will be straight and smooth because it does not lay on the ground.

Harvest. Cucumbers should be picked when they reach an edible size. The sooner and more often you pick cucumbers, the more the plant will produce. Do not wait until cucumbers turn yellow to pick or they will be past their prime. Should cucumbers turn yellow, pick them and add them to the compost pile, so the plant that they came from can direct energy toward producing more cucumbers. Do not handle cucumber plants when they are wet or you may spread disease.

Varieties. Long slicing: China Long (75 days) and Sunnybrook (60 days); medium slicing: Black Diamond (58 days), Burpee M&M Hybrid (60 days), Marketer Improved (70 days), and Smoothie (75 days); pickling: Burpee Pickler (55 days), Galaxy (60 days), Mariner (53 days), and Salty (50 days).

DILL

This annual herb should be grown if you intend to pickle cucumbers. It can also be used to add zest to salads and pasta dishes. Dill grows throughout the United States.

Planting. After the last frost, plant dill by sprinkling seeds over a small area or into rows and cover with a thin layer of dirt. Dill can also be started in flats or peat pots and transplanted into the garden after all danger of frost is past.

Culture. Dill grows in almost any soil and seems to prefer marginal soils. This herb should be grown in full sun. It does not require extra watering except in cases of severe drought. Dill beds should be weeded and mulched. Since this plant grows on a fragile stem, it should be staked when 1 foot tall to prevent wind damage.

Harvest. When harvested for fresh leaves, pick a few from each plant to prevent setting the plant back too much. When harvesting for seed, allow seed heads to dry on the stalk, but pick them just before seedpods break open and drop their seeds. Hang in a dry shady place until seeds fall from heads. Leaves can be dried by pulling up the plant and hanging in a dry shady place until crumbly. Store in airtight containers.

Varieties. Since dill is still closely related to its wild cousins, little selection has occurred and specific varieties have not been developed.

EGGPLANT

Eggplants can be a problem to grow for some gardeners, but for others they grow quite readily. The 3-foot-tall tree-like structure of this plant adds an interesting touch to the garden, as does its unique purple fruits. There are two basic types of eggplants: oval and cylindrical. The oval varieties produce egg-shaped fruits up to five inches in diameter; the cylindrical types produce longer, thinner plants of equally good quality.

Planting. Eggplants will not stand frost and should be started indoors in flats or individual peat pots 7 to 8 weeks prior to planting out in the garden. Plant out after danger of frost has passed and soil has warmed to 60° F. Protect plants from sun and wind a few days after transplanting.

Culture. Eggplants demand an ample supply of nutrients and water as well as plenty of heat for good production. Soil should be very rich with a light texture. Dig in substantial amounts of compost or well-rotted manure prior to planting. Side-dress with compost during the growing season to keep a steady supply of nutrients available. Soil should be slightly acid with plenty of moisture so that nutrients are readily available. Mulch heavily after plants have established themselves and soil is warm to conserve moisture.

Harvest. Fruit should be picked when shiny, glossy, and deep in color. Cut the stem to prevent damaging the plant. Do not leave fruit on the plant once it begins to dull, or further fruit production will be slowed.

Varieties. Oval: Black Beauty (80 days from transplanting), Black Magic (73 days from transplanting), and Midnite Hybrid (70 days from transplanting); cylindrical: Dusky (60 days from transplanting), Long Black (100 days from transplanting), and Royal Knight (65 days from transplanting); non-purple: Albino (68 days from transplanting) and Golden Yellow (75 days from transplanting).

ENDIVE

Endive is a little-known salad crop that grows much the same as lettuce, but produces greens with a sharper flavor. Endive is often called escarole and comes with either curled or uncurled leaves.

Planting. Endive should be sown as soon as soil can be worked in the spring. Cover seeds with a thin layer of soil. Since this plant is hardy until the first frost of the fall, it is often grown as a fall crop. Sow in midsummer for a fall crop.

Culture. Endive prefers rich, well-drained loam soils. This plant likes a lot of nutrients close to the soil's surface since it is shallow-rooted. Dig compost into the soil prior to planting. During growth, side-dress with compost or well-rotted manure. Endive requires adequate moisture to ensure quick growth. Water heavily during dry spells and mulch to reduce water loss due to evaporation.

Harvest. Endive is grown for the loose head produced at the center of the plant. Many gardeners say the taste of this head is improved when it is blanched. Two weeks prior to harvest, tie outer leaves together so they shade the central head. When the central head has turned white, cut the plant and discard the outer leaves which will be more bitter than the blanched central head.

Varieties. Curled: Deep Heart Fringed (90 days) and Green Curled (90 days); uncurled: Batavian Full Hearted (85 days) and Broad Leaved Batavian: (90 days).

GARLIC

This strongly flavored and pungent member of the onion family is a perennial, but in most gardens it is treated like an annual. There are two types of garlic: regular and elephant. The regular type is familiar in most kitchens. The elephant garlic has regular garlic's flavor, but lacks its pungency.

Planting. Garlic is planted as individual cloves, which have been separated from the bulb, as soon as the ground can be worked in the spring. Although garlic can be planted in rows or beds, many people like to scatter it throughout the garden as a means of insect protection.

Culture. Garlic prefers a loose soil that is moderately rich and moist. This plant is shallow-rooted, so be careful when cultivating near it. Garlic left in the ground will keep coming back year after year, but the cloves get increasingly smaller. This is why garlic is best grown as an annual instead of a perennial.

Harvest. Bulbs should be pulled or dug up when tops fall over and die. In very rich soil this may not happen, and tops should be broken over at the end of the season and allowed to die back before digging. Garlic should be cured by drying in a shady place for a week prior to storage.

Varieties. California White Garlic (110 days) and Elephant Garlic (100 days).

JERUSALEM ARTICHOKE

This member of the sunflower family is native to America and is grown for the tubers it produces (Fig. 11-9). Jerusalem artichokes grow to 8 feet and produce an abundance of showy yellow flowers. Although the tubers of this plant are potato-like, they do not store starch. Instead, carbohydrates are stored as insulin and sugar is stored as levulose. It is highly recommended for diabetics. This plant will spread rapidly throughout the garden, so it is best grown in a separate bed where it will not invade other crops.

Planting. Plant in early spring by burying tubers 4 inches deep. Although Jerusalem artichokes require a long growing season of 125 days, they can be grown throughout most of the United States.

Fig. 11-9. The tubers of Jerusalem artichokes make a nice change of pace from potatoes.

Culture. This plant grows in almost any soil, although rich, loose soils produce the best-shaped tubers. Jerusalem artichokes are disease-and pest-free, and they will do well with little attention.

Harvest. Dig tubers after the plant has begun to die back in the fall. The tubers do not keep well out of the ground, but when left in the ground and mulched heavily they can be dug throughout the winter as needed.

Varieties. American (125 days).

KALE

This member of the Brassica (cabbage) family is grown for its leaves, which are used for greens. The two basic types of kale are Scotch, which has curled blue-green leaves, and Siberian, with flat gray-green leaves.

Planting. Kale is cold-hardy and becomes bitter when grown in heat. Plant in spring in the north where summers are cool or in midsummer for a fall crop in the south where summers are hot. Frost improves the flavor of this plant. Sow seeds sparsely and thin when plants are 5 to 6 inches tall. Thinnings can be used for salad greens.

Culture. Like other Brassica crops, kale likes fertile loam soils that are neutral to slightly alkaline. Their location should be sunny, well-drained, and a place where other cabbage family members were not grown the previous year. Dig in a liberal amount of compost or well-rotted manure prior to planting and work in enough limestone to reduce the soil's acidity when necessary. Keep kale well-watered for quick growth, which prevents leaves from becoming tough and stringy. Mulch to conserve moisture and reduce weeding. Plants can be mulched at the end of fall to overwinter in the garden and produce an early crop the following spring.

Harvest. Kale can be harvested by removing outermost leaves, allowing inner leaves to continue growing. The traditional method of harvest is to cut every other plant, allowing more room for remaining plants. Frost enhances kale's flavor so cut after the first frost.

Varieties. Scotch: Blue Curled Scotch (65 days) and Dwarf Blue Curled Vates (55 days); Siberian: Hanover Late Seeding (45 days) and Siberian (65 days).

KOHLRABI

Kohlrabi is a strange-looking member of the cabbage family that produces a swelled stem just above ground (Fig. 11-10). Cabbage-like leaves grow out of this globe. For this reason, kohlrabi is often called a turnip cabbage. Purple and white types are available, although both have white flesh.

Planting. Plant seeds as soon as soil can be worked in the spring. For an earlier crop, begin seeds inside 6 to 8 weeks prior to last frost date. Plant in flats or individual peat pots. For a fall crop, sow in midsummer. Seeds should be soaked overnight in water prior to midsummer planting to enhance germination rate.

Culture. Like other members of the Brassica family, kohlrabi prefers rich, moist, loose soils with plenty of lime and available nutrients. This plant will stand slight shade. Dig in a healthy helping of compost prior to planting. This plant requires a lot of water in order for it to take in the nutrients it needs for quick growth. Mulch heavily to keep soil cool and to preserve soil moisture.

Harvest. The globe-like section of kohlrabi should be harvested when it is between the size of a golf ball and a baseball. The smaller it is, the more tender the interior flesh will be. Late crops should be harvested after the first fall frost, as the cold tends to increase its flavor. Late harvests can be stored in a root cellar until early winter.

Fig. 11-10. Kohlrabi has a strange shape and produces a flesh with a taste between cabbage and turnip.

Varieties. White: Early White Vienna (60 days) and Grand Duke (50 days); purple: Blue Danish L.D. (65 days) and Early Purple Vienna (60 days).

LEEKS

This bland, sweet member of the onion family does not form bulbs. Instead, leeks are grown for their thick stems which are often used in salads and delicately-flavored dishes. Leeks can be grown in most areas in the United States where the growing season is at least 4 months long.

Planting. Leek seeds should be planted in flats 8 weeks prior to last spring frost. When transplanting leeks outside, dig a trench 6 inches deep and line the bottom with compost. Cut off one-half of each plant's green leaf growth and place the remainder of the plant in the trench (Fig. 11-11). Pull an inch or two of soil around each plant and water. As the leeks grow soil and compost should be filled into the trench. In this way the stem of the leek is supported and blanched to enhance its flavor.

Culture. Leeks prefer a rich, deep loam with a neutral reaction. They respond well to heavy applications of fertilizer when supplied in the form of well-rotted manure or compost. Early growth requires a good amount of nitrogen that can be supplied by side-dressing with cottonseed meal or dried blood. Adequate amounts of moisture should be applied during the early stages of growth and during drought to keep leeks crisp.

Harvest. Leeks require a full summer of growth and are harvested in early to late fall by digging up the desired plants. The blanched white stalk is eaten. These plants can be left in the ground through heavy frost and finally mulched in place for winter storage. Dig as needed.

Varieties. American Broad Flag (90-130 days), Broad London (130-150 days), Elephant Leek (85-120 days), and Titan (70 days).

LETTUCE

Lettuce is one of the easiest crops to grow. This vegetable does well wherever there is a cool

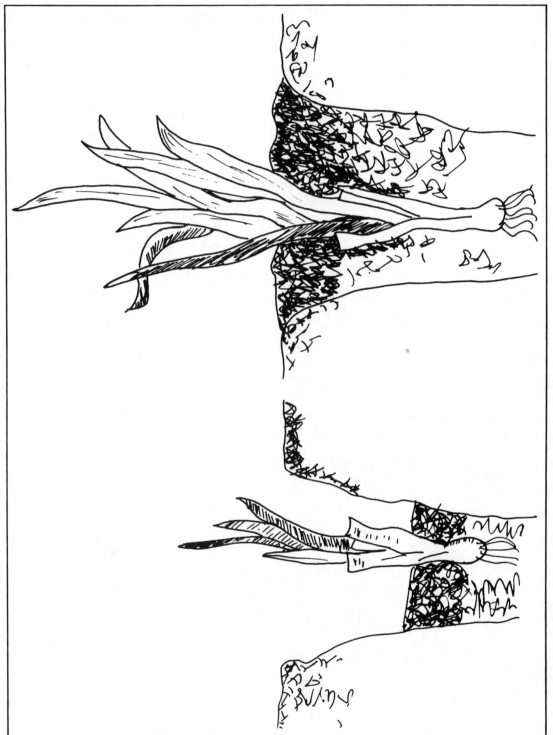

Fig. 11-11. Plant leeks in a trench (left), filling in around the plant as it grows, right.

season. Lettuce comes in a multitude of shapes, sizes, colors, and textures. There are four types of lettuce: head, butterhead, romaine, and looseleaf. Head lettuce is the type most often found in supermarkets. Butterhead is a looser version of true head lettuce and is easier to grow than the commercial head lettuces. Romaine lettuce produces an upright cylindrical plant with thicker stems and a smaller central head than head or butterhead lettuce. Looseleaf lettuce produces no head. Instead, it grows in a rosette pattern with individual leaves that can be picked as needed.

Planting. Lettuce is usually sown directly into the garden as soon as the soil can be worked in the spring. You can produce an earlier crop by starting it indoors several weeks prior to transplanting outside. Transfer seedlings to the garden when soil can be worked. When you transplant lettuce, also make a sowing of seeds so that lettuce will mature through the spring instead of all at one time. Early fall plantings will result in an abundance of lettuce through the severe killing frosts. The small seed of this plant should not be buried too deeply—less than ¼ inch of dirt will usually do the trick. Thin head, butterhead, and romaine lettuce so that individual plants do not touch. Leaf lettuce plants can touch, but they will grow better when thinned.

Culture. Lettuce prefers a rich, loose soil with plenty of moisture for quick growth. Since lettuce is a cool-weather crop, do not attempt to grow it during the heat of summer or the plants will send up seed stalks. When lettuce starts to bolt, it becomes bitter and worthless. Lettuce will grow in slight shade. Compost or well-rotted manure should be dug into the top few inches of soil where lettuce is to be grown. The shallow roots of this plant will limit cultivation, but a fine sprinkling of compost or other loose mulch can be spread around plants to reduce weeds and to keep moisture in the soil. Water frequently and heavily during dry periods. Lettuce should be weeded and cultivated late in the day to avoid damaging plants that are suffering from midday heat. Make several sowings of different types of lettuce through the season in order to keep a ready supply available for table use.

Harvesting. Lettuce is crispest early in the morning. Pick it in the morning before midday wilt and store for use later in the day. Old plants tend to turn bitter, so when a particular planting begins to loose its taste turn it under and replace it with another vegetable. Head, butterhead, and romaine lettuce are usually harvested by cutting off plants at ground level. Leaf lettuce can be picked by pulling the outermost leaves and allowing the innermost leaves to achieve desired size.

Varieties. Head: Fairton (90 days), Great Lakes (95 days), Imperial (80 days), and Iceberg (85 days); butterhead: Bibb (65 days), Dark Green Boston (80 days), Fordhook (78 days), Buttercrunch (70 days), and Butter King (80 days); romaine: Crisp Mint (70 days), Paris Green (70 days), and Paris White Cos (75 days); Looseleaf: Black Seeded Simpson (45 days), Grand Rapids (45 days), Oak Leaf (45 days), and Ruby (55 days).

LIMA BEANS

Like snap beans, limas are available in both bush and pole types. Both types of limas have plump and baby lima bean variations. The plump are large flat beans; the baby are smaller in size. Limas require a somewhat long growing season and do best with at least two months in which the nighttime temperature does not dip below 50° F.

Planting. Limas must be planted after all danger of frost is past, preferably when soil has warmed to at least 65° F. Early planting in cool, wet soil may result in rotting of the seed prior to germination. Since limas are legumes, they benefit from a seed inoculation with nitrogen-fixing bacteria. When placing limas in the ground, seed eyes should be positioned down to help this large seed push through the soil's surface.

Culture. Limas prefer better soil than snap beans. Soil should be loam and well-drained, with a normal complement of humus. This bean prefers sunshine and lots of it. Although limas do not require substantial amounts of fertilizer, a side-dressing of compost is beneficial. Limas are shallow-rooted and should not be cultivated deeply. Mulching is preferred. This bean likes a moist soil, so water it during droughts. Do not handle plants when they are wet to prevent the spread of disease.

Harvest. Limas tend to ripen all at once, unlike snap beans, so be prepared to do a lot of picking during the short time they are at their peak. Harvest can be extended somewhat by making two or more plantings of the bean 1 to 2 weeks apart. Limas can be picked when they first start to swell the pod. These green beans make a fine fresh bean dish. They can also be allowed to dry on the vine and shelled out for winter storage.

Varieties. Bush plump: Fordhook 242 (75 days); bush baby: Henderson Bush Lima (75 days) and Dixie Butterpea (75 days); pole plump: King Of The Garden (88 days) and Giant Podded (90 days); pole baby: Carolina (80 days) and Climbing Baby Lima (70 days).

MINTS

Mints comprise a large family of aromatic herbs that can be grown quite easily in the home garden. Spearmint, peppermint, apple mint, and long-leaved mint are the four most common varieties. Each has a distinct taste and smell.

Planting. Mints are usually started from cuttings that have been allowed to root in water. Plant cuttings in well-worked soil slightly deeper than the level of the water they were rooted in. Plant them in beds so that they choke out weeds. Most mints propagate quickly by means of runners and will take over the garden if not held in check.

Culture. Mints prefer well-worked, loose soils with a lot of moisture. Frequent waterings during dry spells are necessary to keep these plants at their peak. Mints will stand slight shading. Mints withstand transplanting well and are often dug up and re-potted in flower pots before being carried inside for winter enjoyment.

Harvest. Leaves, stems, and top buds can be picked at any time for use in the kitchen. It is generally better to pinch back the tips of the stalks prior to the time when they send up seed heads. The amount of volatile oil (mint's active ingredient) falls off considerably after flowers have formed. These plants can be dried by hanging them in a shady place with good air circulation. When dry, crumble leaves and store in airtight containers.

Varieties. Mints are closely related to wild plants, so no distinct varieties have been developed.

MUSKMELON

Muskmelons, also known as cantaloupes, are a warm-weather crop that require a growing season with temperatures above 55° F at night and above 80° F during the day. Although many gardeners call all of these sweet, orange-colored flesh melons cantaloupes, cantaloupes are actually a smaller class of muskmelons. Muskmelons come with a wide range of outside skin markings, flesh thicknesses, tolerance to disease, season lengths, and flavors. When deciding on a variety to grow in your area, ask around to find out what other gardeners have grown successfully.

Planting. In the south where summers are long and hot, muskmelons can be sown directly into the ground when the soil has warmed to at least 65° F and all danger of frost is past. In the north, short-season varieties should be planting indoors 1 to 2 months prior to outdoor transplanting. Muskmelons can be planted in rows with at least 1 foot between plants. Rows should be 4 to 5 feet apart. Muskmelons can also be planted in hills with 4 to 5 feet between the hills. Place six seeds in each hill and thin to the two or three strongest plants when 6 inches tall.

Culture. Muskmelons prefer light sandy soils with considerable amounts of humus and good drainage. Plant where they will receive full sun and can be watered frequently during dry spells. Since melons are largely water, the moisture content of the soil must be kept high. A deep mulch and frequent irrigation are essential. Prior to planting, compost or well-rotted manure should be dug into hills or rows to a depth of at least 1 foot. Although the traditional method for growing muskmelons is to allow the vines to trail over the ground, you can reduce this space requirement by training these vines to climb a trellis. When fruits have set, they should be supported with a nylon mesh—old onion bags work well—tied to the trellis. When allowed to trail across the ground, each melon should be set on a stone or board to keep crawling insects at bay.

Harvest. Cantaloupes are ready for harvest when they pass the slip test. To perform the slip test, apply light pressure to the stem at the base of the melon. If the stem slips off, the cantaloupe is ready to eat. If the stem does not budge, the melon has not yet reached maturity. To test Crenshaw and Persian melons, smell the blossom end of the fruit. When it smells fruity and sweet and gives a little when pressed with your finger, the melon is ripe. Honey Dew and Casaba melons are ripe when the rinds are totally yellow. Do not pick melons early and expect them to ripen. Once the melon has been picked, it will not ripen further; in fact, it begins to lose some of its sweetness.

Varieties. Cantaloupes: Mammoth (95 days), Hearts of Gold (90 days), Hale's Best (85 days), and New Ideal (80 days), cantaloupes, green: Burpee's Fordhood Gem (80 days); Green Nutmeg (63 days), and Rocky Ford Green Flesh (85 days); honeydew: Honeydew (110 days), Honey Mist (92 days), and Kazakh (70 days); casaba/crenshaw: Crenshaw (100 days), Persian Medium (95 days), and Santa Claus (110 days).

MUSTARD GREENS

These greens are a favorite in the south, although mustard greens will grow virtually anywhere in the United States. Two types, smooth and curled leaf, are available.

Planting. Sow mustard seed as soon as the soil can be worked in the spring. Space seeds at 2- to 3-inch intervals in the row and thin to 6 inches when plants have established themselves. Mustard can be planted in late summer or early fall for an end-of-the-season crop.

Culture. This crop prefers a sandy loam soil with ample moisture to promote quick growth. The faster the growth, the less chance of the leaves becoming stringy and tough. Mulch around individual plants to keep down weeds, enhance soil moisture, and encourage cool soil.

Harvest. Mustard greens are quick growers and will become knee-high 5 to 6 weeks after planting. When greens are to be used in salads, cut them when plants are 4 to 6 inches tall. For cooking greens, cut off larger leaves, allowing the central stem to continue growing and producing more leaves. Mustard will turn bitter and hot-tasting when warm weather arrives.

Varieties. Curled: Green Wave (50 days) and Southern Giant Curled (50 days); smooth: Florida Broad Leaf (45 days) and Large Smooth Leaf (40 days).

NEW ZEALAND SPINACH

New Zealand spinach is not a true spinach, but it looks and tastes close enough to fool most taste buds. This plant can be grown as a spinach substitute in areas where the cool growing conditions necessary for a true spinach do not exist. New Zealand spinach will keep its flavor during the heat of summer while most other greens turn bitter and tough.

Planting. Plant seeds in well-worked soil a week or two after the last frost date. Soaking seeds for a day prior to planting will encourage germination. Plant sparsely, as this plant produces heavily on its sprawling, almost vine-like, stems.

Culture. New Zealand spinach needs a thoroughly worked soil that is rich in nutrients (especially nitrogen) and plenty of water to encourage quick growth. Side-dress plants with cottonseed or dried blood after germination. Mulch to reduce evaporation of moisture from the soil and to hamper weed competition.

Harvest. Cut back 6 inches of the tips of growing plants and prepare like other greens. The beauty of New Zealand spinach is that it does not become bitter as the summer becomes hot. You can often harvest from the same plants right through the summer and fall until heavy frosts set in.

Varieties. New Zealand Spinach (70 days).

OKRA

This Southern favorite, also known as Gumbo, will add a distinctly tropical look to your garden. This plant has a tree-like structure with purple and orange flowers through the summer. The flowers produce the seedpods for which this plant is noted (Fig. 11-12). This vegetable will add a unique flavor to soups and fish dishes. Plants come in standard sizes, 5 to 10 feet in height, or in dwarf sizes up to 5

Fig. 11-12. The seedpods of okra are a favorite in Southern gardens and are beginning to gain acceptance farther north.

feet tall. Both sizes come in a variety of pod shapes ranging from short to long, round to ridged, in colors of green, light-green, and red. Many types are quite ornamental with their big colorful flowers.

Planting. Seeds should be planted after last frost, when night temperatures are remaining above 50° F. Soak overnight before planting in order to soften the tough shell on this seed. Okra can be started inside in individual peat pots 1 month prior to last frost date for earlier harvest.

Culture. Okra will grow in a soil of average fertility as long as the soil has a decent texture. During its early stages of growth, okra will benefit from a side-dressing of rotted manure or compost. This plant prefers well-drained soils, and excess moisture may cause the roots to rot. When you

mulch this plant, mulch lightly so that the soil dries quickly after each rain. Okra likes full sun.

Harvest. As mentioned earlier, this plant is grown for the pods formed after flowering. Pick pods when small—2 to 3 inches in length—and still tender. The larger a pod gets, the tougher it becomes. Additionally, leaving pods on the plant will slow flowering, reducing the number of small pods on the plant. Okra will produce pods until nights cool to less than 50° F when picked regularly.

Varieties. Standard size: Clemson Spineless (60 days), Green Louisiana Long (60 days) and Perkins Spineless (55 days); dwarf: Dwarf Green Long Pod (50 days), Emerald (56 days) and Gold Coast (60 days); colored: Red Okra (60 days), Red River (65 days), and White Velvet (60 days).

ONION

This member of the lily family is a cool-weather crop grown for the bulbs or stems it produces. Onions grow blade-like leaves during the cool months and form bulbs after the sun has peaked in the sky and the weather grows hot. Since the bulbs store food from the leaves, the bigger the leaves the larger the bulbs. Onions come in a variety of colors from red to yellow to white with sizes ranging from scallions, without bulbs, to the large globe onions with bulbs of 4- to 5-inch diameters. As a general rule, yellow onions keep better than red or white varieties.

A unique onion you may want to try is called the Egyptian or tree onion. This onion produces small onion sets at the top of its stalk where other onions would normally produce a flower and seedhead (Fig. 11-13). These bulbs can be planted like conventional onion bulbs, and when left in the ground for the winter will produce more sets the following season. Shallots are another onion variety that produce small bulbs. Larger shallots are divided into cloves similar to garlic. This variety is usually used as a green bunching onion.

Planting. Onions should be planted as early in the spring as the soil can be worked. Seeds are planted ½ inch deep. Sets (small bulbs) are set 1 inch deep, and onion plants should be set slightly

198

Fig. 11-13. Egyptian onions form sets at the top of their seed stalks. These small onions can be planted or eaten.

deeper than they grew in the flat. The plants and sets will produce onions with bulbs. Seeds will not normally produce bulbs because the season is not long enough. Seed will, however, grow fine early green bunching onions or small sets for planting the following spring. Sets larger than a dime should not be used, since they tend to produce a flower and a seedhead instead of a bulb.

Culture. Onions prefer a rich loam soil, slightly on the acid side. Although onions prefer moist soil, especially during the early stages of their growth, their location must be well-drained to prevent rotting. Onions are heavy feeders during the early stages of their development. Sufficient nutrients can be provided by spreading a layer of well-rotted compost or manure over their bed after planting. Onions are shallow-rooted so fertilizers do not need to be worked in deeply, although a deeply-worked and loose soil will provide the drainage necessary for good growth. Regular onions do not form good bulbs when they are allowed to form flowers. Therefore, flowers should be cut off as soon as they appear to allow for good bulb development. Egyptian onions should not be treated this way since the bulbs formed at the top of the flower stalks are edible.

Harvest. Young onions have a more delicate flavor than old ones and are more easily digested. For table use, onions should be pulled when they are ¼ to 1 inch in diameter. Onions intended for boiling should be slightly larger, up to 1½ inches in diameter. Onions intended for storage should stay in the ground until tops fall over and shrivel brown to the neck of the bulb. When more than one-half of your onion crop has fallen over, knock the tops of the remaining onions over so that they begin to die back. When tops have died back, pull onions and allow them to cure by spreading them on the ground in the sun for a couple of days. Cut off tops 1 inch above bulbs before storing in a cool, dry, dark place.

Varieties. Seeds: Sweet Spanish (110 days), Southport Yellow Globe (115 days), Yellow Globe Danvers (112 days); sets: Ebenezer (100 days), Yellow Bermuda (95 days), Crystal White Wax (95 days); scallions: White Welsh (95 days) and Evergreen Long White Bunching (120 days); Egyptian.

OREGANO

This strong tasting herb is a native of the Mediterranean region. Oregano is widely used in cooking as a tomato sauce for spaghetti, pizza, and pasta.

Planting. Plant seeds in beds when danger of frost has passed. Some types of oregano can also be started from stem cuttings rooted in water prior to transplanting into the garden. Plant on 12-inch centers in bed arrangements.

Culture. Oregano does well in soils of average fertility, provided they are worked deeply and provide good tilth and drainage. This plant does not require much water, but it should be cultivated often during early growth and then mulched heavily when soil is warm. You can get bushy, dense growth by cutting back the entire stand to within 1 inch of the soil about two months into the plant's growth.

Harvest. Unlike most other herbs, which reach their peak flavor just before blooming, oregano reaches its peak just as it begins to bloom.

Cut and hang inside or outside in direct sun for quick drying. When dry, crumble into a fine powder and store in airtight containers. Oregano can also be used green, although its flavor is not as strong as dried leaves.

Varieties. Greek Oregano and Oregano.

PARSLEY

This biennial herb is grown much like an annual, except that is can be overwintered beneath a winter mulch. Parsley produces leaves rich in vitamins and minerals and is relatively carefree once it is established. Plant parsley near the kitchen so that it is convenient for frequent use. It grows well in flower pots on windowsills during the winter. A few varieties are grown for their taproot.

Planting. Sow seeds in well-worked soil when danger of frost is past. Seeds are very leisurely about germinating and may take upward of 4 weeks to break through the soil. Overnight soaking in water will speed germination, but not more than a few days. Germination rate for this seed is low, so sow thickly and thin plants to 6-inch centers when established. Although this plant is a biennial, you need to sow it each year to ensure a crop the following year. Rooted varieties produce a carrot-like root.

Culture. Parsley does best in fertile rich loams, but it will do well in any average garden soil as long as it has a relatively loose texture. During early growth this plant needs a lot of nitrogen for quick leaf production. Side-dress with compost, well-rotted manure, or cottonseed meal when established. A thick mulch should keep soil moist enough for adequate growth. This plant will tolerate slight shading. Although root parsley grows under similar conditions as leaf parsley, the root crop needs a very deep soil. As mentioned earlier, parsley makes a good indoor herb through the winter. Smaller plants can be dug up and transplanted into a flower pot to be carried inside, or fresh seed can be started directly in pots in late summer.

Harvest. Outer leaves should be snipped off with scissors allowing the central part of the plant to continue growing. To store leaves, pick them and spread them out in a shady place until partially dried. Then move parsley to a dry, dark area where drying should continue until crumbly. Crumble into flakes and store in airtight containers. The rooted varieties produce a carrot-like root that can be dug in the late fall.

Varieties. Curled: Banquet (76 days), Emerald (85 days), and Extra Triple Curled (75 days); plain: Dark Green Italian (72 days), Giant Italian (85 days), and Plain Leaf (75 days); long-rooted: Hamburg Long Rooted (90 days) and Rooted Parsley Record (90 days).

PARSNIP

Parsnips are sometimes called white carrots because they produce carrot-like white taproots. This plant does not enjoy wide popularity, although it is a welcome change from most other root crops. Short-, medium-, and long-rooted varieties have been developed.

Planting. Sow seeds in a very deeply worked soil when all danger of frost has passed. Parsnip seed is very fine and is easier to handle when mixed with sifted compost or coffee grounds prior to planting. This plant's seed is very slow to germinate, and you may want to mix a few radish seeds into the parsnip seeds in order to mark the row. You may also want to lay boards or burlap over the rows to help hold in moisture and improve germination. Check beneath boards frequently and remove when first sprouts appear.

Culture. This plant likes a very deeply-worked soil at least two feet deep with a healthy complement of well-rotted manure and compost mixed in. Parsnips prefer open, sunny locations with good drainage. Watering is essential during early growth, but is not necessary once plants have established themselves and a mulch has been applied. Parsnips require a long growing season—upward of four months.

Harvest. Unlike carrots, parsnips cannot be pulled. They should be dug. Frost improves the flavor of this root, and they are best when dug after cold weather has killed off the top growth. Parsnips can be mulched and left in the ground through the winter and dug as needed. Many gardeners like to leave the roots in the ground until the following spring when they are dug before new growth starts.

Varieties. Long: Hollow Crown (95-130 days) and All American (95-145 days); medium: White Model (100 days) and Premium (80 days); short: Improved Stump Rooted (95 days) and Jung's White Sugar (95 days).

PEANUTS

Peanuts are a crop that's widely grown in the south, and they're becoming more popular in the north. This plant has a rather unique growing habit. The bush sends up stems that flower and then bend over, sending peduncles down into the soil. The peanut is formed at the end of the peduncle.

Planting. In the south, plant seed peanuts, shell and all, up to 4 inches deep. In the north, shell peanuts, being careful not to damage the red skin, and plant no more than 1½ inches deep. In cool, cloudy weather peanuts may take more than a week to sprout. Cool wet weather may cause seed to rot in the ground. Plant during dry weather in the north.

Culture. Peanuts do not require a particularly rich soil; however, the soil must be loose. Sandy loams are preferred. Dig in a healthy complement of well-rotted manure or compost before planting. When plants are 1 foot high, hoe the soil around the base of plants, forming a flat, broad hill. Cultivate regularly to keep soil loose until peduncles have pushed down into the soil. Then mulch heavily and leave plants alone.

Harvest. Peanuts are ready for harvest when their leaves turn yellow and die back. In the north this will probably coincide with the first light frosts. Pull up plants and peanuts should remain attached to peduncles. Dig through soil to retrieve any that may have broken off. Peanuts should be spread in a dry place for 2 months or longer to cure before roasting. Roast 20 minutes in a 300° F oven.

Varieties: Standard: Jumbo Virginia (120 days); dwarf; Spanish (110 days).

PEAS

This member of the legume family is one of the best reasons to have a garden. Peas germinate almost as soon as they are in the ground, and they bloom and produce quickly. Although there are hundreds of pea varieties, they can be classed broadly into three groups: early, midseason, and late. Some other variations include smooth and wrinkled seed, edible pods, and dwarf varieties. Different pea varieties also have pods of varying length, number of seeds, and disease resistance.

Planting. Peas are a cool-weather crop that should be planted as soon as the soil can be worked in the spring. In dry soil, soak seed overnight prior to planting. Soaking is unnecessary in moist soil. Peas should be inoculated with nitrogen-fixing bacteria before planting to increase yields and add nitrogen to the soil. Plant peas an inch or two apart along fences, trellises, or other forms of support. Peas can be double-planted one row on each side of a fence or trellis. A good practice is to plant an early side of a fence or trellis. A good practice is to plant an early, midseason, and late type of pea in the early spring. This way you will have a longer picking season. To grow peas for a fall crop, plant them in late summer or early fall. The edible podded peas do best in the fall, since the season may not be long enough for regular peas to develop.

Culture. Peas prefer cool, moist soils that have a loose structure. Soils rich in potassium and phosphorus are also to their liking. Do not overfertilize peas with nitrogen or you will end up with more vine than pea pods. Extra water may be required when plants are beginning to vine and when pods are forming. Mulch heavily when the plants have established themselves to keep the soil cool. Although dwarf peas are advertised as requiring no support, they will do better when a support is provided. Taller peas, of course, need something to climb. Be extremely careful when working around young peas, as any damage to their stems will prevent that vine from producing.

Harvest. Peas are at their peak just after pods fill out. You will notice a swelling of the pod where each pea is. Pick them at this stage for best flavor. Vines should be picked daily so that energy will not go into already-set pods, but into producing more pods. Pick peas in the morning when they are at their best. Cook, freeze, or can as soon after picking as possible to preserve freshness.

Varieties. Main crop: Extra Early Alaska (51 days), Early Frosty (65 days), Lincoln (66 days), Mammoth Early Canner (60 days), and Wando (68 days); dwarf: American Wonder (61 days), Cameo (58 days), Little Marvel (62 days), Perfection (65 days), and Sparkle (60 days); edible podded peas: Dwarf Gray Sugar (65 days), Green Sugar Pods (60 days) and Snow Peas (65 days).

PEPPERS

Pepper plants have shiny leaves on a bushy, tree-like limb structure. Many gardeners consider the leaves and stems of this plant as ornamental as the many shapes and colors of their fruits. Peppers can be grown as much for their beauty as for their taste. The main division among peppers is determined by how hot they are.

The two main categories are sweet peppers and hot peppers. There are hundreds of variations among both sweet and hot peppers in terms of shape, color, and size. You will have to grow several different types to determine which peppers are best for your needs.

Planting. Peppers are most successfully grown from transplants that get set out in the garden when all danger of frost has passed. Soil temperatures of 60° F or more are best for peppers. Start pepper seed indoors 8 to 10 weeks prior to transplanting outside. Although peppers can be successfully grown in flats, best results are achieved when each plant is grown in its own peat pot. This way root damage is kept to a minimum during transplanting. The hole for transplants should be deep enough to allow plants to be set an inch deeper than they grew inside. Water heavily after transplanting to reduce shock. In the south, peppers can be sown directly into the garden when soil has warmed.

Culture. Peppers prefer a loose, textured soil, not overly rich in nutrients. For instance, excess nitrogen will encourage plants to grow lots of foliage and not many peppers. Water heavily until plants have established themselves. Mulch only after soil has warmed thoroughly to keep down weeds and provide moisture for continued growth. Peppers seem to have a mind of their own, and often spend weeks without seeming to grow much. Suddenly, they burst forth in a flower- and fruit-setting frenzy. A lot of this activity has to do with the air temperature. Peppers prefer air temperatures in the 60° to 80° F range and will not grow well beyond these limits. Peppers, more than any other plant in the garden, seem to benefit from foliar feedings of seaweed and mineral supplements like magnesium. In windy locations, you may want to stake pepper plants to keep them from blowing over. Do not handle plants when they are wet, and the likelihood of spreading disease will be minimized. The flavor of peppers is difficult to determine ahead of time, but as a general rule peppers grown in cooler, moist conditions tend to have milder flavor than those grown in hot, dry conditions.

Harvest. Peppers are harvested when fruits are well-formed and no longer expanding in size. They should be collected by cutting the stems to avoid damaging the plant at the base of the fruit stem. Green, or bell peppers usually turn red when left on the plant for a long time. Many people prefer the flavor of the red pepper, while others are partial to the green. Hot peppers will be at their peak when the fruits have reached full size. Leaving them on the plant longer may reduce the pungency of their flavor. When first frosts arrive you can pull up plants. Hanging them in a cool place will allow you to continue picking peppers for up to a month.

Varieties. (All dates to maturity are from the time of transplanting.) Sweet bell: California Wonder (75 days), New Ace (68 days), Titan (80 days), and Yolo Wonder (75 days); sweet yellow: Cal Wonder Golden (75 days), Sweet Romanian Yellow (75 days), and Yellow Belle (65 days); heat or tomato shaped: Early Sweet Pimento (73 days), Pimento (70 days), and Sunnybrook (70 days); sweet long: Hungarian Yellow Wax (65 days), Long Sweet Banana (65 days), and Pepperocini (70 days); hot long tapering: Anaheim Chili (80 days), Cayenne Long Red Slim (75 days) Hungarian Yellow Wax (65 days), and Mexican Chili (75 days); hot cylindrical: Jalapeno (75 days) and Serrano (75 days); hot medium to small tapering: Fresno Chili (78 days) and Tobasco (100 days); hot small yellow waxy: Goldspike (75 days) and Santa Fe Grande (75 days); chili peppers: Large Red Cherry (75 days) and Small Red Cherry (80 days).

POTATO

Many gardeners claim that potatoes are not worth growing in the home garden. Their main complaints are that potatoes take up a lot of space, and that garden-grown potatoes are no better than what they could buy in the supermarket. Those gardeners obviously have not tried new potatoes fresh from the garden topped with butter. Potatoes are members of the nightshade family, which includes tomatoes and eggplants. Major types of potatoes are red, white, and russet.

Planting. Potatoes are started from seed potatoes. Make sure you buy certified seed potatoes as a measure of protection against disease. Seed potatoes should be allowed to cure by setting them in the open air in a shady location for several weeks before planting. The potatoes will green up. A day or two prior to planting, cut potatoes into 1- to 2-inch squares with at least two eyes per piece.

Allow these pieces to dry so that the cut surfaces heal (Fig. 11-14). This precaution will prevent many rotting problems. Early potatoes should be planted a week or two prior to the last spring frost. Late potatoes a month or more later. There are two basic methods of planting potatoes. The first is digging a foot-deep trench, spreading well-rotted compost 2 inches deep in the bottom of the trench, and placing seed potatoes a foot apart in this trench. Cover the seed potatoes with several inches of soil. As the vines grow, more soil is hoed into the trench until a 6-inch mound is produced. The second method involves tilling the soil and then placing seed potatoes on top of or half-buried in the soil's surface. Cover with a foot or more of straw. Allow the vines to grow through this mulch. Add fresh mulch, as the old stuff settles to prevent potatoes from being exposed to sunlight.

Culture. Potatoes prefer light moist soils, slightly on the acid side. When grown in alkaline soils, a disease known as potato scab disfigures the potato's skin. The potato's interior is not usually affected. Potatoes thrive in moist, cool, cloudy weather—hence their popularity in the Northwest. During dry spells, water heavily and always mulch.

Fig. 11-14. Seed potatoes should be cut and allowed to heal before planting.

Potatoes just do not seem to do well without mulch, which keeps soil moist and cool.

Harvest. New potatoes, golf ball or slightly larger can be harvested after vines flower. Dig up a small area of soil next to a vine and remove the potatoes necessary for a meal. Replace the soil and mulch and the potato vine will continue growing. For full-sized potatoes, wait until vines begin dying back before digging. Potatoes should not be washed after digging. Instead, allow them to dry in the open for a couple of hours, and then gently brush off the soil. Store in a cool, moist place. Do not eat skin on potatoes that is green, since the green areas contain a poison. The green skin can be peeled off and the rest of the potato can be eaten.

Varieties. Red: Chieftain (100 days) and Red Pontiac (100 days); white: Irish Cobbler (100 days), Kennebec (115 days) and Sebago (110 days); russet: Norgold Russet (95 days) and Russet Burbank (100 days).

PUMPKIN

This crop is grown primarily so that it can be used as decorations during Halloween and Thanksgiving. Home gardeners can also grow varieties that produce sweet pulp for pies and pumpkin breads. Pumpkin types are determined largely by their size and shape: extra-large, medium-large, and small are the choices. Special types of baking pumpkins are also available. Although most pumpkins produce vines of up to 25 feet in length, many bush types are finding their way into the market.

Planting. Pumpkins should be planted when all danger of frost is past and soil has warmed thoroughly. Most gardeners plant pumpkins in hills with 7 to 10 feet between hills. Plant three to four seeds in each hill and thin to the strongest seedling when plants are 6 inches tall. Pumpkins can be grown between corn rows as a way of utilizing this normally-wasted space. In areas with short growing seasons, seeds can be started indoors 3 to 4 weeks prior to last frost. Start pumpkin seedlings only in individual peat pots. Pumpkins cannot withstand very much root damage. Set out when soil has warmed to 60° F.

Culture. Pumpkins like a loose loamy soil, so dig in a shovelful or two of compost where each seed is to be planted. Mulch heavily after plants have established themselves. Water frequently during early stages of growth, but discontinue the watering after vines are established, except during extreme drought. Pumpkin vines can be trained to grow on strong trellises as long as each fruit is well-supported by netting when it reaches maturity.

Harvest. Pumpkins are harvested when they turn orange. Cut the stem so that a handle 3 inches long remains attached to the fruit. Allow pumpkins to set in the field for a week or two to cure prior to storage. As cool weather approaches, pinch off immature fruits that will not develop before frost. This practice will give already-established fruit ample energy to finish maturing.

Varieties. Extra large: Big Max (120 days), Hundredweight (115 days), and Mammoth King (120 days); medium-large: Connecticut Field (110 days), Jackpot (100 days), and Red Etampes (110 days); small: Alagold (110 days), Jack O' Lantern (110 days), and Young's Beauty (110 days); special: Small Sugar Pie (105 days), Spookie (100 days), and Cushaw (110 days); for edible seeds: Lady Godiva (110 days).

RADISH

Radishes are the most quickly maturing plants grown in the garden. Many varieties are ready to eat 3 weeks after planting. The short maturity date of this vegetable makes it very easy to grow. Radishes can be grouped in two loose classifications: Spring varieties that produce small ball-shaped roots or longer cylindrical roots, and winter radishes that produce long tapered roots suitable for winter storage.

Planting. Scatter seeds in rows or beds as soon as soil can be worked in the spring. Cover with ¼ to ½ inch of finely-sifted soil or compost. You can attain a better spacing between plants by mixing seeds with coffee grounds or clean sand prior to planting. Sow several crops a week apart to assure longer harvest.

Culture. Radishes require a loose moist soil without an overabundance of nutrients. Too much nitrogen, for example, will cause plants to produce a lot of leaf with little or no radish. Water is essential for the quick growth and development of this plant. If radishes are denied water, they develop tough, hot roots and are likely to send up a seed stalk that destroys their quality. Plant radishes close to the kitchen as you will want to pick them often.

Harvest. Pull plants when roots have swelled to proper size. Do not wait to harvest or they will become strong-flavored. Late varieties can be left in ground until after frost and then stored in damp sand in a root cellar.

Varieties. Early round red: Cherry Belle (22 days), Comet (25 days), Fireball (21 days), and Scarlet King (30 days); early white tip: Half Long (24 days), Perfection Extra Early (25 days), and Sparkler (25 days); early white: Giant White Globe (28 days), Hallstone (30 days), and White Prince (28 days); early red long: Firecracker (22 days) and Long Scarlet (30 days); early white long: All Seasons (45 days), Early Icicle (28 days), and White Strassbury (35 days); winter Long Black Spanish (55 days), White Mammoth (58 days), and Miyashiga (60 days).

RUTABAGA

This member of the Brassica (cabbage) family looks like a turnip—only bigger. It is a winter storage crop popular in Sweden—hence a few of its nicknames; Swedish Turnip, Sweed Turnip, and winter turnip. There are two types of rutabaga. One produces a bulb that ranges in color from yellow-purple and white-red to all red. The second, lesser-known type is grown for its leaves, which produce an edible foliage similar in use to spinach, but closer in taste to cabbage.

Planting. Rutabaga seed is normally sown in midsummer for a fall crop. The tiny seeds should be sown no deeper than ¼ inch and thinned after germination to 1 foot between plants.

Culture. This plant prefers a very deep and well-worked soil loaded with nutrients. In order to ensure the quick growth necessary for crisp flesh,

well-rotted compost and manure should be dug into the soil prior to planting. Since this plant prefers a neutral soil, lime should be added as needed. During its growth rutabaga requires a lot of water. Water deeply and frequently during its initial stages of growth and mulch heavily to preserve moisture.

Harvest. Rutabagas should be allowed to produce a 4- to 5-inch diameter bulb and then be pulled. Remove the top and store the bulb in a cool moist place for winter use. Although this plant is frost-hardy and slight frosts improve its flavor, it should be harvested well before severe cold sets in so as not to destroy its keeping ability. Bulbs can be stored in root cellars in moist sand or in a pit dug in the garden. A few gardeners dip this root in wax to further enhance its storage life.

Varieties. Bulbs: American Purple Top (90 days), Golden Neckless (95 days), and Laurentian Neckless (90 days); foliage: Seven Top (50 days) and Shogoin (70 days).

SAGE

Sage is a member of the mint family, which has over 500 species. Although sage is most often used as a cooking herb, it is still officially listed as a medicine in the United States. Its uses include gargles for sore throats and a tea for nervous headaches.

Planting. Plant seeds in beds or rows when danger of frost is past and soil has warmed sufficiently. Soak seeds a few hours prior to planting to aid germination. Only a few sage plants are needed to meet the needs of most families. Sage can also be propagated by rooting stems in moist sand and then transplanting into the garden.

Culture. Sage does best in rich, clay soils. Plenty of nitrogen will ensure vigorous stem and leaf growth. Sage prefers well-drained soils in sunny locations. Many of the hardier sage varieties will overwinter in the garden when protected by a thick loose mulch of hay or straw.

Harvest. Sage leaves can be picked for use when green. Remove the outermost and lowest leaves on the plant to allow plant to continue growing. For best flavor, leaves and tops should be picked before the flowers bloom. Spread picked material on screen in a well-ventilated room away from direct sunlight. When dry, pick leaves and tops from stems and pack whole into airtight containers.

Varieties. Broad Leaved Sage, Clary Sage, Dwarf Sage, Golden Sage, Gray Sage, Holts Mammoth Sage, Pineapple Sage, Purple Sage, and Variegated Sage.

SALSIFY

Salsify is commonly called the oyster plant because the taste of its root is as close to real oysters as many land-locked gardeners ever get. Although this plant is not widely grown, every gardener should try it at least once, if for no other reason than as a topic of conversation. Two types of salsify are available: black and white root.

Planting. Plant seeds as early as possible in the spring in soil worked deeply. Make sure to obtain fresh seed each year. Cover seed with a thin layer of soil. When plants are up, thin to 3 inches between plants.

Culture. This plant requires all season for growth. Although this crop will do well in a light loam soil that is well drained, many gardeners take the extra precaution of digging a trench where salsify is to grow. The trench, should be filled with a mixture of soil and well-rotted manure or compost in order to achieve the best root growth possible. Do not use fresh manure or forked roots will result. During the early stages of its growth, salsify may need to be watered, but once it is established and roots have penetrated deep into the ground it will grow without supplemental water if it is mulched.

Harvest. Roots are best when they're dug after the tops are killed off by frost. Dig the roots carefully, as damage to the root's skin will cause the flavor to deteriorate rapidly. This root can be stored in shallow pits or cool root cellars. Salsify can also be mulched heavily where it grew in the garden and dug as needed through the winter.

Varieties. White: Mammoth Sandwich Island (120 days); black: Gigantia (120 days).

SNAP BEANS

Snap or green beans are one of America's favo-rite garden vegetables and with good reason; they are easy to grow, produce heavily in a short time, and require little attention. Snap beans come in two basic types: short bush beans and vining or pole beans. Each type comes in a wide variety of colors, sizes, textures, disease resistances, and maturity rates.

Planting. Snap beans require warm soil for proper germination and are usually planted a week or two after the last spring frost. Soaking seeds overnight in water before planting will also aid germination. Several plantings should be made 2 to 3 weeks apart to increase the length of time beans are at a harvestable stage. Since beans are a legume, they will produce nitrogen when seeds are coated with a nitrogen-fixing bacteria before planting.

Culture. Snap beans will grow in almost any soil. Since they produce their own nitrogen, little fertilization is needed, although compost dug into

Fig. 11-15. Pole beans are a high-producer that take up relatively little garden space.

206

the soil before planting is beneficial. Beans withstand drought well, although they should be mulched to encourage even growth. Beans prefer full sun, but they can withstand slight shading. Pole beans do best when grown up rough poles or on wire fences that allow vines to become well anchored on the support (Fig. 11-15).

Harvest. Snap beans are best when picked young, before seeds begin to really show in the pods. Pick often to encourage continued bean production. Do not touch plants when they're wet, or virus diseases may be spread from plant to plant.

Varieties. There are hundreds of varieties, but some favorites are Green bush bean: Stringless Green Pod (49 days) and Tendergreen-Stringless (53 days); wax or yellow beans: Brittle Wax (52 days) and Pencil Pod Wax (54 days); pole beans (green): Kentucky Wonder (65 days) and Blue Lake (60 days); yellow: Kentucky Wonder Wax (68 days) and Burpee Golden (60 days); other: Romano (70 days) and Purple Pod (65 days).

SOYBEANS

Long thought of as no more than a meat-extender or an animal feed, soybeans are finding their way into more main dishes, and with good reason: these beans contain up to 40 percent protein. Unless you have plenty of room, soybeans are not worth growing. Their yields are low, about half that of the same amount of bush type snap beans. Make sure to grow the "edible" type of soybeans which have less oil than the commercially-grown varieties.

Planting. Since soybeans are a legume, they will benefit from an inoculation of nitrogen-fixing bacteria prior to planting. Plant when soil is warm—2 to 3 weeks after the last frost date. It is best to plant soybeans in rows so that cultivation will be easy.

Culture. Soybeans require a fertile, well-drained soil that is not overly rich in nitrogen. Soils that are slightly acid to neutral are best. Soybeans develop a shallow root system, so cultivation should be done carefully to avoid damaging roots. Mulch when plants are 4 to 6 inches tall and water-

Fig. 11-16. When soybeans are allowed to dry in their pods on the vine, they can be shelled out for winter storage.

ing should not be a problem. Soybeans require a long hot growing season and may not be suitable for the northernmost reaches of the United States.

Harvest. Several varieties can be harvested when beans and pods are still green. Pod and all are steamed to enhance shelling, then shelled out. The beans are cooked like other beans. Soybeans can also be allowed to dry on the vine and then stored as a dried bean in airtight containers (Fig. 11-16). Pick beans when pods have yellowed but stems are still green to prevent pods from splitting open and dropping seed on the ground. When harvesting as dry pods, place in a burlap bag and beat with a stick or walk on the bag to break beans loose from their pods. Winnow by pouring beans back and forth from one bucket to another on a windy day or in front of a fan to remove chaff. Store in a cool dry place.

Varieties. Green: Disoy (100 days), Edible Soy Bean (103 days), and Kanrich (95 days); dry: Envy (104 days) and Traverse (111 days).

SPINACH

Spinach is one of America's favorite greens despite its unpopularity with comic-strip children. All true spinach loves cold weather. If you plant it in the fall, it will probably be the last green you get to pick from your garden. On the other hand, spinach is very sensitive to hot weather, and a few steamy days is all it takes to cause this plant to bolt. In warm regions with short periods of cool weather, try New Zealand Spinach. Although New Zealand spinach is not a true spinach, it is close enough for most palates. Different varieties have characteristics ranging from savoyed (crinkled) leaves through semi-savoyed to smooth, and with plant shapes from erect through semi-erect to prostrate.

Planting. Sow as early in the spring as the soil can be worked. Scatter seeds in a bed or in rows and sift up to ½ inch of fine soil over seeds. Firm soil slightly. Because seeds are small, you may want to mix them with coffee grounds or clean sand before sowing. This will keep the seeds from clumping together. When plants have grown to the point where leaves touch, thin and eat the thinnings. Eventually, mature plants should stand so that leaves barely touch. Purchase seed fresh each year to ensure good germination. A fall crop of spinach should be sown in late summer or early fall. Keep the seedbed well watered to prevent heat-related damage. Succession plantings will provide several crops of tender leaves.

Culture. Although this plant does well in average garden soils, it will do even better in loose soils rich in nitrogen. Before planting, dig in a healthy amount of well-rotted manure. Do not use raw manure or diseases may develop. When plants are established, side-dress with cottonseed meal or dried blood. Keep them watered to ensure quick growth. Mulch lightly with nonacidic materials. Spinach prefers neutral to slightly alkaline soils. Heat will quickly destroy the flavor of this plant, turning leaves bitter. When seed stalks appear, remove the plants and replace them with another crop. Many varieties of spinach will survive the winter when tucked beneath a loose but deep mulch. Spinach's season can be extended even further by using cloches or cold frames over your beds. Spinach that has been protected through the winter will produce a second round of growth the following spring—two crops for the price of one.

Harvest. Spinach can be harvested in one of two ways. The most common method involves cutting off an entire plant at ground level and then stripping the leaves for salads and cooking. Another method involves removing only the outer leaves and allowing the center of the plant to produce more leaves. Thinnings pulled to allow remaining plants more room to grow should also be used for the table. Most spinach freezes well.

Varieties. Savoyed upright: America (50 days), Bloomsdale (45 days), and Savoy Supreme (45-50 days); semi-savoyed: Avon (44 days), Old Dominion (40 days), and Giant Thick Leaf (43 days); smooth erect: Big Crop (40 days), Nobel Giant (45 days), and Viking (46 days); prostrate and semi-erect: Nores (48 days), Northland (45 days), and Spinoza (45 days).

SUMMER SQUASH

Summer squash, like its relative winter squash, is one of the domestic vegetables native to America. It produces heavily in virtually all parts of the United States. Summer squash is quick to produce plants of tremendous size which produce fruit at an alarming rate. There are hundreds of varieties of summer squash that grow fruits ranging in color from green to yellow and in shapes from cigar-like to crook-neck, gourd-like, and flying saucer shapes. You will want to grow several types each season while you're deciding which colors and shapes you think taste the best.

Planting. Most summer squashes grow on vines and are traditionally planted in hills, two seeds to a hill. Because seeds are almost 100 percent viable you will not normally need to plant more seeds than you want plants. It might be a good idea to plant at least one extra seed so that the weakest plant can be thinned. The distance between hills for vining squashes should be about 6 feet, and half that for bush types. Squash seeds keep well, so what you do not plant this year can be used next year. Plant the seeds well after the last spring frost when soil has warmed to 60° F or more. Make two or three plantings 3 to 4 weeks apart for continuous crop.

Culture. Squash plants prefer loose, well-drained soils with large amounts of humus. When making hills for planting, add several shovelfuls of well-rotted manure or compost to each hill and mix thoroughly with the soil. These plants are relatively heavy feeders, especially on nutrients like potassium and phosphorus. Squash will do well in slightly acid soils. Watering is essential, since fruits are almost totally water. Water frequently and deeply during the early stages of growth and mulch heavily to preserve moisture during dry spells. A good space-saving idea is to plant this crop next to the edge of the garden so that vines trail out of the garden and do not occupy garden soil that could be used for another crop.

Harvest. Summer squash is best if it's immature when picked. Maturity is reached when seeds are well-formed. If you discover hard seeds in your squash, you have been picking them too late. Summer varieties grow quickly, often reaching the picking stage within a week after flowering. Pick often so that plants are encouraged to set more flowers and produce more squash.

Varieties. Bush scallop or pattypan: Early White Bush (54 days), Golden Bush (60 days), and Silver Dollar (55 days); crookneck: Crookneck (55 days), Giant Crookneck (55 days), Goldneck (50 days), and Sundance (50 days); straightneck: Butterbar (50 days), Golden Summer Straightneck (55 days), and Squash Creamy (50 days); zucchini dark green: Ambassador (55 days), Chefini (51 days), Elite (48 days)), Blackini (60 days), and Burpee's Fordhook (57 days); zucchini yellow: Burpee Golden (54 days), and El Durado (49 days).

SUNFLOWER

Tall-growing sunflowers are herbs! This plant is native to the Americas and will grow well in virtually all parts of the United States. Sunflowers are good plants to let young gardeners cut their teeth on. Sunflowers grow to an impressive height (up to 12 feet), are quite colorful (yellow blossoms up to a foot in diameter) and are almost pest-free.

The seeds of both tall and bushy varieties are delicious snacks for humans and birds alike.

Planting. Sow seeds a week or two prior to the last spring frost. Plant in the north edge of the garden to prevent shading shorter crops. Sow at a rate of one seed every 2 feet and later thin to one plant every 4 feet. Overcrowding will cause plants to be weak and susceptible to wind damage.

Culture. Sunflowers like fertile loams, deeply worked and with a lot of organic matter dug in. Sunflowers are heavy feeders. Soil should be about neutral in reaction and mulched heavily to preserve moisture. When stalks reach heights of 6 to 8 feet, drive a tall stake in next to the stem and tie it loosely to the stake high up on the stem. This will prevent the heads from bending over and touching the ground as they mature (Fig. 11-17). Flowers of the bush varieties can be cut at the beginning of their bloom for table arrangements.

Fig. 11-17. Sunflowers are native to the Americas. They add beauty to the garden while producing heavily.

Fig. 11-18. Sweet potato vines form a thick mat that acts as a living mulch to choke out weeds and keep the soil moist.

Harvest. Seed heads should be harvested when the backs of the heads turn brown and are dry. Cut off heads, leaving a foot of stalk attached. Hang them in an airy place until thoroughly dry. Seeds can be removed by rubbing with a stiff brush. Extra drying may be needed. Store in airtight containers.

Varieties. Mammoth Russian (80 days) and Manchurian (83 days).

SWEET POTATO

This tropical plant is closely related to the morning glory. Although traditionally a southern crop, more and more northern gardeners are finding success with this tuber. Most sweet potatoes produce a vine, but bush varieties have been developed. Root (potato) texture ranges from moist to dry in colors from deep orange to white.

Planting. Since sweet potatoes are very sensitive to frost and cold weather, they should be planted as slips when all danger of frost is past and soil has warmed to 60° F. You can start your own slips by laying several sweet potatoes on their sides in a shallow pan of moist potting soil. Sprouts with leaves and roots will develop from the eyes of the potato. When they're ready to plant, detach the slips by pulling and twisting and set them immediately in the garden. Water heavily so that roots settle in quickly.

Culture. Sweet potatoes do not require an overly-rich soil—in fact, too many nutrients in the soil will produce a lot of vine and few roots. These plants do, however, like loose soils. Heavy soils will produce thin misshapen roots. Water is not required in great amounts, since sweet potatoes prefer hot dry conditions. Sweet potatoes should be planted in hilled rows. This will reduce the amount of digging required for harvest as well as providing a loose soil in which root expansion is unrestricted. Sweet potatoes do not need to be heavily mulched since they vine profusely and these vines often root. A thick mulch would slow this process. In most cases the heavy vine growth of this plant will thwart weeds (Fig. 11-18).

Harvest. Sweet potatoes can be dug as soon as they reach suitable size. All sweet potatoes should be dug prior to the first frost. When leaves turn yellow, it is time to harvest. Frost on the leaves will destroy this root's keeping ability. Cure potatoes in the sun for several hours. Carry them to a storage area with temperatures of 85° to 90° F to finish curing. After 2 weeks at this temperature, roots should be moved to a storage area with a temperature not lower than 50° F and with a high humidity. Under these conditions, sweet potatoes will keep 3 months or more.

Varieties. Centennial (150 days), Jersey Orange (150 days), Georgia Reds (150 days), and White Yams (150 days).

SWISS CHARD

This member of the beet family is not grown for its taproot. Instead, it is grown for its leaves and stems. Chard leaves resemble spinach, and the stems resemble celery (Fig. 11-19). Swiss chard will withstand both long hot summers and freezing temperatures, making it a truly versatile plant. Types of chard range from white-stemmed with dark green crumpled leaves, to white-stemmed with smooth leaves, and red-stemmed types.

Planting. Plant seed in garden as soon as the ground can be worked in the spring. Soak seeds in water 24 hours before planting to soften their tough outer shell. Sow sparsely 4 inches apart and later thin plants to stand 12 inches apart.

Culture. Swiss Chard prefers open sunny locations and soils on the light side with plenty of humus and nutrients. This plant does not do well in acidic soils, so lime should be added as needed. When plants are 6 inches tall, mulch heavily to conserve moisture and prevent weeds from taking over. Swiss chard can be grown virtually anywhere

Fig. 11-19. Swiss chard is a double-duty vegetable. Its leaves can be used as a green and its stalk as a celery substitute.

in the United States and is used in many hot climates as a spinach substitute.

Harvest. When young and thinning is necessary, the whole plant can be pulled. Leaves and stems are added to salads or steamed and eaten as cooked greens. When plants are mature, cut only the outer leaves so that inner leaves will continue producing. Outer stems and leaves should be cut occasionally, even if you are not in the mood to eat them, or center growth will stop. Chard can be overwintered by mulching with a deep loose material. Growth will start again in the spring.

Varieties. Dark-green crinkly leaves: Burpee's Fordhook Giant (60 days), Fordhook (60 days), and White King (55 days); red: Red Burgundy (60 days), Rhubarb Chard (60 days), Ruby Red (60 days), Perpetual (50 days), and Silver Giant (50 days); light-green: Giant Lucullus (50 days), Lucullus (55 days), and Spanish Green Perpetual (55 days).

TOMATO

America's favorite garden vegetable is the tomato. Tomatoes seem to grow by themselves, and they have hundreds of uses in the kitchen. Tomato seeds are available for a wide range of fruit sizes, shapes, colors, and tastes. You will have to experiment with the hundreds of varieties on the market to determine which do best in your climate and which tickle your palate the most.

Planting. The tomato is one plant that loves to be transplanted. Start seeds indoors in flats 6 to 8 weeks prior to the date of last frost in your area. When seedlings develop their first set of true leaves, transplant them into individual peat pots. When all danger of frost is past and the soil has warmed to at least 60° F, transplant them into the garden. Add a spadeful of compost to each hole during planting. If seedlings are short and stocky, plant them straight up and down, burying each plant at least to where the first set of leaves meet the stem. If plants are long and lanky, lay the plant on its side and bury the stem to the first set of leaves. When the stems of tomato plants are buried, they will send out masses of roots. Do not worry about burying tomatoes too deeply—the deeper the better. Place a stiff cardboard collar around each plant to fend off cutworms. If plants are to be staked, drive the stake in when seedlings are planted. This precaution allows the plant's roots to grow around the stake instead of being injured when the stake is pounded into the ground. Water heavily to encourage quick root growth.

Culture. Tomatoes prefer light loamy soils rich in nutrients. Excess nitrogen can, however, be detrimental since excess leaf and stem growth will result. Tomatoes will stand a slightly acid soil. Water during the first few weeks of growth, until the ground heats up sufficiently to mulch. Tomatoes should be able to withstand all but the hottest dry spells without additional water. Mulch heavily when soil is warm to conserve moisture and to keep the fruit of sprawling plants off the ground. When training tomatoes to grow upward, tie plants to supports with cloth strips, baling twine, or other soft material. Do not tie them tightly as stem will expand during growth. Staking is said to slow the maturation of tomatoes by about a week, although this practice does keep fruits off the ground and away from pests. Additionally, staking or caging tomatoes makes picking easier (Fig. 11-20). Untrained or sprawling tomatoes are said to ripen quicker, but a higher percentage of the crop will be lost to pests and moisture induced rotting. A trait unique to tomatoes is that some continue to grow and produce fruit through the season until frost kills the plant. Others grow to a certain size, set fruit, mature the fruit, and then die back. The first type of tomato is called indeterminate, the second determinate. Determinate tomatoes produce a crop all at one time while indeterminate produce all season long. Do not touch tomatoes when they are wet to prevent the spread of disease. Do not smoke near tomatoes or they may be attacked by tobacco mosaic.

Harvest. Tomatoes are generally harvested when they reach maturity, which is indicated by a full color and softness. Some gardeners, however, pick tomatoes green for slicing and frying. Keep ripe tomatoes picked so that plants will continue to set fruit. Just before the first frost, pull tomato vines and hang them upside down in a cool place.

Fig. 11-20. Tomatoes grown in cages or tied to stakes make picking chores easy while reducing the loss of fruit to moisture-related rots.

Any tomatoes remaining on the vine will ripen, or you can pick green tomatoes and wrap each in a sheet of newspaper. Place in a cool dry place and they will ripen long into the fall.

Varieties. Early: Earliana (60 days), Early Girl (60 days), Pitchard (72 days), Starfire (56 days), and Terrific VFN (70 days); mid-season: Bonanza (75 days), Everbearing (74 days), Marglobe (75 days), Red King (73 days), Supermarket (75 days), and Urbana (78 days); late: California Pole Late (85 days), Manapal (85 days), Market King VFN (80 days), and Rutgers VF (90 days); large: Abraham Lincoln (70 days), Beefsteak (90 days), Burpee Big Boy Hybrid (78 days), Delicious (77 days), and Wonder Boy VFN (75 days); pink: Bradley (80 days), June Pink (65 days), McMullen (74 days), Ponderosa (70 days), and Tomboy (66 days); yellow, gold, orange: Burpee's Jubilee (72 days), Golden Delight (60 days), Jubilee

(75 days), Moon Glow (72 days), and Sunray (75 days); small: Red Cherry (72 days), Starshot (55 days), and Yellow Plum (70 days); paste: Chico (75 days), Roma VF (75 days), and Veepick VF (73 days); white: Jung's Giant Oxheart (90 days), Oxheart Pink (90 days), and Oxheat Red (90 days).

TURNIP

Turnips are another member of the Brassica (cabbage family). They are grown for both their bulbous roots and for their leafy greens. There are many turnip varieties with variations of color (white, yellow, red, black, and combination) and shape (flat-globe and globes). A few varieties have been developed specifically for their greens.

Planting. For spring sowings, seed should be

Fig. 11-21. Turnips are at the perfect eating stage when slightly larger than a baseball.

planted as early in the spring as ground can be worked. Mid-summer planting will provide fresh turnips through frost and for winter storage. Sow thinly, 3 to 5 inches apart in rows. When thinning is necessary, save the greens for salads.

Culture. Turnips do well in soils of average fertility, especially those lacking nitrogen and slightly on the acid side. The soil should be worked deeply, however, so that it is loose enough for deep taproots to penetrate, and so it will give as the turnips expand. Keep plants well-watered so that quick growth will produce crisp bulbs. Dry spells will encourage roots to become woody. Mulch when plants are 4 to 6 inches tall.

Harvest. Pull turnips when roots are 2 to 2½ inches in diameter for best flavor and texture (Fig. 11-21). All spring-planted turnips should be pulled long before hot weather sets in. Fall turnips achieve a good taste when pulled after the first frost of the season. For winter storage pull roots, cut back tops so that about 1 inch of stem remains. Store in a cool dry place.

Varieties. White: All Seasons (28 days), Jersey Lily (40 days), Tokyo Market (50 days), and Vertus (50 days); purple top: Early Purple-Top Milan (45 days), Golden Neckless Purple-Top White Glove (55 days), and Red-Top Glove (58 days); other colors: Golden Ball Turnip (60 days), Large Yellow Globe (70 days), Ohno Scarlet (55 days), and Turnip Longue de Caluire (55 days); for greens: Seven Top (45 days) and Spring (40 days).

WATERMELON

Although watermelons are a tropical fruit requiring a long hot growing season, improving seed strains make it possible to grow this delicious crop in most parts of the United States. Northern gardeners will want to grow one of the quick-maturing bush or icebox type of melons. Farther south, the giant oblong and round watermelons will do quite well. Watermelons come in a variety of shapes (from oblong to round) and sizes (from cantaloupe size to 100-pounders) with solid green and striped rinds around red, orange, or yellow flesh. Experimentation is necessary to find the variety that does best in your area.

Planting. In the south, seeds are planted directly into the soil after the danger of frost has passed and the soil has warmed to at least 60° F. In the north, seedlings should be started indoors 6 to 8 weeks prior to last frost. Grow only in individual peat pots since watermelon roots are very sensitive. Watermelons can be grown in hills spaced 8 feet apart or in rows 4 feet apart with one vine every 2 feet in the row.

Culture. Watermelons require loose soils. Sandy soils containing a lot of humus are best. Work the soil deeply, adding a substantial amount of humus where each vine will grow. The soil should be slightly on the acid side with a healthy amount of nutrients. Do not over-enrich soil with nitrogen, or only vines and leaves will grow. Hoe around the plants several times during early growth to keep weeds down and soil loose. Water as needed to keep the soil moist. When soil has warmed thoroughly, mulch heavily. As melons form, they should be placed on boards or flat stones to keep them from touching the ground (Fig. 11-22). It usually is best to allow only two melons to grow on each vine. Pull off any extra melons so that the remaining two receive enough energy to mature fully. Once melons have formed, vines should not be moved.

Harvest. Judging a watermelon for ripeness can be tricky, but with a little practice you will soon be an expert. Watermelons should be allowed to ripen on the vine. Knock melons with your knuckles to test ripeness. In many cases, ripe melons produce a dull rather than a sharp thud. It is best to test melons early in the day since heat will cause them to sound hollow. Judging for ripeness can also be done by looking at the spot on the bottom of the melon where it rests on the ground. When this spot

Fig. 11-22. As watermelons form, place them on boards or stones to reduce the likelihood of damage by soil microbes.

turns from white to pale yellow, the melon is usually ripe. Old-timers advocate plugging—or cutting a small hole—in the melon with a sharp knife. Pull out the plug of rind and a piece of flesh should be attached. Taste the flesh to tell whether or not the melon is ripe. If not, return the plug to its hole and the melon will continue to ripen.

Varieties. Icebox: Burpee Sugar Bush (80 days), Market Midget (70 days), Sugar Baby (80 days), and Sunny Boy (80 days); giant: Cobb Gem (100 days), Mountain Hoosier (85 days), and State Fair (90 days); oblong solid green: Congo (90 days), Klondike (85 days), New Wonder (88 days), and Tom Watson (90 days); oblong stripes: Early Canada (75 days), Jubilee (95 days), and Rattlesnake (90 days); round green: Black Diamond (90 days), Blackstone (90 days), and Louisiana Queen (70 days); round striped: Crimson Sweet (80 days), Dixie Queen Hybrid (75 days), and Super Sweet (93 days); yellow or orange flesh: Black Diamond Yellow (85 days), Golden Honey Long (90 days), Tendersweet Orange (90 days), and Yellow Doll (75 days); seedless: Burpee Hybrid Seedless (80 days), Gurney's Seedless (85 days), Super Seedless (90 days) and Triple Sweet Hybrid (80 days).

WINTER SQUASH

Like the summer squashes, these plants are native to America. Unlike summer squash, winter squash must be allowed to develop fully and mature on the vine before picking. There are several types of this squash with hundreds of varieties. Some favorites are banana-shaped, Hubbard, acorn, bottle, buttercup, heart-shaped and pumpkin-shaped. They come in a variety of colors, with skins smooth, warty, or ridged. Most squashes grow on long vines, although a few bush varieties are available. Experiment to find out which type your family likes best.

Planting. Plant seeds in hills or rows when all danger of frost has passed. Seeds are very viable and you will not need to plant more seeds than the number of plants you want to grow. If you desire, you can over-plant and thin the weakest plants when they're 4 to 6 inches tall. Space hills at least 5 feet apart and plan to grow only two vines per hill. In rows, vines should be spaced at least 2 feet apart with rows 5 or more feet apart.

Culture. Squash likes loose soil (preferably sandy) that is rich in nutrients and well-drained. Soil should be thoroughly worked, with well-rotted manure or compost added to areas where seeds are to be planted. Vines require a lot of water during the early stages of growth, but will do without water later. As vines form, bury several of the knots where leaves meet the vine so that this area of the vine will form roots. This precaution is a good way of thwarting the squash vine borer. You may want to plant winter squash between corn rows to save garden space. Another idea is to plant squash at the edge of the garden so that vines trail over your yard instead of taking up valuable garden space. The last few fruits to be set on each vine should be pinched off in order to allow earlier fruits enough energy to ripen thoroughly.

Harvest. Harvest fruits when fully mature. The skin will be tough, and you should not be able to mar it with a thumbnail. Cut stems leaving an inch or two attached to the fruit. Allow squash to cure in the sun for a day or two, then move them to a cool dry place for storage. Do not stack squashes. Mold can be prevented by wiping squashes monthly with a rag soaked in vegetable oil.

Varieties. Acorn: Bush Table Queen (80 days), Royal Acorn (82 days), Table King (75 days), and Table Queen (85 days); turban shaped; Bush Buttercup (88 days), Buttercup (100 days), Gold Nugget (90 days), and Perfection (85 days); hubbard: Baby Hubbard (100 days), Blue Hubbard (120 days), Golden Hubbard (100 days), and Warted Hubbard (110 days); others: Big Red (100 days), Blue Banana (110 days), Turks Turban (105 days), Vegetable Spaghetti (100 days), Warren Turban (115 days), Boston Marrow (100 days), and Golden Delicious (100 days).

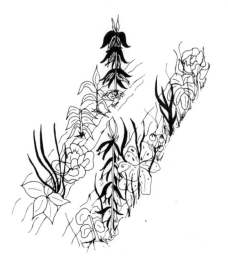

Chapter 12

Irrigation Methods

After the rain cometh the fair weather.
—Aesop's Fables

Farmers and gardeners alike know the truth of a saying similar to Aesop's. It reads, "After the fair weather comes the rain." No matter how you look at it—rain before fair weather, or fair weather before rain—the weather occurs in cycles of wet and dry. Whenever the weather stays in one phase of the cycle for too long, your garden takes a beating.

An extended period of rain will saturate your garden's soil, suffocating plants at the root. On the other hand, when rainless weather lasts for too long, drought conditions develop. It does not take very long for the available moisture in a garden's soil to be used during dry, hot weather. When available moisture is depleted, your plants go thirsty. Whether from too much water or not enough, when extreme weather puts your plants in jeopardy only your helping hands can see them through.

Most of the United States receives enough precipitation during the year to keep soil moist enough for good plant growth. Problems develop in arid areas, where rain is at a premium, or during drought in normally wet areas, because plants are not getting enough to drink. When the weather does not cooperate and your garden goes thirsty, irrigation is the only thing standing between crop failure and success.

The objective of irrigation is to supply plants with water, whenever rain does not do the job. This does not mean that water must be flowing through the soil; it simply means that the soil must be moist enough for the plants to extract their fair share. Your soil's water-holding capacity is related to its condition.

Even a good soil is no insurance against drought. For instance, a properly-mulched soil rich in organic matter has the ability to hold huge amounts of water. In most cases, this stored water is sufficient to carry the garden through a drought. Occasionally droughts will be so severe that a rich soil and heavy mulch will not eliminate the need to irrigate. Irrigation is essential for preventing production lose because of drought-induced problems

216

like wilting, blossom-drop, and inferior vegetable and fruit formation. Irrigation, in one form or another, is the only remedy for drought since a truly effective rain dance has not been perfected.

Unfortunately, gardeners with ready access to irrigation are tempted to use it more often than is good for the garden. When seedlings first emerge, common sense says that these fragile plants need lots of water to help them establish themselves. Just the opposite is true. A heavy supply of water when plants are establishing their roots will make the roots lazy. The roots will remain in the upper levels of the soil instead of growing downward in search of water. Quickly, the plants become dependent on finding water in the top few inches of soil. When a dry spell hits and water disappears from the upper soil levels, the plants do not have roots deep enough to find subsoil moisture. Additionally, plants with shallow roots cannot tap into the mineral-rich water usually found in the lower reaches of the soil. Improper watering places your plants in double jeopardy: they become dependent on frequent applications of water as well as fertilizer. The lesson to be learned from this is that irrigation should be used only when plants need it.

RECOGNIZING DROUGHT

As a general rule, soils that receive an inch of water each week will not suffer drought. This is not an inflexible rule. Your soil type, method of cultivation, climate, and the growth phase of crop plants alter the need for water. Watering at regular intervals, regardless of weather conditions, is a mistake. A better way to head off drought is to learn to recognize drought signs. Then when these signs appear, irrigation can be applied to your garden. Following these signs will save money and prevent the possibility of overwatering.

When garden crops are not getting enough water, they send out distress signals. If you can recognize thirsty plants and then deliver enough water where it is needed, you will be able to pull your plants through the drought season with little, if any, reduction in production. The trick is knowing when to water and how much to water.

How do you know when it is time to irrigate?

Your plants and soil will tell you. Wilting is the best way for plants to tell you that they need water, but wilting can be misleading. Many diseases cause plants to wilt when plenty of soil moisture is available. Also, most plants wilt during the afternoon of hot sunny days as a way of conserving moisture. The soil may have plenty of water, but transpiration (the evaporation of moisture from plant leaves) may be outstripping the ability of roots to take up water. When this happens, the leaves close their stomata and then wilt to slow the rate of transpiration. More water will not do anything except raise your water bill.

The following signs will tell you when the available moisture in your garden is getting dangerously low.

- When deep-rooted broad-leaved plants like squash begin wilting, the soil is close to drought conditions.
- Besides drooping leaves, a loss of normal brightness and color in leaves is an early warning of drought.
- Corn that wilts before noon is an indication that soil moisture is getting very low.
- If you walk through your garden in the evening and notice that your plants have not recovered from their afternoon wilt, it is time to irrigate. Check the leafy vegetables carefully since these crops require more water and tend to be the first to suffer drought.

The soil also has a few conditions that will indicate drought. In most cases, when the top inch of soil is dry, watering time has arrived. You can also check the soil moisture by turning over a shovelful of dirt and checking the lowest portion for moisture. Compare your soil to Table 12-1 and you will get a fairly accurate idea of the moisture level in your soil. In most soils, an available moisture content of less than 50 percent indicates that the soil is approaching drought and irrigation should be considered.

IRRIGATION METHODS

Now that you have decided when your garden needs water, you should decide how it will be applied. There are three basic methods of irrigation: furrow flooding, sprinkler systems, and drip irrigation. The efficiency of each method is quite different.

When 100 gallons of water are run into the furrows of a conventional irrigation method, roughly 50 gallons of water reaches the plant's root zone. The rest evaporates or soaks into the ground out of the reach of most roots. A sprinkler system does better, delivering up to 75 gallons of water to the root zone. A properly used drip irrigation system will deliver from 90 to 95 gallons of water to a plant's root zone. It is easy to see why more gardeners and farmers are turning to drip irrigation to help them through times of drought.

Here are a few tips that will help you choose an irrigation system that is right for you. Some of these tips will also help you water effectively with the system you select.

● Shop around before you buy an irrigation system. Many manufacturers sell irrigation systems. These range in simplicity from a standard lawn sprinkler to the sophistication of fully automated drip irrigation systems. Only by comparing several different types and designs will you be able to determine what is right for you. Ask someone who has a system how it works, what kind of maintenance it requires, and how easy parts are to get. In the end, though, the responsibility rests on your shoulders. The cheapest system may not save you money, and the most expensive system may not work as well as its price tag.

● Check your water source. Will you be able to afford the cost of the water necessary to support the system? Drip irrigation systems are definitely cheaper in terms of water use, but they are more expensive to install.

● Water should be applied at the time a crop usually makes its most rapid growth—provided soil moisture is low.

Table 12-1. Use This Table to Determine the Moisture Content of Your Soil.

Amount of Readily Available Moisture Remaining for Plants	Sand	Sandy Loam	Clay Loam	Clay
Close to 0%. Little or no moisture available.	Dry, loose, flows through fingers.	Dry, loose, flows through fingers.	Dry clods that break down into powder.	Hard, baked, cracked surface. Hard clods difficult to break.
50% or less. Approaching time to irrigate.	Still appears dry, will not form ball.	Still appears dry, will not form ball.	Crumbly, but will hold in ball with pressure.	Somewhat pliable, will ball under pressure.
50% to 70%. Enough available moisture.	Same as sand under 50%.	Tends to ball, but will not hold together.	Forms ball, plastic, may be slick.	Forms ball, will ooze out between fingers when squeezed.
75% to field capacity. Plenty of available moisture.	Tends to stick together slightly. forms weak ball.	Forms weak ball, breaks easily, is not slick.	Forms ball and is pliable, becomes slick.	Easily oozes out between fingers, feels slick.
At field capacity. Will not hold more water.	No free water, but moisture is left on hand,	Same as sand.	Same as sand.	Same as sand.
Above field capacity. Soil is water-logged.	Free water appears when soil is bounced in hand.	Free water will be released with kneading.	Can squeeze out water.	Puddles form on surface.

● Do not apply water faster than the soil can absorb it. Water running out of the garden is wasted.

● Watch the weather forecasts. A heavy rain after irrigation can wash crops out of the soil or waterlog their roots to the point of suffocation.

● In many instances a good soil-building program will meet all the water needs of a garden. Try adding organic material to your soil and mulching heavily before deciding to buy an irrigation system.

Whether you choose furrows, sprinklers, or drip irrigation, there are two basic rules for watering: water deeply and water at the end of the day. When you turn off the water, the soil should be soaked to a depth of at least 6 inches. The deeper the better, since deep watering encourages deep root growth.

There is some debate about whether watering at the end or the beginning of the day is best. Those in favor of watering early in the day suggest that plant diseases such as mildew and fungus may attack plants when water remains on them through the night. This is probably true of sprinkling where water splashes onto the plants. It is less of a possibility with plants watered with a furrow or drip irrigation system. Besides, if you are watering at the proper time, the garden should be close to drought. It is doubtful that water will remain on the plants all night under these low-moisture conditions. Evaporation will dry up the excess water before disease carrying organisms have a chance to attack.

Those that argue for watering at the end of the day suggest that water applied early in the day is subjected to the tremendous evaporative power of the sun. When you irrigate in the morning, a lot of the water you apply will evaporate, doing your plants little good. Watering in the evening, however, will give the water all night to soak into the soil where it will resist evaporative losses.

Generally, watering in the evening seems to make the most sense since it reduces evaporation. If your schedule only allows you to water in the morning, go ahead, but be prepared to irrigate more often than if you water at night.

Sprinkler Systems

Sprinkler irrigation (including spraying the garden with a hand-held hose) is probably the most popular method of watering. Sprinkler systems are popular because they are cheap, simple to use, and can be moved from one area of the garden to another.

Sprinklers water in two basic patterns: circular and rectangular. The circular systems usually have a rotating head that sprays water outward from a central location into a circular or semicircular pattern. The rectangular sprinklers usually have a bar that rotates back and forth watering a rectangular area. Most people prefer the rectangular sprinkler since this is the shape of most gardens. Both sprinklers deliver less water to the edges of their patterns than the middle. Therefore, watering patterns should overlap at least by a third.

Conventional water sprinkling systems are generally the most wasteful way to water your garden. Up to 30 percent of the water used by sprinklers never reaches the ground—it is lost to evaporation. You can reduce evaporation by waiting until late evening to water. Watering on windless days is also advisable.

Sprayed water is also difficult to control. You often end up watering walkways, weeds, and the leaves of plants—none of which need that water. The roots of crop plants need the water, and getting water down to the root zone by sprinkling is a time-consuming chore. It takes anywhere from 45 minutes to an hour to soak 100 square feet of garden to 12 inches deep. Any less time will result in shallow watering, encouraging plants to keep their roots close to the soil's surface (Fig. 12-1). Roots in

Fig. 12-1. Sprinklers soak the soil evenly, wetting the upper layers of soil without much deep penetration.

this position are vulnerable to light droughts which, in turn, means watering more often.

Sprinkler systems can cause a buildup of harmful salts in soil and on plant leaves. Nearly all tap water especially well water and pond or stream water, contains salts. These salts are left behind when the water evaporates. When a lot of water evaporates from the soil's surface, a salt deposit will form. You can reduce this salt problem by sprinkling for at least an hour so that the water soaks into the ground where it is taken up by plant roots instead of evaporated away.

Sprinkler systems are designed to simulate rain. Rain tends to compact the soil when it falls. On clay soils this can result in a crust that prevents seedlings from breaking through the surface. The crust also reduces the aeration of the soil. These conditions are especially noticeable during times of drought.

A somewhat better way to irrigate is with the traditional furrow method.

Furrow Method

Running water in furrows between crop rows is one of the oldest methods of irrigation. As water stands in its furrow, some of it soaks down into the root zone of the soil (Fig. 12-2). This simple method of irrigation has a few advantages over sprinkler systems. For one, water is not wasted on the paths of your garden. The water in a trench has less surface area than the fine mist of a sprinkler, so evaporation losses are reduced. Finally, less soil

compaction takes place since water does not fall onto the soil.

Furrow watering works best on very flat gardens laid out in traditional rows. The trenches or furrows necessary for this method of watering should be dug between rows—every other row is good—to a depth of no more than 8 inches. Make the furrows as wide as possible. Narrow deep trenches encourage water to run, reducing its ability to soak into the ground. Water moving slowly in a wide shallow trench has more time to percolate into the ground. Water should be applied at the high end of the trench, and it should soak at least a foot into the ground before the furrow is allowed to dry.

Furrow irrigation is most effective on soils with a moderate amount of clay and organic matter. Sandy soils tend to allow the water to percolate into the ground at a fast rate that reduces the amount of water delivered to the far ends of the trench (Fig. 12-3). Additionally, clay soils will hold water longer than sandy soils. A mulch added to a furrow will reduce evaporation, but may hinder water movement to all areas of the trench. When mulching in a furrow, use a loose material like straw or hay.

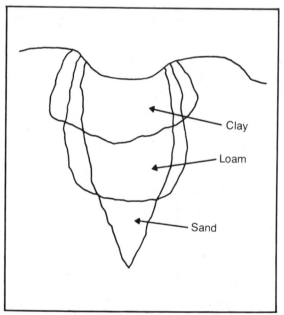

Fig. 12-3. Your soil type has a big influence on how water soaks into the ground from furrows.

Fig. 12-2. The water soaking pattern of a furrow irrigation system is deeper than a sprinkler.

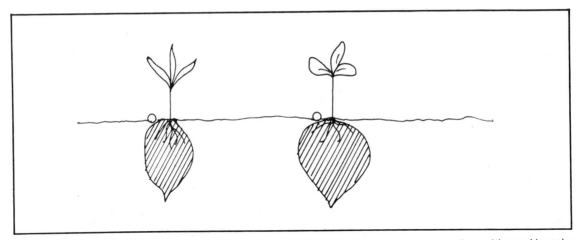

Fig. 12-4. The pattern of water soaking into the ground from a drip irrigation system reduces evaporation and thoroughly soaks the root zone.

Commercial Drip Irrigation Systems

Drip or trickle irrigation was developed more than 40 years ago in Israel where irrigation is a fact of life. This method of irrigation was designed to overcome watering problems, especially losses due to evaporation. A soaker or emitter type or drip irrigation system used under a mulch requires about 50 percent less water than conventional sprinkler systems. Water use is minimized and the water that is used is used effectively.

Evaporation is reduced because water is applied directly to the soil at the top of the root zone. This minimizes the water's exposure to air. Compaction is reduced because the water does not fall onto the soil. The application rate is slow enough to allow water to soak deeply into the ground. Although you may see a small wet spot on the soil's surface, the water entering at this point is spreading out below ground. The result is a cone shaped area of wetness below a drip irrigation emitter or hose (Fig. 12-4). This cone shape roughly resembles the shape of most roots, thereby encouraging correct root growth.

Drip irrigation systems do have a disadvantage when compared to sprinklers or furrows, but it is slight. Once a drip system is in place you will have to till or dig around it. When the whole garden is being worked, the whole irrigation system must be removed. In most of the country, where year-round gardening is not possible, you should drain and remove the system from the garden each fall. It can be reinstalled any time after the garden has been cultivated for planting.

If you decide to install a drip irrigation system, sit down and do a little planning. The first step is drawing a map of your garden. This way you can determine the most efficient use of irrigation hose in addition to how much you will need (Fig. 12-5).

Most drip tubing is about ½ inch in diameter. It will bend enough to allow you to loop from one row to the next; however excessive bending will restrict the flow of water and cause problems. In closely-spaced gardens you might want to consider running one main line down the center of the garden and then placing smaller hoses so that they branch out of the main hose.

So far, our discussion of irrigation has assumed a source of tap or well water. There is a lot of other waste water that can be collected and used to irrigate your crops. Gravity-feed systems that use a holding tank such as a rain barrel, plastic garbage can, or metal drum to deliver otherwise-wasted water are gaining popularity (Fig. 12-6). The only requirement for such holding tanks is that they be higher than the garden they are intended to water. For best results, the holding tank should be on a platform 3 to 5 feet above the garden.

Collected water will drain from this holding

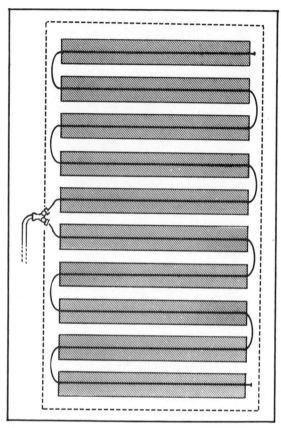

Fig. 12-5. A typical garden drip irrigation layout (courtesy of International Irrigation Systems).

tank through a connector inserted near the bottom of the tank. Special pieces are available for this job through various manufacturers. You can also jerry-rig a length of hose with a male end. Make the hose long enough so that you can raise the end of it above the top of the tank. This will act as a crude faucet, allowing you to turn the water off and on. The hole where water exits the holding tank should be at least 1 inch above the bottom of the tank. This way, debris will settle to a level below the exit and not enter your irrigation system. Still, you should consider applying a filter to the beginning of your irrigation system.

To fill your tank you can collect rainwater from the eaves of a building or save gray water—spent household water such as bathwater. In either case, you will realize considerable savings in cost over the use of city water.

There are many types of drip irrigation systems on the market nowadays, and each year several new products are introduced. There are only two basic types of drip irrigation: emitters and soakers.

Soaker Hoses. These are the most basic of all drip irrigation systems. Soaker hoses are made from plastic or canvas hose with microscopic holes. Water drips in small quantities from the numerous holes along the hose in a way that resembles sweat

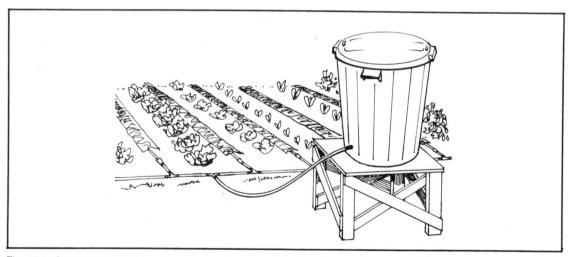

Fig. 12-6. Gravity-fed irrigation systems use waste water. They have become a popular alternative to tap water irrigation systems (courtesy of International Irrigation Systems).

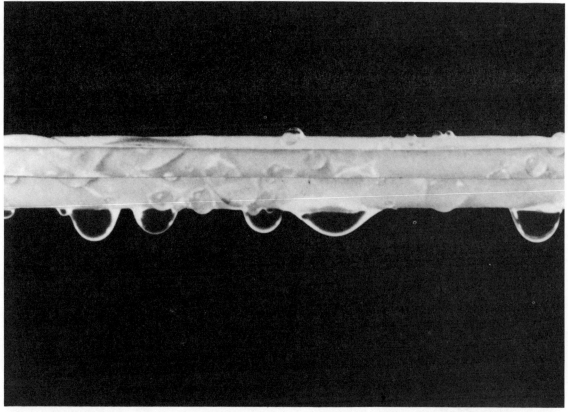

Fig. 12-7. Soaker hoses have microscopic holes through which water drips and soaks into the ground (courtesy of International Irrigation Systems).

(Fig. 12-7). The hose's sweat soaks slowly into the ground.

Soaker systems work best on closely spaced bed vegetables like lettuce and radishes, or in intensive beds. Because the control of water flowing from the system is not quite as good as emitter systems, soaker hoses are not as efficient. They are considerably better than sprinklers and furrow irrigation, however, and the difference between soakers and emitters is slight.

Emitters. Emitter systems come in a variety of sizes and shapes. The crux of these systems is a little valve called an emitter, which allows water to exit the hose at a predetermined rate (Fig. 12-8). Emitters that deliver from 1 to 2 gallons of water per hour should satisfy most gardening needs.

Some systems come with emitters already installed. Most allow you to place emitters where you want them along the hose. The emitters are installed with a special plier-like tool (Fig. 12-9). They can also be removed for cleaning or for use at a new location. Most emitter kits also contain plugs so that you can stop the flow where it is no longer needed.

One of the secrets to getting the most out of an emitter system is providing the right amount of water. A system with 100 feet of hose and an emitter every 2 feet usually needs about 1 gallon of water per minute. To see if your water system can supply this demand, find out how long it takes your hose to fill a 1-gallon bucket. If it takes 20 seconds, your hose provides 3 gallons of water per minute and will easily supply 1 gallon per minute to an irrigation system.

Fig. 12-8. The tiny black square on this hose is an emitter. It allows you to place water right where you need it (courtesy of Submatic).

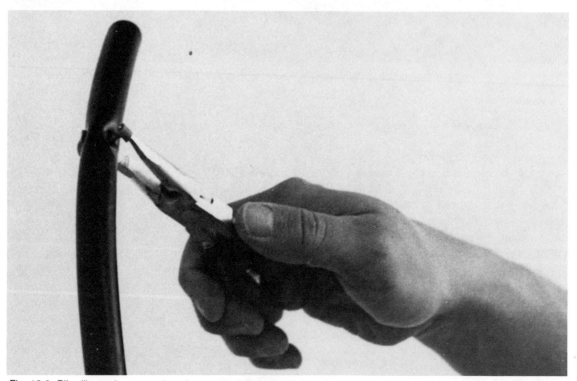

Fig. 12-9. Plier-like tools are used to place emitters on irrigation hoses (courtesy of Submatic).

224

Although emitter systems deliver a regulated flow of water right where you want it, they do have problems. Algae, dirt, and mineral deposits can clog the tiny emitter holes. Algae growth can be discouraged by using a black plastic or opaque hose material. Clogging is rarely a problem with city water, but pond, stream, and well water often carry debris. It is smart, even when using city water, to filter water before it reaches the emitter hose. Several in-line filters are available for this.

When an emitter does become clogged, remove it and blow it to remove dirt. If this fails, poke the hole with a fine wire or boil the emitter in a pan of water for a few minutes to dislodge the problem.

Drip irrigation system manufacturers offer a wide range of additional accessories for their systems. Think carefully before buying any of these extra devices. In-line shutoff valves let you water one part of the garden at a time. Timing units can turn your system on and off automatically, but they are expensive. Tensionmeters (which measure soil moisture and then turn your irrigation system on and off) are nice, but usually unnecessary in most gardens. Fertilizer injectors are not what they are cracked up to be. The nutrients injected into a drip system create excessive algae growth. Many types of natural fertilizers, even liquid seaweed and fish emulsion, can clog both emitters and the pores in soaker hoses.

One accessory is a must for drip irrigation. This is a filter of some sort. Regardless of your water source, a simple in-line filter will prevent many headaches. In drinking-water-supplied systems, a simple screen filter inserted into the coupling right before the system will be sufficient. Systems fed by pond, stream, and well water need a more effective dirt trap. These filters should be placed between the delivery hose and the start of the drip system.

Although emitter systems appear expensive at first glance, they can be built a little at a time, spreading out the cost. If you want to find out how well they work you can buy a starter kit for $15.00 to $20.00. This should provide at least 50 feet of hose with emitters placed every 2 feet. If the system proves worthwhile, you can add on to it and cover more of your garden.

Ideally, drip irrigation systems should be covered with mulch. Not only will this reduce the amount of water lost to evaporation, but it will protect the plastic from sunlight. The ultraviolet rays in sunlight are capable of deteriorating plastic within a few years. Anything from black plastic and newspapers to leaves and other organic matter can be used as a mulch. The best mulch material is organic matter, since it breaks down and adds fertility to your soil.

Homemade Drip Irrigation Systems

If all this talk about commercial drip irrigation systems seems expensive, then you might want to consider making your own system. There are two alternatives: making your own emitter system from

Fig. 12-10. A homemade irrigation system can be made by cutting holes in an old hose.

Fig. 12-11. A plastic jug with holes punched in the bottom makes a cheap and effective irrigation system.

water flow so that it dribbles out instead of squirting. After an hour or two of soaking, move the pipe to the next bed and repeat the process.

To make an emitter system from an old hose the same basic steps are taken. Select a hose with the female end still attached. If this is not possible, then attach a female end. Plug the opposite end with a piece of whittled wood and secure in place. Next, cut ½-to-¾-inch Xs at 8-inch intervals along the length of the hose with a box knife. When all the Xs have been cut, lay the hose on a flat surface, hook up a good hose, and turn on the water. If water does not flow evenly from all openings, enlarge those that do not flow properly. After this fine-tuning, lay the hose in a vegetable bed, turn on the water until it gurgles out, and you have an adequate emitter for most irrigation chores (Fig. 12-10).

Container drip irrigation systems are also easy to make. In this method a bucket, plastic milk container, tin can, or anything that will hold water can be used. Punch or drill holes around the bottom of the container. The container is then dug into the ground next to a plant, filled with water, and the water seeps out of the holes irrigating the plant (Fig. 12-11). This method supplies a constant amount of moisture to the plant and can be used to deliver fertilizers as well.

When using a bucket or tin can, punch holes in the sides of the container slightly above the container's bottom. After the container is dug into the ground and filled with water, place a board weighted down with a rock over the top to reduce evaporation. When using a milk jug or other plastic container, replace the cap after filling, but leave it slightly loose. You can regulate the rate at which air enters the jug in this manner, which will affect the outflow of water. The tighter the lid, the slower the water flow.

Experiment with the size and number of holes until the drainage rate suits your soil. Generally, loose sandy soils drain easily, so the holes should be small and well-spaced. Heavy clay soils reduce the rate of flow, so you will need larger, more frequently placed holes. Do not make the holes too large, or your water will bubble to the surface and drain away.

hose or PVC (polyvinyl chloride) pipe and making a container soaker system.

To make your own emitter irrigation system, all you need is a length of old garden hose or a length of PVC pipe. In both cases the emitter hose or pipe should be cut to match the length or width of your garden. This will make control of water flow and handling easier.

To make an emitter system from PVC pipe, simply cap one end of a ½ inch PVC pipe. Then install the female end of a hose to the open end. You can use two ¾ inch automotive gear-type clamps to hold the hose end in place. Then drill ½ 2-inch holes down each side of the pipe at 8-inch intervals. Place the pipe in the middle of a garden bed, attach a garden hose, and turn on the water. Adjust the

Containers can be used to dispense liquid fertilizers, manure teas, and compost teas to growing plants. Make sure to strain any liquid fertilizer before pouring it into one of these watering containers. This precaution will save you the problem of clogged holes later. If water stays in a container for a long time, chances are the bottom holes are clogged. Pull the container free and unclog the holes. Return the container to its hole.

This container method of irrigation is especially useful for small gardens. It is also a good way to make sure large plants like tomatoes, peppers, and squash get all the water they need. No water is wasted and you have complete control over how much water the plants receive.

By now you are probably convinced that every garden needs some sort of irrigation system. This is not really true. If you are lucky (or have worked hard enough) to have a soil loaded with organic matter, and nature supplies adequate rainfall (approximately 1 inch per week), you probably will not need to irrigate. Unfortunately, nature seldom confers such a blessing on gardeners. Across most of the country an August or September drought is very common and you should be prepared for it. If you live in the arid regions of the country or have a sandy garden soil, you will need to supplement your garden regularly with irrigation. Choose a system that fits into your soil, climate, and schedule, and you will have many happy returns for your efforts.

Chapter 13

Mulch Your Way to a Better Garden

Constant tillage exhausts a field.

—Ovid

Through the ages, mulch has been an integral part of nature's soil-building and plant-growing program. You need only look at the deep carpeting of leaves or pine needles on the floor of a mature forest to convince yourself of this. Mulching—covering the ground with a layer of protective material—has been slow to gain a foothold in the world of vegetable growing. The reason gardeners are reluctant to spread mulch between the plants in their gardens probably has more to do with the way the stuff looks than anything else. Most gardeners consider a clean garden, with exposed soil, the best for vegetable production. Recent and not so recent research indicates that taking after nature by incorporating a mulch into your garden can have significant benefits.

BENEFITS

The reason for mulch's success is that this practice modifies the growing conditions in your garden in a way that helps your plants. Mulch is multi-talented (Fig. 13-1). It has the ability to conserve soil moisture, moderate soil temperature fluctuations, reduce the growth of weeds, and protect perennials against the ravages of winter. When organic materials are used as a mulch, there is also an improvement of soil structure and fertility as these materials decompose and become part of the soil. Today's mulch is food for tomorrow's vegetables.

Conservation of soil moisture is one of the most important reasons for applying a mulch. All mulches slow the rate of water evaporation from the soil by protecting it against the drying effects of sun and wind. Mulching can reduce evaporation by up to 90 percent, a real boon in dry areas where drought can seriously curtail garden production. A few good waterings in a mulched garden will often provide all the moisture necessary to keep plants growing right through the severest of dry spells. Mulch will also reduce both wind and water erosion which are responsible for the loss of valuable topsoil.

Temperature moderation of the soil is also a

Fig. 13-1. Mulch has many benefits. From the left, it moderates soil temperature, reduces evaporation, adds nutrients to the soil as it decays, and chokes out weeds.

benefit of mulch. Since mulch acts as a blanket of insulation, soil temperature changes occur over a longer period of time, allowing the soil and plants living in the soil to adjust gradually. On extremely hot days, mulch will keep the soil cool enough for plant roots to continue taking up moisture and nutrients. In cold soils, mulch will often trap heat present in deeper soil, extending the period of soil activity.

The weed-control characteristic of a deep mulch is one of the most attractive advantages of mulching. When a mulch is laid on bare soil, light is prevented from reaching recently-germinated weeds. Weed seeds will germinate, but without light they soon perish, saving you hours of back-breaking weeding and hoeing. A few of the tougher perennial weeds may find their way through mulch, but because the soil is soft and moist, pulling them is a snap.

As a way of protecting perennials against winter freezing, organic mulches are hard to beat. A layer of mulch does many things to protect hibernating plants. Mulch reduces the depth to which the soil freezes. In many cases this prevents root damage that would set plants back in the spring. A deep winter mulch also reduces the rapid freeze/thaw cycles of the soil, which can cause plants to heave, breaking tender roots in the process. Additionally, soil that has overwintered beneath a mulch will have a lighter, less-packed structure than soils compacted by rain and snow. Earthworms, too, are encouraged by a winter mulch, and they can often be found working the soil in the dead of winter while nearby soil is frozen solid.

Soil structure is improved through mulching. Many soils, especially clay soils, form a surface crust as a result of the compaction caused by rain and wind. When the soil is protected by a mulch, compaction is greatly reduced. As organic mulches decay they create humus, an important ingredient for good soil structure. When decaying mulches are turned under in the fall, they improve soil structure in much the same way a finished compost would.

Nature's tillers—earthworms—are also encouraged by mulching. A layer of mulch will encourage earthworms to burrow close to the soil's surface, producing pore spaces for air, water, and roots. Worms drag bits of nutrient-rich decaying mulch down into the soil where plant roots can utilize it.

Soil fertility is also improved by organic mulches. Many of the materials used as mulch contain a wide assortment of valuable nutrients. As rainwater washes through the mulch, it carries these nutrients down into the soil where plant roots can absorb them. Likewise, when mulches are turned under at the end of the growing season, the remaining nutrients are released into the soil where next year's plants can use them.

A final benefit of mulch is that it keeps vine vegetables such as unstaked tomatoes, cucumbers, and squash off the ground. This reduces the likelihood of the vegetable rotting by keeping it away from moisture and soil microorganisms. Mulches also keep plants and fruit clean by reducing the splashing of dirt by water drops.

DANGERS

Although mulching your garden will result in many desirable effects, improper mulching can cause a few problems. The two biggest dangers of mulch are keeping the soil too wet and too cold for good plant growth. These problems can be overcome by allowing soils to dry out and warm up sufficiently in the spring before applying a mulch. This practice is very important around young seedlings where excessively moist and cool soil will encourage the fungal disease damping-off (Fig. 13-2).

Mulches applied in damp areas may also encourage slug and snail populations. Again, allowing the soil to warm and dry thoroughly before applying a mulch will reduce this problem. Cultivating soil before mulching will also help control excess moisture problems.

Mulch may cause crown rot in some perennials when the material is not applied properly. To prevent crown rot, do not allow mulches to touch the base of perennials during the growing season. Additionally, mulches should not be placed around perennials immediately after a rain. Instead, wait a few days until soil is no longer waterlogged.

Fig. 13-2. Apply mulch after vegetable plants have established themselves to prevent damping-off disease.

ORGANIC MULCHES

Although just about any organic material will make a suitable mulch, some are better than others. A material's texture and nutrient content has a lot to do with its desirability as a mulch, but more important is the availability of the mulching material. If you have to buy your mulch, the bill can quickly price you out of the mulching habit. Fortunately, there are many sources of free mulch—it is simply a matter of looking for them. Many stables, canneries, mills, packing houses, park departments, grain elevators, and lawn services are willing to give away their waste. All you have to do is ask and in most cases you can haul away all the mulch you want. Try to locate a variety of sources so that when one is out of material you can visit another. Many of the materials mentioned in Chapter 5 can be used for mulches. Here are a few of the more common organic (biodegradable) mulching materials and their properties as a mulch.

Cardboard

This material makes an effective mulch when laid between the rows of your garden. In most cases a single layer of cardboard will last throughout the season, but by the fall it should be decomposed enough to be turned under. Steer clear of cardboards printed with colored ink as the ink may contain lead or other harmful materials. Secure cardboard with rocks or dirt around edges to prevent it from being blown out of place by the wind. Once cardboard is in place in your garden, it is virtually impossible for weeds to grow through it.

Compost

Compost should be spread to a depth of 1 to 2 inches when applied as a mulch. Although finished compost is rich in nutrients and does wonders for soil structure, it is not very effective as a weed control since weeds grow in it just as well as vegetables. The best use of compost is beneath another mulching material that has good weed control properties.

Corncobs

Both ground and crushed corncobs are generally available free for the taking at corn mills (Fig. 13-3). This material should be spread to a depth of 3 to 4 inches, which will create an effective barrier against weeds. Corncobs decompose very slowly, hold a lot of moisture, and are heavy enough to stay where you put them. They will rob the soil of nitrogen unless a nitrogenous material is added during application. When mixed with leaves, corncobs will prevent leaves from matting. Corncobs will attract birds and rodents for a short time after application.

Grass Clippings

This plentiful material works best as a mulch when spread at a depth of 2 to 3 inches. Grass clippings decompose rapidly adding valuable humus

Fig. 13-3. Many corn mills give away all the corn cobs you care to haul. Try to get the darkest color cobs you can find, as these have a lower carbon/nitrogen ratio.

to your soil. You will probably need to keep replenishing grass clipping mulches throughout the summer (Fig. 13-4). Grass clippings will stay where you put them and are excellent for use around fragile plants. Although grass clippings do a good job of choking out established weeds, they may contain weed seeds that will sprout and cause problems. Make sure the clippings you collect have not been sprayed with herbicides or pesticides, because these poisons will stunt or kill vegetables as they leach into the soil. It is a pretty safe bet that lawns without weeds are being sprayed. Stay away from clippings from these lawns.

Leaves

Leaves are available as a mulch wherever

trees grow. Leaves should be applied to a depth of 2 to 3 inches. Whole leaves have a tendency to mat down in a soggy mass, but the problem can be reduced by shredding the leaves before application. Shredded leaves make excellent mulches for overwintering perennials when applied in a layer of more than 12 inches. Although leaves are rich in many trace minerals, they often carry weed seeds. Leaves also tend to blow around a lot in windy locations.

Manure

Thoroughly-rotted animal manures can be used as a mulch, although these materials perform better as additions to the compost pile. Fresh manure applied as a mulch is likely to burn plants and therefore should never be used. Although decomposed manure will add valuable nutrients and a lot of humus to the soil, it also tends to contain many weed seeds. Because of this habit of producing rather than reducing weeds, manure is best used under other materials which are effective weed barriers.

Newspaper

Newspaper is a widely available mulching material that works best when applied in sheafs of 10 to 12 pages (Fig. 13-5). Stones or dirt should be heaped around the edges of the newspapers to prevent the wind from blowing them away. Newspaper can also be shredded and applied in 3- to 4-inch-thick mats. Use only newspaper with black print as colored ink contains lead. Do not use the slick paper stock found in magazines as these papers

also contain dangerous chemicals. Newspaper is a very effective control for weeds and will add slightly to the fertility and structure of your soil when it decomposes. Newspaper decomposes so quickly that several applications may be necessary through a season. A good use for newspaper is beneath materials like leaves and hay, which may carry weed seeds.

Peanut Shells

Peanut shells and other nut and seed hulls make attractive mulches which do not blow around much. Apply shells and hulls to a depth of 3 to 4 inches. These materials tend to be high in major nutrients such as nitrogen, phosphorus, and potassium. Although these fiber-rich materials break down slowly, they greatly increase the water-holding capacity of the soil. Beware of using too

Fig. 13-4. Grass clippings are a readily available organic mulch. Lay them on heavily and often during the growing season.

Fig. 13-5. Newspapers make an effective weed control mulch. Do not use colored or slick paper, as these contain dangerous chemicals.

Pine Needles

Pine needles form a light mulch when applied to a depth of 3 to 4 inches. Pine needles mat together in a soft bedding that does not blow around. Although pine needles do not absorb much water, they will trap it in the soil. Pine needles decompose slowly, but add substantial amounts of humus when they do so. Pine needles are acidic and work wonderfully on acid-loving plants. Do not place them around alkaline-loving plants.

Sawdust

Sawdust is one of those mulching materials that is very high in carbon and low in nitrogen. Therefore, application tends to draw nitrogen from

many salted peanut shells. Cottonseed hulls may also be dangerous because many contain high concentrations of pesticides and herbicides.

Peat Moss

Unless you live near a peat bog, peat moss is only available commercially. Peat moss should be applied to a depth of 1 to 2 inches. This material has been used for years as a mulch and with good reason; it is weed-free, pleasant to handle, and greatly increases the water-holding capacity of the soil. Peat moss is acidic, so do not use it on acid soils or around alkaline-loving plants. Peat moss tends to blow around when dry, so wet it thoroughly before applications. Peat moss is expensive, so use other materials when you can find them.

Fig. 13-6. Sawdust makes an attractive mulch. However, it is low in nitrogen and can do more harm than good when applied without a nitrogen-rich material.

the soil. It is best to add a layer of a nitrogen-rich material like cottonseed meal, dried blood, or compost to soil before laying down 1 to 2 inches of sawdust. This material stays in place well, breaks down slowly, and produces a favorable appearance (Fig. 13-6). Sawdust improves a soil's structure and nutrient content following decomposition. Many sawdusts are acidic and should not be used around alkaline-loving plants.

Seaweed

When available in large quantities, seaweed makes an excellent mulch. Apply 2 to 3 inches deep. This material is free of weed seeds and diseases and adds substantial amounts of potassium and humus to the soil. Seaweed decomposes quickly, so you may need to make several applications through the season.

Straw and Hay

These two materials are popular mulches. They should be applied to depths of 4 to 6 inches. These materials are slow to decompose, and one application should last 3 to 4 months. Both materials add valuable nutrients as well as humus to the soil when turned under in the fall. Straw has a high carbon/nitrogen ratio, so nitrogenous materials should be added to the soil before application. Straw and hay stay in place well and will smother most weeds. Beware of freshly cut hay that may contain weed seeds.

Vermiculite and Perlite

These two materials are expensive soil conditioners that work adequately as mulches when layered to a depth of 2 inches. Both materials are very light and tend to blow away, so cover them with a heavier mulch. Vermiculite and perlite are sterile which prevents the spread of weeds and disease. Each holds several times its own weight in water. Unfortunately, these materials have very little nutrient value. They are best used as a mulch over recently planted seed rows to keep soil moist enough for proper germination without smothering the seedlings.

Wood Chips

Wood chips are basically the same as sawdust except that the larger pieces decompose more slowly. Wood chips are most often used as a permanent mulch in pathways and around fruit trees. When used close to plants, make sure to add sufficient nitrogen. Wood chips are best when added after a year of weathering.

This list is far from exhaustive. You may be able to find other mulch materials such as salt marsh hay, cocoa bean shells, spent mushroom soil, tobacco stems, and cotton or wool wastes in your area. Each of these materials will produce an effective mulch.

NONORGANIC MULCHES

Organic materials are not the only stuff that can be used for mulching. Many non-biodegradable materials perform nicely as mulches. Although non-biodegradable materials conserve soil moisture, moderate soil temperature, and reduce weeds they will not improve soil structure and fertility because they do not break down. On the other hand, since these materials do not decompose rapidly, they will have many years of use. Common nonorganic mulches include the following.

Aluminum Foil

This kitchen helper can be used successfully in the garden as a mulch (Fig. 13-l7). It is especially suited for use beneath plants growing where there is less than optimum light, since aluminum foil will reflect light that has already passed the plant back toward the plant. The light-reflecting characteristic of aluminum foil also works as a deterrent to aphids, which prefer the bottoms of leaves to be dark. Aluminum foil will keep soil about 10° F cooler than unmulched soil. It can be used to prolong the life of cool-weather crops like lettuce well into the summer. Do not apply aluminum foil mulches on plants, which prefer warmer soil until the soil has warmed thoroughly. Hold aluminum foil mulches in place with rocks, soil, or boards. When large areas are mulched with foil, you will want to poke holes here and there at low spots so water can find its way into the soil.

Fig. 13-7. An aluminum foil mulch will keep the soil cool while reflecting light back up to the plant.

Boards

Boards form an effective mulch between row crops. Like cardboard or newspaper, boards are very efficient at choking out weeds. The boards will also provide a solid surface on which to walk, reducing soil compaction between plants. Boards used as a mulch also act as a good slug trap. Check frequently under the boards for these pests and remove them to keep slug populations under control.

Carpeting

Discarded carpeting forms a mulch nearly impervious to weeds. You can lay strips of carpeting between plants, or lay out a whole section of carpeting, cutting holes in it where your plants are to

grow (Fig. 13-8). Either way you will achieve a virtually weed-free garden. It is best to lay carpeting with its pile side up. This will provide a nice clean place for mature crops to rest and allows water to trickle down into the soil. Carpeting should be removed each fall to allow cultivation of the soil and to increase the carpeting's life.

Plastic

Plastic is being used much more frequently as a garden mulch. Black plastic 1 ½ mils thick in rolls ranging in width from 3 to 6 feet is the most popular mulch. Many gardeners roll out the plastic to cover their beds following spring cultivation, but before setting out seeds and plants. The black plastic will heat up the soil a little bit quicker than if the

Fig. 13-8. Carpeting is an effective mulch for keeping down weeds, although it does not add to soil fertility.

soil were left uncovered. The plastic also chokes out weeds by denying them light and preserves soil moisture. Because the plastic will force rain to run off instead of soaking into the soil, you will want to poke holes in the plastic here and there. After plastic has been laid out and rocks or dirt piled around the edges to hold it in place, holes are made and plants transplanted into these holes. At the end of the season, roll up the plastic so soil can be worked and to prolong the plastic's life. Because plastic is broken down by the ultraviolet rays of the sun, you will need to replace it every 2 to 3 years.

Stones

Stones are used in several sections of the country as permanent mulches. Although stones do not add to a soil's fertility and structure, they do reduce soil compaction by providing a place to walk. Stone mulches are, however, better at conserving moisture and moderating soil temperatures than most other mulches. Stone mulches are placed so that individual beds of 1 to 2 feet in width are left open. Plants are grown in these spaces. Compost and fertilizers are added to the soil in the open areas between the stones as needed. This controlled application is more efficient than simply broadcasting fertilizers and soil conditioners over the entire garden.

MULCHING TIPS

Here are some mulching tips which will help you put the above mulching materials to good use.

● Organic materials that have been finely shredded or ground, such as grass clippings or leaves, are more effective than coarse materials when applied in a thin layer. The main reason coarse materials do not form an effective thin mulch is that there is a lot of space between individual pieces of the coarse mulch. These spaces have two drawbacks: they allow the soil's moisture to evaporate easily, and they allow the penetration of sunlight, which encourages the growth of weeds. Finely-ground mulches do not present such a problem. When coarse mulches are applied, lay them on thickly.

● Mulches are most effective at choking out weeds of less than 1 inch in height. When mulching over weeds taller than this, you will need to cultvate the soil to knock them down before applying a mulch.

● Try to alter the mulches you apply to different sections of the garden from year to year. By consciously mixing up the materials you use for mulch, you will be ensuring that the garden receives a wide variety of nutrients.

● Mulch applied early in the spring will keep soil moist and cool. This coolness is of benefit to the cool-weather plants like peas, lettuce, radishes, and beets. Mulch these crops as early as possible, and you may be able to keep them from suffering from hot summer days for an extra week or two, thereby prolonging your harvest. A light-colored mulch that reflects sunlight will help keep the soil cool.

● Crops like tomatoes, egglants, and peppers that like warm soil should not be mulched immediately after being set out. Instead, set out the transplants and let them establish themselves (usually signified by a growth spurt) before mulching. The growth spurt is an indication that the soil is warm enough to encourage good growth. When mulch is added, the soil temperature will continue to rise—although slowly—and water will be conserved. A dark-colored mulch, which absorbs light, will help keep soil temperatures high.

● Some crops grow better when mulched heavily at planting time. This is especially true of potatoes, which can be planted by placing seed pieces just below the soil surface and then covering with a 6 to 10 inch mulch. The vines will grow through the mulch and form potatoes in the mulch. No digging is necessary for harvest; simply pull back the mulch to expose the potatoes.

● A light dusting of a fine mulch like sawdust, peat moss, or grass clippings can be made directly over seeds immediately after planting in dry soil. The mulch will hold in moisture, aiding germination without hindering the seeds' ability to push up to sunlight. When a mulch is used in this way, it should be light and not more than ½ inch deep. Do not use a mulch in this way on cool wet soils, or damping-off will be encouraged.

● When frost begins to arrive in your area, a light loose mulch can be used to help plants fend off the cold. Sprinkle a thin layer of loose material like straw over plants. Frost will form on this mulch, protecting the plants against damage. In the morning you can pull back the mulch to expose the plants to direct sunlight. This mulch will also trap some of the ground's heat, allowing growth to continue for a few extra weeks.

● Although newspapers are one of the best methods for keeping weeds down and preserving soil moisture, they tend to blow around. You can prevent this by applying a layered mulch. First, spread newspaper 6 to 10 sheets thick. Then cover it with a mulching material like leaves or corncobs that do not blow around. This combination mulch is very effective against weeds, but is not ugly like newspapers alone may be.

● When applying high-carbon mulches such as sawdust, leaves, and wood chips, which take nitrogen from the soil for decomposition, sprinkle a thin layer of a nitrogen-rich material on the soil before mulching. In the fall, more nitrogenous material should be added when the materials are turned under. This will enhance decomposition in the soil.

● Acid-loving plants like strawberries, blueberries, cranberries, raspberries, peanuts, radishes, sweet potatoes, and watermelon do best when mulched with a slightly acidic mulch. Acidic mulches include hardwood sawdust, pine needles, and oak leaves.

MULCHING METHODS

Every gardener who uses mulch has his or her own method of mulching. Below are some of the more common mulching practices.

Living Mulches

Mulches of living plants are used by many gardeners. The most common form of living mulch is sod. This method is very similar to planting in beds, except that between each rop row sod is allowed to grow. Where each crop is to grow, a strip approximately 1 foot wide is dug up and the soil mixed with organic materials and fertilizers (Fig. 13-9). This strip is then planted and cultivated and mulched in the normal manner. The area between rows (at least 2 feet wide) is left in sod and mowed to prevent the takeover of weeds. Where you have sufficient room, this method can save considerable time because weeding your garden involves little more than running a lawn mower back and forth between the rows.

Permanent Mulches

Using a permanent mulch—leaving a mulch of organic material on the garden year round—carries the idea of mulching to its fullest possible extent. Many gardeners make claims about the tremendous amount of work saved and the fine texture and fertility of their soil under a permanent mulch. They are right, but what they do not tell you is that they had good soil to begin with.

Before you decide to keep your garden covered with a year-round mulch, there are a few things to consider. Those gardeners who have had such success with a permanent mulch either have fine-textured, light soils to begin with, or they have spent several years tilling organic material into their soil in order to achieve adequate soil texture. Fertility is another matter. Since decomposition works mulches into the soil slowly, applying a permanent mulch to an infertile soil will be a disappointment.

If you are beginning a garden for the first time in a particular soil, do not try to garden with a permanent mulch. In most cases, the soil will not be adequately developed to allow good plant growth and you will end up with rather disappointing results. For example, clay soils under a permanent mulch will be too tightly packed for plant roots to find adequate growing room. On the other hand, sandy soils, which are plenty loose for root growth, will probably not hold enough nutrients to maintain the plants' growth. After a year or two of adding compost, manure, rock powders, and organic fertilizers to your soil your garden will be ready for a permanent mulch. It is important that you have

Fig. 13-9. Sod will form an effective living mulch between vegetable beds. Mowing is your major weeding chore.

fertile soil of sufficient depth and structure before attempting to garden with a permanent mulch.

Most gardeners who use a permanent mulch start their garden in the usual manner the first spring. The whole garden is turned, then seeds and transplants are placed in the garden. As the plants establish themselves, the mulch is laid on. The thickness of the mulch will depend on the material used and the length of the growing season. For example, a 6-inch-thick layer of straw will last about 3 months before it decomposes enough for weeds to become a problem. As the mulch decomposes, new mulch is added to keep the ground thoroughly covered. At the end of the season, when most people would till in or remove the mulching material, permanent mulch gardeners add more, covering all the areas of the garden, even where crops were grown. This practice creates a blanket

under which the garden soil remains unfrozen through the winter. The idea is to keep a thick enough mulch on the garden year-round so that the soil is always active.

In the spring, several weeks before an area is planted, the winter mulch is raked back and the sun allowed to warm the soil. After seeds are sown, or transplants are set out and established, the mulch is raked up to the base of the plants. This will keep the soil moist and prevent weeds from taking over. More mulch is added between the rows and around plants as needed to maintain a complete cover.

Although many gardeners report success with permanent mulching by using only one mulch material such as straw or leaves, add as many different materials as you can. Following this practice will ensure that many nutrients are delivered to the soil.

On soils of marginal structure and fertility, a

239

variation of the permanent mulching system can be used. With this method the entire garden is kept under a mulch year round, but in the spring the areas to be planted are raked so that the soils are exposed. The soil in these exposed areas is turned with a tiller or by hand. Compost, rotted manure, and rock or organic fertilizers are added to the soil during this turning phase. Where individual plants such as tomatoes, peppers, or squash are to be set, the mulch is raked off of a circle and this area worked prior to planting. At the end of the growing season, a mulch is once again established over the entire garden. Within a few years the soil should develop to the point where a permanent mulch system can be employed.

Stone Mulches

Stone mulches are an attractive alternative for gardeners in areas where organic material is in short supply. With this method, a permanent mulch of stone or gravel is established between crop rows. Large flat stones have most of the advantages of other types of mulch except that they do not add organic material to the soil, and they are permanent. Once stone mulches are in place your mulching days are over. Stone mulches are better at some things than regular mulches. They help the soil warm more quickly in the spring and in the fall they radiate heat, somewhat delaying the effects of the frost.

As with any permanent mulch, the soil must be up to par for a stone mulch to be effective. Large amounts of organic material, rock powders, and natural fertilizers should be turned into the soil before the stones are laid in place. When placing the stones for this mulch, make the stone paths approximately 2 feet wide with rows of exposed dirt about 1 foot wide. This way you will have adequate room to move around the garden on the stones and still have plenty of room in the foot-wide rows to plant most crops. After plants have established themselves in the rows each spring, you will need to spread a conventional mulch of leaves, hay, or other material on the dirt exposed between plants and stones.

WINTER MULCHES

Winter mulching of perennials should be a normal part of your gardening program. Coarse mulch materials are preferable to finely ground mulches for winter protection of perennials, because the mulch is used primarily as a blanket to trap soil heat. Dead airspace is one of the best insulators there is. Fine materials pack together with little or no airspace, while coarse materials maintain their loft (thickness) better through the winter. When using leaves, which tend to mat when wet, be sure to mix in a rough material like straw or corncobs to prevent suffocating the plants.

Although perennial plants may appear dead during the depths of winter, they are actually hibernating. They are still alive, but at a greatly reduced metabolic rate. The plants are taking up oxygen and giving off carbon dioxide. A coarse mulch will allow the plants to breathe while a tightly packed mulch will often suffocate them. Tightly packed mulches also tend to hold too much moisture near the plants through the winter. As the soil temperatures begin to rise, bacteria and fungi may cause various forms of rot to take hold on the plants. Loose mulches allow much of this excess moisture to evaporate, or at least allow plants a ration of air, which reduces the likelihood of rotting.

Winter mulches should not be applied until the plants have thoroughly died back. A safe way to tell when to mulch is by watching the soil. When the soil freezes to a depth of about 1 inch, you can be relatively certain that the plants are dormant. Lay on the mulch thickly—more than a foot deep in the northern reaches of the United States, slightly less, but certainly not less than 6 inches in the more temperate sections of the country. In most cases the ground will thaw out beneath the mulch, yet remain cool enough to prevent further growth during the winter. If mulches are applied too soon, before the plants are completely dormant, the plants are likely to try to grow beneath the mulch. Since there is no light, the plants cannot manufacture food and they will use up their stored reserves, weakening or dying before spring arrives.

When spring finally arrives and the snow begins to melt (or if you live in an area where it does not snow, when nighttime temperatures begin bottoming out around freezing), it is time to remove the mulch. Do not do it all at once. An unexpected cold snap could kill the plants. Instead, fluff up the mulch with a pitchfork, rake, or spading fork, but do not remove any of the mulch. A few days later, remove an inch or two of the mulch from the top of the blanket. Wait a week and remove all but an inch or two of the mulch from the bed. By now the plants should be acclimated to the harsher conditions. When the danger of killing frost has passed, the remainder of the mulch can be pulled back from the plants. Keep it handy, though, just in case one last frost decides to return.

WEEDS

As to the value of weeds in the garden, the most common theory is that weeds rob the soil of nutrients needed by the crops. To combat this idea, most garden soil is kept bare between rows or else mulched. True, a garden choked with weeds is hardly a garden at all, but weeds can be of use in your garden.

Many weeds have extensive root systems that pull nutrients from deep in the soil to the surface. When weeds die and break down, those subsoil nutrients are released for vegetables. Deep-searching weed roots also break up the soil for less sturdy vegetables.

The type of weed has a lot to do with its effect on the garden. Deep-rooted weeds should be allowed to grow here and there, but not thickly enough to crowd vegetables. Some deep-rooted weeds are ragweed, annual smartweed, dead nettle, sow thistle, ground-cherry, burdock, pokeweed, mullien, annual black nightshade, lamb's quarters, pigweed, and purslane. The ground creepers are usually shallow-rooted and will complete directly with your vegetables for soil nutrients. The secret is keeping the weeds under control so they do not muscle out your vegetables, which is one of the major reasons for using mulch in your garden.

Chapter 14

Fewer Pests Without Chemicals

An ounce of prevention is worth a pound of cure.

—Benjamin Franklin

Gardening organically depends on creating a balance of life in the mini-ecosystem of your garden. A healthy soil is the foundation of this balance of life. Even the healthiest plants, growing in the best of soils, will suffer from attack by insects on occasion.

What should you do when the first bug appears? Reaching for the synthetic (chemical) spray is a typical reaction. Instead, pick the bug off the plant and identify it. If the bug is a harmful one, squash it or drop the pest into a can of kerosene. If the bug is beneficial, let it go so that it can help your garden.

If you automatically reach for a can of insecticide, stop and think a minute. What are pesticides? How well do they work?

Pesticides are man-made or naturally occurring substances that kill insects, be they pest or friend. There are two kinds of pesticides: the man-made chemicals versus those made from plant or animal sources. Both types of insecticides work in similar ways to kill insects, but their source and persistence (ability to stay active) differ.

As a rule, synthetic insecticides are made from petroleum byproducts and the residues of chemical manufacturing processes. The federal government attempts to regulate the several-billion-dollar-a-year chemical insecticide industry, but is doing an inadequate job. For instance, only about 15 percent of insecticides have been tested for carcinogenic (cancer-causing) effects. The government also regulates the amount of pesticide that can be in or on our food. Since many of the synthetic insecticides remain active for several years, they tend to concentrate in the tissue of living organisms. The higher up on the food chain an animal is, the more concentrated the insecticides tend to be in that animal. Man, unfortunately, is at the top of the food chain. Each of us has several pesticides in our system. One of the main reasons for organic gardening is to reduce the amount of poison we eat, resulting in better health and a longer life. Another important reason to garden without chemical pesticides is that these pesticides may not be as effective as their manufacturers would like us to believe.

REASONS FOR NOT USING CHEMICAL PESTICIDES

We all know at least one gardener who grows green beans and has problems with Mexican bean beetles. Chances are he sprays and sprays his beans with a chemical, but the beetles continue to strip his plants of leaves. He just cannot seem to maintain a satisfactory amount of control over the pest, no matter how thickly he lays on the pesticide. This happens because he is upsetting the entire ecosystem by spraying. He should not expect a cure for three good reasons.

The first is that because insects mutate rapidly, new generations quickly become immune to the poison. No matter how often that gardener dusts, it will not kill all the pests. The insects that survive each barrage will become that much harder to eliminate the next time. This ability of insects to resist chemical pesticides leads manufacturers to synthesize over more potent poisons at an ever increasing rate.

The second reason not to use a chemical pesticide is that they are normally designed to kill *all* insects, even the good ones. This indiscriminate killing upsets the ecosystem in your garden which nature works so hard to maintain. Eventually the garden will recover, but the pests will also be back. The same may not be true for beneficial insects. Good bugs, like ladybugs and bees, take longer to rebuild their populations than the pests. Chances are the problem bugs will come back stronger than ever; the helpful bugs barely, if at all. Birds that feed regularly in your garden may also be affected.

The final reason for not using chemical pesticides is that they leave toxic residues in plants and soil. Soil microbes are affected, and the foundation of your healthy garden—healthy soil—is compromised. The plants, too, are hurt. Pests like to pick on unhealthy plants so the cycle starts anew. Meanwhile, you have eaten the fruits and vegetables, adding unnecessarily to your intake of poison.

All this is not to say that chemical pesticides made from plant sources are harmless. Insecticides derived from plant sources are dangerous and should be handled accordingly. The advantage of using a pesticide derived from a plant is that these pesticides tend to break down rapidly. Additionally, the poison breaks down into a nutrient for soil microorganisms and plants. Many synthetic pesticides leave behind salts and other residues which retard instead of benefit plant and soil life.

In many cases, treating your garden with chemical pesticides may be worse than the problem. By using natural methods of control, you can help your garden at the same time you battle bugs.

The organic concept allows for minor insect damage. If you have ever had a garden, you know that certain years different pests plague your garden. Mexican bean beetles may be your biggest headache one year. The next, squash bugs may do the most damage. You cannot really plan ahead, but you can be ready for whatever insect problem presents itself each year.

Like any living organism, a garden gets sick from time to time. Humans visit the doctor. You are the doctor for your garden. How you decide to handle the pest problems will determine how quickly and thoroughly your garden recovers.

There are two strategies for keeping pest controls working properly and in harmony with your garden. They are prevention and treatment.

The idea behind preventative measures is to make it harder for injurious insects to reproduce and create the populations necessary to do real damage to your garden. Treatment, on the other hand, is an attempt to battle a particular insect once it has gotten out of control. Not surprisingly, you will find that breaking an insect problem through adequate prevention will reduce pest problems to the point where you will seldom need to worry about a cure.

PREVENTION

The easiest way to handle pest problems is to prevent them. The foundation for a healthy garden is a good soil, but prevention of large insect populations requires more than a healthy soil. There are several strategies you can incorporate into the way you tend your garden, which will keep insect populations within acceptable limits without resorting to chemical warfare. These are; crop rotation, garden maintenance, resistant varieties, diversified planting, barriers, and altered planting times.

Crop Rotation

Most insects spend the winter as eggs or pupa attached to host plants or in the soil. By moving your plants to a different location each year, you can do much to reduce pest populations.

Take the squash borer as an example. This insect hibernates as a larva or pupa an inch or two deep in the soil. If you continuously plant squash, cucumbers, and melons in the same place each year, when the borers hatch in the spring they do not have to look very far to find their host plants. When you rotate your crops, however, the borer will emerge in the spring and will not find the plant it likes to eat. Instead, it will be faced with the difficult task of trying to locate your squash plants, which may be several yards away or in another plot altogether. Chances are very few of the borers will find a host plant. This will reduce the borer population, resulting in less damage to your plants.

Crop rotation is important for the well-being of the Brassica family. These plants—cabbage, broccoli, cauliflower, kale, kohlrabi, and other cole crops—should not be planted in the same area where they have grown previously until at least 2 years have passed. This rotation is an attempt to break both the life cycle of the insects that feed on these plants and the diseases, such as club root, which attack these fragile plants. Virtually every other crop will receive similar benefits from crop rotation.

Garden Maintenance

Garden maintenance is an important part of preventing insect infestations. Diseased plants, leaf droppings, unplowed soil, and excessive weeds encourage pestiferous insects to breed and produce large populations.

When a plant is not as strong as it should be—you can tell by its stunted growth or unhealthy color—it offers a ready target for pests. Should insect damage become severe on the plant, remove it from the garden. Either burn it or place it in a compost heap that is hot enough to destroy the problem.

Because many garden pests pass the winter in the first few inches of soil, tilling, plowing, or hand-digging in early spring will expose the pupa or larva of many insects to the weather or to birds, which will destroy them.

Applying a clean mulch around plants will also help reduce the spread of harmful insects. By the same token, removing diseased leaves from plants before they fall to the ground will help reduce the spread of disease. If you keep a mulch on your garden year-round, change it every year or two. Mulches that remain in place for long periods of time are a perfect place for insects to hide and breed.

Weeds by themselves are not especially harmful to the garden unless they crowd out your vegetable plants. This crowding weakens the vegetable and encourages attack by insects and disease. Try to keep weeds under control be hoeing or tilling, but go ahead and let a few grow. Many produce pretty flowers later in the summer and others will act as trap plants for harmful insects.

Resistant Varieties

Some pests and diseases can be controlled by planting vegetables that have been bred to be resistant to certain diseases and pests. If drought or extremely wet growing seasons are common to your area, order seeds and plants that have been bred to withstand these adverse growing conditions. Many pests attack plants when they are suffering from drought or soggy soil conditions.

Many types of tomatoes have been bred to resist pests and disease. The capital letters V, F, N, and T after a tomato's description in a seed catalog will tip you off to the resistance bred into various tomato plants. The V stands for resistance to verticillium wilt, F for fursuraium wilt, N for nematodes, and T for tobacco mosaic. Choosing varieties with these characteristics will give your plants a better chance of remaining healthy through the season, thus reducing the ability of pests to attack the plant.

Diversified Planting

Since most insects prefer to eat only one or two types of vegetables you can do much in the way of reducing insect populations by mixing up the types of vegetables you plant in any one area of your garden. When the insect population on a host plant becomes large, some of the insects wander off in search of fresh plants on which to feed. If several of the same family of plants are grown together, the insects will have little trouble finding new plants to eat. If several types of plants are grown together, however, the pests will have a difficult time finding a new host plant.

The common practice of planting a perfectly straight row of only one type of plant makes an insect's movement from one area of the row to another rather easy. Insects will find it harder to stay in a row when it is not straight and does not contain all one type of plant. The idea is similar to the difference between driving down a straight interstate highway and a winding, twisting back road. Do not plant in straight rows, but if you do, place dissimilar plants, such as aromatic herbs or vegetables—onions and garlic, for example—at intervals in the row. Insects will make a detour around these plants and they may end up lost and confused. Their ability to damage your crop will be reduced and they will be exposing themselves to preditors such as birds and other insects.

Diversified planting works the best when plant combinations are based on companion planting methods. Companion planting (covered more thoroughly in the chapter on planning your garden) is a method of planting different vegetables with various other vegetables and herbs so that each plant helps the other grow and fend off insects. Mint, dill, spearmint, onions, and sage are said to reduce pest infestations of cabbage worms and other pests of the Brassica family (Fig. 14-1). See Table 7-4 for a more complete listing of companion plants.

Barriers

There are several materials useful for keeping insects from reaching your vegetables. These preventive measures involve physical barriers.

Fig. 14-1. Interplanting cabbages with onions makes it difficult for cabbage worms to find the cabbages.

Aluminum Foil. Aluminum foil, when placed around the trunk of fruit trees, discourage borers and other crawling insects from boring into or climbing the tree.

Tanglefoot and Stickem. Tanglefoot and Stickem are two sticky toothpaste-like substances that can be put around the base of grape vines, fruit trees, and larger plants suffering from crawling insects (Fig. 14-2). The insects get stuck in the goo and perish.

Netting. Netting is a useful deterent to birds and moths which like fresh fruit just as much as you (Fig. 14-2).

Tar Paper. Tar paper laid around the base of cabbages prevents cabbage maggots. The paper stops the flies from laying eggs close to the host plant.

Altered Planting Times

Try to plant vegetables before or after their major pests have passed through their most active stage. To do this, you will have to keep a sharp eye on insect populations for a couple of years. Also consider when plants are weakest—usually just after transplanting or right after they germinate—then plant so that these phases coincide with a lull in the pest insect's activities.

An example of foiling an insect with an altered planting time is transplanting cole crops as early in the spring as possible. Early planting will allow the plants to grow enough so that they will not be bothered by cut worms which emerge later in the spring. Additionally, planting these crops early means that they are harvested earlier, before the pest population has a chance to grow out of control.

Fig. 14-2. Tanglefoot and other sticky substances keep pests from crawling up and down fruit trees and canes.

Fig. 14-3. Netting placed over strawberries and other fruits keeps pesky birds at bay.

Paper Collars. Paper collars pushed an inch deep in the ground around recently-transplanted seedlings will go a long way toward keeping the nocturnal chomping of the cutworm at bay.

Diatomaceous Earth. Diatomaceous earth, a white powder of fossilized microscopic algae, can be sprinkled around a plant to keep slugs and snails away. Diatomaceous earth has sharp edges that these soft-bodied pests will not crawl over.

Wood Ash. Wood ash is said to do the same job as diatomaceous earth, but acts on the principle that the ash is alkaline and snails and slugs will stay away from it (Fig. 14-4).

Wire Fence. Wire fence will keep many larger pests like rabbits, dogs, and children away from your garden.

Fig. 14-4. A border of wood ash around tender plants keeps many crawling pests away and provides nutrients for the plants.

TREATMENT

The treatment of out-of-control insect populations involves two levels of attack. The first level is chasing the insect away. The second, more final, solution is killing the insect. The common treatments for out-of-control insect populations (in increasing levels of potency) are: mechanical controls, kitchen cabinet sprays, bug juice sprays, traps, commercially available biological controls and biodegradable poisons.

Mechanical

Your first line of defense after deciding to attack an insect population is a mechanical control. This usually means picking as many of the pests off your plants as possible. Do not forget to look for egg cases on the bottoms of leaves and on stems. Insects can be dropped into a can of kerosene or a can of water with a thin film of kerosene on top. If you are a hardy soul, you can simply squash the insects with your fingers. A badminton racket comes in handy for swatting flying insects such as cabbage butterflies and moths out of the air.

If the number of insects present makes picking by hand impossible, spray the undersides and tops of the affected planted with a high-pressure jet of water. This will dislodge many insects. Some will be eaten by predators, others will never find their way back to the plant, and a few will reinfest the plant. Should reinfestation occur, move on to a higher level of treatment.

Kitchen Cabinet Sprays

Kitchen cabinet sprays are made by mixing materials usually found in a well-stocked kitchen with water for use on insect-troubled plants. There are several advantages to using kitchen cabinet sprays. They are cheap, easy to make, and almost harmless, since they are made from foodstuffs of one kind or another.

To make a kitchen cabinet spray, whizz the active ingredient in a quart of water in a blender. Strain this liquid through cheese cloth or another fine-mesh material. Old nylon hosiery are effective filters. Next, pour this concoction into a sprayer. Mix thoroughly with water and add a squirt or two of liquid dish soap so that the spray will stick to the plants. Spray troubled plants with the spray.

Here are some favorite kitchen cabinet sprays. Like most insecticides these sprays should be applied early in the morning or late in the evening when insects are least active. Do not apply when rain is forecast or the sprays will be washed off the plants and you will have to reapply them.

Buttermilk. Buttermilk mixed one to one with water and sprayed on caterpillars is said to clog their breathing pores, causing them to suffocate.

Flour. Flour mixed in water is another spray useful for battling caterpillars. Flour sticks to the worms and dehydrates them as it dries. The flour also clogs the breathing pores of these pests. When using flour, be careful not to overdo it. Excess flour on plants will cut down on their ability to receive light and may clog their stomata as well.

Soap Spray. Soap sprays are the easiest kitchen cabinet sprays to make. Simply add 4 tablespoons of liquid dish soap to a gallon of water and spray on plants infested with aphids, mealybugs, spider mites, whiteflies, spittlebugs, earwigs, stink bugs, crickets, grasshoppers, and other pests. The fatty-acid salts in soap inhibit these pests' growth. Fels Naphtha dissolved in water and sprayed on fruit trees is recommended as a deterrent to many fruit pests.

Sugar. Sugar dissolved in water and sprayed on bean plants is an effective method of discouraging Mexican bean beetles.

Garlic and Onion. Garlic and onion are aromatic plants useful in kitchen cabinet sprays. Whizz the greens of these plants in a blender, strain, and mix with water and soap before spraying on the garden.

Hot Pepper Juice. Hot pepper juice mixed with water is said to discourage many chewing insects. Be careful when using a mix containing hot peppers not to over-apply the spray on delicate plants like eggplants. Additionally, make sure the plant to be sprayed does not dislike hot peppers.

Molasses. Molasses is said to chase many insects from the vegetable patch. This spray is also rich in many minerals that promote plant growth.

Spearmint and Peppermint. Spearmint and peppermint are two aromatic herbs that are said to chase cabbage worms away from Brassica crops.

Cedar Chips. Cedar chips brewed in water, cooled, and sprayed on plants are said to repel bean beetles and squash vine borers. Add liquid soap to this solution to make it stick on the plant.

Dormant Oils. Dormant oils sprayed on fruit trees late in winter, prior to the start of bud growth, are effective controls for many pests. This oil will smother many aphids and other small insects that overwinter in the bark of fruit trees and vines. Do not apply oil after growth has started since oil will interfere with pollination of the flowers and subsequent bud growth.

Bug Juice Sprays

In addition to making insecticides from substances found in your kitchen, you can use the pest insect itself to make what is known as a bug juice spray.

To make a bug juice spray, first determine which bug is causing you trouble. Then gather a couple of handfuls of the pests (keep an eye out for sick ones, and be sure to collect as many of them as possible). Next, place the bugs in a blender, add a cup or two of water and liquefy them. Strain the liquid through a fine mesh material to prevent the solids from clogging your sprayer. Dilute this juice at a rate of 1 part bug juice to 3 parts water. Pour into sprayer and spray on both tops and bottoms of leaves of affected plants. Extra bug juice concentrate can be stored in the freezer for up to a year just in case the pest returns. Within a day or two after the initial spraying you should notice a decline in the population of pest insects.

No one really knows why this method of pest control works, but several theories have been advanced. One theory holds that grinding the insects causes them to release an "alarm" pheromone which scares away other members of that species. Another line of reasoning suggests that diseased insects spread their disease when whizzed and sprayed on healthy insects. Another theory says that healthy bugs do not particularly like to live where their ground brothers and sisters have been sprayed. A final theory suggests that the chopped-up insects attract natural preditors to the area where they feed on the pests. Whatever the reason, bug juice seems to work for many gardeners.

Gardeners will find that bug juice sprays are effective against Mexican bean beetles, June beetles, grasshoppers, cutworms, stink bugs, and many caterpillars. Although pill bugs, slugs, and snails are not really insects, the bug juice method appears to work on these crop-hungry pests as well.

Traps

There are several types of traps that can be used to catch insects before they have a chance to attack your vegetables and fruits. Here are some favorites:

capture many moths. Mix ⅛ cup of molasses in a pint of water and pour into a quart-size wide mouth jar. Hang the jar in a fruit tree, and check often for pests. When molasses water gets solid with bugs empty the jar and renew the molasses solution. Sassafras oil can be used in place of molasses to attract codling moths, while geranium oil does the same for Japanese beetles.

A jar containing the same molasses solution buried so that its mouth is at ground level will attract many ground insects (Fig. 14-6). Cucumber beetles, corn borers, corn earworms, moths, cutworms, tomato hornworms, and cabbage worms are attracted to this sweet-smelling trap. Check this trap a few days after installation to make sure you are not catching excessive numbers of beneficial

Fig. 14-5. Stale beer in a shallow pan will attract many snails and slugs. These pests fall into the trap and drown before they can damage your vegetables.

A shallow pan of stale beer placed in the garden so that the lip of the pan is at ground level will attract slugs and snails (Fig. 14-5). These pests fall into the brew and cannot escape. Empty the pan every few days and replenish the beer to keep the trap effective.

Earwigs can be trapped quite easily. Simply lay 1-foot-long sections of bamboo (open at both ends) or 1-foot-long pieces of hose near plants affected by these pests. The earwigs will crawl into these traps at night. You can destroy them by shaking the earwigs out of the trap and into a can of kerosene or a can of water with a film of kerosene floating on its surface.

A jar with molasses hung in fruit trees will

Fig. 14-6. A jar buried to its lip and baited with molasses traps many insects.

insects. If so, remove the trap. It is doing more harm than good.

There are several traps for Japanese and June beetles available commercially. Most of these traps use a chemical attractant that lures the beetles to the trap. The beetles then fall inside an escape-proof device and are collected in a bag for disposal.

You can stop many fruit-loving insects from attacking your fruit trees by hanging brightly-colored balls (red, yellow, and orange) smeared with Tanglefoot or Stickem in your trees. Insects will be attracted to these fake fruits, becoming stuck in the adhesive where they can do no more damage.

Tanglefoot and Stickem can also be used to keep crawling insects away from fruit trees and grape vines. Smear a band of either of these materials around the base of the plants. Crawling insects will get stuck in the goo before they have a chance to do real damage to your trees.

Biological Controls

Biological controls are a method of thwarting pest insects by pitting the pest against another naturally occurring organism. The field of biological control is a relatively new one. Here are some of the commercially available biological controls.

• *Bacillus thuringiensis* is a bacterium that attacks many caterpillars including European corn borers, gypsy moths, canker worms, tomato hornworms, tent caterpillars, leaf rollers, and the many caterpillars which attack cole crops. The bacteria is sprayed on the host plant and the insect eats the bacteria. The bacteria multiply within the host, causing sickness and rapid death.

BT, as the bacteria is sometimes called, is an effective method of controlling large caterpillar populations. Remember, though, that BT is harmful to almost all caterpillars. It may kill the caterpillars of such lovely butterflies as the swallowtails that visit your garden. Therefore, *Bacillus thuringiensis* should be used only when caterpillar populations are out of control and you know they are a pest.

• *Bacillus popillae* is a bacterium (also known as Milky Spore) which attacks the June beetle when it is in the grub stage. Spray this bacteria on lawns or add as a powder by sprinkling 1 teaspoon every 3 feet. The *Bacillus popillae* bacteria attack only June beetles, so there is little danger of harming helpful insects.

• *Pheromones* are secretions of animal and insects with scents that mean various things to other members of the species. Pheremones can signal the location of food, danger or mating conditions.

Pheromones are used to attract harmful insects away from crops or to confuse pests so that they become incapable of reproducing, quickly reducing the size of the pest population. Pheromones have been synthisized to match the naturally-occuring sex attractant chemicals of insects. Do not use sex pheromones near host plants. This only attracts more pests to your crop. Instead, place pheromone lures on the other side of your yard. This way pests are attracted *away* from instead of *toward* your garden. Commercially available Japanese and June beetle traps often use phermones as a bait.

• *Hormones* are chemicals within the body of an insect. Some insect hormones have been isolated. The ones of importance to gardeners control the growth phases of the insects. These can be used to destroy the normal pattery of growth, leaving the target insect incapable of reproducing and creating large, damaging populations.

Hormones are less widely used than pheromones, because most are still in the developmental stages. The effects of hormones on the ecosystem are not fully known. Therefore, they should be avoided when other controls are available.

Beneficial Insects, Birds, and Animals

No discussion of biological controls would be complete without mentioning some of the insects, birds, and animals that are useful for combating pest insects. Many of the predatory insects can be bought for introduction into your garden. Look in the back of gardening magazines for advertising about these beneficial insects. Many times intro-

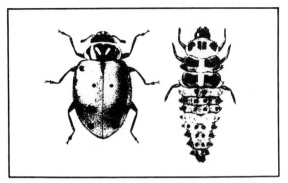

Fig. 14-7. Lady beetles are a pretty and beneficial addition to the garden. Both the adult (left) and nymph (right) feed on many harmful insects.

duced insects will establish themselves and return year after year to help you fight the plant-eating insects. Therefore, it is important to keep an eye open for these garden helpers and try to encourage their growth. If there are large numbers of these beneficial insects living in and around your garden, you should be extremely careful about using poisons which kill insects indiscriminately.

● *Lady beetles,* also known as ladybird beetles, are a favorite beneficial insect because of their looks and their appetite (Fig. 14-7). Adult lady beetles and their larvae roam the garden eating soft-bodied insects such as scales, aphids, and mealybugs. Lady beetles are one of the few insects that will do battle with ants over an aphid colony.

● *Praying mantises* are, perhaps, the most well-known of the predatory insects (Fig. 14-8). These large insects have a big appetite for aphids, beetles, bugs, leafhoppers, flies, bees, wasps, caterpillars, and butterflies. Their appetite is such that they will feed on each other when there are no more pests to eat.

Fig. 14-8. Praying mantises have huge appetites for all kinds of insects, especially those that frequent your garden.

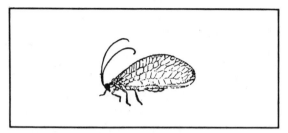

Fig. 14-9. Lacewings, although delicate in appearance, are heavy feeders on insect pests of all types.

● *Assassin bugs* are rare visitors to the garden, but when they arrive welcome them with open arms. Adults are brown or black, flat-bodied, and large-beaked. They feed on larva and adult forms of many plant-eating insects.

● Many types of ground beetles such as the *fiery searcher, mealybug destroyer, soldier beetle,* and

tiger beetle feed on a wide range of insects in the garden. Learn to identify these beneficial insects and keep them around your yard and garden.

● *Lacewings* are one of the most beneficial predatory insects (Fig. 14-9). These delicate insects have distinctive membranous wings and can be found flying about the garden in early morning or late afternoon. The adults as well as the larvae feed on ants, aphids, and the larvae and eggs of various insects. A healthy population of these insects in your garden will keep many garden pests to a minimum.

Wasps. Several types of wasps feed on various insect pests. Many of these wasps are available by mail order.

● *Braconid wasps* are one of the most common beneficial wasps for battling caterpillars in

Fig. 14-10. The white cocoons of the Braconid wasp on this tomato hornworm are a new generation of pest control in the making.

252

your garden. One sign of this wasp is the small white cocoons its lavae spin on the backs of caterpillars such as the tomato hornworm (Fig. 14-10). When you spy a caterpillar with these small white or brown cocoons on it, leave the caterpillar alone. It may eat a few more tomato leaves, but when the wasps hatch they will go a long way toward keeping future caterpillar populations under control.

● *Chalcid wasps* operate in much the same way as the braconid wasps, but they also feed on aphids, beetles, and scales. These wasps do not build nests so the best way of encouraging their populations is by allowing their cocoons to survive.

● *Mud dauber wasps* are another important predator in your garden. These wasps build mud nests and then go out in search of spiders, crickets, cicadas, flies, and leafhoppers, which are paralyzed and dropped into the nest as food for the young.

● The *asparagus wasp* is another efficient ally in the battle against damaging pests, but this one feeds only on the asparagus beetle. The adult wasp lays its eggs in the eggs of the beetle. After the larvae of the beetle has moved into the ground to pupate, the wasp larvae takes over by feeding on the beetle's pupae. Although this wasp may not eliminate the asparagus beetle completely, it will help keep populations of the leaf-eating pest under control.

Birds. Birds are a valuable asset to your garden. Although birds can be pests at certain times—starlings, bluejays, and crows pull up corn shoots, for an example—in general they eat more than their share of bugs, both good and bad. Throwing kitchen scraps into the garden will attract birds. After the birds pick through the garbage, they move out to comb the garden for insects and weed seeds. A water bath helps keep birds returning regularly to your garden.

● *Sparrows* are another insect-hungry bird. Although these and other birds eat insects indiscriminately, pest insects are usually more abundant than beneficial ones. Therefore, birds are more likely to eat harmful insects than beneficial ones.

● *House wrens* are said to feed upward of 500 caterpillars and spiders to their young each day.

Chickadees are said to eat nearly 138,000 canker worm eggs a month. Baltimore orioles can eat up to 17 caterpillars a minute.

● *Robins* search for earthworms, caterpillars, and grubs for their young. These birds dig through mulch with their beaks and do a thorough job of cleaning the soil of insect larvae.

● Do not allow *chickens* into your garden except in late fall or early spring. These birds will eat everything in sight, including vegetable plants and fruits. However, when allowed to roam in the garden prior to planting or after harvest they will scratch out many grubs and larvae that would otherwise attack your plants.

Toads, Bats, and Moles. Toads should be encouraged to live in your garden. These reptiles can be placed in your garden when found in other parts of your yard. Their flypaper tongues will be active at night lapping up insects while you sleep.

Bats are another bug-catching garden helper. Flying at night, these winged rodents snatch moths from the air before they have a chance to lay their eggs on your garden plants.

Moles are a grub-eating rodent of great value in your garden. Although the tunnels these animals leave are often unsightly, they do not usually feed on plant roots. Instead, they seek out grubs that could cause serious root damage.

Insecticides

Biologically-derived insecticides should be the last resort in the war against insect pests. Although these insecticides are said to be harmless to most people and animals, they kill harmful and beneficial insects alike. Insecticides should never be sprayed on flowering plants since they kill the insects which pollinate the plants. It is best to spray only the plants that need it and let the healthy plants be.

Most biologically-derived insecticides upset the balance of life in the garden ecosystem in much the same way chemical insecticides do. The only advantage of biologically-derived insecticides is that they are not persistent. Natural insecticides break down into harmless compounds a few weeks

Fig. 14-11. A dusting of rotenone is a good defense against chewing insects. It breaks down rapidly and must be applied often for best effect.

after application. Still, no insecticides should be sprayed directly on fruit you plan to eat in the next few days. Always wash fruit and leaves of vegetables sprayed with insecticides, even if spraying took place weeks ago.

Here are some of the commercially available biological insecticides. Use them only as a last resort, when other methods of prevention and treatment have failed. Additionally, you should check the label when you buy any of these products to make sure that they have not been mixed with non-biologically derived poisons.

False Hellebore. False hellebore is an insecticide sold as a dust. It can be applied as a dust or mixed in water as a spray. This is a stomach poison which is effective against many chewing pests including leafhoppers, grasshoppers, beetles, caterpillars, and sawflies.

Pyrethrum. Pyrethrum is a contact poison made of a ground-up member of the chrysanthemum species of flowers. This poison is considered the least poisonous to man and leaves little or no residue on vegetables. This poison is not a stomach poison. Instead, it paralyzes the pest and must contact the insect directly to be effective. Pyrethrum is effective against leafhoppers, aphids, caterpillars, bugs, and some beetles.

Rotenote. Rotenone is a contact insecticide and stomach poison made from cube, derris, and other tropical plants. It is also sold as derris. This poison breaks down rapidly, leaving little or no toxic residue (Fig. 14-11). Its effects are short-lived so it must be applied periodically to be effective. Rotenone is non-poisonous to man, but it may harm beneficial insects, fish, and toads. This poison is the responsible gardener's best weapon against insect pests, especially those that chew.

Ryania. Ryania is made from the roots of the ryania shrub and is very potent. It should not be used unless other methods have failed to bring insect populations under control. Ryania is effective against the codling moth, corn borer, cranberry fruit worm, cotton bollworm, and other pests.

Sabadilla Dust. Sabadilla dust is a stomach poison made from the seed of a South American lily plant. This poison is not widely available, although it is effective for some bugs, aphids, caterpillars and some beetles. This poison can irritate mucous membranes, so wear a mask when applying.

The organic concept allows for minor insect damage, but incorporated into the overall garden strategy are two ideas, prevention and treatment, useful for reducing large-scale insect damage. Prevention methods include crop rotation, garden maintenance, resistant varieties, diversified planting, barriers, and altered planting times. If insect populations get out of hand, use treatment methods—mechanical controls, kitchen cabinet sprays, bug juice sprays, traps, commercially-available biological controls, and biodegradable poisons.

Chapter 15

Dealing with
Forty Garden Pests

All worms have an apple, but not all apples have a worm.

—Peter Reeves

Forty major fruit and vegetable pests are listed alphabetically in this chapter. Although this selection of garden pests is far from complete, it should provide you with some pretty good ideas about how to handle certain pest insects. You can use the controls listed in each section to help keep the pest from further damaging your garden. As always, insects beneficial to your garden should be encouraged. You will find brief descriptions of some of these beneficial insects in Chapter 14, "Fewer Pests Without Chemicals."

APHIDS

Aphids come in many colors, green, gray, violet, red, yellow, and brown are the most common. Aphids are extremely small, 1/5 to 1/10 of an inch in length. These pear-shaped, soft-bodied insects gather on the leaves of many garden plants.

They suck juices from plants and, when colonies grow large enough, cause the leaves to curl and become stunted and deformed (Fig. 15-1). Aphids often carry mosaic and other virus diseases.

Small communities of aphids seldom cause much damage, but when herded together by ants, who protect the aphids in return for the excess plant sugars they secrete, these pests can become a major problem. The easiest way to remove them is to rub affected plant parts between your thumb and fingers, squashing the insects. Often, a strong spray of clear water will wash many of the pests from the plant. Sprays of soap, tobacco tea, lime water, and rotenone will disperse the colonies. On fruit trees, aphids can be controlled through the use of an early spring dormant oil spray.

APPLE MAGGOT

This pest is also known as the *apple fruit fly* or the *railroad worm*. Adult flies are 1/4 inch in length with a back body marked with yellow across the abdomen and zigzagged yellow markings on the

Fig. 15-1. Aphids gather on plant stems to suck juices from the plant.

color with yellow/orange squares on each wing. The spotted asparagus beetle is reddish-brown with 12 black spots on its back (Fig. 15-2). The spotted beetle feeds mainly in the spring, the other in the fall. Both beetles range from 1/4 of an inch to 1/3 of an inch in length. The adults overwinter in the soil, emerging to chew foliage and shoots. These insects live throughout North America.

Look for the beetles during early periods of asparagus growth. The insects will be sluggish and are easily picked by hand. Drop picked beetles into kerosene. Good garden sanitation and dustings of phosphate rock or bone meal deter these beetles. Chalcid wasps prey on the adult beetles, while ladybugs eat its larva. For severe infestations apply rotenone.

BEET LEAFHOPPER

This wedge-shaped pest is greenish-yellow to light-brown in color with irregular dark markings (Fig. 15-3). It is slightly less than 1/4 inch in length. Several generations are produced each year after adults emerge from the weeds where they have hibernated through the winter. Eggs are deposited in plant stems, and nymphs emerge from the weeds where they have hibernated through the winter. Eggs are deposited in plant stems, and nymphs emerge looking like smaller versions of adults. This insect carries a disease known as *curly top* that affects beets, beans, tomatoes, cucumbers, spinach, squash, and potatoes. Curly top causes plants to be stunted and deformed, with brittle curled leaves. Distribution is west of Illinois and Missouri with heaviest concentrations in the far west.

The best line of defense is the removal of weeds in and around your garden. Remove any plants that appear affected by curly top to prevent spread of the disease by beet leafhoppers. A light dusting of diatomaceous earth over plants often reduces infestations.

BLISTER BEETLES

These long, soft-bodied beetles swarm over plants feeding on foliage and fruits. The striped blister beetle (yellow with black stripes) feeds on

wings. The adult lays eggs by punching a hole in fruit skin. Maggots or larva hatch from these eggs and eat tunnels through the fruit's flesh, causing the entire fruit to rot. This pest will attack apple, blueberry, cherry, and plum trees.

Adult flies can be trapped by hanging jars filled with 1 part blackstrap molasses and 9 parts water in tree branches. Maggots can be destroyed by collecting dropped apples before maggots exit. Several collections of fallen fruit are necessary for this to be effective. Late-maturing apple varieties are seldom affected as much as early-maturing apple varieties.

ASPARAGUS BEETLE

The asparagus beetle is a metallic blue-black

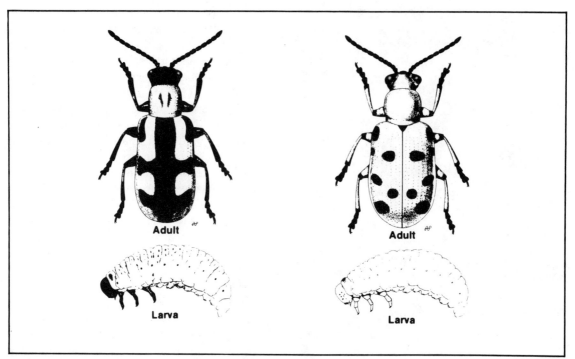

Fig. 15-2. The asparagus beetle (left) and the spotted asparagus beetle (right). Larva of both (bottom).

beans, beets, melons, peas, potatoes, tomatoes, and other vegetables. Blister beetles overwinter as larva in the soil.

The larva of some species feed on grasshopper larva. Adults can be controlled by handpicking. (Make sure to wear gloves since a noxious secretion of this insect may cause a blister). If blister beetles are out of control, dust plants with sabadilla, or a lime and flour mixture.

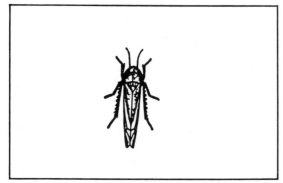

Fig. 15-3. Leafhoppers are small (less than ¼ inch long) and wedge-shaped.

CABBAGE LOOPER

This caterpillar is green with a white stripe down each side. The cabbage looper makes a distinctive loop when it crawls with its 1½-inch-long body. This pest feeds on broccoli, cabbage, cauliflower, beans, celery, kale, lettuce, parsley, peas, potatoes, radishes, spinach, and tomatoes throughout the United States. The adult moth is brownish-gray with a silver spot on each wing. This pest is a prolific breeder, producing several generations per year. Eggs are green-white and round and deposited on the top surface of leaves.

Because this pest overwinters as a pupa attached to leaves, garden sanitation is a must. Handpick mild infestations. For more serious problems, spray plants with Bacillus thuringiensis. Trichogramma wasps are natural predators of this pest.

CABBAGE MAGGOT

The adult cabbage maggot resembles a house fly except that it is dark gray with black stripes on the thorax. The adult fly is ¼ inch long and lays its eggs on plant stems near the soil surface. White blunt maggots emerge to tunnel into roots and stems causing plants to wilt from bacterial or fungal disease. Two to three broods are produced each year, and they pass the winter as a pupa in the soil. Adults lay eggs on cabbage, broccoli, radishes, turnips, cauliflower, cress, celery, and Brussels sprouts. This pest is distributed through the central, western and northern United States.

CANKER WORM

The canker worm is also known as the measuring worm or the inch worm. These small, striped, black-to-green larva feed on spring foliage and on ripening fruit, especially apples and cherries. The adults are brown or gray moths that lay eggs in the bark of the trunk and branches of fruit trees. This pest is especially destructive in the spring and fall. Various forms of this pest are found throughout North America.

Apply Tanglefoot or a similar sticky material to tree trunks early in the spring and in the fall. Bacillus thuringiensis will destroy some species. Trichogramma wasps are natural predators of the canker worm.

CODLING MOTH

The larva of this pest is off-white with a pink tinge and a brown head. The larvae grow to 1 inch in length. The adult is a grayish-brown moth with fringed hind wings. The hind wings are slightly lighter than the rest of the moth. The moth lays its eggs on the blossom end of fruit early in the season. The larvae then enter the fruit, eating until it matures. The larvae exits the fruit to spin a cocoon on the tree's bark. The codling moth spends the winter in the cocoon stage. A second generation may be produced in some areas. The codling moth is common throughout most of the United States. Host fruits include apple, plum, pear, cherry, and peach.

In spring, wrap the tree trunk with corregated cardboard. Larvae will often crawl inside to spin cocoons. At the end of the insect's season, the cardboard can be removed and burned, destroying the cocoons. In the early spring scrape bark of trees with a plastic card to dislodge overwintering co-

coons. Dormant oil sprays may afford some protection. Some braconid and Trichogramma wasps are natural predators of this pest. Woodpeckers, which pull young caterpillars and larvae out of tree bark, are also natural predators.

COLORADO POTATO BEETLE

Colorado potato beetles are slightly larger than ladybugs, but similar in shape (Fig. 15-4). The adult beetle has a yellow body with black stripes. Larvae are red with two rows of black dots and a black head. Yellow eggs are deposited on the underside of leaves. Both adults and grubs feed on leaves. This pest occurs in the northern three-fourths of North America.

Select resistant varieties of potato, and then plant on or above the ground, mulching heavily with straw. Plants that repel this pest include flax, horseradish, garlic, marigold, and green beans. Plant potatoes along with these repellent crops. Hand-picking the pest is the first line of defense. (Do not forget to look for eggs). Next, spray with a kitchen cabinet spray made from basil, or dust plants with wheat bran. Apply rotenone when necessary.

CORN EARWORM

This yellow, green, or brown caterpillar feeds on buds and on the unfolding leaves of young plants, in addition to the tassels and ears of corn (Fig. 15-5). The corn earworm also feeds on buds of potatoes, beans, cabbages, broccoli, and lettuce. When hungry, this 1-inch-long pest also feeds on

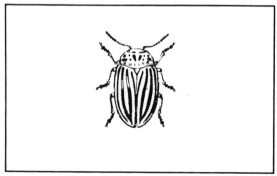

Fig. 15-4. The Colorado potato beetle.

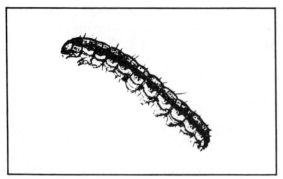

Fig. 15-5. Corn earworms are from ¼ to 1 inch in length.

clover, grapes, okra, peach, pear, peppers, pumpkins, squash, and strawberries. The adult is a green-gray or brown moth with black markings on its fore wing. The corn earworm is a prolific breeder and may produce up to seven generations per year, especially where corn is grown.

On corn, apply mineral oil to the base of the silk where it enters the ear, immediately after the silk has wilted. Removal of silk after wilting also helps. For serious infestations, spray with Bacillus thuringiensis. On garden plants other than corn, spray with garlic juice, onion extract, or rotenone.

CUCUMBER BEETLE

There are two varieties of cucumber beetles. The spotted variety is greenish yellow with 12 black spots on its back and a black head. Striped cucumber beetles have yellow to orange bodies with three black stripes and black heads (Fig. 15-6).

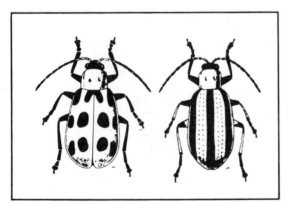

Fig. 15-6. Spotted cucumber beetle (left) and striped cucumber beetle (right).

Both pests average ¼ inch in length. Adults over-winter in garden trash. These insects do not necessarily defoliate their host plants, but they carry several types of wilt diseases. Cucumber beetles infest beans, cucumbers, melons, squash, gourds, asparagus, tomatoes, beets, cabbage, peas, potatoes, and eggplants. They also feed on many ornamental flowers. The larvae of this pest attacks the roots of corn plants. Their range is limited to the eastern half of the United States.

Crop rotation is an important defense against this pest. Frequent cultivation and garden maintenance also reduce grub populations. Heavy mulch and hand-picking are the first lines of defense. Cucumber beetle predators are the soldier beetle and tachinid fly. Use rotenone or pyrethrum as a last resort.

CUTWORMS

Although several species of cutworm occur throughout the United States, their damage and habits are the same. Cutworms range in color from gray to brown with plump, soft bodies and a few bristly hairs (Fig. 15-7). They can range from 1 to 2 inches in length. Adults are brownish to gray moths with wingspans of up to 1½ inches. Larvae are seldom seen during the day because they stay in burrows in the soil. However, these pests venture forth at night to chew the stems of young plants, cutting them off at or below ground level. A few species also climb plants, eating fruits, flowers, and leaves. Cutworms prefer young transplants of the cabbage family, but will also destroy beans, tomatoes, and just about any other young plant.

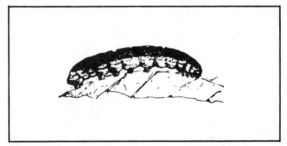

Fig. 15-7. Cutworms chew stems of small plants off at ground level as well as the young leaves on upper parts of some plants.

Preventive measures against the cutworm include garden sanitation, especially in the fall when moths are laying eggs. Frequent cultivation around newly set out plants will often expose this pest. Wood ashes, crushed eggshells, or sharp building sand can be spread around plants as a barrier. The best protection against this pest is to place a stiff paper or plastic collar around new transplants. The collar should be at least 1 inch high and penetrate the soil an equal distance. When plants have grown to the point where the stem is pencil-sized, the collar can be removed. At this size, the plants are too big for the worm to cut. The trichogramma wasp is a natural predator of the cutworm.

EUROPEAN APPLE SAWFLY

Although they are called flies, these insects are actually members of the wasp and bee family. The adult is a brownish-yellow, fly-looking insect with a black spot on its head. Adults are 1/5 of an inch long. Larvae are white to brown with a black head. The eggs are laid on fruit blossoms. When larvae hatch, they burrow into fruit, leaving a sawdust-like residue on the surface and brown tracks on the skin. The European apply sawfly produces only one brood per year and overwinters as a cocoon in the soil. Its host tree is the apple. This pest occurs in the eastern half of the United States.

Spray fruit trees with rotenone when flower petals begin to fall. Make a second application 1 week later.

FLEA BEETLES

These flea-like beetles jump when disturbed. They are rarely more than 1/16 of an inch long. Large populations of flea beetles will skeletonize the leaves of many plants, especially transplants (Fig. 15-8). Host plants are corn, eggplant, potato, spinach, strawberry, sweet potato, tomato, and several ornamentals. Some types of flea beetles can be found in all parts of North America. These beetles carry several viral and bacterial diseases.

Frequent cultivation and good garden maintenance go a long way toward checking populations of flea beetles. Wood ashes, diatomaceous earth, and garlic sprays discourage them from feeding. Seri-

Fig. 15-8. Flea beetles and damaged eggplant leaf.

ous infestations can be battled with frequent dustings of rotenone.

FRUIT TREE LEAF ROLLER

The green caterpillar of the fruit tree leaf roller grows up to 1 inch in length. Its head may range from black to dark brown. Adults are mottled brown and gold moths with two beige spots on their wing edges. Eggs are laid in masses on twigs and small branches. Eggs are covered with a brownish protective cover. The larvae of this pest spins a light web on the upper leaves and twigs of fruit trees where the worms feed on leaves and immature fruit. A distinctive trait of this insect is that leaves on affected trees appear to be rolled into hollow tubes. These caterpillars will feed on apricot, blackberry, cherry, gooseberry, pear, plum, raspberry, and some citrus trees and vines. They prefer apple trees. Fruit tree leaf rollers are distributed throughout the United States.

Dormant oil sprays in early spring, prior to bud opening, will suffocate most eggs. Caterpillars can be controlled to some extent with Bacillus thuringiensis sprays.

GRASSHOPPERS AND CRICKETS

Various forms of these well-known insects live throughout the country. Few crickets are a threat to the garden, and only certain grasshoppers produce much damage. Grasshoppers chew through the stems and leaves of plants causing them to break and die (Fig. 15-9). They are usually only pests in drought-stricken areas. Most species produce only one generation per year.

Keep the garden clean and free of weeds.

Sprays of hot pepper and soap are said to deter chewing. A good trap is made by setting a mason jar half-full of molasses in the ground so that its lip is at ground level. Protect young plants with netting.

GYPSY MOTH

The gypsy moth caterpillar is brown with a lot of long brown hair. The caterpillar reaches a length of 2 inches. The adult male moth is gray and the female white with wingspans of up to 2 inches. Eggs are light brown to yellow, covered with hair, and deposited in batches of up to 400. The emerging caterpillars feed at night on foliage of many trees including fruit trees. They return to the tree's leaf litter during the day. Winter is passed in the egg stage, and one generation of caterpillar and adult is produced each year. Distribution is currently limited to the New England States, but this pest is spreading.

Fig. 15-9. Grasshoppers do minor damage by chewing leaves and stems of vegetable plants.

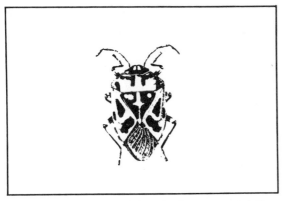
Fig. 15-10. Colorful harlequin bugs feed on many vegetables.

HARLEQUIN BUG

This cheerful-looking red and black, shield-shaped bug emits a disagreeable odor (Fig. 15-10). Only ¼ inch in length, these bugs feed heavily on Brussels sprouts, cauliflower, cherries, citrus crops, collards, horseradish, kohlrabi, mustard, radishes, turnips, lettuce, corn, eggplant, grapes, potatoes, plums, and squash. Harlequin bugs are found mostly in the south. Look for eggs that are small, white, and marked with two black bands. The harlequin bug reproduces three to four times a season and hibernates as an adult in plant debris.

Use Bacillus thuringiensis to destroy the caterpillars. Destroy any egg cases that you find. A sticky barrier such as Tanglefoot is effective in limiting the migration of this pest up the trunk of trees. Trichogramma wasps eat this pest's eggs.

Clean gardening practices and good weeding prevent large harlequin bug populations. Plant trap crops of turnips or mustard greens near members of the cabbage family. Hand-pick bugs and look for eggs on the underside of leaves. For excessive populations, spray or dust with pyrethrum, sabadilla, or soap and nicotine sprays.

Fig. 15-11. The imported cabbage worm has a tremendous appetite for all types of cole crops.

IMPORTED CABBAGE WORM

The velvety, pale green caterpillar of the imported cabbage worm has a yellow stripe down its back and grows to one inch in length (Fig. 15-11). This caterpillar leaves behind dark green excrement pellets and chews holes in all members of the cabbage family. It also attacks mustard, radish, and turnip plants. Eggs are yellow and slightly irregular. They are deposited by the well-known white cabbage butterfly. The butterfly has three black spots on white wings and a 2-inch wingspan. One or two generations per year are produced throughout the United States. Pupa overwinter in soil.

Crop rotation and clean gardening practices keep early spring populations under control. Out-of-control populations should be sprayed with Bacillus thuringiensis. Try sprays made from a mix of flour and salt, garlic or sour milk. As a last resort, rotenone can be used. Natural predators include some trichogramma wasps.

JAPANESE BEETLE

The Japanese beetle is metallic-green with copper-brown wings. It grows up to ½ inch in length, with short hair around the edges of its wings and in patches along its abdomen (Fig. 15-12). Eggs are deposited in soil, where grubs—grayish-white with a brown head up to ¾ of an inch in length—chew plant roots. Adults emerge in early summer and attack many types of fruit including apple, cherry, grape, peach, plum, quince, raspberry, rhubarb, and others. This beetle skeletonizes

Fig. 15-12. Japanese beetle to 1 inch in length.

leaves and devours flowers. Its range is east of the Mississippi River, but expanding westward.

Hand-pick Japanese beetles and, if infestation is large, make a bug juice spray from collected insects. Shaking Japanese beetles off of trees early in the morning onto a dropcloth for removal is often effective. The fall and spring tiphia wasps are predators, as are the tachinid flies. Biological control includes spreading milky spore disease on garden and lawn to control grubs. Rotenone spray will destroy the adults.

JUNE BEETLE

This sturdy brown beetle is also known as the *June bug*. The adult may damage the leaves of some berries and fruits, but the insect is more of a problem during its grub stage. The larvae are white to grayish-brown and plump. June beetle grubs are larger than Japanese beetle grubs, with an appetite to match. The grubs feed on the roots of bluegrass, corn, timothy, potatoes, strawberries, and soybeans, in addition to decaying vegetation. The June beetle is a slow breeder, producing one generation every 3 years. Two of those years are spent in the destructive grub stage.

Rotation of plants susceptible to June beetles is essential. Yearly cultivation of your soil and clean garden pratices are also effective preventive measures. Hand-picking and spraying with bacillus popilliae are simple controls. Most of Japanese beetle controls will also work on the June beetle.

LEAF MINERS

The larvae of several species of this widely-distributed pest tunnel between the upper and lower layers of leaves resulting in a telltale trail of yellow foliage. Some tunnel in long convoluted patterns, others in blotches. The adult is a black fly with yellow stripes one-tenth of an inch in length. Eggs are attached to leaf surfaces. When stout, worm-like larvae hatch out, they tunnel through leaves. Host plants include apple, blackberry, cabbage, bean, lettuce, pepper, potato, spinach, and beet. Various species are distributed throughout the United States.

The best line of defense is removal of affected

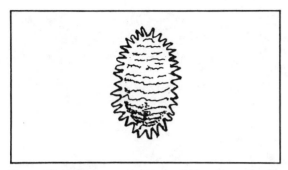

Fig. 15-13. Mealy bugs resemble small bits of cotton on the undersides of leaves.

leaves. Destroy the leaves by burning them or by adding them to an active compost pile. Clean gardening practices, especially removal of weeds from the garden area are helpful. Some resistant vegetable varieties have been developed.

MEALY BUG

Several species of this insect are distributed throughout the United States. Mealy bugs look like tiny tufts of cotton (up to 1/10 of an inch in length) attached to leaf bottoms, young stems and fruits of apples, grapes, peaches, pears, potatoes, plums and some citrus fruits (Fig. 15-13). Mealy bugs suck juices from the plants. Large populations can siphon away large amounts of the plant's fluids. Mealy bugs excrete sweet residues that will attract ants. Some carry plant diseases while others cause fungal growth. Mealy bugs spend the winter as eggs attached to garden debris—usually the host plant.

Spray the underside of infested foliage with soapy water or a light kerosene and water emulsion. Chalcid wasps are natural predators to some mealy bugs. Garden sanitation is a good preventive measure.

MEXICAN BEAN BEETLE

Mexican bean beetles are closely related to the lady beetle. Mexican bean beetles range from copper to yellowish-brown with 16 black spots arranged in three rows down the back (Fig. 15-14). They are the same size as lady beetles, up to ¼ inch. Eggs, larvae and pupa are yellow. Two to three generations are produced each year,

skeletonizing various bean plants. The Mexican bean beetle is found in all states east of the Mississippi River and in Texas, Colorado, Arizona, and Utah west of the Mississippi. Overwinters in garden trash.

Clean garden debris from garden in fall. Plant beans as early as possible to get plants off to a good start ahead of this pest. Hand-pick beetles, eggs, and larvae when they first appear. Interplant beans with trap plants such as nasturtium, savory, garlic, and potatoes. Certain assassin bugs and wasps (Pediobius foveolatus) are predators. Sprays of sugar water and dish soap work well in chasing off Mexican bean beetles. As a last resort, dust with rotenone, pyrethrum, or derris.

NEMATODES

Nematodes are not really insects; they are microscopic worms. Many nematode species feed on plant tissues. Nematodes are often called ellworms. Various nematode species are widely distributed throughout the United States. Symptoms of infestation by this pest include malformation of flowers, leaves, stems, and roots. Although nematodes do not do much damage directly, the lesions they make on plants allow the entry of disease. Some nematodes cause swollen growths on roots. The growth restricts the flow of nutrients to the above ground parts of the plant.

Nematodes are difficult to control, but some success has been reported by scattering marigold plants throughout the garden. Crop rotation and plowing fallow garden areas during midsummer can reduce populations. Many common vegetables have been bred for nematode resistance. (Look for a capital "N" in the plant's catalog description.) Additionally, increasing the organic content of the soil will reduce damage.

ONION MAGGOT

The adult fly of the onion maggot is ¼ inch in length with a gray to brown body and a humped back. The adult lays white cylindrical eggs at the base of onion plants during all stages of the onion's growth. Larvae or maggots hatch from these eggs. Larvae are about 1/3 inch long, Larvae tunnel into

Fig. 15-14. Mexican bean beetle and damage.

bulbs and stems ruining the crop. This pest produces two to three broods each year and hibernates as a pupa in the soil. Distribution is limited to the northern reaches of the United States and most of Canada.

Plant onion sets as early as possible. The type of onion grown will have a decided effect on infestations. White onions tend to be more readily attacked than yellow or red onions. Red varieties are the most resistant. Scattering onion crops through the garden will prevent maggots from moving easily from one plant to the next. Some measure of protection is achieved by sprinkling wood ash around the base of onions.

PARSLEYWORM

This colorful caterpillar is green with a white spotted black band on each body segment. The parsleyworm grows to 2 inches in length and emits a strong, sweet odor. Two orange horns project from its head when it is disturbed. This caterpillar is the larva of the beautiful black swallowtail butterfly. It feeds on celery, carrot, dill, and parsley, chewing leaves and stems. Since populations are rarely large, little damage results. You might consider letting this caterpillar live since the butterfly will add beauty to your yard and garden. The parsleyworm is distributed throughout the United States.

Hand-pick parsleyworm when necessary. Bacillus thuringiensis is also effective. Rotenone or derris can be used as a last resort.

PEACH TREE BORER

Damage to apricot, cherry, peach, and plum trees results from the white to pale-yellow grub of this moth. The male moth is shiny blue and clear winged, with a yellow stripe. The female has a wide orange band around the abdomen. Eggs are deposited around the base of trees. Larvae hatch and

266

burrow into the tree at or below ground level. The tree is weakened by the girdling effect of this insect's feeding habits. Damage appears as a gummy sawdust at the base of injured trees. Many peach tree borers carry a wilt fungus. One generation per year is produced and larva spend the winter in their burrows. The borer emerges from a brown cocoon in the soil each spring. It ranges throughout the United States and Canada.

To keep peach tree borers away from fruit trees, circle the base of each trunk with aluminum foil 2 inches from the trunk. Fill the area between the trunk and the foil with tobacco dust. Coat the base of young trees with Tanglefoot or another sticky substance, which will snare adults and larvae before they can do their damage. Garlic planted next to tree trunks repels peach tree borers. Mothballs are also said to repel this pest. Slit trunk and dig out borers as a last resort.

POTATO LEAFHOPPER

This translucent green wedge-shaped insect has white spots on its head, wings and thorax. It is 1/5 of an inch long. Although potato leafhoppers do not damage plants very much, they do carry a disease known as hopperburn. Hopperburn has symptoms such as pronounced leaf veins, stunted growth, and curled, brittle leaves. Leaves of affected plants usually turn brown around the edges, later curling upward. Crop yields are reduced on host plants. Potato leafhopper feeds on beans, celery, eggplant, potato, rhubarb and some citrus crops. Distribution is limited to eastern half of the United States with similar species occuring in the west.

Cover plants with fine gauze netting during first month of growth to prevent insects from reaching plants. Adults can be trapped at night with black fluorescent lamps and collected for elimination. Diatomaceous earth and rotenone dusted on plants may reduce infestations.

ROUNDHEADED APPLE BORER

The roundheaded apple borer is the larva of a beetle. This brown-red or whitish grub has a brown head and a round, thick area just behind its head.

The tan, brown, or gray beetle is marked with two longitudinal white strips, white head, and white underside. The grub is 1½ inches long. The beetle is 1 inch long. Eggs are laid in slits made in apple tree bark. The grub feeds on the bark during the first year if its 2- to 4-year life. Following years are spent burrowing deeper until heartwood is reached. A rusty brown material shows at the borer's hole along with sawdust-like castings. This borer attacks apple, quince, peach, and plum trees. The borer's girdling weakens trees, and adults occasionally feed on flowers and leaves of the tree. The roundheaded apple borer is found eastward from Texas.

Tanglefoot or another sticky trap can be spread around the base of tree trunks to trap adults and hatching larvae. Once a borer has started a hole, it can be removed by slitting the trunk or by pouring boiling water into the hole.

SLUGS AND SNAILS

Although slugs and snails are not insects, they can be serious pests in some gardens. Various species of slugs and snails have different markings. Most slugs are plump-bodied, gray to black or brown, covered with mucous membrane, with eyes at the end of tentacles (Fig. 15-15). Both animals leave a wet path where they have crawled. Snails have hard shells, but in other ways are similar to slugs. The size of these pests ranges from ½ inch to 3 inches in length. Most slugs and snails are nocturnal (feeding only at night.) They spend the day beneath garden litter, under boards, or in the soil. Slugs and snails chew off the outer layers of plant leaves which exposes the plants to attack by disease or fungus. Some snails are predators, eating small garden insects. Several years are required to complete the life cycle of these garden dwellers. Adults overwinter in the soil or beneath garden trash. They are distributed throughout the United States.

Hand-pick slugs and snails when they emerge at dusk. A sprinkling of salt will destroy these pests. An effective trap can be made by placing a shallow pan in the soil and filling it with stale beer. Slugs and snails will be attracted to the beer, fall in,

Fig. 15-15. Slugs can be a problem in the garden.

and drown. Diatomaceous earth can be spread around plants to discourage these pest.

SQUASH BUG

Squash bugs are ½ inch long, and dark brown to black. They emit a peculiar odor when crushed (Fig. 15-16). Because of this trait, they are also known as stink bugs. Eggs are red and attached to the bottom of leaves. Nymphs have reddish-brown heads and legs on green or brown bodies. Squash bugs feed on all vine crops, especially squash, pumpkin, and melon. These pests cause plants to wilt, blacken, and die. Various species are found throughout the United States. The squash bug produces one generation per year and hibernates as an adult.

Crop rotation and clean gardening are big preventive measures. Radishes, nasturtiums, and

Fig. 15-16. The coloring of squash bugs makes them difficult to see.

marigolds should be planted as repellant crops. Hand-pick both insects and eggs when they first appear. For out-of-control populations, dust with sabadilla. The tachinid fly is a natural predator.

SQUASH VINE BORER

The squash vine borer is a wrinkled, white caterpillar with a brown head. It bores into the stems of cucumbers, gourds, melons, pumpkins, and all types of squash. The first sign of infestation is a sudden wilting of the vine and a yellow sawdust-like deposit at the entrance hole. This 1-inch-long borer produces one to two generations per year and is found east of the Rockies. Adults are moths with clear wings and an orange and black abdomen. The moths are 1 to 1½ inches long.

An early planting to get host plants off to a good start is the first step in thwarting the squash vine borer. Occasionally, borer damage can be reduced by burying sections of vine at 1-foot intervals. New roots will form under the dirt, reducing the severity of damage. As a last resort, slit stems of affected plants to reveal the borer. Remove the borer and heap dirt over the wound.

STALK BORER

This thin, striped caterpillar feeds on almost all garden plants (Fig. 15-17). Favorites of this 1½-inch-long pest include tomatoes, rhubarb, peppers, and many weeds. The stalk borer causes stems to break and leaves to wilt. The adult stalk borer is a gray moth with white spots on its wings. This pest is found east of the Rockies.

Remove damaged plant parts and debris from your garden.

STINKBUGS

There are several species of this pest, ranging

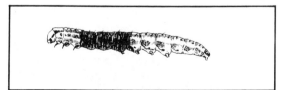

Fig. 15-17. The stalk borer feeds on many weeds and garden vegetables.

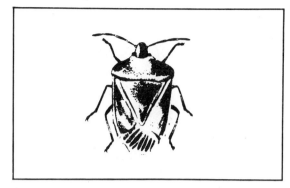

Fig. 15-18. Shield-shaped stinkbugs produce an offensive odor when handled.

from the green (Southern) stinkbug to the brown (eastern) stinkbug (Fig. 15-18). These shield-shaped bugs feed on beans, potatoes, tomatoes, cabbage, corn, and citrus fruits. Stinkbugs prefer new growth. Most species range in size from ½ to ¾ inch in length. Stinkbugs emit a distinctly offensive odor when disturbed. Adults hibernate in garden trash, producing up to five broods per season. Eggs are laid in groups or singly on the underside of the leaves of host plants.

Keeping garden clean through cultivation and weed control are the best preventive measures against the stinkbug. Hand-picking may be objectionable because of the bug's odor. Serious infestations can be dusted with sabadilla.

THRIPS

There are several species of thrips, ranging in color from brownish-orange to black. All have fringed wings. Thrips are barely visible, as they grow to only 1/50 of an inch in length. These pests damage plants by sucking juices out of leaves, fruits, and flowers. Thrips are most often found on flowers where they cause the petals to become streaked with brown. Affected blossoms wither prematurely, hindering fruit set. The leaves of plants suffering from thrips often become bleached or slightly silver before withering. Host plants are grapes, peach, citrus fruits, and beans. Various species are widely distributed.

Weed control will limit the infestation of thrips. Since thrips prefer darkness, aluminum foil

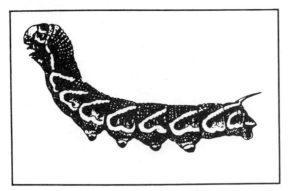

Fig. 15-19. The tomato hornworm has a distinctive horn on its rear end and diagonal stripes on its sides.

pillar (3 to 4 inches long) with white diagonal bars along its sides (Fig. 15-19). This caterpillar is obvious because of the horn protruding from its rear end. A red horn indicates the tobacco hornworm. One to two generations per year are usual for this pest. Hornworms feed on eggplants, tomatoes, peppers, potatoes, and tobacco. They are distributed throughout North America.

Since tomato hornworms are so large, they are easy to hand-pick. Bacillus thuringiensis will destroy large infestations of these worms. Natural predators include Braconid wasps that lay eggs on the caterpillar. The wasp's larvae form small white cocoons on the worm's back. Worms with these cocoons should not be picked in order to enhance Braconid wasp populations. Tricogramma wasps paralyze hornworm eggs.

mulches may retard population growth. Rotenone or diatomaceous earth will control extreme infestations.

TOMATO HORNWORM

The tomato hornworm is a large green cater-

VEGETABLE WEEVIL

The adult vegetable weevil is ½ inch in length

Fig. 15-20. The white powder on whiteflies make them easy to see on the bottom of leaves.

with a gray to brown body. Wing covers have a pale V-shaped mark near their ends. Larvae of this pest are clear and greenish with a dark head. Both adults and larvae chew on tender new growth of plants, skeletonizing the leaves. The vegetable weevil feeds mainly at night and hides in the soil during the day. Adult weevils spend the winter in garden debris, emerging in the spring to produce one generation per season. This pest feeds on beet, cabbage, cauliflower, carrot, lettuce, onion, potato, radish, spinach, tomato, and turnip foliage. The vegetable weevil is widely found in the southern United States.

Crop rotation and garden sanitation are the best preventive measures against the vegetable weevil. Adults and underground pupae can be destroyed by deep cultivation in early spring or late fall. To combat infestations, dust plants with diatomaceous earth or rotenone.

WHITEFLIES

The whitefly gets its name from the white powdery substance that covers its wings. Although 1/50 of an inch in length, this pest's white color makes it easy to see (Fig. 15-20). Eggs are placed on small projections on the underside of leaves. Several generations are produced each year. Whiteflies overwinter as nymphs. Nymphs are translucent green with fine waxy, filaments. Adults and nymphs feed on plants by sucking juices from the underside of leaves. Severely infested leaves will often wither and die but because of the many diseases and fungi associated with whitefly damage. Whiteflies are widely distributed throughout the United States with severest infestations occurring in the south and coastal states.

Nicotine sprays or tobacco dusts will control this pest. The encarsia formosa wasp is a natural predator of whiteflies. Garden sanitation is a must.

Chapter 16

Seed Saving Savvy

Who soweth good seed shall surely reap.
—Julia R. C. Dorr

Up until the middle of this century, saving seeds was as much a part of gardening and farming as plowing. In fact, it was the only way people who grew food could make sure they would have seeds to plant the following year. Sadly, most of today's gardeners and farmers depend heavily on being able to get seeds from seed companies each year.

Although mass distribution seed companies are a recent development in agriculture, the lure of convenience has convinced Americans to buy seeds from distant companies rather than saving their own. The habit of buying seeds each year became firmly entrenched when breeders developed hybrids that promised higher yields and a measure of disease resistance. Unfortunately, the seeds produced by hybrid plants cannot be saved from year to year, further increasing gardeners' and farmers' dependence on seed companies.

Nowadays, almost all gardeners buy seeds each winter through mail-order catalogs or through a local greenhouse or seed store. Gardeners are at the mercy of the seed companies, since they can buy and grow only the seeds offered for sale. Although this arrangement means that seeds are relatively inexpensive, there is at least one serious consequence. The number of varieties available in this country is narrowing rapidly as the seed industry consolidates its holdings. Whenever regional companies are purchased by multi-national corporations, many locally-adapted varieties are often discontinued in favor of high-profit hybrids. This could have serious consequences for gardeners, especially in terms of finding a vegetable variety suited to a particular climate and soil.

There are several reasons to save your own seeds. Among them is the fact that not all seeds do well in all locations. However, each crop tends to have one or two plants which do exceptionally well. By saving the seeds from these plants you will develop a variety adapted to your soil, climate, and personal taste. When this selection process is carried on over a period of years, the plants and soil become a more tightly-knit unit, growing better and better each year. The same cannot be said for seeds grown in Iowa and planted in Florida. Saving your own seeds is one way of helping your plants grow their best in the conditions of your garden.

Another good reason to save your own seeds is that it reduces the total cost of your garden. Sacrificing one or two fruits from each crop is not a heavy price to pay to avoid the expense of ordering seeds the following winter. Once seed saving becomes a standard part of your gardening routine, you will hardly notice the little extra work that it involves. Saving seeds from year to year is one more step toward self-sufficiency.

When breeders select characteristics for their hybrid plants, disease resistance and large, well-formed fruits tend to be items high on the list of desirable traits. Many people think that these new improved varieties are just not as flavorful as the older strains of seeds. Seed exchanges and seed companies that offer old-time varieties are popping up around the country. These growers as well as the people who order from them are keeping many old-time varieties from becoming extinct. When a friend gives you seeds from an old-time variety or when you buy an old-time variety, saving the seed may be the only way to keep the strain from going out of existence.

The major seed-saving force in the country is the Seed Savers Exchange Organization. Founded in 1974 by Kent Whealy, the Seed Savers Exchange seeks to find people who keep long-vanished and heirloom vegetable varieties. Kent's organization helps bring together people desiring to share old-time or heirloom seeds with the hope of preserving these unique varieties from extinction. The Seed Savers Exchange address is: Kent Whealy, RFD 2, Box 92, Princeton, MO 64673.

HOW TO SAVE YOUR OWN SEEDS

The easiest way to learn how to save seeds is to select a few seeds labeled "open-pollination" when you order from seed companies. Try to pick varieties that sound like they will be suited to your growing area, soil, and taste. Once the seeds have germinated and the plants are established in your garden, you will need to begin paying attention to their growth patterns.

Seed development is a season-long job, not just a quick trip through the garden after the first killing frost collecting whatever seeds happen to be around. When choosing plants to save for seed, select those that are healthy, vigorous, productive, and have the best-tasting fruit. Plan to save seeds from several plants so that there is a good mix of genetic material. Saving seed from only one plant year after year can lead to trouble, as genetic quirks in the vegetables become more pronounced.

Do not base your choice on just one trait, like earliness or size of fruit, and do not make up your mind completely until the season is nearly finished. To assure full ripening, select and mark one fruit on each potential parent early in the season and then keep an eye on it (Fig. 16-1).

On your first attempts, choose vegetables that tend to self-pollinate. Tomatoes, green beans, lima beans, lettuce, and muskmelons are good for starters. The flowers of these plants are constructed such that when insects gather pollen from them, the flowers fertilize themselves. This ensures that the seed is true to the strain.

In order to maintain the quality of the strain of a particular seed, you must take the same precautions that professional seed growers take. Only your best plants should be used for seed. The plant that produces the largest seedpod or fruit is not necessarily the one with the best seed. Seed from such a plant may produce fruit that is tougher than seed from a normal-sized fruit. Additionally, seed from such a fruit may not produce fruit as tasty as that from an average size fruit. Plants that grow and produce fruit the way you want next year's crop to look and taste should be marked with a string or a stake to be saved for seed. Do not try to select specific characteristics, such as earliness—concentrate instead on choosing the healthiest plants in your garden.

For instance, lettuce that is early to head and slow to bolt should be marked and allowed to go to seed. Spinach plants that produce the most leaves should also be saved and allowed to bolt. Radishes that form fat, edible roots should be allowed to bolt to preserve this trait.

Fig. 16-1. Well-shaped fruit for seed saving should be marked early in the season.

Hybrids, and Open and Self-Pollination Plants

Vegetables that produce seed fall into three basic catagories in terms of their reproductive traits: hybrids, open-pollinated, and self-pollinated.

Self-pollinating plants are the easiest for home gardeners to keep true to the parent strains because insects collecting pollen and nectar from the flowers of these plants almost always fertilize the *pistil* (female part) of the flower with pollen from the *stamen* (male part) of the flower with the pollen from the same flower (Fig. 16-2). This keeps the genetic traits of the seed true to the variety. A surprising number of vegetable plants fall into this self-pollination category. Usually, these plants require wind or insects for pollination. Tomatoes,

muskmelons, and lettuce have blossoms that encourage self-pollination. The seed is normally at least 90 percent true to the parent.

Hybrid and open-pollination plants present a couple of problems for the seed saver. Hybrid seeds are produced by seed companies through the selective crossbreeding of two plants of known characteristics. This combination produces a plant with fruit of known traits. Seeds from plants grown from hybrid seeds should not be saved because they often revert to a parent variety that does not have the same traits as the hybrid plant (Fig. 16-3). Many hybrid plants are not fertile at all. Corn is one good example of a sterile hybrid.

Crossbreeding or cross-pollination means that the pollen of a flower has come in contact with a

Fig. 16-2. Bees pollinate many self-pollinating plants.

274

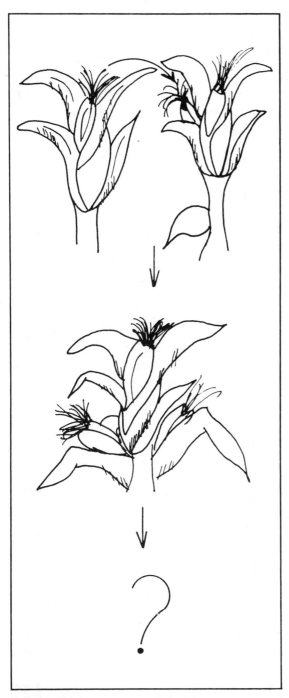

Fig. 16-3. Hybrids are cross-pollinated from two parents of known traits. The seed then produces a better plant, but seeds from this better plant will have unknown characteristics.

flower of a plant of another variety or species. The resulting seed will not be true to either of the parents. Although crossbreeding is used by seed companies to produce seed for plants of known characteristics, the same is not normally possible in the home garden because wind and insects are hard to control.

Open-pollination plants are those with flowers designed so that they usually are not self-fertilized. Eggplant, squash, and peppers, for example, have blossoms not designed for self-pollination. Only about 50 percent of the seed from these plants will be true to the parent varieties unless precautions are taken to prevent crossbreeding. If you have several types of peppers—for instance, bell, chili and banana—growing close together, you may end up with some strange peppers the following year. The cabbage family also does a lot of crossbreeding. Their offspring will vary unpredictably unless you use a few of the professional plant breeder's tricks to create true seed. Summer squashes are so closely related to some varieties of pumpkins that the two will cross, but any change in flavor even after cross-pollination will not be noticed until the seed of this mix is grown the following year and allowed to fruit. Two varieties of cucumber will cross, but winter and summer squash will not. Corn is another heavy cross-pollinator, so do not plant sweet corn anywhere near field corn or you will loose the sweetness of the sweet corn the following year. Beets are another open-pollination plant and should not be planted close to chard or sugar beets.

The safest way to propagate open-pollination plants true to the present plant is to be sure that there are no other varieties of the same species, or in some cases the same genus, growing in the neighborhood. A distance of 100 feet is usually enough to prevent cross-pollination, but insects and wind can easily carry pollen this far. Where cross-pollination may be a problem, the blossoms of the plant selected for seed production should be protected against pollination by stray pollen (Fig. 16-4).

Paper bags can be used to cover the flowers which may then be hand-pollinated when flowers open. Hand pollination is accomplished by rubbing a

Fig. 16-4. Paper bags can be placed over flowers to prevent pollen from unknown sources from affecting seed genetics.

small soft brush or cotton swab over the stamens and pistils of each flower (Fig. 16-5). Replace the paper bag until fruit has begun to form. Sometimes it is necessary to cover the seedpod, or fruit, again when the seed is almost ripe to prevent birds and other critters from eating the seeds.

Let us run through the hand pollination of corn in order to get a better idea of how this technique is accomplished. When ears form, but before the silk appears, secure a paper bag over the ears you want to save for seed. When the silk has emerged, cut off a tassel from the seed plant (the same plant is fine) and shake pollen onto the silk. Replace the bag. Pollinate the ear 2 days in a row to increase the chances of full pollination. (You should use a new tassel from another plant of the same variety.) The

paper bag is left on the ear until the ear matures and dries thoroughly on the stalk. The paper bag will keep many corn pests and diseases like corn ear worm and smut away from the seed ear. The dried cob and seed can then be stored for the next year.

Squash can be pollinated in much the same way except that a brush or cotton swab is used to transfer pollen from male to female flowers. The female flowers are those that form on what looks like a miniature fruit near the vine. Use a new swab or brush every time you switch varieties.

Collecting Seed

Seeds form either in a seedpod or embedded in the fruit of the plant. Those that grow in seedpods (beans for example) are much easier to dry and store than those found in soft fruits, like tomatoes. In all cases the seedpod or fruit should be allowed to mature on the parent plant as long as possible. However, seedpods and fruits should not be allowed to ripen to the point where they begin to decay.

Seeds from non-pulpy fruits and vegetables present few problems for the seed saver. Peas and beans should be allowed to dry on the vine as long as possible. When they turn brown and brittle, pull up the plants and hang them inside until pods are quite hard. Shell out and dry them further, if necessary, before storage.

Sweet corn should be allowed to ripen thoroughly on the stalk. Seed can be stored on the husked ear. Although peppers form seeds within their fruit, they are usually clean enough to dry without washing. The seed from fleshy fruits needs to be separated from the fruit, washed, and dried prior to storage.

The seed of cucumbers, squash, melon, tomato, and eggplant are all taken from ripe fruit. Remember that many vegetables, such as summer squash and cucumbers, are usually eaten before ripe. Therefore, the fruits chosen for seed production must be left on the vine until they change color, which is an indication of ripeness. Tomatoes, winter squash, and melons are borderline cases—sometimes they are fully ripe when harvested; at other times they are not.

Fruit harvested for its seed should be taken

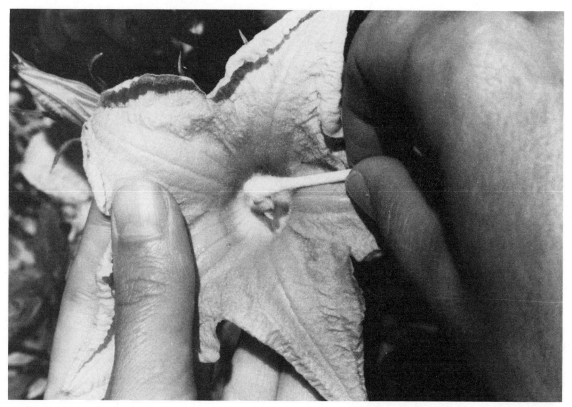

Fig. 16-5. You can control pollination by using a cotton swab to fertilize vegetable flowers selected for seed production.

inside when it's ripe and the seeds scraped out when possible. Pepper seeds can usually be removed and dried immediately. Soft fruits like tomatoes should be soaked in water a day or two. Careful watching is required at this stage. When fruit has fermented a little, the pulp can be loosened by rubbing it between your hands. Rinse seeds in cold water, and dry them on sheets of paper.

Clean seeds can be rid of bacteria, fungus, and insect eggs by soaking them 5 to 10 minutes in a 1 to 5 solution of clorox bleach and water. (Use 1 to 10 for fragile seeds like tomatoes.) Following this soaking, wash seeds in running water 5 to 10 minutes, then dry thoroughly.

Seeds can be dried in full sunlight or in an oven, provided they are not allowed to reach a temperature of more than 95° F. Mix the seed occasionally during drying to prevent mold. Seeds store the best when their internal humidity is be-tween 4 and 8 percent. A food dryer can also be used to dry seed, but remember not to let the temperature stray above 95° F. Another drying method is placing the seeds in a cardboard box with a 25 watt bulb. A thermometer is also necessary to control the temperature. When drying seeds outside, keep a close eye on them so that birds do not have a feast.

Some vegetables are biennials (2-year plants) that do not produce seed during the first year of growth. Some of the biennial vegetables are members of the cabbage family, endive, kale, onion, spinach, and all the root crops except radishes. Each of these crops must be stored through the winter and allowed to regrow the following year in order to produce seed. There are two storage techniqes, depending on whether the plants are winter-hardy or not.

Winter-hardy plants like parsnips, salsify, leeks, kale, spinach, and parsley, can be mulched with straw, leaves, or other materials directly in the garden where they grew. They are uncovered after the last killing frost of the spring and allowed to grow and bolt.

The fragile plants that are not winter-hardy must be dug up, and the plant kept in cold storage through the winter in order to keep the plant alive. When frost sets in in the fall, dig up the roots of these plants and brush off the dirt. Keep the roots in a cool, dark place through the winter and return them to the garden in the spring. Gather the seed heads just before they break open and scatter their seed.

Storing Seeds

Storing seed through the winter is not very

difficult as long as you keep a few things in mind. The colder your storage area the better your seeds keep, provided humidity is low. You can keep the humidity low by making sure seeds are thoroughly dry before storing them in an airtight container. A small cloth bag of powdered milk in each seed container will soak up excess moisture (Fig. 16-6). The volume of powdered milk should roughly equal the volume of seed.

How long a seed remains viable depends on the conditions under which it is stored and the particular vegetable seed (Table 16-1). In general, seed

Table 16-1. Use This Table to
Determine the Storage Capabilities of Various Seeds.

Fig. 16-6. A small bag of powdered milk placed in a seed storage jar is good insurance against moisture.

Short-Lived Not Good After 1 or 2 Years	
Corn	Parsley
Leek	Parsnip
Onion	Salsify

Moderate Not Good After 3 to 5 Years.	
Asparagus	Kale
Bean	Kohlrabi
Beet	Lettuce
Brussels sprouts	Okra
Cabbage	Peas
Carrot	Peppers
Cauliflower	Pumpkin
Celery	Radish
Celeric	Rutabaga
Chicory	Spinach
Chinese cabbage	Swiss chard
Collard	Turnip
Cress	Watermelon
Endive	

Long-Lived Often Good for More Than 5 Years.	
Broccoli	Mustard
Cucumber	New Zealand spinach
Eggplant	Squash
Muskmelon	Tomato

will keep longer when stored in cool, dry, dark areas than when stored in warm moist areas exposed to light.

Refrigerators or freezers are the best place to keep seeds. Most seeds retain their highest viability when stored at humidities below 65 percent. Optimum temperatures for long-term storage (several years) are between 0 and 32° F. For single-winter storage, a relative humidity of 50 to 60 percent at a temperature of 32° to 50° F is preferred.

Check your seeds frequently for insect or mold damage. When spoiled seeds are spotted, remove them immediately. Mold usually indicates that the seeds are not dry enough. The presence of insects usually indicates that the storage temperature is not low enough. Clear jars allow you to see what is going on with your seeds.

Although many people save seeds in paper packages because they are easy to handle and allow the seeds to breathe, this method is not really good because insects and rodents can get into the seeds easily. A much better storage method is in airtight glass jars or cans. Moisture in these containers may be a problem, but the powdered milk trick mentioned earlier should reduce this problem.

Germination Test

All of your seed-saving efforts will be wasted if the seed you save will not germinate next spring. To test seeds for germination, place 20 to 40 seeds on a moist blotter or newspaper. Cover them with another layer of paper. Keep this makeshift seedbed moist and warm, but not wet. Lift the upper layer once a day for a few seconds to give the seeds air.

Another method that works well for large seeds such as beans, corn, peas, and squash is folding a couple of sheets of newspaper into quarters. Roll up the paper and place it in a small jar so that the upper edges of the paper extend beyond the jar. Poke the seeds you want to test down between the layers of paper 1 to 1½ inches. Water thoroughly, making sure that there are 1 or 2 inches of water standing in the jar. The newspaper will act as a wick, drawing moisture up to the seeds. As

seeds sprout count and remove them (Fig. 16-7). When the standard germination time plus 1 week has elapsed, unroll the newspaper and count the ungerminated seeds. This will double check your

Fig. 16-7. Newspaper rolled up and stuck in water will act as a good germination test for large seeds.

count of germinated seeds. Figure the percentage of germination.

A germination rate above 80 percent is good. A percentage in the 70s is considered adequate. When a germination rate is less than 50 percent occurs consider using other seeds.

SEED SAVING
METHODS FOR DIFFERENT PLANTS

Beets are cared for in the same way as carrots. Select the beets that are formed the best and show the least woodiness. Beets will cross with chard and sugar beets, producing a worthless vegetable, so do not allow these plants to seed at the same time.

Brassicus

The brassicus, also known as the cole or cabbage family, is an incestuous lot. Virtually every member of this family will cross-pollinate every other member. Weird crosses like broccoli and cabbage produce seed that will not produce a plant worth eating. Different varieties should be grown only with a great deal of distance between them to prevent cross-pollination. If this is not possible, only one member of this family should be allowed to produce seed each year.

The plants with the best fruit should be selected for seed and stored over winter, or sow seed in the fall and pull up the best-looking immature plants for storage. Dig or pull the plant out of the ground and brush off the dirt. Store it wrapped in newspaper in a root cellar or a cool, dark, dry place. The following spring the plant should be replanted and allowed to bolt.

Most members of the cabbage family are self-sterile, so at least two are needed for proper fertilization. The seed stalks formed by these plants need to be staked for support and the seeds should be protected from birds. Stalks are hung indoors after seed has matured and then seeds are removed from the seedheads when dry.

Carrots

The carrot is a close relative to the weed *Queen Anne's Lace* or *wild carrot*. Therefore, saving the seeds from carrots grown near this weed does not make sense since cross-pollination is likely. This cross-pollination will make your carrots tough and tasteless.

Keep those carrots with straight roots, medium tops, and small cores in a root cellar through the winter. Replant the following spring and allow to grow normally. When seed heads are formed and seed is well developed, cut and dry them in the shade. Rub off chaff with your hands and save the seed.

Corn

Corn is an open-pollinated plant that loves to cross-breed. Take the necessary precautions and hand-pollinate ears intended for seed. Allow the ears to ripen fully and remain on the stalk until the husks turn straw colored. Husk corn and tie two ears together, hang in a dry place and allow to dry thoroughly. Seeds can be left on the cob until shelled for planting the next spring.

Cucumbers

The earliest-maturing and well-formed cucumbers should be saved for seed. Allow them to remain on the vine until they're ripe (yellow in color). Take them inside, scrape out the seed, ferment in water a day or two, and then spread them on paper to dry.

Herbs

Most herbs are relatively easy to gather seeds from. Since these plants are the closest to weeds of all the plants we grow, they produce seed prodigiously. For biennials, save the roots or mulch and gather seed the following year. Annuals like basil will produce seed the first season. When seedheads are near the breaking-open point, pull up the herb and hang it inside (Fig. 16-8). A paper bag can be placed under the seed head so that as seeds fall they are collected. Herb seeds are usually highly viable and true to their strain.

Lettuce

Choose the first lettuce to form a head and the

Fig. 16-8. Herbs like parsley produce a lot of seed with little effort. Knock seed from seedheads when fully mature.

last to bolt. Allow the plant to form a stalk and then stake the stalk. When the seeds are well-formed, they look tiny and black. Cut the stalk and hang it inside to dry. When it's dry, rub out the seeds with hands.

Onions

Onion seeds from which sets are grown are produced during the second summer of this plant's life when onions are started from seed. Choose several firm and well-shaped onions grown from sets, and store in a cool dry place. Plant out as early as possible the following year. When stalks form, stake them and allow them to mature. When the first few seeds begin to drop, cut the stalk, carry it inside and allow it to dry over a newspaper. Most

seeds will drop from the seedhead as it dries. Those that do not should be rubbed out by hand.

Peas and Beans

These are some of the easiest plants from which to save seed. Early in the season, mark several of the best plants and do not pick from them. Allow the selected plants to ripen until the seed pods turn brown. Pull up the whole vine and hang it where it can dry until pods turn brittle. Then shell out the beans and dry them in the sun or in an oven until they're extremely hard. Store them in a jar with powdered milk.

Radishes

Choose plump, non-woody radishes for seed production. Allow the plant to send up a seed stalk and stake the stalk. When heads have matured, pull the entire plant and allow it to hang in the shade and dry. Protect it from birds.

Spinach

Spinach should be planted in the fall and then mulched in place to overwinter. When seed stalks form the following spring, stake them and allow the head to mature. Cut it and hang it inside until the seeds begin to fall. Remove remaining seeds by hand.

Tomatoes

Choose the best-formed fruits from the healthiest plants for seed. Allow seed-producing tomatoes to ripen past edibility, but do not allow them to rot. Cure seed the same way you handle other vegetables with soft flesh because tomatoes are self-pollinating, very little crossing occurs. Different varieties can be grown close together without much chance of cross-pollination.

To save seeds or not to save seeds is a decision only you can make. Choosing to save you own seeds will provide the benefit of keeping old-time varieties that are suited to your soil and climate, but you will be giving up the convenience of store-bought seeds. Saving your own seeds will bring you a step closer to nature.

Chapter 17

Tucking Your Garden in for the Winter

One of the best things about a garden,
large or small, is that it is never finished.
It is a continual experiment.

—Margery Bianco

If you are like most gardeners, once you have harvested the last of your fall crops the garden fades quickly from mind. The tools get put away, and you do not give the garden another thought until the colorful seed catalogs begin arriving in the mail. Fall seems to be a low point for most gardeners' interest in the garden. Chores go unfinished until one day it is time to start preparations for spring planting. A little time and effort at this time of year, though, will help the garden wake up fresh and rested next spring.

There are at least five things every gardener should do to prepare a garden for winter: removing crop residues, planting cover crops, spreading rock fertilizers, mulching perennials, and sheet mulching. Not only will these chores give you an excuse to get out in the garden a few more times, but they will increase the fertility of your soil, reduce wind

and water erosion of your soil, minimize harmful insect populations next year, and protect perennials against the icy blasts of winter.

A few other fall procedures are storing crops in the garden, making fall plantings of some spring vegetables, making a fall compost pile, sharpening and cleaning tools, extending the season with a cold frame, and reviewing your garden plan.

CLEANING UP THE GARDEN

If you do not have time to do anything else in the fall, at least clean up all the dead and dying vegetable plants in your garden. Many insects overwinter as eggs, cocoons, or larvae attached to crop leaves and stems. Removing this debris will break the reproduction cycle of many insects, putting them at a disadvantage next spring. Cleaning up crop residues will also reduce the chance of harmful diseases reappearing next year (Fig. 17-1).

Many gardeners like to pull up all their crop debris and burn it. While this is an effective way of destroying insects and diseases, it does not add

Fig. 17-1. Crop residues left in the garden through the winter give pests and diseases an easy way to overwinter. They will be back in full force next spring.

much to the soil. A better method is to turn the crop residues into the soil (Fig. 17-2). Make sure all sticks, wires, cloth ties, and strings have been removed from the garden before tilling, or you will end up having a difficult time turning crop residues under. Tilling will destroy many insects, but it is not as effective a disease control as removal of vegetable residues.

The most sensible treatment of crop debris is to remove them from the garden, chop or shred them, and then add them to a compost pile. This practice will not only destroy insects and disease, but it will also recycle the nutrients in the residue back into the soil next season when the compost is used on your garden.

Do not forget to rake up fallen fruit leaves and fruits around fruit trees and bushes. Many insects and diseases hide in this material.

Stakes, ties, wire cages, and other garden structures should be stored in a dry place so that they will be ready to use next spring.

COVER CROPS

Cover crops are quick-growing plants that are not used for food. Instead, they reduce wind and water erosion and add to the soil's fertility by reducing the leaching of soil nutrients, add humus to the soil when tilled under in the spring, and have strong, deep roots that help soil aeration and drainage. After you have removed crop debris from the garden, your soil should be protected with a cover crop or by sheet mulching. Sheet mulching is covered in the next section.

There are two basic types of cover crops: legumes and non-legumes. The legume cover crops—field peas, clover and alfafa, for instance—fix nitrogen from the air. This nitrogen is fixed by being built into the plant's tissue. Nitrogen is added to the soil when the cover crop is turned under. Non-legume cover crops—usually grasses like rye, buckwheat, and winter wheat—do not fix atmospheric nitrogen. Instead, they draw it from the soil. Still, they are favored as a short term, quick-growing source of organic matter.

The best winter cover crops are rye, winter wheat, rye grass, and buckwheat, because they establish themselves quickly in cool weather. Rye can be planted as late as mid-October in many areas of the United States with good results.

When choosing seed for a cover crop, chose varieties listed as annuals. Annuals will be killed by winter freezes, but the stubble they leave on the garden will act as a mulch until turned under in the spring. Perennial cover crops, on the other hand, will die back during the coldest part of the winter, but as the ground begins to warm they will green back to life. Even if you turn them under in the spring, their tough root systems may not be totally eliminated. They will compete with early crops for nutrients, light, and water. In this respect, they are no better than a weed.

Chances are not all parts of your garden will be ready for cover cropping at the same time. If, for example, you have planted late crops of peas, spinach, lettuce, turnips, and collards, you will not want to turn these under while they are still productive simply to plant a cover crop. Warm weather crops like corn, eggplant, peppers, and tomatoes, which stop producing early in the fall, can be turned under or removed from the garden and their spaces

Fig. 17-2. Turning crop residues under when they have finished producing is an effective cleanup method (courtesy of Troy Bilt Rototillers.)

planted to a cover crop. Remove crop debris as soon as the crop quits producing. Sow the area to a cover crop. You do not have to sow the entire garden all at once. You can progress one area at a time as different vegetables quit producing. Corn usually ends first—eggplants shortly thereafter. Tomatoes and peppers do not quit until near the first frost.

Before planting a cover crop, work the soil the same way you would prior to planting vegetable crops. Till or dig the soil and rake it smooth. You may want to add rock fertilizers prior to tilling, so you can accomplish two tasks, turning in the rock fertilizer and preparing the soil for a cover crop, in one operation. When the bed is prepared, broadcast cover crop seed on the soil and then rake the area to work the seeds into the soil. If soil is extremely dry, you may want to water it and mulch with a thin sprinkling of straw or other loose mulch material. The following spring, the cover crop residues are turned under while preparing seedbeds (Fig. 17-3).

Here are some common cover crops and a few of their characteristics.

Alfalfa. Sow in late summer. Alfalfa is a legume so you need to inoculate it with nitrogen-fixing bacteria prior to planting. It's high in protein and nitrogen, with moderate amounts of calcium, magnesium and potassium. Turn under in late fall or early spring, after 2 or 3 months of growth.

Buckwheat. Sow in early fall in the north, late fall in the south. Non-legume. Annual. Turn under in the spring.

Crimson Clover. It's a winter legume, so it needs to be inoculated. Plant 60 days before killing frost. Turn under in the spring.

Persian Clover. A winter legume for Southern and Pacific states. Inoculation is necessary. Sow in fall and turn under in spring.

Rye. Non-legume. The annual variety lasts until killing frost when planted in late summer. Plant where early spring crops are to follow. The perennial variety survives winter until tilled under in late spring.

Ryegrass. Non-legume. Sow in fall and turn dead plants under in the spring.

Vetches. Legume, so inoculation is advised.

Fig. 17-3. Cover crops should be turned under early in the spring during normal garden preparation (courtesy of Troy Bilt Rototillers).

Sow in late fall in the south, early fall in the north. Turn under in spring. It can become a problem when allowed to grow unchecked. Tilling prior to the plant's maturity is recommended.

Winter Wheat. Non-legume. Sow in fall and turn under the stubble in spring.

SHEET MULCHING

In the sections of your garden that cannot be planted to cover crops because of late-maturing fall vegetables, sheet mulching should be practiced. Sheet mulching is no more than spreading a layer of organic material over the soil to protect it against wind and water erosion. Additionally, a thick sheet mulch will prevent the ground from freezing very deep. This will allow some soil organisms to remain active. By spring, all but the top layer of mulch should be broken down into humus. When turned under, this humus will release valuable nutrients for spring crops.

Virtually any organic material can be used for sheet mulching. Refrain from using crop residues because they may carry insect eggs or cocoons and various plant diseases. Materials with a good C/N (carbon/nitrogen) ratio are the best. A few recommended materials are alfalfa hay, grass clippings, and spoiled hay. Low nitrogen materials such as corncobs, leaves, sawdust, and straw will require the addition of a nitrogen-rich material such as dried blood or cottonseed meal to prevent nitrogen deficiency in the soil. Add the nitrogen-rich materials to the bare soil before covering with a mulch. Rock fertilizers can also be added to the soil before covering with a winter mulch.

After the garden has been cleared of vegetable debris, spread organic material in a uniform layer over the area being mulched. Chop or shred large bulky materials prior to spreading. Not only will shredding make handling the materials easier, but it will speed decomposition and help keep the material in place through the winter.

Tree leaves are one of the most widely used winter mulches because of their availability, but they have a few problems you should keep an eye on. First, whole leaves tend to mat together as they settle. This causes the soil beneath them to suffer a lack of oxygen. The activity of soil microorganisms is reduced and decomposition slows. Secondly, leaves tend to blow around a lot. Shredding will reduce this somewhat. Laying boards, wire cages, or a coarser organic material over the leaves will reduce this problem.

Here are some common winter mulches.

Alfalfa Hay. High in nitrogen. Breaks down easily and stays in place well. Best when shredded prior to spreading.

Corncobs. Low in nitrogen. Add nitrogen materials before spreading and in the spring prior to turning under. Stays in place well, but breaks down slowly. Great water-holding capacity.

Grass Clippings. Rich in nitrogen when green. Decomposes rapidly and stays in place well.

Leaves. Somewhat low in nitrogen, so add nitrogen prior to spreading leaves and in spring prior to turning under. Rich in trace minerals. Chop or shred to prevent matting or mix with coarse material like straw or corncobs. Leaves tend to blow around a lot.

Pine Needles. Slightly acidic, so do not use them where non-acid loving plants are to grow. Slow to break down. Stays in place well. Add nitrogen in spring prior to turning under.

Sawdust. Low in nitrogen, so add nitrogen to soil prior to spreading this material. Sawdust that is one year old is best. Stays in place well. Some hardwoods will produce an acidic soil. Add nitrogen in spring prior to turning under.

Straw. Low in nitrogen, so nitrogen should be added. Breaks down slowly, but stays in place well. Good complement to leaves since it prevents matting. Chop or shred for best results. Add nitrogen in spring before turning under.

For a more thorough description of mulch materials, see Chapter 13.

ROCK FERTILIZERS

Fall is the best time to add rock fertilizers to your soil. Rock fertilizers need to be in contact with soil microorganisms and acids to become available to plant roots. The longer they are in the soil, the more the rock minerals become available. Granite dust, phosphate rock, greensand, and other powdered rocks dissolve slowly, adding nutrients to the soil over a long period. When these rocks are added in the fall, they are readily available the following spring and summer. Yearly application is seldom necessary since rock fertilizers stay active for years. Application once every 3 to 5 years should suffice.

Since the nutrients in rock fertilizers are released when in contact with the soil, they should be applied under sheet mulches or prior to tilling when a cover crop is planted. Soil microorganisms under mulches will work on rock fertilizers through the winter, making them available for the following season. The roots of cover crops do the same thing. Cover crops may be a little better at holding minerals in the soil because these plants incorporate minerals into their root, stem, and leaf tissues. In the spring when the cover crop is turned under, these nutrients are re-released as the cover crop decomposes.

As a general rule, rock fertilizers should not be worked too deeply into the soil. Their nutrients are carried naturally into the soil to the root zone by rainwater. When buried too deeply in the soil, water will carry the nutrients out of the reach of hungry roots.

Here are some common rock fertilizers and a few of their characteristics. You will find more information about rock fertilizers in Chapter 4.

Basalt Rock. Contains significant amounts of phosphorus, potassium, calcium, magnesium, and iron. Slow to release. Ten pounds per 100 square feet of garden should last several years.

Basic Slag. Contains lime, magnesium, silicon, aluminum, magnanese, and many trace minerals. Basic slag is alkaline, so avoid using it where acid-loving plants are to grow. Avoid using slags with high sulfur content.

Dolomite Limestone. This alkaline material is used to neutralize acidic soil conditions. Although dolomite is rich in magnesium, it should be used only to counteract pH problems. Suggested application rates are 30 pounds per 1,000 square feet on sandy soil, 50 pounds on sandy loam, 70 pounds on loam, and 80 pounds on heavy clay to change pH one unit.

Granite Dust. This material contains 3 to 5 percent potassium as well as many valuable trace minerals. Granite dust is released slowly over a period of years. Suggested application rate is 10 pounds per 100 square feet.

Greensand. This material contains 5 to 6 percent potassium. It also contains traces of more than 30 elements—many important to plant growth. Spread at the rate of 15 pounds per 100 square feet.

Rock Phosphate. This material contains 25 to 30 percent phosphorus. It does not leach from the soil and is lost mainly through cropping. Rock phosphate works best when applied with manure at a rate of 10 pounds per 100 square feet.

MULCHING PERENNIALS

A mulch spread over perennials in early winter will protect these plants against the ravages of winter. Mulches protect plants against the heaving associated with freezing and thawing soil in addition to reducing the drying out of the soil due to windy conditions. When spring rolls around, mulch protected perennials are rested and ready to come on strong for another season of quality food production (Fig. 17-4).

Mulches should not be applied until several frosts have killed back most of the plant's top growth, and the soil has frozen to a depth of about 1 inch. Waiting this long will ensure that the plants are completely dormant and that they will stay this way throughout the winter.

Leaves make an effective mulch and are available in abundance. However, leaves should be mixed with a rough material like straw or corncobs

Fig. 17-4. Uncover mulch-protected perennials when danger of killing frost has passed.

prior to being applied over perennials. Mixing leaves with another material will prevent matting, which could suffocate the plants. Shredding or chopping the leaves prior to application will also reduce matting problems. Perennials, although they do not appear to be alive, are living. They need an exchange of oxygen and carbon dioxide to remain healthy through the winter. Matted mulch sets up a barrier through which these gases cannot pass, and plants are likely to suffocate under these conditions.

Loose materials like straw, chopped leaves, peat moss, salt marsh hay, and corncobs form an effective mulch when used alone. Pine needles make a good mulch, although their acidity makes them the preferred mulch for acid-loving plants like strawberries, blueberries, and raspberries.

Winter mulches should be layed to a depth of up to 1 foot or more. Most mulches settle to a thickness of 2 or 3 inches during the winter. In the spring, remove the mulch a little at a time to allow plants to adjust gradually to daily temperature changes.

Plants that need a winter mulch include asparagus, rhubarb, strawberries, overwintering spinach, perennial herbs like parsley, and oregano. Fruit trees and grapes will also benefit from a ring of mulch around the base of their trunks. The mulch will protect shallow roots from hard winter freezes.

Rock fertilizers can be applied around perennials prior to mulching to give them a little extra time to become available. Nitrogenous materials should not be applied to perennials before winter mulching, because excess nitrogen may cause the plants to try to come to life during the winter. The limited oxygen and light beneath the mulches will cause the plant to struggle to stay alive and use up its stored energy. If the plant escapes death, it will be severely weakened the following spring.

FALL COMPOST PILES

If you have the time, it is a good practice to construct a compost pile each fall. Autumn is the time of year when most native plants shed their summer leaves, stems, twigs, and smaller branches. These materials should be gathered and used in the construction of a compost pile. Unfortunately, in most areas of the United States winter temperatures are too cold for the compost to be very active, but by constructing the pile in the fall it will begin to work at the earliest possible date in the spring. By midsummer, the pile should be ready for use on your garden.

Gather leaves, grass clippings, vegetable debris, and anything else you can get your hands on to make your fall compost pile (Fig. 17-5). Since winter tends to be a wet time of year, you will probably want to protect the pile with plastic, sod, or another semi-waterproof or waterproof material. This protection will prevent many of the nutrients in your pile from leaching out.

A good location for fall compost piles is over the spot where you want the first spring crops to

Fig. 17-5. Tear down spent vegetable plants and add them to a winter compost heap. Shred tough materials like tomato vines prior to composting.

288

grow. If the pile has any height at all—2 feet or more—it will prevent the ground beneath it from freezing. In the spring, a week or two prior to when you want to plant those first crops, the pile is moved off of the area reserved for the early crops. The ground will be easy to work and warmer than surrounding soil.

Another idea is building low compost piles not over 2 feet high at strategic areas in your garden. As soon as the snow melts, go out and turn over the piles. Chances are that some decomposition has already taken place, and turning will aerate the pile, speeding up the process. Within a few weeks it will be partially broken down. You can then spread the half-made compost over the garden and turn it under as part of the normal spring cultivation process. You may need to add some nitrogen-rich material during tilling to prevent the organic material from robbing this nutrient from your soil.

STORING ROOT CROPS IN THE GARDEN

If inside storage space is limited at your house, you may want to try storing potatoes, carrots, turnips, salsify, cabbages, apples, and beets right in the garden. Fruits should be stored separately from vegetables. Fruits give off a gas that causes most vegetables to overripen and spoil.

The most common name for such a storage method is *pit storage*. As the name implies, this practice involves hollowing out a shallow pit in the garden in which crops can be stored. Barrels, boxes, and hardware-cloth containers can also be used, but the basic construction methods are the same.

Pits for winter storage should be made only in gardens with adequate drainage. To make a storage pit, dig a shallow hole less than 1 foot deep that's about 3 feet in diameter. Line the bottom of the hole with 6 or more inches of a dry material such as straw or leaves. Place the vegetables to be stored on this bed. Continue placing alternating layers of vegetables and straw in the pit until a mound 1 to 2 feet high has been made. Cover the entire mound with a foot-thick layer of straw so that a teepee-like structure is formed. The straw at the top of this pyramid should be about 2 feet thick. Finish the pit

by spreading 6 inches or more of soil over the straw. Firm the sides to prevent wind from blowing the soil away and to repel water. A little bit of straw should stick through the top of this configuration so that the pile can breathe. A pit constructed in this manner will keep most vegetables at about 35° F through the winter. Unfortunately, once the pit has been opened during the winter it cannot be reclosed, and all vegetables must be removed. For this reason, it is advisable to construct several smaller pits instead of one large one.

If rodents are a problem in your garden, you may want to consider using a barrel instead of a pit storage system. This method is similar to a pit storage area except that the vegetables are placed in a barrel.

To make a barrel storage area, dig a trench slightly larger than the barrel to be used. Place stones or gravel on the bottom of the trench. Then place the barrel in the trench so that it rests at a 45° angle. Pack straw or dry leaves around the barrel. Fill the barrel with alternating layers of vegetables and straw or sawdust until it's full. Place a lid over the barrel and lay a foot-thick layer of straw or leaves over the whole area. Cover mulch with 6 inches of soil and pack in place. Again, the straw or leaves should stick through the highest point of the soil to provide ventilation for the pit.

In gardens where drainage is questionable, you can store vegetables on a low, flat mound instead of in a pit. Scrape dirt into a circle so that it forms a flat-topped mound approximately 3 feet in diameter and about 6 inches high. Place a few inches of straw or leaves on the mound and then a layer of vegetables. Alternate layers of vegetables and straw until a 2-foot-tall pyramid is built. Cover this pyramid with a 1-foot layer of straw so that a cone is made. Cover the straw with dirt and pack it in place. Again, a vent should be created by allowing the straw to poke through the top of the mound.

Many root crops can be stored in the ground right where they grew. A thick mulch layed over carrots, turnips, beets, salsify, and parsnips will keep these roots from freezing. They can be harvested as needed during the winter simply by pulling the mulch away from the roots and digging them

Fig. 17-6. Root crops like carrots can be stored right where they grew. Place bagged and loose leaves over them and dig them up for a fresh winter treat.

up. If you place bags of plastic leaves directly on the soil and then cover the bagged leaves with loose leaves, removal of the leaves will be much easier (Fig. 17-6). Additionally, when all the roots have been removed from beneath one bag, that bag can be removed from the row. This will indicate where the end of the row is. Stakes should be driven into the soil to mark the ends of any root crops stored under a mulch. The stakes should be taller than expected snows so that you will be able to find your crops during the winter.

COLD FRAMES

A good way of extending the fresh salad season well into late fall or early winter is through the judicious use of a cold frame (Fig. 17-7). Not only can cold frames be used in the spring to harden off

transplants, but you will be amazed at how much cold cold-tolerant plants can stand in the late fall if they're under glass.

Plant short-season crops like radishes and leaf lettuce 2 or 3 weeks prior to the first frost. Later maturing crops such as spinach, endive, and butterhead lettuce should be planted 1 to 1½ months prior to the first frost. Many seeds will germinate poorly under these conditions. Remedy this by sowing heavily and deeply, watering regularly and thoroughly, and by shading seedbeds with boards or loosely-woven cloth until the seedlings have established themselves. Should plants come up too thickly, thin the weakest ones for use in salads.

There are two basic ways of planting for a cold frame. The first is planting in beds, slightly smaller than the size of the frame, and then placing the frame over the beds as the nights begin to frost. Leave the lid open the first few days so that the plants can adjust to their new home. This method allows you to move fall crops from one place to another in the garden each fall. Hence, it is good for crop rotation.

The second method is planting directly in the cold frame. This method is the only way to plant in permanent cold frames. Prepare the seedbed in the frame and then plant. Leave the lid open until nights begin frosting. Permanent beds should have their soil enriched with compost at least once each year. The enrichment should be added prior to each sowing. Normal side-dressing and mulching practices can be used in the cold frame, but keep an eye out for damping-off disease.

When nights begin frosting, close the cold frame's lid before sundown to hold in the day's heat. Open the frame early each morning to prevent overheating the plants and to provide air circulation. When nights grow very cold, close the glass and cover with a blanket or tarp. Hay, straw, or leaves banked around the sides will also help hold in heat. When days begin to remain cold (30° F or less), leave the lid closed throughout the day. Light will enter and be trapped, keeping the interior of the cold frame warm.

Toward the end of the cold frame season, plants may freeze occasionally during the night.

Fig. 17-7. Cold frames are an easy way to extend the season of cold weather crops in the fall.

You can warm them without damage by sprinkling them with *cold* water and leaving them in the dark for an hour or two. Beware of leaves that touch the cold frame's glass because they are more likely to suffer cold damage. Harvest any leaves that touch the glass when you first notice them to prevent cold damage.

Some vegetables that do well in the cold frame include Chinese cabbage, endive, kale, lettuce (leaf and butterhead), and spinach.

TOOL CARE

The next to last thing you will want to do each fall is store your tools, stakes, wire cages, and other garden structures and implements for the winter. It is generally a good idea to wait until your garden has been buttoned up for the winter before performing these tasks since you will need many tools during the fall.

You will find more information about cleaning, sharpening and storing tools in Chapter 6. Other garden equipment like stakes, trellises, and wire cages should have all the dirt cleaned off them and then be stored in a dry place.

Those of you with irrigation systems will also want to bring them inside for winter storage. If you have a drip irrigation system, it should be removed first thing, right after crops are finished producing. This not only protects the system from winter's harmful effects, but it also allows you easier access to the soil for tilling, mulching, and composting chores. Make sure to drain all irrigation systems prior to storage.

REVIEWING YOUR GARDEN PLAN

When everything else has been done in the garden and you are ready to settle down to the wait for next season, it is time to reveiw your garden plan. Reviewing your plan now while your garden is fresh in your mind will allow you to find mistakes and see ways of improving next year's garden. It is easier to remember which planting methods, seed varieties, and culture techniques worked best in the fall than next spring. You will also remember mistakes to avoid in next season's plan.

To effectively review last season's garden, you will need to get out the garden plans you drew up. Think about plant and row spacing. Did your garden have too much or not enough? Was shading a problem? Do you grow too many of one vegetable and not enough of another?

You should keep a list of varieties you grew. Notes on how well they did are also helpful. It is also handy to record where seed was purchased. Fall is an excellent time to compare notes with other gardeners. You can also gather soil samples, which may be impossible to dig early next spring.

Winter is a good time to visit garden centers and greenhouses. They are usually not busy, and many owners are willing to talk freely with interested gardeners. You can also buy fertilizers, rock powders, and other garden equipment and supplies during the winter and avoid the spring rush.

Working in the garden in the fall is a good way to improve your chances of success next season. Besides, it gives you an excuse to get out in the garden a few more times before winter sets in.

Chapter 18

The Year at a Glance

In order to live off a garden, you practically have to live in it.

—Kin Hubbard

Although this last chapter is short and sweet, it can be used as a way of planning your gardening activities for the coming year, or as a checklist for what needs to be done. Below you will find four sections: spring, summer, fall, and winter. Each lists what needs to be done during that particular season to keep your garden productive and on schedule for maximum yields.

SPRING

- Plant seeds in flats indoors for vegetables to be transplanted into the garden.
- Start compost piles or finish off those begun in the fall.
- Cultivate garden.
- Plant cold-hardy crops outside.
- Prune fruit trees and vines.

- Use dormant oil sprays on fruit trees and vines.
- Remove mulch from overwintering perennials.
- Apply balanced organic fertilizers to perennials.
- Prepare seedbeds for summer crops.
- Set out cold-weather transplants.

SUMMER

- Transplant warm-weather crops like tomatoes, peppers, and eggplants into garden.
- Plant summer crops after last frost, when soil has warmed thoroughly.
- Weed the garden.
- Fertilize plants beginning new phases in their growth cycles.
- Mulch, mulch, mulch.
- Practice insect prevention measures.
- Irrigate as necessary.
- Stake and trellis tall and climbing plants.

- Harvest and store early crops.
- Save seeds for next year.
- Plant fall garden.
- Make more compost from garden debris.
- Thin apples, peaches, and other fruit to improve size and quality of fruit.
- Maintain pest control measures on fruit trees.
- Prune damage or diseased wood from fruit trees and vines.

FALL

- Harvest summer and fall crops.
- Clean all debris from garden.
- Spread rock fertilizers.
- Sow cover crops.
- Mulch perennials.

- Start fall compost piles.
- Rake all fallen leaves and spoiled fruit from around fruit trees and vines.
- Mulch around fruit trees and vines.
- Put tools, stakes, wire cages, and other garden equipment away for the winter.

WINTER

- Sharpen and repair tools.
- Make flats, trellises, cloches, cold frames, and hot beds.
- Plan garden.
- Order seeds.
- Order spring-planted fruit trees and vines as well as other perennials.
- Wrap base of young trees with burlap or tree guards for winter protection.

Sources of Untreated Seeds

D.V. Burrell Seed Growers Co.
Rocky Ford, CO 81607

Johnny's Selected Seeds
Organic Seed and Crop Research
Albion, ME 04910

Nichols Garden Nursery
1190 North Pacific Highway
Albany, OR 97321

Stokes Seeds, Inc.
Box 548
Buffalo, NY 14240

Appendix B

Organic Product Suppliers

(Not all have mail-order service.)

Name	Products
Atlantic & Pacific Research P.O. Box 14366 North Palm Beach, FL 33408	Seaweed extracts and fish emulsion
Atlantic Laboratories Route 32 Waldoboro, ME 04572	Liquid Seaweed, kelp meal, liquid fish emulsion
Beneficial Bio-systems 1523 63rd Street Emerybille, CA 94608	Biological pest controls
Bio-Syn Research P.O. Box 451 West Des Moines, IA 50265	Soil products and foliar nutrients
Carpale's Inc. Box 32 Garfield, MN 56332	Fish-based fertilizers

Comstock, Ferre & Company 263 Main Street Wethersfield, CT 06109	Natural organic plant food
Earth & Sea Products, Inc. Box 1305 Watsonville, CA 95076	Compost, seaweed concentrates, and related products
Farmer Seed & Nursery Co. Fairbault, MN 55021	Liquid seaweed, fish fertilizers
Garden Way Associates 299 Westport Avenue Norwalk, CT 06851	Seeds, tools, and material for energy-saving farming and gardening
Geo. Tait & Sons, Inc. 900 Tidewater Dr. Norfolk VA 23504	Bone meal, dried blood, cottonseed meal, organic garden food
Gurney Seed & Nursery Co. Yankton, SD 57078	Dried blood, fish emulsion, seeds
Henry Field Seed & Nursery Shenandoah, IA 55021	Fish emulsion, fish meal, bone meal, dried blood
H.R. Shumway Rockford, IL 61101	Dried blood, bone meal, fish emulsion
International Diatoms Industries, Ltd. 2629 South 21st Street Phoenix, AZ 85026	Diatomaceous earth
JDL Speciality Sales Inc. 1459 West 5th Street Winona, MN 55987	Soft phosphate, potash, hi-calcium lime, liquid fish concentrate, and kelp meal
L.L. Olds Seed Co. P.O. Box 7790 2901 Packers Avenue Madison, WI 53707	Bone meal, compost, dried blood, Fertilite compost, fish emulsion, fish meal, liquid seaweed
Lonfosco 811 North Bluff Road Greenwood, IN 46142	Collodial phosphate

Name	Products
Mellinger's 2310 West South Range North Lima, OH 44452	Fish emulsion, greensand, rock phosphate, cottonseed meal, cattle and sheep manure, dried blood, bone meal, organic garden food
Meyer Seed Company 600 South Caroline Street Baltimore, MD 21231	Dried blood, bone meal, cow manure, cottonseed meal, Electra Organic food, Fertrell Organic fertilizers, rock phosphate
Natural Development Co. Box 215 Bainbridge, PA 17502	Liquid plant food from the sea, Sudbury Sea Power, organic plant food
Necessary Trading Company Box A New Castle, VA 24127	Trace minerals, fertilizers, seaweed, biological pest controls, and compost aids
Nichols Garden Nursery 1190 North Pacific Highway Albany, OR 97321	Liquid seaweed
Ohio Earth Food, Inc. 13737 Duquette Avenue NE Hartville, OH 44632	Seaweed meal, rock phosphate, pest control materials
Sea Born, Inc. 2000 Rockland Road Charles City, IA 50616	Liquified seaweed, meal, fish and blends of seaweed and fish
Steve Carlsen & Associates 4767 Candleberry Street Seal Beach, CA 90740	Compost, seaweed, and related products
Sudbury Laboratories 572 Dutton Road Sudburry MA 01776	Liquid seaweed and fish fertilizers
The Organic Farm Center 193 Marinwood Ave. San Rafael, CA 94903	Humates, kelp products, rock minerals, beneficial insects
Zook & Ranck, Inc. RR 1 Gap, PA 17527	Full line of natural and energy-saving fertilizer materials, seaweeds, and compost

Orchards Specializing in Old-time Fruit Varieties

Baum's Nursery
New Fairfeld, CT 06810

Leuthardt,
East Moriches, NY 11940

Mellinger's
2366 West South Range Rd.
North Lima, OH 44452

Waynesboro Nursery
Waynesboro, VA 22980

Appendix D

Soil Testing Laboratories

A + L Midwest Agricultural Lab
119-2 Elam Street
Omaha, NE 68144

Analytical Chemistry Lab
3913 Cumings
Omaha, NE 68131

Brookside Farm Laboratory Association, Inc.
New Knoxville, OH 45871

Chemical Service Laboratory, Inc.
P.O. Box 220
Jeffersonville, IN 47130

Erickson Lab
519 First National Bank Building
Fremont, NE 68025

Harris Laboratories, Inc.
624 Peach
Lincoln, NE 68502

Inter-American Corporation
Box 94
Cozad, NE 69130

Iowa Testing Lab, Inc.
Box 188
Eagle Grove, IA 50533

Minnesota Valley Testing Lab, Inc.
202-214 Woolworth Building
New Ulm, MN 55073

Nature's Way Farm
Route 1, Box 218
Vestaburg, MI 48891

Necessary Trading Company
Box A
New Castle, VA 24127

Nutritional Products, Inc.
15280 South Roberts Trail
Rosemount, MN 55068

Ohio Earth Food, Inc.
13737 Duquette Avenue NE
Nartville, OH 44632

Viterage
Box 16
Kidron, OH 44636

Woods End Laboratory
P.O. Box 50
Ashville, ME 04640

Index

Index

Greensand, 52, 287
Grinding wheel, 95
Ground oak bark, 40
Gynoecious cucumbers, 122
Gypsy moth, 262

H

Hammer mills, 94
Hand cultivators, 85
Hand tools, 81
Hardening-off, 133
Hardpan, 19
Harlequin bug, 263
Hay, 235
Hay bale bins, 75
Heeling-in, 169
Herbs, 280
Hoeing, 27
Hoes, 83
Hormones, 250
Horse manure, 72
Horseradish, 162
Hot beds, 136
Hot pepper juice, 248
House wrens, 253
Humus, 7
Hybrids, 122, 274

I

Imported cabbage worm, 264
Indeterminate, 123
Indore composting method, 73
Insect control 115
Insecticides, 253
Intercropping, 113
Interplanting, 113
Iron, 36
Irrigation methods, 216-227

J

Japanese beetle, 264
Jerusalem artichoke, 191
Jerusalem artichoke, culture, 192
Jerusalem artichoke, harvest, 192
Jerusalem artichoke, planting, 191
Jerusalem artichoke, varieties, 192
June beetle, 264

K

Kale, 192
Kale, culture, 192
Kale, harvest, 192
Kale, planting, 192
Kale, varieties, 192
Kitchen cabinet sprays, 247
Kohlrabi, 192
Kohlrabi, culture, 193
Kohlrabi, harvest, 193
Kohlrabi, planting, 192
Kohlrabi, varieties, 193

L

Lacewings, 252
Lady beetles, 251
Leaf mills, 93
Leaf miners, 264
Leaves, 70, 232, 286
Leeks, 193
Leeks, culture, 193
Leeks, harvest, 193
Leeks, planting, 193
Leeks, varieties, 193
Legume seeds, 152
Lettuce, 193, 280
Lettuce, culture, 195
Lettuce, harvesting, 195
Lettuce, planting, 195
Lettuce, varieties, 195
Lima beans, 195
Lima beans, culture, 195
Lima beans, harvest, 196
Lima beans, planting, 195
Lima beans, varieties, 196
Limestone, 53
Linseed oil, 97

M

Macronutrients, 10, 33
Magnesium, 36
Manganese, 36
Manure, 50, 70, 232
Manure tea, 60
Mealybug, 265
Mealybug destroyer, 252
Mexican bean beetle, 265
Microbes, 9
Micronutrients, 35
Mints, 196
Mints, culture, 196
Mints, harvest, 196
Mints, planting, 196
Mints, varieties, 196
Mississippi River, 49
Moisture, 64
Molasses, 248
Moles, 253
Molybdenum, 30, 36
Mosaic indexed, 123
Mulches, living, 238
Mulches, permanent, 238
Mulches, stone, 240
Mulches, winter, 240
Mulching, 228-241
Mulching, dangers of, 230
Mulching methods, 238
Mulching perennials, 287
Mulching tips, 237
Muskmelon, 196
Muskmelon, culture, 196
Muskmelon, harvest, 197
Muskmelon, planting, 196
Muskmelon, varieties, 197
Mustard greens, 197

Mustard greens, culture, 197
Mustard greens, harvest, 197
Mustard greens, planting, 197
Mustard greens, varieties, 197

N

National Garden Bureau, Inc., 122
Nematodes, 124, 265
Netting, 245
Newspaper, 233
New Zealand box, 75
New Zealand spinach, 197
New Zealand spinach, harvest, 197
New Zealand spinach, planting, 197
New Zealand spinach, varieties, 197
Nitrogen, 10, 32-33
Nonorganic mulches, 235
No-till method, 26
Nutrient cycles, 32

O

Oak leaves, 40
Oak sawdust, 40
Okra, 197
Okra, culture, 198
Okra, harvest, 198
Okra, planting, 198
Okra, varieties, 198
Onion, 198
Onion, culture, 199
Onion, harvest, 199
Onion, planting, 198
Onion, varieties, 199
Onion maggot, 265
Onions, 281
Open pollination, 123
Orchards specializing in old-time fruit
    varieties, 299
Organic matter, 7
Organic matter, benefits of, 8-11
Organic mulches, 231
Organic product suppliers, 296
Oregano, 199
Oregano, culture, 199
Oregano, harvest, 199
Oregano, planning, 199
Oregano, varieties, 200

P

Paper collars, 246
Parsley, 200
Parsley, culture, 200
Parsley, harvest, 200
Parsley, planting, 200
Parsley, varieties, 200
Parsleyworm, 266
Parsnip, 200
Parsnip, culture, 200
Parsnip, harvest, 200
Parsnip, planting, 200
Parsnip, varieties, 201
Pathogens, 56